The Townsend Lectures

The Department of Classics at Cornell University is fortunate to have at its disposal the Prescott W. Townsend Fund—established by Mr. Townsend's widow, Daphne Townsend, in 1982. Since 1985, income from the fund has been used to support the annual visit of a distinguished scholar in the field of classics. Each visiting scholar delivers a series of lectures, which, revised for book publication, are published by Cornell University Press in Cornell Studies in Classical Philology.

During the semester of their residence, Townsend lecturers effectively become members of the Cornell Department of Classics and teach a course to Cornell students as well as deliver the lectures.

The Townsend Lectures bring to Cornell University, and to Cornell University Press, scholars of international reputation who are in the forefront of current classical research and whose work represents the kind of close reading of texts that has become associated with current literary discourse, or reflects broad interdisciplinary concerns, or both.

CORNELL STUDIES IN CLASSICAL PHILOLOGY

EDITED BY

FREDERICK M. AHL ★ KEVIN CLINTON
JOHN E. COLEMAN ★ JUDITH R. GINSBURG
G. M. KIRKWOOD ★ DAVID MANKIN
GORDON M. MESSING ★ ALAN J. NUSSBAUM
HAYDEN PELLICCIA ★ PIETRO PUCCI
JEFFREY S. RUSTEN ★ DANUTA SHANZER

VOLUME LVI

Ammianus Marcellinus and the Representation
of Historical Reality
by Timothy D. Barnes

ALSO IN THE TOWNSEND LECTURES

Artifices of Eternity: Horace's Fourth Book of Odes
by Michael C. J. Putnam

Socrates, Ironist and Moral Philosopher
by Gregory Vlastos

Culture and National Identity in Republican Rome
by Erich S. Gruen

Horace and the Dialectic of Freedom: Readings in "Epistles 1"
by W. R. Johnson

Animal Minds and Human Morals: The Origins of the Western Debate
by Richard Sorabji

Platonic Ethics, Old and New
by Julia Annas

Ammianus Marcellinus and the Representation of Historical Reality

Timothy D. Barnes

Cornell University Press

Ithaca and London

First published 1998 by Cornell University Press

Printed in the United States of America

Cornell University Press strives to use environmentally responsible suppliers and materials to the fullest extent possible in the publishing of its books. Such materials include vegetable-based, low-VOC inks and acid-free papers that are recycled, totally chlorine-free, or partly composed of nonwood fibers.

Library of Congress Cataloging-in-Publication Data

Barnes, Timothy David.
Ammianus Marcellinus and the representation of historical reality / Timothy D. Barnes.
p.   cm. — (Cornell studies in classical philology ; v. 56.
The Townsend lectures)
Includes bibliographical references and index.
ISBN 0-8014-3526-9 (cloth : alk. paper)
1. Ammianus Marcellinus.   Rerum gestarum libri.
2. Rome—History—Empire, 284–476—Historiography.
3. Historiography—Rome. I. Title. II. Series.
DG316.B37   1998
937′.007′202—dc21   98-19791

Cloth printing   10 9 8 7 6 5 4 3 2 1

CONTENTS

[v]

Contents

PREFACE

The present book is a twice rewritten and greatly expanded version of the seven Townsend Lectures that I composed and delivered at Cornell University in the Fall Term of 1994. I am most grateful to Prescott and Diana Townsend for their generosity in leaving the bulk of their estate to support an endangered academic discipline, to the Cornell Department of Classics for inviting me to spend a term with them, and to all those who made my time in Ithaca so very pleasurable, especially Carol Kaske and Danuta Shanzer.

My serious interest in Ammianus Marcellinus goes back to 1986, when I made the surprising discovery that, virtually without exception, those who had written about the historian since Otto Seeck in 1906 had misunderstood both the chronological principles on which Ammianus arranges his narrative and the literary structure of the *Res Gestae*. My interest was further kindled as I came to realize how much the Roman Empire of Ammianus differed from the mid-fourth-century world that my researches into the career of Athanasius were revealing to me—a discrepancy that clamored for explanation.

Since I started to think about Ammianus, both graduate and undergraduate students in Toronto have helped me constantly by compelling me to clarify my ideas in class; and I am extremely grateful to Paul Burton, Angela Kalinowski, Ron Pathen, and Sarah Pothecary for allowing me to use essays on Ammianus that they wrote for me and to Rodney Ast, Gordon Nixon, Michael Redies, and Aara Suksi for practical assistance. I owe more than I can easily express in words to my colleagues in the Toronto Department of Classics not only for letting me pester them with questions arising from a text in which hardly any of them has a real interest, but also, more generally, for collectively creating a lively academic environment in which it is a delight to teach and

to conduct research. I know that the others will excuse me if I single out for
mention Alexander Jones, who gave me lucid guidance on astronomical matters. I am also grateful to Rob Prichard and Paul Gooch for teaching me how
autocratic and bureaucratic structures of power normally react to incompetence and corruption.

It was only after I had formulated most of my conclusions about Ammianus' treatment of Christians and Christianity that I became aware of the work
of David Woods, whose acute researches into the imperial bodyguard under Julian have produced results convergent with mine. I am most grateful to
Dr. Woods for his generosity in allowing me to read several of his articles before publication: they have rescued me from uncritical acceptance of received
views on a number of important points.

I must also record with gratitude the generous financial support given me
by the Social Sciences and Humanities Research Council of Canada.

The preparation of the final text has led me to reflect on some important
lessons that I learned before I became a pupil of Ronald Syme in 1964. The
first serious book of history that I can remember reading (in 1956) was the
first edition of Alan Bullock's remarkable *Hitler, A Study in Tyranny* (London,
1952): the passage of time has powerfully confirmed the sureness and accuracy of Bullock's historical judgments and established his book as a model of
how a historian can write objectively about men and events for which he feels
the deepest repugnance. Bullock's *Hitler and Stalin: Parallel Lives* (London,
1991) imparts the same lesson—and reading it has reinforced my conviction
that Ammianus failed in his obligation as a historian to strive to transcend personal bias.

When I was an undergraduate at Oxford, I studied Plautus and attended
Eduard Fraenkel's seminars. From Fraenkel I learned both to be attentive to
the Greek elements in any Latin writer and to respect the classical scholarship
of Wilhelmine Germany. Hence, when I began to read Ammianus closely and
discovered that Ulrich von Wilamowitz-Moellendorff, Friedrich Leo, Eduard
Norden, and Fraenkel himself all believed that Ammianus thought in Greek
rather than Latin, I took the idea seriously—and soon saw that it provides the
interpretative key to a difficult author.

TIMOTHY BARNES

Toronto
31 August 1997

EDITIONS, TRANSLATIONS, AND COMMENTARIES

References to Ammianus Marcellinus are normally given as bare numbers in parenthesis in the main text (e.g., 14.1.1). The text of Ammianus used or quoted is that of the Teubner edition by W. Seyfarth (Leipzig, 1978), unless a deviation is explicitly signaled. The following editions, translations, and commentaries are cited by the name of the editor(s), translator(s), and/or commentator(s) alone when it is clear which passage is under discussion and which edition or commentary is intended.

1. Henri de Valois (Valesius). *Ammiani Marcellini Rerum Gestarum qui de XXXI supersunt libri XVIII*. Paris, 1636. (Notes are reprinted in the variorum edition of J. A. Wagner and K. G. A Erfurdt. Leipzig, 1808).
2. C. U. Clark. *Ammiani Marcellini Rerum Gestarum libri qui supersunt*. Berlin, 1910, 1915.
3. The Loeb edition by J. C. Rolfe. *Ammianus Marcellinus*. London, 1935, 1940, 1939.
4. The Budé edition, *Ammien Marcellin: Histoire*, of which the following volumes have been available to me:

    E. Galletier and J. Fontaine. Tome 1: *Livres XIV–XVI*. Paris, 1968.

    G. Sabbah. Tome 2: *Livres XVII–XIX*. Paris, 1970.

    J. Fontaine. Tome 3: *Livres XX–XXII*. Paris, 1996.

    J. Fontaine. Tome 4: *Livres XIII–XXV*. Paris, 1977.

    M.-A. Marié. Tome 5: *Livres XXVI–XXVIII*. Paris, 1984.
5. P. de Jonge. *Sprachlicher und historischer Kommentar zu Ammianus Marcellinus XIV 1–7*. Groningen, 1935.

    ——. *Sprachlicher und historischer Kommentar zu Ammianus Marcellinus XIV, 2. Hälfte (c. 7–11)*. Groningen, 1939.

    ——. *Philological and Historical Commentary on Ammianus Marcellinus XV, 1–5*. Groningen, 1948.

———. *Philological and Historical Commentary on Ammianus Marcellinus XV, 6–13.* Groningen, 1953.

———. *Philological and Historical Commentary on Ammianus Marcellinus XVI.* Groningen, 1972.

———. *Philological and Historical Commentary on Ammianus Marcellinus XVII.* Groningen, 1977.

———. *Philological and Historical Commentary on Ammianus Marcellinus XVIII.* Groningen, 1980.

———. *Philological and Historical Commentary on Ammianus Marcellinus XIX.* Groningen, 1982.

J. den Boeft, D. den Hengst, and H. C. Teitler. *Philological and Historical Commentary on Ammianus Marcellinus XX.* Groningen, 1987.

———. *Philological and Historical Commentary on Ammianus Marcellinus XXI.* Groningen, 1991.

J. den Boeft, J. W. Drijvers, D. den Hengst, and H. C. Teitler. *Philological and Historical Commentary on Ammianus Marcellinus XXII.* Groningen, 1995.

(The three most recent volumes are cited collectively as "the Dutch commentators.")

6. W. Seyfarth's edition with a German translation and brief commentary: *Ammianus Marcellinus: Römische Geschichte. Schriften und Quellen der alten Welt.* Berlin: 1, 1968; 2, 1968; 3, 1970; 4, 1971.

7. J. Szidat. *Historischer Kommentar zu Ammianus Marcellinus, Buch XX–XXI. Teil I: Die Erhebung Julians; Teil II: Die Verhandlungsphase; Teil III: Die Konfrontation. Historia Einzelschriften* 31, 38, 89. Wiesbaden, 1977, 1981, 1996.

8. The Penguin translation by W. Hamilton and A. Wallace-Hadrill. *Ammianus Marcellinus: The Later Roman Empire (A.D. 354–378).* Harmondsworth, 1986.

The English translations of Ammianus are my own. For passages of narrative I have freely adapted the version by Hamilton and Wallace-Hadrill, modifying it wherever I thought that I could recapture Ammianus' tone or precise meaning more faithfully. For passages omitted by Hamilton and Wallace-Hadrill, I have consulted Rolfe's translation in preparing my own.

ABBREVIATIONS

The names of ancient authors other than Ammianus are normally given in full: for the abbreviations used for the titles of their works and for the standard collections of inscriptions and papyri, the following works of reference should be consulted.

Hornblower, S., and A. Spawforth, eds. *The Oxford Classical Dictionary*[3]. Oxford, 1996, xxix–liv.

H. G. Liddell and R. Scott. *A Greek–English Lexicon*[9], rev. H. S. Jones. Oxford, 1940, xvi–xlii.

G. W. H. Lampe. *A Patristic Greek Lexicon*. Oxford, 1961, ix–xliii.

The full titles of periodicals and serials that are cited in the notes by conventional abbreviations are given in the bibliography, but the following books (plus a recently reedited chronicle) are always cited with abbreviated titles.

Alföldi, *Conflict* (1952)
A. Alföldi, *A Conflict of Ideas in the Late Roman Empire. The Clash between the Senate and Valentinian I*, trans. H. Mattingly. Oxford, 1952.

Athanasius (1993)
T. D. Barnes, *Athanasius and Constantius. Theology and Politics in the Constantinian Empire*. Cambridge, Mass., 1993.

Bitter, *Kampfschilderungen* (1976)
N. Bitter, *Kampfschilderungen bei Ammianus Marcellinus*. Diss. Erlangen-Nürnberg, 1975; publ. Bonn 1976.

Blockley, *Ammianus* (1975)
R. (P.) C. Blockley, *Ammianus Marcellinus. A Study of His Historiography and Political Thought*. Collection Latomus 141. Brussels, 1975.

Blomgren, *Quaestiones* (1937)

S. Blomgren, *De Sermone Ammiani Marcellini quaestiones variae*. Uppsala Universitets Årsskrift 1937: 6. Uppsala, 1937.

Chastagnol, *Fastes* (1962)

A. Chastagnol, *Les Fastes de la Préfecture de Rome au Bas-Empire*. Études Prosopographiques 2. Paris, 1962.

Cognitio Gestorum (1992)

J. den Boeft, D. den Hengst, and H. C. Teitler, eds., *Cognitio Gestorum. The Historiographic Art of Ammianus Marcellinus*. Koninklijke Nederlandse Akademie van Wetenschappen: Verhandelingen, Afd. Letterkunde, Nieuwe Reeks 148. Amsterdam, 1992.

Constantine (1981)

T. D. Barnes, *Constantine and Eusebius*. Cambridge, Mass., 1981.

Consuls (1987)

R. A. Bagnall, Alan Cameron, S. Schein, and K. Worp. *Consuls of the Later Roman Empire*. Atlanta, 1987.

Demandt, *Zeitkritik* (1965)

A. Demandt, *Zeitkritik und Geschichtsbild im Werk Ammians*. Diss. Marburg, 1963; publ. Bonn, 1965.

Descr. cons.

R. W. Burgess, ed., *The Chronicle of Hydatius and the Consularia Constantinopolitana. Two Contemporary Accounts of the Final Years of the Roman Empire*. Oxford, 1993, 215–45.

Burgess' text supersedes the standard edition by Mommsen, T. *Chronica Minora. Monumenta Germaniae Historica* 1, Auctores Antiquissimi 9. Berlin, 1892, 205–47. References are given to the relevant consular year, and where there is more than one entry for the year, to the number assigned to it by Mommsen and Burgess (e.g., 378.3).

Drexler, *Ammianstudien* (1974)

H. Drexler, *Ammianstudien*. Spudasmata: Studien zur Klassischen Philologie und ihren Grenzgebieten, ed. H. Hommel and E. Zinn. Hildesheim / New York, 1974.

Elliott, *Ammianus* (1983)

T. G. Elliott, *Ammianus Marcellinus and Fourth Century History*. Sarasota/Toronto, 1983.

Ensslin, *Ammianus* (1923)

W. Ensslin, *Zur Geschichtschreibung und Weltanschauung des Ammianus Marcellinus*. Klio 16. Leipzig, 1923.

History and Historians (1984)

History and Historians in Late Antiquity, B. Croke and A. M. Emmett, eds. Sydney, 1983.

Jones, *LRE*

A. H. M. Jones, *The Later Roman Empire, 284–602.* Oxford, 1964.
In the American reprint in two volumes, pages 1071–1518 correspond to 3.1–448 in this edition.

Julian Apostata (1978)

R. Klein, ed., *Julian Apostata. Wege der Forschung* 509. Darmstadt, 1978.

Matthews, *Ammianus* (1989)

J. F. Matthews, *The Roman Empire of Ammianus.* London, 1989.

Matthews, *Aristocracies* (1975)

J. F. Matthews, *Western Aristocracies and Imperial Court, A.D. 364–425.* Oxford, 1975: photographic reprint with postscript, 1990.

New Empire (1982)

T. D. Barnes, *The New Empire of Diocletian and Constantine.* Cambridge, Mass., 1982.

Pack, *Städte und Steuern* (1986)

E. Pack, *Städte und Steuern in der Politik Julians. Untersuchungen zu den Quellen eines Kaiserbildes.* Collection Latomus 194. Brussels, 1986.

PLRE 1

A. H. M. Jones, J. R. Martindale, and J. Morris. *The Prosopography of the Later Roman Empire. 1: A.D. 260–395.* Cambridge, 1971.

PLRE 2

J. R. Martindale, *The Prosopography of the Later Roman Empire. 2: A.D. 395–527.* Cambridge, 1980.

Reading the Past (1990)

G. Clarke, ed., with B. Croke, A. Emmett Nobbs, and R. Mortley. *Reading the Past in Late Antiquity.* Rushcutters Bay, 1990.

Rike, *Apex Omnium* (1987)

R. L. Rike, *Apex Omnium. Religion in the "Res Gestae" of Ammianus. The Transformation of the Classical Heritage* 15. Berkeley, 1987.

Rosen, *Ammianus* (1982)

K. Rosen, *Ammianus Marcellinus. Erträge der Forschung* 183. Darmstadt, 1982.

Rosen, *Studien* (1970)

K. Rosen, *Studien zur Darstellungskunst und Glaubwürdigkeit des Ammianus Marcellinus.* Bonn, 1970. This work is a reprint, with a slightly modified title, of Rosen's Heidelberg dissertation of 1966, previously revised and published in Mannheim in 1968.

Sabbah, *Méthode* (1978)

G. Sabbah, *La Méthode d'Ammien Marcellin. Recherches sur la construction du discours historique dans les "Res Gestae."* Paris, 1978.

Seeck, *Regesten* (1919)

O. Seeck, *Regesten der Kaiser und Päpste für die Jahre 311 bis 476 n. Chr. Vorarbeit zu einer Prosopographie der christlichen Kaiserzeit.* Stuttgart, 1919.

Syme, *Ammianus* (1968)

Syme, R. *Ammianus and the Historia Augusta.* Oxford, 1968.

Thompson, *Ammianus* (1947)

E. A. Thompson, *The Historical Work of Ammianus Marcellinus.* Cambridge, 1947.

Vanderspoel, *Themistius* (1995)

J. Vanderspoel, *Themistius and the Imperial Court. Oratory, Civic Duty, and Paideia from Constantius to Theodosius.* Ann Arbor, 1995.

Viansino, *Lexicon*

G. Viansino, *Ammiani Marcellini rerum gestarum Lexicon.* Hildesheim/Zürich/New York, 1985

(two volumes with separate pagination)

Wanke, *Gothenkriege* (1990)

U. Wanke, *Die Gotenkriege des Valens. Studien zu Topographie und Chronologie im unteren Donauraum von 366 bis 378 n. Chr.* Europäische Hochschulschriften, Reihe III: Geschichte und ihre Hilfswissenschaften 412. Bern/Frankfurt/New York, 1990.

Ammianus Marcellinus
and the Representation
of Historical Reality

A truly great historian would reclaim those materials which the novelist has appropriated.

—Macaulay

[I]

THE IMPARTIAL HISTORIAN

At the close of his history, Ammianus Marcellinus described himself as "a soldier and a Greek" (31.16.9). He was born about 330 into the local aristocracy of one of the cities of Roman Syria or Phoenicia, and his father was probably a career soldier who rose to a position of some importance in the reign of the emperor Constantius, who ruled the East from 337 to 361 (Chapter VI). Ammianus entered the Roman army as an officer in an élite corps around 350 and first appears in his narrative as extant in the year 354 (14.9.1, 11.5). It is not known how long he served beyond 359, when he disappears from his narrative after escaping from Amida when the Persian king took it by storm and returning safely to Antioch (19.8.5–12).

Ammianus reappears in his narrative in 363, when his use of the first-person plural indicates that he joined Julian's expedition into Persia at Circesium (23.5.7, cf. 6.30) and returned to Antioch with the defeated Roman army after its failure (25.10.1: Antiochiam venimus). After 363, however, Ammianus disappears from his narrative completely, except for isolated first-person statements that reveal that he was residing in or near Antioch in 372, no longer a soldier (29.1.24, 2.4), and a remark that implies that he was still there in 378 (31.1.2).

Subsequently, Ammianus traveled in Greece, where he saw a ship carried almost two miles inland near Mothone in Laconia by the tsunami of 21 July 365 (26.10.19), saw at least part of the coasts of Thrace and the Black Sea (22.8.1, 27.4.2), and probably traversed the Balkans, seeing the bones of Romans and Goths killed in fighting near Marcianople in the autumn of 377 (31.7.16).[1] He had also toured Egypt (17.4.6, 22.15.1) before he came to

---

[1] The precise location seems to be uncertain: Wanke, *Gotenkriege* (1990), 157–60.

Rome, probably shortly after 380. There, it is plausibly inferred from the bitterness with which he refers to the event (14.6.19), he had the misfortune to be expelled as a foreigner during a food shortage, probably in 384 on the orders of Symmachus as *praefectus urbi*.[2]

Ammianus was a Greek, his native language was Greek, and he thought in Greek (Chapter VII). Yet he wrote a history on an enormous scale in Latin, which covered a period of almost three centuries, from the accession of the emperor Nerva in 96 to the disastrous Battle of Adrianople on 9 August 378 and its immediate aftermath, probably in a total of thirty-six books (Chapter III). Only the second half of the *Res Gestae* has survived. The extant part begins in the middle of the historian's account of the activities of the two emperors during the campaigning season of 353 (14.1.1), and it occupies six hundred pages in modern critical editions. It is by far our fullest, most precise and most reliable narrative source for military campaigns and political events at the imperial court in the fourth century.[3] Hence Ammianus has inevitably provided the basis for all modern narrative accounts of the period from 353 to 378. He has also pervasively influenced all modern interpretations of the period, including those by innovative historians who refuse to give narrative sources their traditional privileged position.[4]

Ammianus' history is thus fundamental to modern understanding and interpretation of the fourth century. All the more necessary, therefore, to investigate its strengths and weaknesses, its biases, its literary quality—in short, to ask how Ammianus depicts a period that is usually seen through his eyes. Ammianus has traditionally been regarded as belonging to the select canon of great historians who have penned reliable and impartial histories of their own times. Edward Gibbon included in his "vindication" of the last two chapters of the first volume of his *History of the Decline and Fall of the Roman Empire*, which analyzed the development of Christianity down to the early fourth cen-

[2] Alan Cameron, *JRS* 54 (1964), 28. The expulsion of *peregrini* from Rome is explicitly attested in 384: Symmachus, *Ep.* 2.7; Ambrose, *De Officiis* 3.7.47–51, cf. J.-R. Palanque, *REA* 33 (1931), 349–52, 355, who points out that a similar expulsion is not documented during any of the other known food shortages of the late fourth century. Ammianus complains that, while the practitioners of the liberal arts, though very few in number, were all expelled, the fans and pretended fans of *mimae* were allowed to remain, together with 3,000 dancing girls, their accompanying choruses, and their trainers (14.6.19).

[3] For a full appreciation of the scope and virtues of Ammianus' narrative, see Matthews, *Ammianus* (1989), 33–228.

[4] See, recently, Averil Cameron, *The Later Roman Empire, A.D. 284–430* (Cambridge, Mass., 1993), esp. 19–21, 73–74, 85–89, 133–37. Much greater independence of Ammianus is shown by Peter Brown, whose classic *World of Late Antiquity* (London, 1971) seems to mention him only twice and very briefly (115, 120).

tury in a manner that offended many of his Christian contemporaries, an assessment of the "character and credit" of the ecclesiastical historian Eusebius
of Caesarea, whom he disparaged and compared unfavorably with Ammianus,
and three early modern historians whom he greatly admired:

> Since the origin of Theological Factions, some historians, Ammianus Marcellinus,
> Fra-Paolo, Thuanus, Hume, and perhaps a few others, have deserved the singu-
> lar praise of holding the balance with a steady and equal hand. Independent and
> unconnected, they contemplated with the same indifference, the opinions and
> interests of the contending parties; or, if they were seriously attached to a par-
> ticular system, they were armed with a firm and moderate temper, which en-
> abled them to suppress their affections, and to sacrifice their resentments. In this
> small, but *venerable* Synod of historians, Eusebius cannot claim a seat.[5]

The three "independent and unconnected" historians whom Gibbon names
with Ammianus reflect his own interests and predilections—and one of them
conspicuously lacks the qualities for which Gibbon commended him.

Gibbon had praised de Thou as "a moderate philosopher" in his second
commonplace book in the early 1770s.[6] Jacques Auguste de Thou (1553–1617)
was a moderate Catholic who supported political accommodation with protes-
tants and was one of the drafters of the Edict of Nantes in 1598 granting toleration to the Huguenots. His *History of His Time*, which covers the period
from 1543 to the early seventeenth century and was frequently reprinted in
French and English after its original publication in Latin in Paris between
1604 and 1620, was placed on the index of forbidden books by the Spanish
Inquisition.[7]

David Hume (1711–1776) was a friend whom Gibbon admired deeply
both as a philosopher and a historian.[8] His *History of England from the Invasion
of Julius Caesar to the Revolution in 1688*, first published in three separate pairs
of volumes between 1745 and 1762, commended itself to Gibbon by both its

---

[5] E. Gibbon, *A Vindication of Some Passages in the Fifteenth and Sixteenth Chapters of the History
of the Decline and Fall of the Roman Empire* (London, 1779), 110–11; *The English Essays of Edward
Gibbon*, ed. P. A. Craddock (Oxford, 1972), 299.

[6] *English Essays* (1972), 203.

[7] The multifarious editions of the *History* are catalogued by S. Kinser, *The Works of Jacques-
Auguste de Thou* (The Hague, 1996), 6–78.

[8] *Decline and Fall*, 7.308, n. 101 (B) = 3.1057, n. 89 (W) (quoted at n. 14). See also 1.255,
n. 90 (B) = 1.251, n. 86 (W); *English Essays*, 338 (I, 2: "Mr. Hume told me," etc.). References to
Gibbon's *Decline and Fall* are given by volume and page numbers in both the 1926–1929 reprint
of J. B. Bury's "revised library edition" in seven volumes, which is often styled the second edition (London, 1909–1914) (B), and the critical edition in three volumes by David Womersley
(London, 1994) (W).

Tory standpoint and its distinguished style, which enabled it to remain a standard work for more than a century,[9] and Gibbon alluded to Hume as a preeminent Scotsman in terms that tempted a modern historian of Rome to indulge in a rare moment of self-revelation.[10]

Pietro Sarpi (1552–1623) is a very different character. He was a servite friar who enjoyed the protection of the city of Venice in political battles against contemporary popes: he wrote about the Reformation and Counter-Reformation of the sixteenth century with passion, not detachment, and no one now would seriously claim any degree of objectivity for his *Istoria del concilio tridentino*, which was first published in London in 1619 under the anagrammatical pseudonym Pietro Soave Polano and "represent[s] the Council of Trent as being solely a conspiracy against reform of the church."[11] Gibbon read Sarpi in his youth: his early commonplace book of 1755 commends him as "one of the most learned men of his time."[12] In the first volume of *Decline and Fall*, Gibbon adduced a rescript of Diocletian (without giving the relevant reference to the *Codex Justinianus*) "on the respectable authority of Fra-Paolo" and praised him most warmly as "in learning and moderation . . . not inferior to Grotius."[13] And in the penultimate chapter of his sixth volume he delivered a final and highly commendatory verdict: Sarpi was a "worthy successor" of the "noblest historians," the Florentines Guicciardini and Machiavelli, and this trio, together with Davila, "were justly esteemed the first historians of modern languages, till, in the present age, Scotland arose to dispute the prize with Italy herself."[14]

Literary taste and intellectual fashions have changed greatly since Gibbon's day. Although his *Historia delle guerre civili in Francia*, published in Venice in 1630, went through some two hundred printings in several European languages during the seventeenth and eighteenth centuries, Enrico Caterino Davila (1576–1631) is today completely forgotten. Hume's philosophical works are still read with profit, but not his history of England; de Thou is

---

[9] See, for example, the appreciative notice by Leslie Stephen, *Dictionary of National Biography* 10 (London, 1921 [1892]), 215–26.

[10] Syme, *Ammianus* (1968), 22. n. 3, quoting Gibbon, *Decline and Fall*, 3.47 (B) = 1.1001 (W): "Such reflections tend to enlarge the circle of our ideas, and to encourage the pleasing hope that New Zealand may produce, in some future age, the Hume of the Southern Hemisphere."

[11] F. L. Cross and E. A. Livingstone, *Oxford Dictionary of the Christian Church*[2] (Oxford, 1974), 1236–37, cf. H. Jedin, *Der Quellenapparat der Konzilgeschichte Pallavicinos: Das Papstum und die Widerlegung Sarpis im Lichte neuerschlossener Archivalien* (Rome, 1940); *Geschichte des Konzils von Trient*, 2 (Freiburg, 1957), 441–44.

[12] *English Essays* (1972), 23–24.

[13] *Decline and Fall*, 2.52, n. 139 (B) = 1.492, n. 137 (W); 2.148, n. 187 (B) = 1.580, n. 186 (W): the first quotation is taken from Gibbon, *Vindication* (1779), 12–13 = *English Essays* (1972), 238.

[14] *Decline and Fall*, 7.308, n. 101 (B) = 3.1057, n. 89 (W).

generally ignored, except by historians with a professional interest in the sixteenth century;[15] and Sarpi's voluminous tomes remain unopened even by those who proclaim his supreme importance as an intellectual figure.[16]

Gibbon's library contained two copies of Hume's history and the historical works of Sarpi and de Thou in both French and their original language of publication (Italian and Latin, respectively).[17] He had naturally read Ammianus long before he penned his *Vindication*, but at the time of its composition he was already at work on the next installment of his history, whose second volume draws heavily on the *Res Gestae*.[18] Gibbon pays Ammianus a series of fulsome tributes that, although justly both famous and familiar, will bear yet another repetition. For they show how little the prevailing estimate of Ammianus changed during the next two centuries. When Gibbon considered the ecclesiastical politics of the reign of Constantius, he gave Ammianus a privileged position as an unbiased witness:

> The sentiments of a judicious stranger who has impartially considered the progress of civil or ecclesiastical discord are always entitled to our notice; and a short passage of Ammianus, who served in the armies, and studied the character, of Constantius, is perhaps of more value than many pages of theological invectives.[19]

When he came to Julian, Gibbon appealed to "the unexceptionable testimony of Ammianus Marcellinus" and commended the intrinsic value of his account of the reign both in general and in particular:

> The philosophic soldier, who loved the virtues without adopting the prejudices of his master, has recorded, in his judicious and candid history of his own times, the extraordinary obstacles which interrupted the restoration of the Temple of Jerusalem.[20]

---

[15] See, W. McCuaig, *Carlo Sigonio: The Changing World of the Late Renaissance* (Princeton, 1989), 70–72; B. B. Diefendorf, *Beneath the Cross: Catholics and Huguenots in Sixteenth-Century Paris* (New York, 1991), 4, 81, 83, 97, 169–71.

[16] G. Steiner, *No Passion Spent: Essays, 1978–1996* (London/Boston, 1996), 4: "I have, a dozen times, slunk by Sarpi's leviathan history of the Council of Trent (one of the pivotal works in the development of western religious–political argument)." J. H. Plumb, *The Death of the Past* (Boston, 1970), 126, makes the less momentous claim that "Sarpi was a far greater historian than Livy."

[17] G. Keynes, *The Library of Edward Gibbon*[2], St. Paul's Bibliographies No. 2 (Dorchester, 1980), 156, 245, 267.

[18] On Gibbon's use of and attitude toward Ammianus, see D. Womersley, *The Transformation of "The Decline and Fall of the Roman Empire"* (Cambridge, 1988), 169–81.

[19] *Decline and Fall*, 2.380 (B) = 1.793 (W).

[20] *Decline and Fall*, 2.485 (B) = 1.890–91 (W).

And when he reached the accession of Theodosius, he bade Ammianus an emphatic and moving farewell:

> It is not without the most sincere regret that I must now take leave of an accurate and faithful guide, who has composed the history of his own times without indulging the prejudices and passions which usually affect the mind of a contemporary.[21]

Gibbon was not blind to the subjective and personal elements in Ammianus: he noted "the sarcasm of an impartial historian" and argued that in the two angry digressions on the city of Rome "the judicious reader" would "perhaps detect the latent prejudices and personal resentments which soured the temper of Ammianus himself."[22] Gibbon sensed that there was an apparent contradiction between the impartiality of historical judgment that he prized so highly and the often emotional style of the historian, but he made a rigid distinction between the content of Ammianus' work and his manner of presentation: "The sincerity of Ammianus would not suffer him to misrepresent facts or characters, but his love of *ambitious* ornaments frequently betrayed him into an unnatural vehemence of expression."[23] Leading Roman historians and Latin scholars in Wilhelmine Germany wrote in virtually identical terms. Otto Seeck declared Ammianus to be cool and unbiased in his judgments, unmoved by the religious conflicts of his time, a pagan whose beliefs were purely theoretical, not a living creed.[24] Hermann Peter contrasted the "rhetorical whitewashing" of Ammianus' account of Julian's victory at Strasbourg with "the calm and moderation which constitute the main feature of his being."[25]

Gibbon's high estimate of Ammianus as an impartial historian has continued to be shared and repeated by most who have written about both the historian and the Roman Empire in the fourth century until very recently: Hugo Jones, for example, saluted him as "a great historian, a man of penetrating intelligence and of remarkable fairness."[26] One of the most lucid and precise statements of this traditional view can be found in M. L. W. Laistner's Sather Lectures of 1947, whose intelligent chapter on Ammianus remains worth reading and pondering. Laistner picked out "conspicuous fairmindedness" as

---

[21] *Decline and Fall*, 3.128 (B) = 1.1073 (W).

[22] *Decline and Fall*, 2.262 (B) = 1.686 (W); 3.311–18 (B) = 2.175–81 (W), where Gibbon blends and paraphrases Ammianus 14.6 and 28.4.

[23] *Decline and Fall*, 2.264, n. 18 (B) = 1.687, n. 16 (W).

[24] O. Seeck, *RE* 1 (1894), 1851.

[25] H. Peter, *Wahrheit und Kunst: Geschichtschreibung und Plagiat im klassischen Altertum* (Leipzig/Berlin, 1911), 403.

[26] Jones, *LRE* 116.

Ammianus' salient characteristic and pronounced that, apart from a general and undisguised dislike of Germans, he displays an obvious bias on only two matters:

> One of these is the description of Roman society, which is a kind of satire inspired by a long-established literary tradition and perhaps by the rigors of his earlier life; the other is a bitter outburst near the end of his work against the whole tribe of lawyers. Was this invective . . . inspired merely by certain general notions aroused by observing frequent malpractices in the administration of justice? It may be so, but it is tempting to imagine that behind his vitriolic bitterness lay some personal experience of having been bested by a smart attorney.

With his sensitivity to Latin, Laistner recognized the tendentious nature of Ammianus' excursus on Rome and lawyers (14.6.2–26; 28.4.6–35; 30.4.3–22), and Ammianus himself confesses his personal animosity against lawyers when he refers to the indignity that he had suffered at their hands in the East (30.4.4: super eius indignitate . . . quam in illis partibus agens expertus sum). Nevertheless, Laistner accepted the prevailing scholarly estimate of the quality of Ammianus' narrative without enquiring whether personal animus, concealed in apparently judicious language rather than openly avowed, could be a pervasive feature of his work.[27]

Gibbon's favorable assessment of Ammianus has recently received a full and able restatement in John Matthews' large book of 1989, which conveys its main message in its very title. The *Roman Empire of Ammianus* argues both that the historian depicted the society in which he lived fairly and accurately and that the Roman Empire of the second half of the fourth century really was as Ammianus depicts it:

> It will be obvious that he is a wonderfully eloquent witness of almost every aspect of the life and society of his times. In breadth of interest, wealth of circumstantial detail and power of observation, he rivals any other Greek or Roman historian known to us from any period, and outclasses most. As contemporary historians, only Thucydides and possibly Polybius have any prior claim to our admiration, and Ammianus' world is so much vaster, its political structures more forbidding, and its cultural complexity far greater than theirs: all seen with the observant eye of an individual fascinated by all forms of human conduct, a still living challenge to the modern historian of his age.[28]

[27] M. L. W. Laistner, *The Greater Roman Historians* (Berkeley, 1947), 141–61, 181–83: the passage quoted occurs on p. 158.

[28] Matthews, *Ammianus* (1989), 228.

Moreover, a subsequent essay by Matthews defends the accuracy of Ammianus' excursus on lawyers, which Laistner diagnosed as the product of personal resentment: it argues that the historian described "the real world" in which he lived, that "his accounts of it are full of precisely observed detail, which often occur when the rhetoric is most intense," and that the rhetorical aspects of his narrative method should not be overrated in relation to the circumstantial.[29] Thus, although Matthews concedes the force of Ammianus' rhetoric, he consistently emphasizes the "precisely observed detail" over the possibility that such details may be subservient to rhetoric and prejudice.

The traditional estimate of Ammianus that has held sway from Gibbon to Matthews confronts the obvious problem that this supposedly impartial and dispassionate historian writes with unusual violence and ferocity. How can a method of expression that so often distorts and contorts the phrase, the sentence, even the paragraph, be reconciled with Ammianus' postulated serenity of historical judgment? Appeal has naturally been made to modern artistic and literary analogies. Jacques Fontaine depicted Ammianus as a "romantic historian" comparable to Chateaubriand, while simultaneously arguing that the subjective and emotional elements in his text reflect the world in which he lived, and hence do not impair the lucidity, equanimity or detachment of his historical judgments.[30] But that is to treat the contradiction as if it were unimportant and to avoid rather than to solve a real problem.

When Sir Ronald Syme came to Ammianus at the age of sixty as a result of his newly discovered interest in the *Historia Augusta*, he immediately and instinctively recognized the problem:

> At the outset an historian proclaims that he will tell the truth. What else was he to say? The profession belongs to standard convention. . . .
>
> With Ammianus the thing is not a mere convention. Rather an obsession and a passion. It is insistent and pervasive. Truth and honesty will not be found in the court and the councils of the Caesars. . . .
>
> Ammianus was a truthful man. His portrayal of Julian verges on panegyric, but conveys pertinent criticism and permits a balanced estimate. Elsewhere he is dominated by a number of prejudices. He has nothing good to report of the lower classes, for example. In general, emotion (of the more honourable sort), the im-

[29] J. F. Matthews, *Cognitio Gestorum* (1992), 57.

[30] J. Fontaine, *BAGB* (1969), 417–35, esp. 418: "ce vieil officier, lucide, équanime, moralisateur, un peu distant." Fontaine rejects the application of the favorite term "baroque" to Ammianus, and he has recently tried to relate his style to a "Theodosian aesthetic" (*Cognitio Gestorum* [1992], 27–37).

portance of the theme, and the style he has elected impel him to exaggeration. That has happened to other historians.

The History (as extant) depends largely on his own experience and meditation: the memoirs of an old soldier developed, adorned, and reinforced by other information. . . . His own testimony is firm, valid and not to be discounted.[31]

Syme's analysis, although explicitly reasserting the traditional estimate of Ammianus as an impartial historian, also consciously subverts it. For Syme sees distortion not merely in a handful of passages and in Ammianus' confessed predilection for Julian, but as a pervasive and characteristic feature of the *Res Gestae*: although Syme's Ammianus was at heart "a truthful man," he is nevertheless "dominated by a number of prejudices," and he habitually exaggerates under the influence of emotion, theme, and style.

Some years after Syme wrote, the traditional assessment of Ammianus was subverted in another, even more troublesome, fashion. Tony Woodman adduced the third of the brief paragraphs quoted from Syme to redeem the reputation of Velleius Paterculus, whose history, dedicated to M. Vinicius during his consulate in A.D. 30, has usually been regarded as sycophantic and mendacious. Specifically, Woodman claimed that Syme's verdict on Ammianus "could with equal justice be applied to the Tiberian portion of Velleius' narrative."[32] Syme immediately protested against this revaluation of Velleius, for the obligation to produce panegyric does not excuse mindless repetition of the official version of events when it is patently false—and Velleius' language reflects the propaganda and rhetoric of the government of Tiberius while Sejanus was his chief minister.[33] As concerns Ammianus, the parallel is valid in at least one particular. Ammianus' loyalty to and partiality for his old commander Ursicinus inevitably recalls that of Velleius for his old commander-in-chief Tiberius.[34] Hence Woodman's misguided attempt to rescue the reputation of Velleius as a historian indirectly impugns that of Ammianus. The

---

[31] Syme, *Ammianus* (1968), 94.

[32] A. J. Woodman, *Velleius Paterculus: The Tiberian Narrative (2.94–131)* (Cambridge, 1977), 55–56.

[33] R. Syme, *Roman Papers*, 3 (Oxford, 1984), 1090–1104. Syme adduced Velleius' statement that the war against Tacfarinas in Africa, which lasted seven years, "auspiciis consiliisque eius [sc. Tiberius] brevi sepultum est" (2.129.4) as the clearest example of "mendacity in Velleius." The phrase *bellum/a sepultum/a*, which Velleius also uses four times in his account of Augustus (2.75.1, 82.1, 89.3, 90.1) is now known to reflect contemporary official phraseology: the *senatus consultum de Cn. Pisone patre* proclaims that Piso tried to arouse a civil war by invading Syria after the death of Germanicus, although "all the evils of civil war had been buried by the *numen* of Augustus and the virtues of Tiberius" (lines 45–49, esp. 47: omnibus civilis belli sepultis malis).

[34] Ammianus' partiality for Ursicinus was demonstrated by Thompson, *Ammianus* (1947), esp. 42–55—without noting the parallel.

comparison of the two writers poses an awkward and unavoidable question: can the traditional estimate of Ammianus withstand scrutiny in the light of modern techniques of both historical research and literary criticism? It has in fact begun to crumble. Half a century ago, a classic of modern literary criticism offered a fundamental reassessment of Ammianus, which most historians of Late Antiquity have been strangely reluctant to apply consistently to the evaluation of his narrative.[35]

[35] The present work deliberately refrains from any general assessment of modern scholarly research into the *Res Gestae*: For guidance readers should consult the full and helpful bibliographies in Seyfarth's preface to his Teubner edition, 1.xxv–xlvii; Rosen, *Ammianus* (1982), 183–221 (more than 400 items); Matthews, *Ammianus* (1989), 554–71 (with an introductory discussion of earlier bibliographical surveys). On the date of composition, a compelling case that Ammianus completed the *Res Gestae* no later than 390 or 391 has been made by C. P. T. Naudé, *AJAH* 9 (1984, publ. 1990), 70–94; Matthews, *Ammianus* (1989), 17–27.

[II]

REALITY AND ITS REPRESENTATION

Erich Auerbach published his classic study *Mimesis* in 1946, and it was superbly translated into English by Willard Trask in 1953.[1] Unfortunately, Trask rendered Auerbach's subtitle in a way that has unintentionally misled many readers and some critics. What is rendered into English as *The Representation of Reality in Western Literature* is subtly, but significantly, different from *Dargestellte Wirklichkeit in der abendländischen Literatur*. Whereas the original German means "reality (as) represented in western literature" with emphasis on the first noun, the English version replaces the noun qualified by a participial adjective by two nouns and thus shifts the emphasis from "reality" to its "representation." It is mistaken, therefore, to criticize Auerbach as if his book were exclusively a work of literary criticism.[2] On the contrary, as Rene Wellek noted in an important and influential review, Auerbach always moves beyond the analysis of style "to reflections on the attitude of a writer toward reality and his technique of reproducing it" and thence to "reflections about periods and cultures, social conditions and assumptions," so that his book "can be viewed as

[1] E. Auerbach, *Mimesis: Dargestellte Wirklichkeit in der abendländischen Literatur* (Bern, 1946); English translation by W. R. Trask, *Mimesis: The Representation of Reality in Western Literature* (Princeton, 1953). In an epilogue, Auerbach defined his subject as "die Interpretation des Wirklichen durch literarische Darstellung oder 'Nachahmung'" (494). Trask translates this as "the interpretation of reality through literary representation or 'imitation'" (534), thereby concealing Auerbach's subtle shift from the abstract "Wirklichkeit" of the book's title to the concrete "das Wirkliche" in the epilogue.

[2] On the historical or historiographical aspects of *Mimesis*, see esp. W. W. Holdheim, *CLIO* 10 (1981), 143–54; T. Bahti, *After Strange Texts: The Role of Theory in the Study of Literature*, ed. G. S. Jay and D. L. Miller (Univ. Ala., 1985), 127–45.

a short history of the human condition."[3] For it is a study of the development
of Western culture from its twin roots in Homer and the Old Testament to
the twentieth-century novel.

As is natural with a work of genius and profound originality, *Mimesis* was
seriously misrepresented by reviewers and commentators. Ernst Curtius, for
example, appealed to Otto Regenbogen for the proposition that one of Auerbach's two main theses was that only modern realism broke through the ancient doctrine of the three styles,[4] even though Auerbach had expressly asserted that "the rule of differentiated styles cannot possibly apply" to the
account of Peter's denial of Christ in the Gospel according to Mark, since the
depiction is "entirely realistic" and the mingling of styles "was rooted from
the beginning in the character of Jewish-Christian literature."[5] When Auerbach penned a dignified reply to Curtius, he not only corrected his critic's
misapprehension about his view of stylistic doctrines, but also explained the
nature of his book: his method (he asserted) was not sociological; what he had
offered was an interpretative essay written by a particular individual in a particular situation at a particular date.[6]

Ammianus' history, too, was written by a particular individual in a particular situation at a particular date, but it also claims to describe the world in
which he lived. From Ammianus, Auerbach selected for discussion an episode
in Book XV, which he thereby made famous.[7] In his review of the English
translation of *Mimesis*, Wellek commended Auerbach for selecting passages
"known to only a few specialists" and posed a question that was obviously not
intended to be rhetorical when he asked "Who has read the gruesome story
of the arrest of Peter Valvomeres in Ammianus Marcellinus?"[8] Ammianus' account of the arrest of Peter Valvomeres (15.7.4–5) provides both the title and
the starting point of the third chapter of Auerbach's book. In his discussion of
this episode, as throughout *Mimesis*, Auerbach combines literary criticism
with general verdicts about the temper of the age:

> The incident is so treated that it produces a strongly sensory impression—to
> such an extent in fact that many readers will feel it unpleasantly realistic. Am-
> mianus has oriented it entirely towards gestures: the compact crowd set against
> the imposing prefect as he domineers over them. This element of the sensory and

---

[3] R. Wellek, *Kenyon Review* 16 (1954), 299; cf. C. Landauer, *German Studies Review* 11 (1988),
84: "Auerbach is constructing a model of Western culture which is all-inclusive."

[4] E. R. Curtius, *Romanische Forschungen* 64 (1952), 57.

[5] Auerbach, *Mimesis* (1953), 41.

[6] E. Auerbach, *Romanische Forschungen* 65 (1954), 5–15, 17: "ein Buch, das ein bestimmter
Mensch, in einer bestimmten Lage, zu Anfang der 1940er Jahre geschrieben hat."

[7] Auerbach, *Mimesis* (1953), 50–60.

[8] Wellek, *Kenyon Review* 16 (1954), 299.

the gestural is prepared for from the first—through the choice of words and similes . . .—and reaches its climax in the scene at the Septemzodium when Leontius,
sitting in his carriage with flashing eyes confronts the "snakily" hissing mob like
an animal tamer, unmoved as they rapidly vanish. A riot, a solitary man trying
to quell it by the power of his eyes, then stepping in—some harsh words, a ring-
leader's muscular body raised high, finally a flogging. Then all is quiet, and, by
way of conclusion, we get a rape and the subsequent capital punishment.

For Auerbach, the world of Ammianus is a grim world, and the historian himself a profound pessimist:

Everywhere human emotion and rationality yield to the magically and somberly
sensory, to the graphic and the gestural. . . .

Ammianus' world is somber: it is full of superstition, blood frenzy, exhaustion,
fear of death, and grim and magically rigid gestures; and to counterbalance all
this there is nothing but the equally somber and pathetic determination to ac-
complish an ever more difficult, ever more desperate task: to protect the Empire,
threatened from without and crumbling within. . . .

With glittering words and pompously distorted constructions language begins to
depict the distorted, gory, and spectral reality of the age. . . .

Grotesque and sadistic, spectral and superstitious, lusting for power yet constantly trying to conceal the chattering of their teeth—so do we see the men of
Ammianus' ruling class and their world. . . .

Judged by classical standards, the style, both in diction and syntax, is overrefined
and exaggeratedly sensory; its effects are powerful, but distorted. Its effects are as
distorted as the reality it represents. Ammianus' world is very often a caricature
of the normal human environment in which we live; very often it is like a bad
dream. . . . Striking only in the sensory, resigned and as it were paralyzed despite
its stubborn rhetorical passion, his manner of writing history nowhere displays
anything redeeming, nowhere anything that points to a better future, nowhere
a figure or an act about which stirs the refreshing atmosphere of a greater freedom, a greater humanity.[9]

[9] Quoted from Auerbach, *Mimesis* (1953), 53, 53–54, 55, 56, 57, 59–60. Auerbach provided
his own translation, which "attempts to preserve the strangely baroque style of the original"
(51–52). The original reads as follows:
   dum has exitiorum communium clades suscitat turbo feralis,/ urbem aeternam Leontius
regens/ multa spectati iudicis documenta praebebat,/ in audiendo celerior,/ in discep-
tando iustissimus,/ natura benevolus/ licet auctoritatis causa servandae/ acer quibusdam

This analysis contains an inherent contradiction. Does Ammianus' style faithfully reflect the world that he describes? Or does it turn it into a "bad dream" that caricatures and distorts it? Auerbach appears to assert both these mutually incompatible propositions. What is "the normal human environment in which we live"? Is Auerbach's "we" here the human race in general or modern western men and women? It is necessary to distinguish between the literary analyses in *Mimesis* and its historical interpretations.

John Matthews has already drawn this distinction in a paper with the programmatic title "Peter Valvomeres, Re-arrested." [10] Matthews accuses Auerbach of being evasive and scores easy points against some of the historical assumptions that underlie his literary observations, particularly against Auerbach's claim that Ammianus fails adequately to indicate the social and historical context of the riot that the prefect Leontius suppressed. Yet, like most who have recently written about Ammianus, Matthews accepts the central contention of Auerbach's analysis—that "the prime quality of the passage is the pictorial imagery." Nor does Matthews reject Auerbach's diagnosis of the relation between Ammianus' text and the historical reality that it depicts. For Matthews argues that Ammianus' emphasis on pictorial effect and gesture corresponds to central aspects of public life in Late Antiquity: hence, where Auerbach emphasizes the elements of unreality and distortion, Matthews contends

---

videbatur et inclinatior ad damnandum. / prima igitur causa seditionis in eum concitandae vilissima fuit et levis. / Philoromum enim aurigam rapi praeceptum/ secuta plebs omnis velut defensura proprium pignus/ terribili impetu praefectum incessebat ut timidum,/ sed ille stabilis et erectus / immissis apparitoribus/ correptos aliquos vexatosque tormentis/ nec strepente ullo nec obsistente/ insulari poena multavit. / diebusque paucis secutis/ cum itidem plebs excita calore, quo consuevit,/ vini causando inopiam/ ad Septemzodium convenisset, celebrem locum,/ ubi operis ambitiosi Nymphaeum/ Marcus condidit imperator. / illuc de industria pergens praefectus/ ab omni toga apparitioneque rogabatur enixius,/ ne in multitudinem se arrogantem immitteret et minacem/ ex commotione pristina saevientem. / difficilis ad pavorem recta tetendit/ adeo, ut eum obsequen . . . desereret/ licet in periculum festinantem abruptum. / insidens itaque vehiculo/ cum speciosa fiducia contuebatur acribus oculis/ tumultuantium undique cuneorum/ veluti serpentium vultus/ perpessusque multa dici probrosa/ agnitum quendam inter alios eminentem/ vasti corporis rutilique capilli interrogavit,/ an ipse esset Petrus Valvomeres, ut audierat, cognomento. / eumque, cum esse sonu respondisset obiurgatorio,/ ut seditiosorum antesignanum olim sibi compertum/ reclamantibus multis / post terga manibus vinctis suspendi praecepit. / quo viso sublimi/ tribuliumque adiumentum nequiquam implorante/ vulgus omne paulo ante confertum/ per varia urbis membra diffusum/ ita evanuit, ut turbarum acerrimus concitor/ tamquam in iudiciali secreto/ exaratis lateribus/ ad Picenum eiceretur,/ ubi postea ausus eripere virginis non obscurae pudorem/ Patruini consularis sententia/ supplicio est capitali addictus. (15.7.2–5)
I have marked all the clausulae with a hasta [/]: my clausulation sometimes diverges from that of Seyfarth.)
[10] Matthews, *Homo Viator: Classical Essays for John Bramble* (Bristol/Oak Park, 1987), 277–84.

that in the fourth century both reality and social relations "conform to a the-atrical mode of expression."[11] In this attempt to establish that "reality and social relations" conformed to "a theatrical mode of expression" in the fourth century, however, Matthews blurs an important distinction that Auerbach had emphatically asserted. Auerbach acknowledged that Ammianus resembled Tacitus in certain ways, but he saw a fundamental difference between both the historical reality and its representation in the two historians: "a comparison with Tacitus (he wrote) serves to show how much stronger the magical and the sensory has become at the expense of the objectively rational."[12] For Matthews, in contrast, the similarities outweigh the differences. In his hands, Ammianus' representation of reality becomes dramatic in the sense of depict-ing historical action in the manner of a tragedy, as Tacitus does. For Matthews, the arrest of Peter Valvomeres, like other episodes in Ammianus, "is presented almost like a scene from a play, the contrasting emotions and postures of the sides preparing for the dialogue between the central characters." Matthews sees dramatic action in Ammianus, not merely dramatic tableaux: "the urban prefect Leontius approaches the rioting crowd almost as if in a crowd scene from a Shakespearean play, addressing the mob leader man to man, in a con-frontation of startling intimacy."[13]

The Shakespearean analogy is deeply misleading. It confuses two distinct senses of the word *theatrical*—and it ignores the profound differences between what could be seen on the dramatic stage in Tacitus' day and in the fourth century.[14] If Tacitus and Ammianus are both "theatrical," they are so in two very different ways (Chapter XV). Ammianus focuses not on the development of plot or the internal attitudes, emotions, and motives of the historical actors, as Tacitus does, but on the visual aspects of the historical drama, and he presents the drama itself not as a developing plot, but as a series of dramatic tableaux, that are discontinuous even when they succeed one another closely.[15]

Like contemporary poets, Ammianus practices what Michael Roberts has called "the jeweled style."[16] The analysis that Roberts gives of Ammianus' fa-

---

[11] Matthews, *Homo Viator* (1987), 279, cf. *Ammianus* (1989), 460–61. The visual character of Ammianus' portrayal of persons and events was illustrated in a justly famous paper by R. Mac-Mullen, *Art Bulletin* 46 (1964), 435–55.

[12] Auerbach, *Mimesis* (1953), 53.

[13] Matthews, *Homo Viator* (1987), 279, 280.

[14] For a brief description of these changes, see *Roman Theater and Society*, ed. W. J. Slater (Ann Arbor, 1996), 161–80.

[15] J. Fontaine, *Le Transformazioni della Cultura nella tarda Antichità: Atti del Convegno tenuto a Catania, Università degli Studi, 27 sett.–2 Ott. 1982* (Rome, 1985), 795–808. He attributes to Am-mianus an "optique nécessairement théâtrale, voire, si l'on ose ce néologisme, amphithéâtrale" (803).

[16] M. Roberts, *The Jeweled Style: Poetry and Poetics in Late Antiquity* (Ithaca, 1989), esp. 132.

mous description of Constantius' triumphal entry into Rome in 357 (16.10.4 –
12) can be applied to many scenes in his work, including the arrest of Peter
Valvomeres: "the effect is of a series of brilliantly eye-catching but discrete visual impressions, which in part by their very brilliance deter the viewer from
attempting to piece together the individual scenes into a coherently ordered
whole."[17] If this analysis of Ammianus' method of presenting reality and historical events is correct, it raises the question of how far this stylization has
distorted his depiction of historical reality. For such stylization must operate
at the unconscious and semiconscious levels as well as the conscious. The historian's representation of reality cannot be, as Gibbon asserted, merely a matter of surface rhetoric. Nor may it simply be assumed that his distorted style
and presentation faithfully reflect an unpleasant and distorted historical reality. Auerbach made that assumption, and it could be correct, but such an assumption needs to be proved before being made the basis of either a historical or a literary interpretation.

Do the findings of historical research confirm Ammianus' essential veracity or
call it into doubt? Much recent work on both Ammianus and the fourth century either delivers or implies a negative verdict on one whom Arnaldo
Momigliano characterized as "the lonely historian,"[18] a designation that subtly emphasizes the disjunction between the historian and the world he depicts.

Edward Thompson's slim volume of 1947 marked a watershed in historians'
approaches to Ammianus. Although Thompson reiterated that "the general
accuracy of Ammianus' monumental work even in matters of the minutest detail cannot seriously be called in question,"[19] he demonstrated how unfair in
general, and how misleading and even inaccurate in detail, is Ammianus' account of the actions and policies of the emperor Constantius. Thompson's
specific arguments were too often a priori and too often based on unexamined
assumptions, yet he established two central facts about the Res Gestae beyond
all reasonable doubt. The first was that Ammianus' account of Constantius'
court and military policies is colored by his admiration for his commanding
officer and friend Ursicinus.[20] Thompson showed that there is good reason to
believe that Ammianus has exaggerated the merits of Ursicinus and that sympathy for the general after he was dismissed as magister militum led the historian to his hostile view of the emperor, which was then strongly reinforced

[17] M. Roberts, Philologus 132 (1988), 183.
[18] A. Momigliano, Annali della Scuola Superiore Normale di Pisa, Classe di lettere e filosofia,
Ser. 3.4 (1974), 1393–1407.
[19] Thompson, Ammianus (1947), 40.
[20] Thompson, Ammianus (1947), 40–55.

by his admiration for Julian, whose propaganda against Constantius he sometimes repeats.

Second, as a Marxist and a Communist, Thompson was sensitive to Ammianus' class bias. Thompson recognized a textbook bourgeois when he read one. He did not invent the idea that the historian was a *curialis* by legal origin and status: Wilhelm Ensslin had already argued in 1923 that curial status helps to explain Ammianus attitudes and *Weltanschauung*.[21] But Thompson detected the attitudes of a *curialis* in so many passages that it seemed impossible any longer to doubt that Ammianus belonged to the "upper middle class," the curial class that was both "oppressed and oppressive," and that his status as a *curialis* provided a basis for understanding both his career and much in his history.[22]

The task of reassessing the quality of Ammianus as a historian has subsequently been prosecuted with vigor by several scholars with very different approaches.[23] Yet not all such enquiries have applied the relentless logic that such a reevaluation requires. In the 1970s, although Roger Blockley produced both a monograph on the historiography and political thought of Ammianus and a series of articles in which he consistently called the historian's factual accuracy into question, he too often appealed to Ammianus' political and moral assumptions or invoked the copying of rhetorical models as omnibus explanations for postulated distortion rather than employing all the available evidence to prove specific inaccuracies, unfair bias, or the suppression of relevant facts.[24] Moreover, despite the implications of his arguments about individual episodes, Blockley paradoxically reaffirmed the traditional general estimate of Ammianus as a sincere and honest historian, "faithful to the truth."[25]

---

[21] Ensslin, *Ammianus* (1923), esp. 4–6.

[22] Thompson, *Ammianus* (1947), 2, 15, n. 6, 68, 81–85, 128–29, followed by R. Pack, *CP* 48 (1953), 80–85; G. A. Crump, *Ammianus Marcellinus as a Military Historian* (*Historia Einzelschriften* 27, 1975), 5–13; N. J. E. Austin, *Ammianus on Warfare: An Investigation into Ammianus' Military Knowledge* (*Collection Latomus* 165, 1979), 12–13; T. D. Barnes, *Reading the Past* (1990), 62.

[23] Esp. C. P. T. Naudé, *Ammianus Marcellinus in de Lig van die Antieke Geskiedskrywing* (Diss. Leiden, 1956); *Acta Classica* 1 (1958), 92–105 (battles and sieges); Demandt, *Zeitkritik* (1965); Rosen, *Studien* (1970); Bitter, *Kampfschilderungen* (1976): for critical comments on some of Rosen's main arguments, see N. J. E. Austin, *Historia* 22 (1973), 331–35; G. Calboli, *Bollettino di Studi Latini* 4 (1974), 67–103. J. Szidat, *Cognitio Gestorum* (1992), 107–16, has recently argued that exaggeration does not lead Ammianus to distort historical reality in any important way.

[24] R. P. C. Blockley, *AJP* 93 (1972), 437–50: Ammianus was "strongly influenced" by Julian's propaganda and hence "must be used with caution"; *Latomus* 31 (1972), 433–68: Ammianus' account of Gallus is "suspect on grounds both literary and historical"; *Ammianus* (1975); *Phoenix* 31 (1977), 218–31: the account of the Battle of Strasbourg is shaped so as to produce "a microcosm of Ammianus' overall attitude toward Roman-German relations"; *Studies in Latin Literature and Roman History* 2 (*Collection Latomus* 168, 1980), 467–86: Ammianus had an "almost paranoid dislike" of Constantius.

[25] Blockley, *Ammianus* (1975), 100, 101, 136.

Some recent assessments of Ammianus have been markedly more critical. In 1979, Chantal Vogler published an analysis of the administration of Constantius in which she was perforce compelled to evaluate the main sources for his reign: she stigmatized Ammianus' account of Constantius' dealings with his Caesars as a mass of subjective impressions requiring correction because the historian was carried away by his sympathies for Julian, and she observed that "historical truth does not always win." [26] In a monograph on Ammianus published in 1983, Thomas Elliott correctly identified some cases of gross distortion, although he formulated his case too brusquely and sometimes too carelessly to convince others that he was right.[27] In particular, the thesis argued by Elliott (following Salvatore D'Elia) [28] that Ammianus is a pagan apologist who treats Christianity unfairly was answered by David Hunt in an article that was hailed as a definitive refutation[29]—prematurely, since its central arguments are demonstrably fallacious.[30]

Most recently, John Drinkwater has called the historian's bluff over his account of the alleged rebellion of Silvanus, which he helped to suppress (15.5.15−34).[31] Although Ammianus' account of this "reluctant usurper" has always been accepted largely at face value,[32] there are strong grounds for scepticism. Admittedly, it very quickly came to be accepted that Silvanus proclaimed himself Augustus at Cologne (15.5.16) and reigned for twenty-eight days.[33] But the alleged usurpation leaves no trace whatever in the Roman imperial coinage of nearby Trier.[34] Hence Silvanus never minted coins in his name. That fact implies that in reality he never laid claim to the imperial power:

[26] C. Vogler, *Constantius II et l'administration impériale* (Strasbourg, 1979), 44.

[27] Elliott, *Ammianus* (1983), cf. J. M. Alonso-Núñez, *JRS* 76 (1986), 328: "Elliott has exaggerated the bias introduced by Ammianus in his narrative, to reach the surprising conclusion that he was not an impartial historian. . . . His verdict that Ammianus was a pagan apologist and thus an anti-Christian historian representing the pagan reaction is completely distorted." That does not do justice to Elliott's recognition of how bias can be disguised (*Ammianus* [1983], 12−13, with a telling modern analogy).

[28] Elliott, *Ammianus* (1983), 205−21, cf. S. D'Elia, *Studi romani* 10 (1972), 372−90, partly anticipated by A. Selem, *Rivista di Cultura Classica e Medioevale* 6 (1964), 224−61.

[29] E. D. Hunt, *CQ*, N.S. 35 (1985), 186−200: heartily commended by Matthews, *Ammianus* (1989), 435−51, 546, n. 22, 547, n. 32−33.

[30] See *Reading the Past* (1990), 75−82; *CP* 88 (1993), 67−70; Chapter IX.

[31] J. F. Drinkwater, *Studies in Latin Literature and Roman History* 7 (*Collection Latomus* 227, 1994), 569−76.

[32] Syme, *Ammianus* (1968), 5, 11. Unlike many others, Syme correctly allowed for the lacuna in 15.5.30.

[33] Julian, *Orat.* 1, 48bc; *Pan. Lat.* 3(11).13.3; Eutropius, *Brev.* 10.13; Jerome, *Chronicle* 239[d] Helm; *Epitome* 42.10.

[34] *RIC* 9.165−67. The contrast to the revolt of Poemenius against Magnentius in 353 is striking (ib. 164−5). It need hardly be added that *CIL* 10.6945 = *ILS* 748 (Aversa) cannot be a milestone of Silvanus.

paradoxically, once that is granted, most of Ammianus' account of the suppression of Silvanus becomes more (not less) plausible.[35]

The time is thus ripe for a systematic investigation of the structure, nature, and quality of Ammianus' *Res Gestae*, which combines literary and historical approaches. In the chapters that follow, the formal structure of the *Res Gestae* and its arrangement of material are laid out (Chapters III–V). Next, the historian's origin, social status, culture, and attitudes are investigated (Chapters VI–IX). Third, Ammianus' presentation of both the main historical actors and several supporting characters in the period for which the history is extant are assessed (Chapters X–XIII). Then it is asked how Ammianus interpreted the whole sweep of Roman history and what he expected of the future (Chapter XIV). In conclusion, Ammianus is compared briefly with two other great historians: Tacitus, whom he had read and whom he imitated in various ways, and Macaulay, who uncannily resembles him as a historian (Chapter XV). The aim is to provide a companion to Ammianus on the model of Sir Charles Firth's classic companion to Macaulay's *History of England*, which concentrated on the modern historian's fundamental historical beliefs and his manner of depicting persons and events.[36]

[35] Drinkwater, *Studies in Latin Literature*, 7 (1994), 575–76, suggesting that Ursicinus had Silvanus killed "out of self-interest."

[36] C. Firth, *A Commentary on Macaulay's History of England*, ed. G. Davies (London, 1938). Macaulay's unfair denigration of the Duke of Marlborough and William Penn and his whitewashing of his hero William III had been exposed in a series of essays by John Paget published between 1858 and 1860 and later collected together in book form as *The New "Examen"* (Edinburgh/London, 1861). Although the great historian's reputation all but obliterated Paget's criticisms at the time, as Winston Churchill complained in the preface to his reissue of his book ([Halifax, 1934], ix–xv), their basic validity is now taken for granted by all who write about Macaulay: Firth, *Commentary* (1938), 263–76; H. R. Trevor-Roper, *The Romantic Movement and the Study of History* (London, 1969), 8–9; J. Clive, *Not by Fact Alone* (New York, 1989), 72.

[III]

SYMMETRY AND STRUCTURE

The twentieth century, or at least English-speaking culture in the twentieth century, has lost the feeling for symmetry and formal structure that came instinctively to earlier ages. Formal structure, that is, the division of long works into books among the ancients and their division into volumes in the modern age, was important for all historians in the classical tradition until the nineteenth century. The subsequent loss of this sense of the architecture of a history that also sets out to be a literary masterpiece can be charted through a comparison of the original publication of Edward Gibbon's *History of the Decline and Fall of the Roman Empire* in the late eighteenth century and the edition by John Bagnall Bury, which has been the standard edition of Gibbon's work used by scholars during the twentieth century.[1]

Gibbon published the first volume of his *Decline and Fall* in 1776, the second and third together in 1781, and the last three of the six volumes together in 1788.[2] Each installment has a carefully balanced structure and each volume a careful and deliberate internal arrangement, though without any perceptible concern for formal symmetry in the number of chapters. The first volume had a total of sixteen chapters. The central block of eleven chapters is a political

[1] First published in 1896–1900. For the normal mode of referring to *Decline and Fall* in the present work, see Chapter I, n. 8.

[2] For the pervasive differences between the three installments of 1776, 1781, and 1788 on practically every level, see D. Womersley, *The Transformation of "The Decline and Fall of the Roman Empire"* (Cambridge, 1988). Womersley's subsequent critical edition (London, 1994) preserves the architecture of Gibbon's masterpiece. For, although each of its three volumes includes two of Gibbon's original six, a facsimile of the title page of the first edition of each of Gibbon's original volumes and Gibbon's prefaces to his second and fourth volumes are printed in their original positions, immediately preceding Chapters I, XVII, XXVII, XXXIX, XLVIII, and LVIII.

and military narrative of the history of the Roman Empire from 180 to 324; these are framed by three introductory chapters that survey the stable empire of the Antonines and two concluding chapters that describe and analyze the rise of Christianity down to the "Great Persecution" of 303–313. The second and third volumes had ten and twelve chapters, respectively. They took the main narrative to 476 and concluded with an epilogue discussing the causes of the "Fall of the Roman Empire in the West," which Gibbon had composed as a separate brief essay before the publication of the first volume.[3] The final three volumes, with a total of thirty-three chapters, formed a clear compositional unit too, whose function was not merely to take the story down to 1453, but also to explain the origin of the world in which Gibbon lived.[4]

Each volume of the second installment (though not perhaps of the third) exhibits a deliberate and careful arrangement of the historical material. The second volume covers the five and a half decades between Constantine's defeat of Licinius in 324 and the Battle of Adrianople, concluding with an epilogue on the settlement of the Goths. Hence it includes the whole of the period covered by the extant books of Ammianus. Gibbon follows his principal source for the years 353–378 in giving generous space and great prominence to the emperor Julian, but he balances this by assigning an emphatic and important place to Athanasius as bishop of Alexandria from 328 to 373.[5] The volume has ten chapters in all. It begins with one chapter on the foundation of Constantinople and Constantine's organization of the "new empire" and two chapters that narrate the political and military history of the Roman Empire from 324 to Julian's proclamation as Augustus in 360. The central place is filled by two chapters on the Christian church in the fourth century and three on the brief reign of Julian. Athanasius, whom Ammianus had deliberately treated as a marginal figure (15.7.7–10),[6] occupies a position close to the very middle of Gibbon's second volume, where he is presented as a champion of religious freedom who defied the tyranny of Constantius, and as a man who possessed

---

[3] The precise date of composition (1772 or 1773) is disputed: see P. R. Ghosh, *JRS* 73 (1983), 1–23; P. B. Craddock, *Edward Gibbon, Luminous Historian, 1772–1794* (Baltimore/London, 1989), 8–11; P. R. Ghosh, *JRS* 81 (1991), 132–56.

[4] P. B. Craddock, *Roman Images*, ed. A. Patterson (Baltimore, 1984), 63–82. Chapter LV, for example, observes at the outset that "the disciples of Mahomet still hold the civil and religious sceptre of the Oriental world" and concludes with the words "the light of knowledge which arose on the western world" (6.129, 166 [B] = 3.440, 470 [W]).

[5] On Gibbon's treatment of Athanasius, his dependence on Tillemont, and his disingenuous answer to the charge of plagiarism, which has too often been accepted uncritically, see *Corolla Torontonensis. Studies in Honour of Ronald Morton Smith*, ed. E. I. Robbins and S. Sandahl (Toronto, 1994), 14–25.

[6] Ammianus here writes as if he had not mentioned Athanasius before, despite his importance in imperial politics in the 340s and in 350: see *Athanasius* (1993), 166–68.

"a superiority of character and abilities which would have qualified him, far better than the degenerate sons of Constantine, for the government of a geat monarchy."[7] The final pair of chapters reflect the final books of Ammianus: one takes the main narrative down to 375, and the last frames an account of the campaigns of 376–378 between a digression on the Huns and the settlement of the Goths after the Battle of Adrianople.

All this (and much more) is very clear about the structure of Gibbon's *History of the Decline and Fall of the Roman Empire*, which recent studies have done much to illuminate in detail.[8] But it entirely escaped Bury, who believed that, because Gibbon was a great historian who (unlike David Hume) was still read, he could and should be corrected and brought up to date by judicious additions to his footnotes and appendices supplied by a scientific historian, so that twentieth-century readers could not only enjoy Gibbon's masterly prose but also imbibe accurate and up-to-date information about the period that the *Decline and Fall* covered.[9] Bury's edition contains seven volumes, not six, and it ignores every single one of Gibbon's carefully chosen divisions between volumes.

Two of Bury's deviations from Gibbon's original structure are particularly unfortunate. Bury put the pair of intimately connected chapters in which Gibbon analyzed the rise of Christianity at the beginning of the second volume instead of at the end of the first as the author did. These famous chapters adopted a tone of barely concealed hostility toward the Christians of the first three centuries, and they were greeted with an avalanche of angry clerical ripostes, to which Gibbon replied in 1779 with *A Vindication of Some Passages in the Fifteenth and Sixteenth Chapters of the History of the Decline and Fall of the Roman Empire*.[10] Because of this controversy, the subsequent five volumes of the *Decline and Fall*, published in 1783 and 1788, adopt a significantly different tone toward Christianity and Christians: Gibbon mocks gently with an air of amused detachment where he had earlier mounted a frontal attack employing outright ridicule.[11] Worse still, Bury put Gibbon's "General Observations on the Fall of the Roman Empire in the West," which he printed with separately numbered footnotes as an epilogue to both his second instal-

---

[7] *Decline and Fall*, 2.384 (B) = 1.796 (W).

[8] Esp. L. Braudy, *Narrative Form in History and Fiction* (Princeton, 1970), 225–68; Craddock, *Gibbon* (1989), 101–3, 149–59, 184–93, 213–16, 241–44.

[9] See the "Introduction by the Editor" in Bury's first edition of *Decline and Fall* (1 [London, 1896], xxxi–lxviii).

[10] On Gibbon's immediate reaction to criticism of these two chapters, which he later misrepresented, see the illuminating essay by D. Womersley, *Edward Gibbon and Empire*, ed. R. McKitterick and R. Quinault (Cambridge, 1997), 190–216.

[11] M. C. Noonkester, *HTR* 83 (1990), 399–414.

ment and the third volume of his *Decline and Fall*, in a completely unemphatic position in the middle of his fourth volume.[12]

The ancients were extremely sensitive to formal, balanced, symmetrical structure in literary works on a large scale. Dictionaries and grammars in Late Antiquity, it was observed long ago, all comprised exactly twenty books, no more and no less, "in accordance with the fashion which regulated Latin lexicographical works."[13] Creative and more original writers in less academic genres either observed the conventions of symmetry or used them to convey or insinuate an implicit message. Quintilian wrote his *Institutio Oratoria* in twelve books. He could have chosen ten or possibly fifteen instead, but hardly eleven or thirteen. When Apuleius composed his *Metamorphoses* in eleven books, he was deliberating flouting, or rather exploiting, convention in order to set the eleventh and last book outside the narrative of Lucius' adventures in Greece: he could trust his readers to draw the desired inference that it marked an ascent to a higher realm of reality and describes a genuine conversion that stands outside the story of the "golden ass."[14] Augustine knew the convention and tried to observe it. His *City of God* has a total of twenty-two books, but it falls into two parts, of ten and twelve books respectively, which could in their turn be divided into two groups of five books and three of four.[15]

A century ago Curt Wachsmuth identified two patterns widely employed by Greek and Roman authors who wrote long histories divided into many books: some historians arranged their work in multiples of five or ten books (pentads and decades), and the total number of books remained a multiple of ten even when the complexity or proportions of the material destroyed the internal symmetry of the work. Others composed in hexads, or groups of six books. Examples of the first pattern are easy to find: the history of early Rome by Dionysius of Halicarnassus, the Elder Pliny's *Bella Germaniae* and Josephus' *Jewish Antiquities*, each in twenty books; Polybius and Diodorus Siculus in forty books; and the eighty books of Cassius Dio's *Roman History*, much of

[12] *Decline and Fall*, 4.172–81 (B) = 2.508–16 (W).

[13] W. M. Lindsay, *Nonius Marcellus' Dictionary of Republican Latin* (Oxford, 1902), 1–2, adducing also Aulus Gellius and Isidore of Seville. Lindsay held the fact all the more significant because Nonius' materials "did not lend themselves readily to this division, so that the books are awkwardly uneven in size."

[14] J. Tatum, *Apuleius and "The Golden Ass"* (Ithaca, 1979), 21–37, 80–91.

[15] Augustine, *Ep. ad Firmum* = *Ep.* 1A.1 Divjak. For groups of five books of larger historical works (e.g., Livy) transmitted together, C. Wachsmuth, *Rh. Mus.*, N. F. 46 (1891), 329–31. The thirteen books of the *Confessions* are widely believed to result from Augustine's insertion of the tenth book into an original twelve (*CP* 89 [1994], 294).

which falls naturally into sections embracing five or ten books.[16] And it may be argued that Livy, who clearly divided the extant part of his history *Ab Urbe Condita* into pentads and decades, continued this strict arrangement to the very end of his work, composing a total of one hundred and forty books rather than one hundred and forty-two, as the manuscripts of the *Periochae* imply (Appendix 2).

The prime example of composition in hexads, often themselves divided into balancing triads, is Tacitus.[17] His *Annals* originally contained eighteen books, his *Histories* twelve. In the fourth century they circulated as a combined work in thirty books.[18] No reader of Tacitus can miss the clear division between *Annals* I–III and IV–VI: Book IV opens with a character sketch of Sejanus and a survey of the Roman Empire, both deliberately deferred from Tacitus' account of the year 14 in the first book, and Book VI closes with the death of Tiberius and an analysis of his character.[19] There is a similar division in the six books devoted to the reign of Nero: the second half of Book XV narrates the suppression of the Pisonian conspiracy of 65, and XVI opens with a symbolic foreshadowing of Nero's impending downfall.[20] As for the *Histories*, Books I–III narrate the civil wars of 69 and conclude with the death of Vitellius, whereas the fourth book opens with the consolidation of the Flavian regime in Rome and a senatorial debate in which Helvidius Priscus confronts Eprius Marcellus, through which Tacitus sets the tone of his treatment of Vespasian by contrasting the philosopher who criticized him with a *delator* who was one of his closest advisers until he perished in 79, presumably toward the end of Book VI.[21]

Hexadic composition can be detected even in the forty-four books of Pompeius Trogus' *Historiae Philippicae*, which Wachsmuth analyzed as seven groups

---

[16] Pliny, *Ep.* 3.5.3/4; C. Wachsmuth, *Einleitung in das Studium der alten Geschichte* (Leipzig, 1895), 83–89 (Diodorus), 440 (Josephus), 639 (Dionysius), 597–600 (Dio), 644–48 (Polybius). For pentadic and decadic structure in Dio, which is obscured by textual losses, see A. von Gutschmid, *Kleine Schriften*, 5 (Leipzig, 1894), 561–62; F. Millar, *A Study of Cassius Dio* (Oxford, 1964), 39.

[17] E. Wölfflin, *Hermes* 21 (1886), 157–59.

[18] Jerome, *Comm. in Zach.* 3.14.1/2 (*PL* 25.1522 = *CCL* 76A.878): Cornelius quoque Tacitus, qui post Augustum usque ad mortem Domitiani vitas Caesarum triginta voluminibus exaravit. For proof that the *Annals* had eighteen books and the *Histories* twelve, see R. Syme, *Tacitus* (Oxford, 1958), 211–15, 263–66, 686–67. For subsequent discussion, G. Wille, *Der Aufbau der Werke des Tacitus* (Amsterdam, 1983), 222–341, 358–647.

[19] Tacitus, *Ann.* 4.1–2, 5–6, 6.57, cf. R. H. Martin and A. Woodman, *Tacitus: Annals, Book IV* (Cambridge, 1989), 12–14.

[20] Tacitus, *Ann.* 16.1–3 (Dido's gold); cf. A. J. Woodman, *Tacitus and the Tacitean Tradition* (Princeton, 1993), 127–28.

[21] On the structure of the *Historiae*, see esp. Syme, *Tacitus*, 211–16.

of six books with a virtual postscript of two.[22] What then of Ammianus' thirty-one books? The number is anomalous. It cannot be justified by appeal to the thirty-seven books of the Elder Pliny's *Natural History* because that total is reached by prefixing an index and lists of authorities used, which is numbered as Book I, to thirty-six books of the *Natural History* proper. Wachsmuth accordingly accepted the theory endorsed (though not invented) by Alfred von Gutschmid that a book has been lost between XXX and XXXI, so that the original number of books was the aesthetically acceptable total of thirty-two.[23] This theory is not merely implausible, but impossible, since Ammianus does not in fact completely omit western events after 22 November 375: he omits the political history of the West after the proclamation of Valentinian II as Augustus (described in 30.10.4−6) so that he can avoid writing about the execution of the general Theodosius in Carthage during the winter of 375−376, an event too embarrassing for a historian to describe during the reign of his son.[24] Moreover, Ammianus follows Tacitus, who may be his conscious model, in adopting a triadic and hexadic structure.

The extant eighteen books of the *Res Gestae* have the following obvious hexadic structure:

XIV–XIX	Gallus and Julian as Caesars (353−359)
XX–XXV	Julian as Augustus (360−363)
XXVI–XXXI	The reigns of Valentinian in the West (364−375) and Valens in the East (364−378)

Furthermore, the first two of these hexads divide neatly into pairs of triads with identifiable main themes:

XIV–XVI	The fall of Gallus, the appointment of Julian as Caesar, and his initial successes in Gaul
XVII–XIX	Julian's continuing success in Gaul contrasted with Constantius' failure in Mesopotamia
XX–XXII	The proclamation of Julian as Augustus, his conflict with Constantius, and his rule as sole emperor until the end of 362
XXIII–XXV	Julian's Persian expedition and its immediate consequences

---

[22] Wachsmuth, *Einleitung*, 113, commended by R. Syme, *Roman Papers*, 6 (Oxford, 1991), 370.

[23] Wachsmuth, *Einleitung*, 682−83, cf. A. von Gutschmid, *Kleine Schriften* 5 (Leipzig, 1894), 572−73. The theory that a whole book has been lost between Books XXX and XXXI goes back to Chifflet and Valesius in the seventeenth century.

[24] On this obscure episode, see esp. A. Demandt, *Historia* 18 (1969), 598−636; R. M. Errington, *Klio* 78 (1996), 443−47.

It may be deduced by extrapolation, therefore, that the *Res Gestae* had a hexadic structure throughout: accordingly, it may be proposed that the full text contained the aesthetically acceptable total of thirty-six books. That hypothesis may seem too adventurous, too speculative, yet it solves the otherwise intractable problem of the scope and content of the lost books.

The *Res Gestae* began with the reign of Nerva, who was proclaimed emperor after the assassination of Domitian on 18 September 96, and they end with the aftermath of the Battle of Adrianople, which was fought on 9 August 378 (31.16.9, 12.10). Book XIV, the first to survive, opens with a reference back to Constantius' invasion of Gaul in the summer of 353 and a transition to eastern affairs during the same summer (14.1.1), and Book XXXI, which concludes the work, concentrates on the events leading up to the disastrous battle in which the emperor Valens perished. Neither pair of facts is in itself either controversial or problematical. Taken together, however, they imply a series of questions that are both troublesome and unavoidable. The first six extant books (XIV–XIX) cover a period of six years (353–359), the next six (XX–XXV) a mere four, from January 360 to February 364. At what point precisely did Ammianus begin to describe events in such amplitude? Where in his narrative did he make the transition from dependence on written sources to contemporary history? And, above all, how was he able to cover two and a half centuries in thirteen books? The vast majority of modern scholars who have studied Ammianus have found no insuperable difficulty in believing that his account of the years 96–353 occupied only thirteen books. Too often, however, the problem has been mitigated or removed by making the tacit and mistaken assumption that Ammianus' narrative expanded to the amplitude of the first extant books exactly where the surviving portion commences.[25] Thus a standard history of Latin literature declared that we can reconcile ourselves to the loss of the first thirteen books "because the more valuable part, in which Ammianus describes the events of his own time, has been spared destruction."[26] Similarly, G. B. Pighi suggested that Ammianus covered the century between the assassinations of Domitian and Commodus in four books, the next ninety years to the accession of Diocletian in another four, and the period from 20 November 284 to the summer of 353 in five,[27] a reconstruction that entails a very cursory treatment of the reigns of Diocletian and Constantine.

[25] H. Peter, *Wahrheit und Kunst: Geschichtschreibung und Plagiat im klassischen Altertum* (Leipzig/Berlin, 1911), 401: "der das Werk des Tacitus als Reichsgeschichte . . . fortgesetzt hat, zuerst kurz, von dem vierzehnten an (dem J. 353), dem ersten erhaltenen, schon ausführlich."

[26] M. Schanz, *Geschichte der römischen Litteratur*, 4.1² (Munich, 1914), 95.

[27] G. B. Pighi, *Ammiani Marcellini Rerum Gestarum capita selecta* (Neuchâtel/Paris, 1948), ix (with minor errors of chronology).

There have so far been two sharp challenges to this uncomfortable orthodoxy. In 1880 Hugo Michael developed the hypothesis, stated baldly at the
end of his dissertation of 1874,[28] that Ammianus either wrote two separate
works separately numbered or composed a history in two parts: he argued that
the first work or part, of unknown size and scale, comprised a history of the
Roman Empire from Nerva to Constantine, whereas the other was a history
of his own day from the death of Constantine, of which the first thirteen
books are lost. Michael employed two principal arguments, which he based
on extant cross-references to the lost portions of the work: first, Ammianus'
lost account of the period 337–353 was as full as the extant account of the
years 353 onward, so that the lost Books I–XIII covered only the years 337–
353 and cannot have begun at any point earlier than the death of Constantine;
second, Ammianus' references in extant excursus to earlier lost excursus imply that he wrote two separate works because he avoided repeating digressions
on the same subject within the second, partially extant work, but readily repeated the substance of digressions that had occurred in the first.[29]

Michael's theory soon encountered trenchant criticism from Ludwig Jeep,
who was generally held to have disproved it.[30] In the 1960s, however, Henry
Rowell reiterated Michael's conclusions and argued again that the extant Books
XIV–XXXI are the last eighteen books of a contemporary history commenc-
ing in 337 "when Constantine died and a new era began with the accession
of his sons."[31] Although Alan Cameron declared himself "wholly convinced"
by Rowell's reformulation of Michael's theory,[32] Ronald Syme and Frank
Gilliam, who both considered it carefully, were more sceptical and rejected it.
Yet neither was completely categorical in his denial. Syme appeared to accept
the possibility of "two works, perhaps, not one," but argued that "two separate works, separately numbered, do not have to be accepted," and avowed a
preference for envisaging a single work in two parts, Books I–X covering the
years 96–337 with Book XI beginning in 337 and constituting the first book

[28] H. Michael, *De Ammiani Marcellini studiis Ciceronianis* (Diss. Breslau, 1874), 50, Thesis IV.

[29] H. Michael, *Die verlorenen Bücher des Ammianus Marcellinus* (Prog. Breslau, 1880): following the fashion of his time, Michael also believed that a book had been lost between XXX and
XXXI (17, adducing the unfulfilled promises in 28.1.57; 22.8.35).

[30] L. Jeep, *Rh. Mus.*, N. F. 43 (1888), 60–72, accepted by M. Petschenig, *Bursians Jahres-
berichte* 72 (1892, pub. 1893), 3–4.

[31] H. T. Rowell, *Ammianus Marcellinus. Soldier-Historian of the Late Roman Empire* (Cincinnati,
1964), 16–21. The same scholar later argued, unconvincingly, that Ammianus refers to the city of
Rome in 14.6.2 in a fashion that would be impossible if the same work had included accounts of
the imperial visits of Diocletian in 303 or of Constantine in 312–313, 315, and 326 (H. T. Rowell, *Mélanges d'archéologie, d'épigraphie et d'histoire offerts à Jérôme Carcopino* [Paris, 1966], 845–48).

[32] Alan Cameron, *Claudian. Poetry and Propaganda at the Court of Honorius* (Oxford, 1970),
359, n. 2.

of Ammianus' history of his own time.[33] Gilliam commended Syme's conclusions as reasonable and therefore approximately correct, yet explicitly conceded that the results of his survey of Ammianus' references to the period 117–285 "do not exclude a longer account in a separate work."[34] Hence it was claimed, as recently as 1984, that "the ghost of two works cannot yet be laid to rest."[35] But five years later John Matthews reformulated the orthodox view and asserted that the *Res Gestae* was not really a history of the Roman Empire from 96 to 378, as Ammianus appears to state, but "in essentials a history of the present age, its nature defined by the methods outlined in the preface to Book XV," to which the early books served as "little more than a substantial introduction."[36]

Neither the orthodox view, even with this modification, nor the hypotheses of Michael and Rowell remove a very real difficulty. It is not possible to postulate two separate works, since Ammianus refers back to his account of the sack of Seleucia by the generals of Lucius Verus in the winter of 165–166 with the words "as we have related before" (23.6.24: ut ante rettulimus). On the other hand, it would be an extraordinary coincidence if Ammianus' history suddenly expanded to its present scale precisely at the point where the surviving books happen to begin—surely too extraordinary to be believed except on strong and compelling evidence. Hence there appears to be a dilemma: Ammianus cannot have compressed his history of the Roman Empire from 96 to 353 into a mere thirteen books, yet the books that survive are the last eighteen books of a single historical work that began with 96 and ended in 378. Because the dilemma cannot be escaped in either of the two ways so far attempted, a new solution of the problem must be sought. One is available in the hypothesis that the transmitted book numbers are erroneous and that each book originally bore a number five greater than its transmitted number. In other words, let it be postulated that Ammianus wrote a total of thirty-six books, not thirty-one, arranged in six hexads as follows:

1–6 (lost)   From Nerva (96–98) to Diocletian (284–305)

7–12 (lost)   Constantine (306–337)

13–18 (lost)   Constantius' rise to sole rule over the Roman Empire (337–353)

19–24 (= XIV–XIX)   Gallus and Julian as Caesars (353–359)

25–30 (= XX–XXV)   Julian as Augustus (360–363)

31–36 (= XXVI–XXXI)   The reigns of Valentinian and Valens (364–378)

[33] Syme, *Ammianus* (1968), 8–9. Similar opinions are repeated by Blockley, *Ammianus* (1975), 12–15; Sabbah, *Méthode* (1978), 2.

[34] J. F. Gilliam, *Bonner Historia-Augusta-Colloquium 1970* (1972), 125–26.

[35] A. Emmett, *History and Historians* (1984), 49, 42.

[36] Matthews, *Ammianus* (1989), 27, 30.

This hypothesis cuts the Gordian knot of the traditional problem by changing its terms. It postulates that what survives is precisely the second half of Ammianus' work, and it thus provides enough space in the early books to accommodate long and frequent excursus on the scale implied by Ammianus' cross-references (Appendix 3). Can anything more be said in its favor?

The preface to Book XV confirms that the narrative reached the amplitude of the extant books before 353. After concluding Book XIV with the execution of the Caesar Gallus and an obituary, Ammianus opens the following book with a personal or programmatic statement:

> utcumque potui veritatem scrutari,/ ea, quae videre licuit per aetatem/ vel perplexe interrogando versatos in medio scire,/ narravimus ordine casuum exposito diversorum;/ residua, quae secuturus aperiet textus,/ pro virium captu limatius absolvemus/ nihil obtrectatores longi, ut putant, operis formidantes. / tunc enim laudanda est brevitas,/ cum moras rumpens intempestivas/ nihil subtrahit cognitioni gestorum. (15.1.1)
>
> Using every effort to investigate the truth, I have set out, in the order of their occurrence, events which my age allowed me to see myself or to know by thorough questioning of those who took part in them. The rest of my task, which the section to follow will reveal, I shall discharge to the best of my ability in a more polished style, with no fear of those who denigrate a work which they think too long. For brevity is only laudable when it prevents tedium and irrelevance without diminishing knowledge of the course of events.

This brief paragraph should not be misunderstood. Ammianus here announces no change in historical method whatever, nor does he state that that his narrative is about to become more detailed than it had been for the immediately preceding period.[37] On the contrary, he continued to use autopsy and the questioning of eyewitnesses for the period after 354 as before: it follows that he must have marked the change from using written sources to contemporary history at some earlier point, most probably when he came to the death of Constantine.[38] Ammianus does not promise a more expansive narrative from the beginning of Book XV, and in fact the scale of treatment does not expand

---

[37] As has often been assumed, as by Peter, *Wahrheit und Kunst* (1911), 410 ("mit erklärter Vollständigkeit"); Blockley, *Ammianus*, (1975), 12 (who contrasts the narrative of Book XV onward with "a previous, less detailed style, of which XIV was the last book"); Rosen, *Ammianus* (1982), 76 ("grössere Ausführlichkeit"); C. W. Fornara, *Cabinet of the Muses*, ed. M. Griffith and D. J. Mastronarde (Atlanta, 1990), 164 ("more expansively than hitherto").

[38] Fornara, *Cabinet of the Muses* (1990), 169, argues that the prefaces to Books XV and XXVI provide "independent and substantial support" to this natural assumption.

significantly until the account of Julian's Persian expedition in Books XXIII–XXV: Books XV–XXII cover approximately one calendar year each (from autumn 354 to the end of 362). What Ammianus promises at the start of Book XV is neither greater detail nor even probably greater accuracy,[39] but greater literary polish.[40] His promise should be interpreted in the light of his later statement that his account of Julian as emperor, though factually accurate and carefully verified, will be a virtual panegyric (16.1.3: ad laudativam paene materiam pertinebit). The paragraph that introduces Book XV foreshadows the opening of Book XVI: it offers an anticipatory justification or apology for the full treatment of Julian, whose imminent entry into the narrative as Caesar it heralds.

The transmitted book numbers constitute an obvious obstacle to the hypothesis that Ammianus Marcellinus originally wrote a history in thirty-six books. The obstacle, however, is not insuperable. The grammarian Priscian in the early sixth century is the sole writer of Late Antiquity to show any acquaintance with Ammianus' work, with the possible exception of the author of the *Historia Augusta*.[41] Priscian quotes Ammianus once to illustrate a linguistic phenomenon that is common in Ammianus and his quotation comes from the very beginning of Book XIV.[42] Since the majority of Priscian's quotations come from the first book of any work that he cites, this fact encourages the suspicion that Priscian did not know the preceding books, from which it may be deduced with a high degree of probability that they had already been lost within little more than a century after their publication.[43] If that is so, then the numbering of the extant books soon became vulnerable to accidental alteration. Because the manuscripts of Ammianus and Priscian concur, the transmitted book numbers must go back at least to the Carolingian period. Is it far-fetched to suggest that the process of alteration began either with Priscian

[39] For this interpretation of 15.1.1, see Rowell, *Ammianus* (1964), 18 ("with still greater accuracy"); I. Lana, *La storiografia latina del IV secolo d.C.* (Turin, 1990), 64 ("con maggiore accuratezza"). It must be conceded, however, that *limatius* appears to have one of these senses in 15.13.2.

[40] The *Oxford Latin Dictionary* gives a single meaning for the adjective *limatus*: "(of writings, etc.) Carefully composed, polished; (also, of writers and orators)" (1030). That Ammianus uses the word in exactly this sense is confirmed by the passages quoted at TLL 7.2.1422.16–48, 1423.49–52. Despite his earlier misleading gloss, Fornara, *Cabinet of the Muses* (1990), 165, translates correctly as "in a more polished style."

[41] Argued by Syme, *Ammianus* (1968), 25–71.

[42] Priscian, *Inst. Gramm.* 9.51 = H. Keil, *Grammatici Latini* 2 (Leipzig, 1855), 486.27–487.3: nam quartae (sc. conjugationis) in "tum" faciunt supinum -, ut "indulsi indulsum" vel "indultum," unde Marcellinus rerum gestarum XIIII: tamquam licentia crudelitati indulta (14.1.4).

[43] L. Jeep, *Philologus* 67 (1908), 21.

himself or with an early copyist who corrupted "xviiii" into "xiiii"? Priscian was widely read and authoritative.[44] Moreover, where the book numbers given for his quotations can be checked, as for example in the case of Livy, they are not invariably correct:[45] indeed, a survey designed to estimate the value of Priscian's testimony about book numbers for the structure of Sallust's lost *Historiae* concluded that his book numbers were erroneous one time in ten.[46] It is not implausible, therefore, to suppose that some conscientious scribe or reader "corrected" the book numbers in a manuscript of the rarely read Ammianus Marcellinus to make them conform to what he had read in Priscian. And if a parallel case of erroneous numbers be demanded, appeal can be made to Seneca's *Natural Questions*, where the content of its preface establishes that the traditional Book III must originally have stood at the beginning of the work.[47]

The preceding argument can be summed up succinctly. The transmitted book numbers cannot be reconciled with what Ammianus himself says about the scale and compass of his history, and they fail to correspond to the observable symmetrical structure of the extant books. Hence it is reasonable to conclude that they may be erroneous and that the extant Books XIV–XXXI were originally numbered XIX–XXXVI, so that the first eighteen books of the *Res Gestae* have been lost and the second eighteen books have survived.

[44] Nearly eight hundred surviving manuscripts were listed by M. Passalacqua, *I codici di Prisciano* (Rome, 1978), including 128 of the ninth and tenth centuries. G. Ballaira, *Per il catalogo dei codici di Prisciano* (Turin, 1982), added another one hundred and thirty.

[45] L. Jeep, *Philologus* 68 (1909), 19–20.

[46] G. Perl, *Philologus* 111 (1967), 286–88.

[47] H. M. Hine, *An Edition with Commentary of Seneca, Natural Questions, Book II* (New York, 1981), 2–23; *L. Annaei Senecae Naturalium Quaestionium libri* (Leipzig, 1996), xxii–xxv.

[IV]

NARRATIVE AND EXCURSUS

In a history with a formally symmetrical structure of triads and hexads, there can be no formal or proportional symmetry in the historical narrative itself without the danger of distortion. Any historian must allow himself the freedom to treat some matters briefly, others at greater length—and all readers feel that Ammianus has devoted an excessive amount of space to Shapur's campaign of 359 in northern Mesopotamia and, within that campaign, to the siege of Amida, which lasted seventy-three days and from which the historian himself barely escaped with his life (19.1–9). On the other hand, Ammianus' conscious choice to expand his narrative in 363 so that Julian's Persian expedition occupies almost three books (XXIII–XXV), although only seven months intervened between the departure of the Roman army from Antioch on 5 March 363 and its return to Antioch in October (23.2.6–25.10.1), whereas the preceding nine books had covered on average just over one year each, from eastern events in 353 (14.1–4) to events in Antioch in the autumn of 362 (22.13–14), reflects the historical importance of the failed expedition, and Ammianus' emphasis has an obvious justification. But precisely how has Ammianus constructed his narrative? What are the blocks of material from which he has put it together? And how has he arranged them?

Following the fashion of the nineteenth century and himself setting an example for many scholars in the twentieth, Otto Seeck invoked *Quellenforschung*: in Books XIV–XXV, he contended, Ammianus derived the organization of his material from a mechanical combination of two main written sources; one of these sources was purely annalistic and arranged events by the consuls of each calendar year, whereas the other used the chronological ordering principle adopted by Thucydides, who dated events by successive summers and winters.[1] But there is no good reason to deny an author who has devoted such care to the overall architecture of his history the ability to choose and organize his own material.[2]

Since Seeck, only two attempts have been made to analyze the overall structure of Ammianus' narrative. Unfortunately, both proceed from mistaken premises, so that, although each established something important, neither produced a simple, elegant, and systematic analysis. G. B. Pighi saw that Ammianus put his narrative together as series of narrative sections corresponding to different centers of activity in succession, but he went astray by accepting the false proposition that Book XIV begins with the winter of 353–354 (instead of eastern affairs during the summer of 353), and he vainly attempted to see symmetrical composition within each book.[3] Christa Samberger saw the subjective nature of much of Ammianus' presentation, the biographical emphasis of much of his narrative, and the division of his material into blocks of narrative dealing separately with the activities of the emperor (or emperors), events in the city of Rome, and eastern or western affairs not directly connected with the imperial court, but she attempted to fit Ammianus' narrative into the straitjacket of a primary annalistic structure,[4] which it simply does not possess (Chapter V).

---

[1] O. Seeck, *RE* 1 (1894), 1848–49; *Hermes* 41 (1906), 493–94, 527–39.

[2] *Reading the Past* (1990), 68–70.

[3] G. B. Pighi, *I discorsi nelle storie di Ammiano Marcellino* (Milan, 1936), 61–81, esp. 81: "abbiamo primo dimostrato che il libro Ammianeo è costituito da serie di sezioni narrative, corrispondenti a centri d'attività, press'a poco contemporanei oppure successivi secondo le vicende della storia dell'Impero . . . , e che le sezioni sono disposte simmetricamente e collegate spesso per mezzo di formule speciali." Pighi analysed Book XIV as being composed of the following five narrative or thematic blocks:

I, East (Gallus), autumn 353–September 354;

II, West (Constantius), 10 October 353–February/March 354;

III, Rome (first prefecture of Orfitus), 8 December 353–356;

IV, East (Gallus), summer 354;

V, West (Constantius), April/May–November 354.

Besides allowing no structural function to the two excursus explicitly marked as such (14.4, 6.2–27), this analysis paradoxically treats the last journey, the execution, and the obituary of Gallus all as belonging to "la narrazione dei fatti di Costanzo" (67). Pighi's similar analyses of other books produce equally implausible corollaries (68–74). Pighi subsequently reproduced his analysis in summary form in his *Ammiani Marcellini rerum gestarum capita selecta* (Neuchâtel, 1948), xxiv–xxx.

[4] C. Samberger, *Klio* 51 (1969), 349–482. She speaks continually of "der annalistische Aufbau" of Books XIV–XXV (352) and "die gewohnte annalistische Methode" (378), asserting that "die kleinste kompositionelle Einheit ist der Jahresbericht" (400). She falsely assumes that Book XIV begins with Gallus' activities during the winter of 353–54 (465, 472), while accusing Ammianus of having no concern for accurate chronology (405: "der Historiker, ungeachtet der genauen Chronologie").

Ammianus in fact organized his material in compositional blocks using the following basic types of unit for constructing his narrative:

1. The activities of an emperor during the campaigning season
2. Events at or connected with his court during the succeeding winter
3. Events at Rome under successive prefects of the city
4. Provincial events of a particular summer or winter
5. Formal excursus explicitly designated as such by a formula of transition either at the beginning or end or at both beginning and end (Appendix 5)

The complexity of the narrative, therefore, varies considerably according to whether or not Ammianus must coordinate (or even relate to each other) the activities of more than one emperor in separate theaters of action and on how strictly he observes the principle of describing the actions of eastern and western emperors in each successive summer and winter.

For almost all of the period covered by Books XIV–XXI there were two emperors resident and active in different places. In these books, therefore, six separate and constant categories of material can be identified:

(A) The activities of Constantius and political and military events at his court
(B) The activities of Gallus (XIV) and Julian (XVI–XXI) and political and military events at their courts
(C) Prefects of the city of Rome;[5]
(D) Eastern events narrated separately from imperial activities
(E) Western events narrated separately from imperial activities
(F) Formal excursus

The material in Books XIV–XXI can be assigned to each of these categories as follows:

Book XIV

1	Crimes of Gallus (B)
2–4.1	Events of summer 353 (D)
4.2–7	The Saraceni (F)
5.1–5	Constantius winters at Arles, 353–354 (A)
5.6–9	Paul "the Chain" (E)
6.1	Orfitus, 8 December 353 to summer 355[6] (C)

---

[5] The certain or probable dates at which each prefect entered and left office are, except where otherwise stated, taken from Chastagnol, *Fastes* (1962), 139–93.

[6] For proof that Orfitus was replaced by Leontius in 355, not 356, *Phoenix* 46 (1992), 257–59; *CP* 88 (1993), 65–66.

6.2–27   Rome (F)

7 + 9   The government of Gallus, 353–354 (B)

8   Provinces of Oriens (F)

10   Campaign of Constantius to the upper Rhine in 354 (A)

11.1–26   Gallus' recall, arrest, and execution (B)

11.27–34   Obituary of Gallus (B)

Book XV

1–2   Accusations at court (A)

3.1–6   Punishment of Gallus' supporters (D)

3.7–11   The affair of Africanus (E)

4.1 + 7–13   Campaign of Constantius, 355 (A)

4.2–6   The Bodensee (F)

5.1–34   Silvanus (E)

5.35–36   Reaction of Constantius to the suppression of Silvanus (A)

6   Repression by Paul (E)

7   Leontius, summer 355 to winter 356–357 (C)

8   Julian proclaimed Caesar (6 November 355) and sent to Gaul (A)

9–12   Gaul (F)

13   The corruption of Musonianus and Prosper[7] (D)

Book XVI

1–5   Julian in 356 (B)

6–8   Accusations at court (A)

9   Persian raids and their sequel (D)

10   Constantius visits Rome (28 April–29 May 357), then departs in haste
      for Illyricum (A)

11–12.66   Campaign of Julian in 357 (B)

12.67–70   Constantius' reaction to Julian's victory (A)

Book XVII

1–3   Campaign of 357 continued (B)

4.1   Orfitus for the second time, spring 357 to spring 359 (C)

4.2–23   Obelisks in Rome (F)

5   Exchange of letters between Shapur and Constantius (A)

6   Iuthungi invade Raetia (E)

---

[7] Seyfarth's clausulae in 15.13.3 are potentially misleading. Since Prosper was the deputy of Ursicinus in the East while the latter was absent in Gaul (14.11.5, cf. 17.5.15, 14.1), the sentence should be articulated as follows: hunc Prosper adaequitabat/ pro magistro equitum agente etiamtum in Galliis/ militem regens.

7.1–8　Earthquake of 24 August 358[8] (D)

7.9–14　Earthquakes (F)

8–10　Julian's campaign of 358 (B)

11.1–4　Reaction at the court of Constantius (A)

11.5　Artemius *vicarius* of Rome in place of the deceased Bassus[9] (C)

12–13　Constantius' campaign of 358 (A)

14　Negotiations with Persia (D)

Book XVIII

1　Administration of Julian (B)

2　His campaign of 359 (B)

3　Execution of Barbatio (A)

4–10　Sapor invades Roman territory (A)

Book XIX

1–9　The siege and capture of Amida (D)

10　Tertullus, ?360 to autumn 361[10] (C)

11　Campaign against Sarmatae Limigantes (A)

12.1–18　Trials for treason (D)

12.19–20　Prodigy at Daphne (D)

13　Isaurian raids (D)

Book XX

1　Julian sends Lupicinus to Britain (early 360) (B)

2　Recall of Ursicinus (A)

3.1　Eclipse of the sun[11] (D)

3.2–12　Eclipses (F)

4–5　Julian proclaimed Augustus, spring 360 (B)

6–7　Shapur attacks Singara, summer 359 (D)

8.1　Constantius winters in Constantinople, then goes east (A)

8.2–22　Julian writes to Constantius (B)

9.1–5　Constantius sends Leonas to Gaul, spring 360 (A)

9.6–8　Julian receives Leonas and replies (B)

9.9　Suspicion of Lupicinus (E)

10　Julian's campaign of 360 (B)

11　Constantius takes the field against the Persians (A)

11.26–30　Rainbows (F)

---

[8] Ammianus' exact date is confirmed by *Descr. cons.* 358.2.

[9] Orfitus was still prefect on 25 March 359 (*CTh* 14.6.1), and Bassus died on 25 August 359 (*ILS* 1286).

[10] The date at which Tertullus became prefect is not certain (Appendix 7).

[11] On the problems raised by this notice, see Chapter IX.

Book XXI

  1–5   Julian prepares for war (B)

  1.7–14   Divination (E)

  6   Activities of Constantius during the winter of 360–361 (A)

  7   Constantius advances into Mesopotamia (A)

  8–10   Julian advances into Illyricum (B)

  11–12.20   Resistance of two legions at Aquileia (E)

  12.21–25   Actions of Julian at Naissus (B)

  12.24ᶜ   Maximus, autumn 361–spring 363 [12] (C)

  13–15   Constantius prepares for war against Julian, but dies (3 November 361) shortly after leaving Antioch (A)

  16   Obituary of Constantius (A)

Between the deaths of Constantius on 3 November 361, whose obituary and burial conclude Book XXI, and of Jovian on 16–17 January 364, with which Book XXV closes, there was only a single Roman emperor. For this period, therefore, Ammianus' narrative structure is correspondingly simpler, and he continues this simpler structure with a single main narrative into Book XXVI, which describes the proclamation of Valentinian and Valens as emperors and their activities until they separated and divided the empire in 364. Hence the narrative structure of Books XXII–XXVI may be analyzed as follows:

(A) Main political and military narrative

(B) Prefects of Rome (with certain or probable dates of tenure noted as before)

(C) Other events

(D) Excursus, methodological and reflective as well as formal

The material in Books XXI–XXVI can be assigned to each of these four categories as follows:

Book XXII

  1–2   Julian waits until he hears of Constantius' death, then proceeds to Constantinople (A)

  3   New appointments to high office (A)

  4   Reorganization of the palace (A)

---

[12] Maximus is attested as prefect on 28 January 362 (*ICUR*, N.S. 4.11758 = *ILCV* 3904), cf. *CIL* 6.31401; Symmachus, *Rel.* 34.5 [both undated]): his successor was L. Turcius Apronianus Asterius, whom Julian appointed in Antioch in January 363 (23.1.4,; 26.3.1–6). In defense of the transmitted date of *CTh* 14.4.3 (9 December 363), which Seeck, *Regesten* (1919), 84, 211, followed by Chastagnol, *Fastes* (1962), 156–157, emended to 9 December 362, see *Cognitio Gestorum* (1992), 5–6.

5 Reestablishment of paganism (A)

6 Julian and the Egyptian litigants (A)

7 Other activities of Julian in Constantinople (A)

8 The coasts of Thrace and Pontus (D)

9 Julian travels across Asia Minor to Antioch (A)

10 Julian in Antioch (A)

11.1−3 Three executions (C)

11.4−11 The death of bishop George in Alexandria[13] (C)

12 Julian's religiosity (A)

13.1−4 The burning of the temple of Apollo and its sequel (A)

13.4 Earthquake at Nicomedia and Nicaea (C)

14.1−3 Julian's difficulties with the Antiochenes (A)

4−5 He ascends Mount Casius (A)

14.6 Report of an Apis bull (C)

14.7−8 The Apis bull (D)

15−16 Egypt (D)

Book XXIII

1 Julian's fourth consulate: events, appointments, and omens of January 363 (A)

2−3 The start of the Persian expedition (A)

4 Military engines (D)

5 Julian at Cercusium and Zaitha (A)

6.1−84 Persia (D)

6.85−88 Pearls (D)

Book XXIV

1−6 Julian's advance into Persia as far as Ctesiphon (A)

7.1−2 + lacuna The Romans before Ctesiphon (A)

<lacuna> The actions of Arsaces, Sebastianus, and Procopius (reference back at 7.8) (A)

8 The start of the retreat (A)

Book XXV

1−3.14 The Roman retreat and the fatal wounding of Julian (A)

3.15−23 The death of Julian (A)

---

[13] George was killed on 24 December 361 (*Historia acephala* 2.10 Martin), long before Julian reached Antioch on 18 or 19 July 362: Ammianus 22.9.15, cf. F. Cumont, *Syria* 8 (1927), 339−41. On Ammianus' error, see Appendix 7.

4   Obituary of Julian (A)

5   The election of Jovian as emperor (A)

6   The Roman retreat continues (A)

7   Shapur offers peace and his harsh terms are accepted (A)

8   The Roman army marches to Nisibis (A)

9.1–6   The surrender of Nisibis (A)

9.7–11   Comparison to earlier Roman defeats (D)

12–13   Procopius escorts the body of Julian to Tarsus, then disappears (A)

10.1–2   The Roman army reaches Antioch (A)

10.3   Comets (D)

10.4–13   Jovian proceeds from Antioch to Bithynia, where he dies (A)

10.14–17   Obituary of Jovian (A)

Book XXVI

1.1–2   The problems of writing recent history (D)

1.2–2.11   The election of Valentinian as emperor (A)

1.8–14   Leap years (D)

3   Apronianus, spring 363 to early 364[14] (B)

4.1–3   Valentinian proclaims Valens his colleague (A)

4.4   Illness of the emperors (A)

4.5–6   Rome's frontiers menaced by enemies (C)

5.1–5   The emperors go to Sirmium and divide the empire, then depart for Milan and Constantinople (A)

5.6–8   The year 365 brings trouble: the Alamanni cross the frontier and Procopius rebels (A)

5.9–14   Valentinian and the northern frontiers (A)

5.15   The structure of the narrative (D)

6–10.14   The rebellion of Procopius, its suppression by Valens and the subsequent purge (A)

10.15–19   The tsunami of 21 July 365[15] (C)

It is significant that Ammianus felt himself impelled to digress to explain the necessity of narrating separately contemporaneous events in East and West as soon as he began to describe the activities of Valentinian and Valens after they set up separate administrations in East and West (26.5.15). In Books XXVII–XXX this separation is scrupulously observed, but without treating the activ-

---

[14] Apronianus was appointed by Julian in Antioch in January (23.1.4), but Ammianus implies that he had reached Rome by 19 March (23.3.3).

[15] For the widespread damage caused by this tsunami and the significance read into it by contemporaries, see B. Bousquet and F. Jacques, *MEFR* (A) 96 (1984), 423–61; C. Lepelley, ibid., 463–90; M. Henry, *Phoenix* 39 (1985), 36–61; C. Lepelley, *Kokalos* 36–37 (1990–91), 359–72.

ities of each of the two emperors summer by summer and winter by winter as compositional units, as in Books XIV–XXI. Hence the structure of Books XXVII–XXX can be analyzed as follows:

(A) Eastern political and military events
(B) Western political and military events[16]
(C) Prefects of the city of Rome
(D) Formal excursus and authorial comments

The material in Books XXVII–XXX can be assigned to each of these four categories as follows:

Book XXVII

1–2   Trouble with the Alamanni (early 366) (B)
3.1–2   Portent at Pistoria (B)
3.3–4   Symmachus, April 364–March 365 (C)
3.5–10   Lampadius, April–September 365 (C)
3.11–13   Viventius, October 365–May 367 (C)
3.14–15   Bishops (D)
4.1   Valens prepares for war against the Goths (A)
4.2–14   Thrace (D)
5   Valens' Gothic war, 367–369 (A)
6   Illness of Valentinian and proclamation of Gratian as Augustus, 367 (B)
7   Condemnations of various persons by Valentinian (B)
8   Problems in Britain (B)
9.1–5   Romanus in Africa (B)
9.6–7   Isaurian raids (A)
9.8–10   Praetextatus, August 367–September 368 (C)
10   Valentinian campaigns on the Rhine (B)
11   Probus as praetorian prefect of Illyricum[17] (B)
12   Conflict with Persia over Armenia (A)

Book XXVIII

1.1, 5–56   Trials at Rome, 369–370 to 374[18] (B)
1.2–4   Phrynichus (D)

---

[16] On the movements of Valentinian and Valens, see, respectively, Seeck, *Regesten* (1919), 216–46; Appendix 10.

[17] Petronius Probus was prefect of Illyricum, Italy, and Africa from 368 to 375: Ammianus 27.1.1; 30.5.4–11; Rufinus, *HE* 11.12, cf. *PLRE* 1.737–39.

[18] On the chronology of this chapter, see Appendix 9.

1.57   The deaths of Maximinus, Simplicius, and Doryphorianus[19] (D)

2.1–10   Valentinian on the Rhine (B)

2.11–14   The Maratocupreni in Syria (A)

3   Theodosius in Britain (B)

4.1–2   Olybrius, January 369–August 370 (C)

4.3–5   Ampelius, January 371–July 372 (C)

4.6–35   The Roman aristocracy (D)

5.1–7   Raid by Saxones, 370 (B)

5.8–15   The Rhine frontier (B)

6   Troubles in Tripolitania, 364 onward (B)

Book XXIX

1–2   Treason trials in the East, 372 onward (A)

3   The cruelty of Valentinian (B)

4   Valentinian campaigns across the Rhine (B)

<lacuna>   Bappo   (attested 22 August 372) (C)

<lacuna>   Eupraxius   (attested 14 February 374)[20] (C)

5   Theodosius' campaign in Mauretania (B)

6.1–16   The Quadi invade Illyricum (B)

6.17–19   Claudius, 21 May–19 July 374 (C)

Book XXX

1   The killing of King Pap of Armenia, probably 374[21] (A)

2.1–8   Conflict with Sapor over Armenia and Iberia (A)

2.9–12   The death of Remigius (B)

3   Valentinian campaigns on the Rhine, 374 (B)

4.1–2   The adminstration of Valens (A)

4.3–22   Lawyers (D)

5–6   Valentinian leaves Trier in the spring and goes to Pannonia where he
        dies, 17 Nov. 375 (B)

7–9   Obituary of Valentinian (B)

10   Valentinian II proclaimed Augustus, 22 Nov. 375[22] (B)

---

[19] Ammianus here promises to describe their deaths, which occurred in the early months of
376 (Appendix 9), but in the event breaks off his continuous narrative of western affairs with the
proclamation of Valentinian II as Augustus on 22 November 375 (30.10.4–6).

[20] On the large lacuna in Book XXIX, see Appendix 8.

[21] *PLRE* 1.665–66.

[22] Ammianus' dates of 17 and 22 November are confirmed by *Descr. cons.* 375.2, 3; Socrates,
HE 4.31.6–7.

After the proclamation of the infant Valentinian as Augustus (30.10.4–6), Ammianus does not attempt to give a full or connected account of western events. Hence there are no notices of the prefects of the city of Rome who held office after Claudius (29.6.17–19). Book XXXI focuses on the events leading to the disaster of Adrianople, and its structure may be analyzed as comprising (A) a single main narrative with (B) two formal excursus and an epilogue:

1   Portents predicting the death of Valens (A)

2   The Huns and Alans (B)

3–5.9   Under pressure, the Goths request and are granted permission to settle south of the Danube, where exploitation by Roman officials leads to insurrection (A)

5.10–17   Roman recovery from past disasters (B)

6–9   The Goths and Roman troops in 376 and 377 (A)

10   Despite trouble with the Lentienses, Gratian prepares to assist Valens against the Goths (A)

11.1–5   Valens leaves Antioch and travels to Thrace (A)

11.6   Gratian reaches Castra Martis (A)

12–13   The campaign of Adrianople (A)

14   Obituary of Valens (A)

15–16.7   The immediate aftermath of the battle (A)

16.8   Killing of Goths throughout the East (A)

16.9   Author's farewell to his readers (B)

[V]

DATING, EMPHASIS, AND OMISSION

As an annalistic historian, Tacitus could manipulate both his annalistic framework and the interplay between it and the division into books in order to emphasize an event or an episode of his choosing, which he wished to invest with
particular significance.[1] Unlike Livy, moreover, Tacitus did not always begin
his account of each year with the entry of the consuls into office and events
in Rome at the start of the year, nor did he record even events at Rome in
strict chronological order.[2] His account of the year 15, for example, begins
with an anticipatory notice that a triumph was decreed to Germanicus for
victories won in a spring campaign against the Chatti and a summer campaign
against the Cherusci: Tacitus then proceeds to describe the two campaigns,
concluding with the award of *insignia triumphalia* to A. Caecina, L. Apronius,
and C. Silius, the lieutenants of Germanicus, for their services during these
campaigns (which the Senate must have decreed at the same time as it decreed
the triumph recorded earlier), before turning to affairs in Rome and Tiberius'
refusal to allow oaths to be sworn to accept his *acta*, presumably on 1 January.[3]
Similarly, Tacitus' account of the year 17 begins with a formal notice that Germanicus celebrated a triumph over the Cherusci, Chatti, Angrivarii, and the

---

[1] J. Ginsburg, *Tradition and Theme in the "Annals" of Tacitus* (New York, 1981), 96–100;
R. H. Martin and A. Woodman, *Tacitus: Annals Book IV* (Cambridge, 1989), 15–19.

[2] See the analysis of material in the first six books of the *Annals* in Ginsburg, *Tradition* (1981),
57–79, 128–43.

[3] Tacitus, *Ann.* 1.55–72.1, cf. D. Timpe, *Der Triumph des Germanicus: Untersuchungen zu den
Feldzügen der Jahre 14–16 n. Chr. in Germanien* (Bonn, 1968), 43–58; Ginsburg, *Tradition* (1981),
21, 67–72. Ginsburg reconstructs the actual sequence of the events recorded by Tacitus for 15
as follows: *Ann.* 1.72.2–81 (January to March), 55.1^b–71 (spring and summer), 55.1^a, 72.1
(autumn).

other tribes up to the Elbe on 25 May.[4] This technique is sometimes relevant to evaluating Tacitus' accuracy. He begins the year 61 with the stark assertion that "in the consulate of Caesennius Paetus and Petronius Turpilianus a grave disaster was sustained in Britain," then describes the events leading up to the rebellion of Boudicca, the rebellion itself, and the appointment of a new governor, presumably during the winter of 61–62, before turning to the events of 61 in Rome.[5] Many modern students of Roman Britain have shown a perverse resolve to reject Tacitus' explicit and emphatic date for the rebellion in favor of 60 simply because he notes that Petronius Turpilianus had relinquished his consulate before he was sent to Britain to replace Suetonius Paulinus.[6]

For the most part in the *Annals*, Tacitus made the beginning and end of each book coincide with the beginning and end of his acount of a consular year. Sometimes he exploited the coincidence to great effect. The year 57 and Book XIII of the *Annals* end with the withering of the *ficus ruminalis* and its subsequent revival: Tacitus did not need to tell his readers explicitly that the withering of the tree portended an early death for Nero, its recovery the advent of the Flavian dynasty.[7] But Tacitus can also make the break between books and the start of a new year diverge to telling effect. After the death of Germanicus in 19 and Piso's rash attempt to recover control of the province of Syria, the second book of the *Annals* closes with a series of annalistic notices that lead up to an obituary of Arminius.[8] Book III then opens with the winter journey of Agrippina from Antioch to Rome carrying the ashes of her dead husband: the consuls of 20 appear as both participants in the action and as marking the transition from 19 to 20 when they greet her after she has landed in Italy.[9]

Ammianus was not an annalistic historian. For him the primary chronological units of his main narrative were the actions of an emperor during cam-

---

[4] Tacitus, *Ann.* 2.41.2. The date is confirmed by the *Fasti Ostienses* and the *Fasti Amiterni* (*Insc. Ital.* 13.1.185, 3.187).

[5] Tacitus, *Ann.* 14.29–39 (Britain), 40–47 (events in Rome).

[6] Tacitus, *Ann.* 14.39.3. In favor of accepting Tacitus' explicit statement that "Caesennio Paeto et Petronio Turpiliano consulibus gravis clades in Britannia accepta" (29.1), see K. K. Carroll, *Britannia* 10 (1979), 197–202.

[7] Tacitus, *Ann.* 13.58; C. Segal, *Ramus* 2 (1973), 107–26; H. Y. McCulloch, *Phoenix* 34 (1980), 237–42.

[8] Tacitus, *Ann.* 2.84–88, cf. Ginsburg, *Tradition* (1981), 36–38. There is, however, no compelling reason to reject Tacitus' date of 19 for the death of Arminius in favor of 21, as is often done: D. Timpe, *Arminius-Studien* (Heidelberg, 1970), 24–25; F. R. D. Goodyear, *The Annals of Tacitus, Books 1–6*, 2 (Cambridge, 1981), 447.

[9] Tacitus, *Ann.* 3.2.3, cf. Ginsburg, *Tradition* (1981), 19, 58, 106, n. 3, who draws attention to the very first words of Book III: "nihil intermissa navigatione hiberni maris Agrippina etc." (3.1.1).

paigning seasons and the intervening winters (Chapter IV). Hence he could not use the interplay of annalistic and formal structure as Tacitus had. In Ammianus the consuls appear for the most part almost incidentally. Moreover, his continuous and consecutive narrative of imperial activities season by season ends with the rebellion of Procopius. The transition between Books XXVI and XXVII is managed as previous transitions had been. Book XXVI concludes its account of eastern events in 366, then explicitly regresses to register the tsunami of 21 July 365, whose date is given by day, month, and consuls (26.10.15). Book XXVII opens with a reference to the kalends of January (27.1.1), which are later specified as those of the year 367 (2.1). Thereafter, however, Ammianus ceases to register the consuls with any consistency: those of 368 are nowhere named, those of 369 only in passing to date a Saxon raid (28.5.1), and the *Res Gestae*, at least as extant, name the consuls of only two years after 369 (viz., 374 and 377) (Appendix 4). Nonetheless, Ammianus was not unaware that consular dates could be used for emphasis—and he so uses them in relation to his hero Julian.[10]

For two of the ten years between 354 and 363, Ammianus notes the transition from one consular year to the next with incidental notices that have no literary function in ordering his narrative. Thus the consuls of 354 and 357 are noted when Constantius and Julian depart from winter quarters in the spring of these years (14.10.1; 16.11.1). For the other eight years, Ammianus exploits the consular formula in a variety of ways, but almost always to enhance his favorable depiction of Julian.

The entry into office of Arbitio and Lollianus as the consuls of 355 is not signaled at all when the narrative moves from 354 into 355 with Constantius' departure from winter quarters into Raetia on campaign (15.4.1). Instead, Ammianus holds back his annalistic notice until he can state that Julian was proclaimed Caesar on 6 November in the consulate of the year when Arbitio and Lollianus were consuls (15.8.17). On 1 January 356 the newly proclaimed Caesar assumed the consular fasces in Vienne, which provides Ammianus with the opportunity to add a brief panegyric of the new ruler (16.1).

For 358, for the first time in the extant books, Ammianus uses the traditional consular dating formula with two names in the ablative case: it stands in the middle of a book, where it marks a sudden, stark transition from Julian's success in Gaul to the impending danger on the eastern frontier (16.5.1: Datiano et Cereali consulibus). The entry into office of the brothers Eusebius and Hypatius on 1 January 359 opens Book XVIII and introduces a vignette of Julian as an excellent civil administrator and judge (18.1). Similarly, Book XX

[10] *Cognitio Gestorum* (1992), 1–8.

opens by noting the consuls of 360 in its second sentence as the narrative turns from events in Illyricum to the proclamation of Julian as Augustus (20.1.2). In 361, by contrast, the entry into office of the consuls Taurus and Florentius (21.6.5) does not mark the progression of the narrative from one year to the next: that has already occurred when Julian, after celebrating his *quinquennalia* (21.1.4), attends a Christian service on the festival "which Christians celebrate in the month of January and call Epiphany" (21.2.5). The consuls of 362, however, are noted no fewer than three times: in comment on Julian's complaint that Constantine conferred consulates on "barbarians" (21.10.8), when Julian, then still at Naissus, designated Mamertinus and Nevitta (21.12.5), and in describing Julian's behavior on 1 January 362 in Constantinople (22.7.1). But Ammianus' most elaborate use of a consular notice occurs at the very start of the triad of books devoted to Julian's Persian expedition.

On 1 January 363 Julian assumed the consular fasces in Antioch. The emperor was consul for the fourth time, with Flavius Sallustius, the praetorian prefect of Gaul as his colleague (23.1.1). By 363 the Kalends of January had become an important festival throughout the Greek East, especially when the day inaugurated an imperial consulate.[11] Ammianus uses the opportunity to enhance his presentation of Julian as a hero possessing *civilitas*, which was one of the traditional virtues of a pagan Roman emperor, to demythologize an episode of which Christian writers made much, and to show how the Persian expedition was from the start doomed to defeat as contrary to the expressed will of the gods.

After a sentence marking the transition from one calendar year to the next, Ammianus names the consuls of 363. An authorial comment follows. It was a novelty for an emperor to take as his consular colleague a *privatus*, that is, a man not related to him, for no one could recall such a pair of consuls since Diocletian and Aristobulus. The precedent that Ammianus alleges is doubly peculiar. First, there had been a similar consular pair three years after Diocletian and Aristobulus: the consuls of 288 were Maximian, the Augustus of the West, and Pompeius Januarianus.[12] Second, although the consular lists that survive from Late Antiquity do indeed have *Diocletiano et Aristobulo* for the

---

[11] M. Meslin, *La Fête des kalendes de janvier dans l'empire romain. Étude d'un rituel de Nouvel An* (*Collection Latomus* 115, 1970), 51–70; J. R. Rea, *Proceedings of the XVIII International Congress of Papyrology*, Athens 25–31 May 1986, 2 (Athens, 1986), 203–08; *Oxyrhynchus Papyri* 55 (London, 1988), 198 (on *P. Oxy.* 3812.5–6). It may be inferred that it owed its increased importance in the Christian Roman Empire to the fact that it took over the functions of, and hence provided an alternative to, the irremediably pagan Saturnalia of late December: Meslin, *Fête des kalendes* (1970), 79–93.

[12] *Consuls* (1987), 110–11.

consuls of 285, Diocletian's original colleague in that year seems to have been Caesonius Bassus:[13] Aristobulus began as the consular colleague of Carinus and only became Diocletian's colleague after Diocletian defeated and replaced him as ruler of the western empire in the late spring of 285.[14] Disregarding the genuine precedent of 288 in favor of 285, Ammianus compares Julian to Diocletian, not to Maximian, the grandfather of Constantius, with whom he contrasts him.

Ammianus surely intended the reader of Book XXIII to recall the comment that Book XVI had made on Constantius' hieratic pose as he entered the city of Rome in 357: "during the whole time of his reign he never took anyone to sit with him in his carriage nor made a private citizen his consular colleague, as consecrated emperors have done" (16.10.12). That comment, in turn, acquires significance when one asks who the *principes consecrati* were who as emperors had a *privatus* as consular colleague. The list of such consular pairs between 288 and 395 (besides the consuls of 363) is brief:

371 Gratian II and Sex. Petronius Probus
374 Gratian III and Fl. Equitius
377 Gratian IV and Fl. Merobaudes
385 Arcadius and Fl. Bauto
387 Valentinian III and Eutropius
388 Theodosius II and Maternus Cynegius
390 Valentinian IV and Fl. Neoterius
392 Arcadius and Fl. Rufinus
393 Theodosius III and Fl. Abundantius (East)

The apparently plural *principes consecrati*, therefore, are precisely Gratian, although the remark incidentally reflects praise on Theodosius for the consular appointments of the later 380s.

Ammianus follows his notice of the consuls of 363 with a brief account of Julian's attempt to rebuild the Jewish temple in Jerusalem.[15] It falls into three

---

[13] See *JRA* 9 (1996), 537, n. 26, arguing from *AE* 1978.782.

[14] *Consuls* (1987), 104–5. On the date of Carinus' death, see now *JRA* 9 (1996), 536–37.

[15] This episode has often been discussed: among recent treatments, note F. Blanchetière, *JJS* 31 (1980), 61–81; Y. Lewy, *Jerusalem Cathedra* 3 (1983), 70–96; G. Stemberger, *Juden und Christen im Heiligen Land. Palästina unter Konstantin und Theodosius* (Munich, 1987), 163–74; J. W. Drijvers, *Cognitio Gestorum* (1992), 19–26.

Jewish sources are notoriously silent about Julian's attempt to rebuild the Temple: D. Levenson, *Of Scribes and Scrolls*, ed. H. W. Attridge, J. J. Collins, and T. H. Tobin (Lanham, 1990),

unequal sections. First, and at greatest length, comes the emperor's motive. Although he was busy with preparations for the military expedition that was about to begin, Julian did not neglect other duties: he intended to restore in a lavish fashion the once-famous temple in Jerusalem, which had been besieged by Vespasian and stormed by Titus because he wished his reign to be remembered for its great building achievements (23.1.2: imperiique sui memoriam magnitudine operum gestiens propagare). Second, Ammianus notes the issuing of the order for rebuilding: Julian entrusted Alypius of Antioch with the speedy performance of the task. Third comes the fate of the undertaking. When (or perhaps although) Alypius was eagerly tackling the task with the active assistance of the governor of the province, fireballs devastated the site and the project was abandoned, as the elements themselves forbade its completion (23.1.3: hocque modo elemento destinatius repellente cessavit inceptum).

Julian's attempt to rebuild the temple in Jerusalem is obviously central to any interpretation of his personality, his reign, or his religious policies as a whole, and Ammianus' treatment of the episode is very relevant to determining his interests and biases. The placing of the episode in Ammianus' narrative is careful: it deliberately minimizes its significance by including it among the annalistic notices that introduce the year 363. Ammianus does not and cannot intend to date the attempted rebuilding in Jerusalem to January 363. Julian entered on his consulate in Antioch, and what Ammianus dates to the very beginning of the year is Julian's charge to Alypius. He then avails himself of the historian's freedom to look forward from the immediate context to the consequences of what he has just described before returning to his chronological point of departure. If he needed to learn such a procedure from an earlier historian, Tacitus could be his model. For Tacitus divided what could have been a virtually continuous account of Roman dealings with Parthia during the reigns of Tiberius, Claudius, and Nero into narrative sections each of which usually covers several calendar years, yet he is careful to anchor each section of eastern narrative to his main annalistic narrative by linking it, sometimes

---

261–79. Admittedly, a passage in the Palestinian Talmud is transmitted as referring to Julian (Nedarim 3.2, 37d), and the reference has sometimes been taken as authentic, as by W. Bacher, *JQR* 10 (1898), 168–72. But an identical passage elsewhere names Diocletian (Shebuot 2.9, 34d): this must be correct, since the emperor in question visited Palestine, as Diocletian did several times (*New Empire* [1982], 50–51, 54–55). Hence the translation of Nedarim 3.2 by J. Neusner, *Talmud of the Land of Israel* 23 (Chicago, 1985), 52, has "when Diocletian went down there" with no hint that the transmitted reading has been emended. Although deliberate suppression has sometimes been inferred, the natural deduction is that the Palestinian Talmud, which has several mentions of Ursicinus' presence in Galilee during the rebellion of 351–352, underwent its final redaction in Tiberias between 352 and 363: M. Adler, *JQR* 5 (1893), 626, n. 1; G. Stemberger, *Introduction to the Talmud and Midrash*[2], trans. and ed. M. Bockmuehl (Edinburgh, 1996), 170–73.

with specific detail, to events in Rome in a particular consular year.[16] Ammianus knew and used this standard technique. It is clearest in Book XIV, where the beginning of the Isaurian raids is set in the narrative of eastern events during the summer of 353, but Ammianus marks the passage of time, refers to winter, and follows the episode through to its end in 354.[17] Similarly, at the start of Book XXIII, Ammianus puts the order to Alypius in early January, but says nothing about how long the preparations for rebuilding took. It is a misunderstanding of the historian's technique to argue that "Ammianus dates the whole episode, including its failure, to the time when Julian was in Antioch."[18] It is only the order to rebuild that he unambiguously assigns to the beginning of the year.[19]

From the abortive attempt to rebuild the temple in Jerusalem, Ammianus turns back to events in Antioch in early January. He marks the transition with the words *isdem diebus* (23.1.4), which take the reader back to Julian's assumption of the consulate on the first day of the year. The paragraph into which Seyfarth divides the rest of the chapter comprises two parts that are very unequal in length—four official appointments (4), then four omens (5–7) that set the scene and create the mood for Julian's departure from Antioch on his expedition into Persia.

Ammianus marks the sequence of events carefully and precisely. First, Julian gave offices and honors to senatorial ambassadors who had come to Syria from Rome; then, after he had made these appointments, he was alarmed by an omen that portended his death. Despite frequent modern assertions to the contrary, Ammianus is correct in dating these three senatorial appointments to January 363 —Apronianus as prefect of the city of Rome (he received instructions from Julian in Antioch on 17 January on how to prevent Christians from practicing as lawyers in his court in Rome),[20] Octavianus as proconsul of Africa (to take office in April), Venustus as *vicarius Hispaniarum*, and Aradius Rufinus as *comes Orientis* in place of the emperor's uncle Julianus, who had just died.[21]

---

[16] Note esp. Tacitus' treatment of the eastern campaigns of Corbulo in *Ann.* 13.5–9, 13.34.2–41; 14.23–36; 15.1–17, 15.24–31, cf. K. Gilmartin, *Historia* 22 (1973), 583–626.

[17] *HSCP* 92 (1989), 418–19.

[18] Bowersock, *Julian* (1978), 121.

[19] J. Vogt, *Kaiser Julian und das Judentum. Studien zum Weltanschauungskampf der Spätantike* (*Morgenland* 30, 1939), 46. The text should probably be articulated as follows: negotiumque maturandum Alypio dederat/ Antiochensi qui olim Britannias curaverat pro praefectis. For Ammianus' use of the pluperfect with a perfect or aorist sense, see Jonge on 14.7.12 and the Dutch commentators on 20.3.1, 4.4. *Dederat* is translated correctly by Seyfarth and Hamilton, incorrectly by Rolfe and Fontaine.

[20] *Constitutio de postulando*, published by B. Bischoff and D. Nörr, *Abh. München*, Phil.-hist. Kl., N.F. 58 (1963), 7.

[21] On the date of Julianus' death, see *Cognitio Gestorum* (1992), 5–6.

After these four appointments had been made, Julian was terrified by an omen that he experienced directly. Felix, the *comes sacrarum largitionum* (an office in which he had probably served since the death of Constantius), had died suddenly just before the emperor's uncle Julianus, and when the Antiochene crowd saw the traditional phrase "Felix Iulianus Augustus" in an announcement posted publicly, they read it aloud with a malicious twist: by adding the enclitic word for "and" after "Augustus," they transformed the meaning of the phrase from the loyal "Happy <be> Julian the Augustus" to the sinister and ill-wishing "Felix, Julianus—and the Augustus." In relating the death of Felix, Ammianus has been deliberately and significantly selective: he declines to mention that the Christians of Antioch, who formed the larger part of the vulgus to whom he attributed the ill-omened witticism, saw the death of Felix as a divine punishment.[22] For Felix was a convert from Christianity to paganism who accompanied Julianus and Helpidius, *comes rerum privatarum* and himself another convert to paganism, when they entered the great church in Antioch: on this occasion, Felix is reported to have commented sarcastically on the luxurious sacred vessels with which Constantine and Constantius had equipped the church.[23]

Previously, Ammianus continues, on the kalends of January, as Julian ascended the steps of "the temple of the Genius," that is, the shrine of the goddess Tyche, patron deity of the city of Antioch,[24] an elderly priest collapsed and died. The spectators proclaimed that this portended the death of the elder of the consuls of the year, that is, of Sallustius. Ammianus remarks that this interpretation was mistaken, either out of ignorance or because of a desire to flatter: as it turned out, the senior consul of the year did soon die, since the emperor was senior to any *privatus* by virtue of his rank, regardless of the age of each man.

Next, as preparations were begun for the departure of the expedition, news arrived of an earthquake in Constantinople. In this case, there were experts to proclaim to Julian that the earthquake was an unfavorable omen that predicted the victory of the side whose territory was being invaded by foreign arms: they therefore urged the emperor to desist from an enterprise that had been shown to be untimely.[25]

---

[22] *PLRE* 1.332, quotes the relevant passages. The earliest is Gregory of Nazianzus, *Orat.* 5.2: although Gregory was writing after Julian's death, there can be little doubt that his interpretation, which reproduces the familiar pattern of the death of a persecutor, was advanced as soon as Felix fell ill.

[23] Libanius, *Orat.* 14.36; Theodoretus, *HE* 3.12.4. For Helpidius' career, see *PLRE* 1.415, Helpidius 6.

[24] G. Downey, *A History of Antioch in Syria* (Princeton, 1961), 73–75, 384.

[25] On earthquakes as omens in the Greco-Roman world, see the rich collection of material assembled by A. S. Pease, *M. Tulli Ciceronis de Divinatione libri duo* 1 (Urbana, 1920), 109, 227–28.

Finally, at about the same time, presumably about the same time as news of the earthquake arrived, Julian received a letter from Rome reporting that the Sibylline books had been consulted, as he had ordered, and that they expressly forebade the emperor to advance beyond his frontiers that year.

Each of these four omens is of a familiar type—the utterance that unexpectedly predicts the future, the sudden death, an earthquake, a divine message through an acknowledged medium of communication between gods and men. Each is connected with the beginning of the year, the two in Antioch explicitly, those at Constantinople and Rome implicitly (23.1.7: eo anno), and all four omens convey a clear apologetic message that is reiterated in Ammianus' reports of discouraging omens during the march to Ctesiphon: the gods gave Julian clear and unambiguous warnings of the disaster that would overtake his Persian expedition.[26]

This elaborate notice of happenings in Antioch in January 363 omits or glosses over certain episodes that illustrate antipathy between Julian and the largely Christian populace of Antioch and the tensions that his anti-Christian policies produced even in the imperial bodyguard. Ammianus does not conceal the hostility that existed between Julian and the Antiochenes. The emperor's arrival was ill-omened: he reached the city during the annual festival of Adonis, so that he was greeted with wailing and lamentation instead of rejoicing (22.9.15). And when he left, he appointed one Alexander of Heliopolis as governor of Syria: Alexander was cruel and bad-tempered, not suitable for such a post at all (Julian conceded), but the greedy and abusive Antiochenes deserved him (23.2.3). The most striking and unusual manifestation of the hostility was the emperor's composition and publication of one of the strangest literary products of antiquity, which combines the literary elements of a cynic diatribe and a speech in praise of a city—hence its double title *Antiochikos* or *Misopogon* (*On the City of Antioch* or *The Beard-hater*).[27] In it, Julian poses as a cynic philosopher delivering an invective against himself while he lavishes on the city and its inhabitants heavily sarcastic praises that make no attempt to conceal his bitterness and resentment.[28] The occasion of the ridicule that infuriated Julian was the celebration of the kalends of January and the work was posted up ouside the imperial palace for all to read during that month.[29] Am-

---

[26] On these later omens, see Chapters XIII, XIV.

[27] A. Marcone, *REAug* 30 (1984), 226–39. J. M. Alonso-Núñez, *Ancient Society* 10 (1979), 311–24, discounts the religious tensions evident in the work and asserts that "among the inhabitants of Antioch there was no religious interest, neither pagan nor Christian" (324).

[28] Bowersock, *Julian* (1978), 103–4; J. Long, *Ancient World* 24 (1993), 15–23.

[29] Malalas 328.3–4 Bonn, cf. M. Gleason, *JRS* 76 (1986), 106–19.

mianus notices the *Misopogon*, but he displaces it from its original context and transfers it to the preceding autumn (22.14.2).

Modern techniques of research reveal significant episodes from Julian's stay in Antioch, which Ammianus plays down or leaves out altogether. The future emperor Valens, it may be argued, was tribune of the Ioviani Cornuti in the imperial bodyguard until he was discharged after he punched a pagan priest who sprinkled him with holy water as he entered the temple of Tyche during the ceremonies of 1 January.[30] This conclusion is admittedly speculative, since the ecclesiastical historians Theodoretus and Sozomenus tell the story of Valentinian, not Valens.[31] But it is plausible and persuasive, despite the fact that when Ammianus refers to the same episode, he asserts that the priest fell without being struck by anyone (23.1.6: nullo pulsante). Again, it has convincingly been inferred from hagiographical evidence that the trial and execution in Antioch of Bonosus and Maximilianus, the tribunes of the Cornuti Seniores Ioviani and Cornuti Seniores Herculiani, apparently on 21 August or 20 September 362, clarifies an otherwise totally unexplained allusion in Ammianus.[32] The standard bearer of the Ioviani (Ammianus records) deserted to the Persians immediately after Jovian was proclaimed emperor because of a quarrel with him before his accession:

> The standard-bearer of the Joviani, whom Varronianus had once commanded, had been on bad terms with the new emperor while he was still a private citizen because he had insulted and denigrated his father. Fearing danger from an enemy who had now risen above the common level, he deserted to the Persians and, when he was given an opportunity to tell what he knew, he informed Shapur, who was already close at hand, that the man he feared was dead and that an unruly throng of camp-followers had proclaimed the obscure, lethargic and effeminate Jovian, who was still a mere *protector*, as pseudo-emperor.[33] (25.5.8)

Ammianus fails to explain the nature or origin of the quarrel between Jovian and the standard bearer of the Ioviani: an explanation must be sought in the fact that the latter (whose name is unknown) replaced Bonosus when he was executed, perhaps over objections voiced by the future emperor.[34]

---

[30] D. Woods, *Studies in Latin Literature and Roman History*, ed. C. Deroux, 9 (Brussels, 1998), 463–86. Valentinian had been discharged in 357 (16.11.1–7) and lived in retirement at Sirmium until the late summer of 363 (25.10.6–9): D. Woods, *Ancient Society* 26 (1995), 273–77.

[31] Theodoretus, *HE* 3.16.1–5; Sozomenus, *HE* 6.6.4–6.

[32] D. Woods, *Hagiographica* 2 (1995), 25–55.

[33] It is hard to find an exact translation that adequately conveys the contempt expressed by Ammianus' Latin: turbine concitato calonum ad umbram imperii Iovianum adhuc protectorem ascitum, inertem quendam et mollem.

[34] Woods, *Hagiographica* 2 (1995), 45–51; *Journal of Roman Military Equipment Studies* 6 (1995), 61–68.

A still more significant episode omitted by Ammianus is an abortive plot to assassinate Julian. Libanius alludes to it in three of his Julianic speeches: ten guardsmen intended to kill Julian on the parade ground during exercises, but they got drunk and incautiously revealed their plans.[35] Two of the ten, Juventinus and Maximinus, were Christians offended by the constant smell of pagan sacrifice: according to John Chrysostom, they complained at a banquet that God was being dishonored and his holy laws trampled upon.[36] Later Christian writers and calendars identify the pair as Scutarii Gentiles and supply the date of their martyrdom as 29 January.[37] The other eight alleged plotters were released.[38] Why has Ammianus left out a matter so important as disloyalty in the palace guard? His motive seems clear. The failed assassins were celebrated as martyrs after their execution, but Ammianus' account of Julian gives the impression that there were no Christian martyrs at all during his reign. Ammianus thus faithfully reflects the emperor's official propaganda that any Christian put to death had been justly condemned for crimes that had nothing to do with his religion.[39] Christian sources name several dozen martyrs under Julian.[40] Ammianus notes the death of precisely one of them, and he goes out of his way to deny that he was in any sense a martyr. He presents Artemius, who had been *dux* of Egypt under Constantius, and who was later venerated as a saint and martyr in Constantinople,[41] as a notorious malefactor who was accused by the people of Alexandria and executed "for a mass of horrible crimes" (22.11.2).

[35] Libanius, *Orat.* 15.43; 16.19; 18.199.
[36] John Chrysostom, *In sanctos martyres Iuventinum et Maximinum* (PG 50.574).
[37] Theodoret, *HE* 3.15.4−9; P. Peeters, *Anal. Boll.* 42 (1924), 77−82.
[38] Libanius, *Ep.* 1120.
[39] Hence the complaint of Gregory of Nazianzus that Julian tried to deprive the church of martyrs (*Orat.* 4.58).
[40] H. C. Brennecke, *Studien zur Geschichte der Homöer* (Beiträge zur Historischen Theologie 73, 1988), 114−57; R. J. Penella, *Ancient World* 24 (1993), 31−43.
[41] On Artemius' posthumous reputation, see S. M. C. Lieu, *From Constantine to Julian: Pagan and Byzantine Views*, ed. S. Lieu and D. Montserrat (London, 1996), 213−23.

[VI]

ORIGIN AND SOCIAL STATUS

Who was Ammianus Marcellinus? Where did he come from? What was his social status? There is no direct and explicit evidence beyond the little that Ammianus has chosen to vouchsafe about himself in the extant books of his history. He was a soldier and a Greek (31.16.9). Both terms require further definition before their precise import becomes clear (Chapters VII, VIII). The extant books disclose Ammianus' approximate age and the outlines of a career. He was an *adulescens* in 357 (16.10.21): when his extant narrative begins, he was serving in the Roman army as a *protector domesticus* (14.9.1, 18.8.11), attached by imperial command to the general Ursicinus, whom he acompanied as a staff officer on various postings and missions between 354 and 359.[1] In 363 Ammianus took part in Julian's Persian expedition and returned to Antioch with the defeated Roman army (23.5.7–25.10.1). Thereafter, he resided in the East for at least fifteen years until he migrated to Rome, where he completed his history about 390.[2]

In order to discover Ammianus' origin and social status, therefore, it is necessary to use both indirect indications in his text and any explicit evidence external to the *Res Gestae* that may be relevant. A letter of Libanius has traditionally been used not only to date the composition of the work, but also to establish Ammianus' precise local origin. During the second half of the year 392, the aged Antiochene sophist dispatched a letter to one Marcellinus, a fellow-Antiochene who was in Rome and engaged in literary activity there. Since so much depends on its interpretation, the letter must be quoted in full:

---

[1] Conveniently summarized in *PLRE* 1.547–48, Marcellinus 13; for a fuller exposition, see L. Dilleman, *Syria* 38 (1961), 91–98; Matthews, *Ammianus* (1989), 34–66, 81–83.

[2] Matthews, *Ammianus* (1989), 13–32.

Libanius to Marcellinus

(1) I envy you for possessing Rome and Rome for possessing you. For you possess a thing to which there is nothing similar on earth, and Rome one not inferior to her own citizens, who descend from demi-gods. (2) It would, therefore, have been a great thing for you just to live in such a city in silence and to listen to speeches delivered by others: Rome produces many orators who follow in the footsteps of their forefathers. But in fact, as one can learn from those who arrive from there, you yourself (I gather) have given some public recitations and are going to give more, since your work has been divided into many sections and the praise bestowed on what has already appeared invites another installment. (3) I hear that Rome herself is crowning your labor and has rendered a verdict that you have shown yourself superior to some and equal to the rest. This adorns with honor not merely the author, but us too to whom the author belongs. (4) Please do not stop composing such things and taking them from the study to literary salons, and do not weary of being admired, but become still more famous yourself and give us fame. For it is a mark of the truly celebrated citizen to adorn his native city with his achievements.

(5) May you continue in your present happy state! As for me, unless one of the gods aids me in my state of mourning, it will be impossible for me to bear it. For he who was my only son, not a bad fellow and born of a good mother, even if she was not of free birth, is gone and buried after dying from grief which was the result of an outrage. Who they were who insulted him, you must discover from others: even though I have suffered, I must refrain from naming them. (6) While the evil was still seething, Calliopius was snatched from among his books and his labors. Wound follows wound, and the education of the young degenerates. This you can learn too from those who have divided up his estate. For me, what happened before his death, his death itself and what has happened after have occasioned lamentation and tears, most of which flow copiously over what I write.[3]

---

[3] Libanius, *Ep.* 1063: my translation of R. Foerster's Teubner text, adapted slightly from *CP* 88 (1993), 58. There are three other recent English translations: (1) C. W. Fornara, *Historia* 41 (1992), 332, which I saw before publication and to which my own rendering owes much; (2) A. F. Norman, *Libanius: Autobiography and Selected Letters* 2 (Cambridge, Mass., 1992), 429–33 (no. 188), whose translation of the crucial terms *syngraphe/eus* assumes that the recipient of the letter is the historian—which is precisely the central point in dispute; (3) J. F. Matthews, *CQ*, N.S. 44 (1994), 252–53, who correctly translates the words in dispute as "composition" and "writer," respectively. Since Libanius' epistolary style is difficult and frequently elliptical, I have tried to bring out his train of thought a little more explicitly than Fornara, Norman, and Matthews—and I have occasionally translated rather freely in order to produce reasonably idiomatic English.

For a German translation of Foerster's text, see G. Fatouros and T. Krischer, *Libanios, Briefe griechisch-deutsch* (Munich, 1980), 154–57. A French translation of sections 1–5 is offered by

Until very recently, it was universally assumed that the recipient of the letter must be the historian Ammianus Marcellinus.[4] In 1987, however, Charles Fornara challenged this traditional identification in a paper that was eventually published in 1992—after he had generously allowed Glen Bowersock and the present writer to use his typescript in advance of publication.[5] Fornara argued that the Marcellinus to whom Libanius wrote was not the historian Ammianus Marcellinus: he drew the corollary that the Antiochene origin deduced for the historian from this letter of Libanius must be discarded; instead, he suggested that the historian came from Thessalonica.[6] In a long review of Matthews' study of Ammianus, Bowersock accepted Fornara's thesis that the correspondent of Libanius could not be the historian and suggested that he might be the Marcellinus to whom one Magnus (presumably Magnus of Nisibis, who taught rhetoric and medicine in Alexandria) dedicated two sets of acrostic iambic verses incorporated in the medico-magical treatise *Cyranides*.[7]

In a reconsideration of the problem published in 1993, I concluded that, although Fornara's demolition of the traditional view was effective, neither the Macedonian origin that he proposed nor the Alexandrian origin suggested by Bowersock was likely to be correct, since Matthews had made a good case for believing that Ammianus could speak Syriac and hence came from the region of Syria, if not from Antioch itself.[8] In 1994 Matthews restated his case for the traditional view,[9] which shows signs of being reinstated as the *communis opinio* of enlightened scholarship.[10] Now Matthews' restatement stands or falls on

---

P. M. Camus, *Ammien Marcellin, témoin des courants culturels et religieux à la fin du IVe siècle* (Paris, 1967), 278−79: it is based on the translation of Reiske's text by J. Gimazane, *Ammien Marcellin. Sa vie et son œuvre* (Diss. Bordeaux, pub. Toulouse, 1889), 403−4.

[4] Matthews, *Ammianus* (1989), 8: "the identity of Libanius' correspondent as Ammianus Marcellinus is inescapable"; 454: Libanius' letter is "the one certain external reference to Ammianus."

[5] Matthews, *Ammianus* (1989), 478−79, n. 1, reports Fornara's conclusion (from a paper delivered in Oxford in February 1987) and argues against it.

[6] Fornara, *Historia* 41 (1992), 333−44.

[7] G. W. Bowersock, *JRS* 80 (1990), 247−48, citing the brilliant detection of the acrostics by M. L. West, *CQ*, N. S. 42 (1982), 480−81, who also improved the text printed by D. Kaimakis, *Die Kyraniden* (Meisenheim am Glan, 1976), 50−51, 96−97. Magnus of Nisibis was an iatrosophist, and his presence in Alexandria is attested in 364 and 388 (*PLRE* 1. 534, Magnus 7). West reedited two more acrostic poems in the same text that have the author's name in the genitive as *Magnou*: a third was subsequently added by R. Führer, *ZPE* 58 (1985), 270, and possible additional evidence about Magnus is noted by D. Bain, *"Owls to Athens." Essays on Classical Subjects Presented to Sir Kenneth Dover*, ed. E. M. Craik (Oxford, 1990), 296, n. 4.

[8] *CP* 88 (1993), 59−61, cf. Matthews, *Ammianus* (1989), 65−70.

[9] J. F. Matthews, *CQ*, N.S. 44 (1994), 252−69. Comments on Fornara's arguments have also been offered by S. Rota, KOINΩNIA 18 (1994), 165−77.

[10] K. Rosen, *Der neue Pauly* 1 (1996), 596: Ammianus "war zweifellos der Empfänger des Briefes."

the proposition that the two related nouns in the letter, which are translated above as "author" and "work," must mean specifically "historian" and "history." However, outside the letter to Marcellinus, Libanius uses the nouns *sungrapheus* and *sungraphe* only five and nine times respectively.[11] Hence, even if Libanius always used the two words elsewhere in the more restricted sense, the inference that they must have the same sense in the letter to Marcellinus would would have a weak statistical basis. For other authors use the word *sungrapheus* in the wider sense. Libanius' frequent model Isocrates uses it of himself as a writer of speeches, Libanius' contemporary the emperor Julian to mean "writer of prose" as opposed to poet, and the ecclesiastical historian Theodoretus even applies it to the Syriac poet Ephrem.[12] Moreover, Libanius himself employs this wider sense: he uses the verb *sungrapho* and the noun *sungraphe* for the activity and products of orators, and styles himself *sungrapheus* as the alleged author of a panegyric on the usurper Procopius.[13] Furthermore, it is pure *petitio principii* to assert that it is implausible to imagine two Marcellini from Antioch in Rome in 392:[14] Marcellinus is not a rare name, and the Antiochene origin of the historian is in dispute. But doxography does not decide truth. What in the letter tells for or against the traditional identification of its addressee?

The crucial point is one that would surely have been realized long ago, had the letter been read without preconceptions. Both Libanius' tone and the contents of his letter imply that his addressee has recently arrived in Rome and has recently made his literary début there: they do not suit a man of sixty or so who had lived in Rome for nearly a decade.[15] Indeed, the remark that it would have been a great thing for the Antiochene Marcellinus merely to live in Rome in silence and to listen to others would have been intolerably offensive and patronizing if addressed to an established historian, especially one who had recently completed a history on the grand scale. Libanius' tone precludes his identification as the historian Ammianus Marcellinus. The letter im-

---

[11] G. Fatouros, T. Krischer, and D. Najock, *Concordantiae in Libanium* 1.2 (Hildesheim/Zürich/New York, 1987), 640; 2.3 (1989), 391. Somewhat surprisingly, Matthews nowhere refers to the published concordances to Libanius' speeches and letters: he appeals instead to a search in the electronic Thesaurus Linguae Graecae conducted for him by H.-U. Wiemer (*CQ*, N.S. 44 [1994], 263–64, n. 58).

[12] Isocrates, *Antidosis* 35; Julian, *Misopogon* 338b; Theodoretus, *HE* 2.30.11.

[13] Libanius, *Orat.* 58.40; *Ep.* 406.1, 793, cf. 826.1; *Orat.* 1.163. The normal usage is well stated by Fornara, *Historia* 41 (1992), 334: "these words . . . define generally either the process of prose composition or its result."

[14] As does Matthews, *CQ*, N.S. 44 (1994), 267.

[15] Bowersock, *JRS* 80 (1990), 247; Fornara, *Historia* 41 (1992), 333–34; T. D. Barnes, *CP* 88 (1993), 58.

plies that its recipient, who listens to speeches in a city famous for its orators and gives *epideixeis*, is an orator or sophist rather than a historian. He need not be a rhetor composing and reciting a collection of speeches,[16] but he could be an iatrosophist who has recited part of a treatise on medical rhetoric.[17]

There is thus no certain external contemporary evidence for Ammianus' career or literary activity.[18] What then does the text of the *Res Gestae* indirectly reveal about the origin and social status of its author? The latter is the easier to discover. Two passages denouncing Julian's policy of forcing men of curial origin to perform curial duties have long been recognized to reflect the personal anger of one who was affected by the policy:

> It was harsh and reprehensible that under him only with difficulty did anyone whom town-councillors wished to co-opt obtain fair treatment under the law, even if he was protected by special privileges, by length of service, or by clear proof that his origin was elsewhere altogether, to such a degree that many in terror bought exemption from molestation by secret payments. (22.9.12)

> Equally intolerable was the fact that he allowed some persons to be wrongfully drafted into membership of town councils who were either from another city or far removed from liability to such conscription through special privileges or by their origin. (25.4.21)

The implicit self-reference is hard to mistake. Yet the precise import of these passages requires careful consideration. It is mistaken to deduce that Ammianus had been threatened with inclusion in the municipal *ordo*, "although he thought that his military service entitled him to exemption."[19] In both passages emphasis falls very heavily on the Latin word *origo*. How many different categories of person does Ammianus specify whom Julian unjustly compelled or allowed to be compelled to serve as decurions? One category is described in identical terms in both passages: those who had been granted specific exemption from curial service (*privilegia*). Moreover, those who are *originis penitus alienae* in the first passage must surely be identical to the *peregrini*, that is, the citizens of another city, in the second. In the first passage the remaining

[16] As argued by Fornara, *Historia* 41 (1992), 336−37.

[17] As suggested by Bowersock, *JRS* 80 (1990), 247−48.

[18] O. Seeck, *RE* I (1894), 1846, suggested that the unnamed addressee of Symmachus, *Ep.* 9.110, might be Ammianus ("Symm. ep. IX 110 könnte wohl an ihn gerichtet sein"). The conjecture, promoted to a certainty by many who subsequently wrote about the historian, was disproved by Alan Cameron, *JRS* 54 (1964), 15−18. For a full bibliography, see S. Roda, *Commento storico al Libro IX dell'Epistolario di Q. Aurelio Simmaco* (Pisa, 1981), 242−45.

[19] Thompson, *Ammianus* (1947), 81: accepted in *Reading the Past* (1990), 62.

category is defined in terms of *stipendiorum numerus*, whereas in the second the third exempt group are *origine longe discreti*. Hence the correct deduction from the pair of passages taken together is that Ammianus claimed exemption from curial obligations both on the grounds of his own service as a soldier and because his father or grandfather had removed himself from the curial class and the attendant obligations by entering imperial service.[20]

The inference that Ammianus came from a family that had already risen above curial status is confirmed by the fact that he was a *protector domesticus* as a young man in his twenties. The standard study of the *scholae palatinae* documents the fact that *protectores domestici* were normally the sons of military officers of high rank.[21] Eight are known from the fourth century besides Ammianus himself: although the origin of three of them is unknown,[22] Ammianus records the parentage of the other five. They all came from very similar backgrounds. Herculanus was the son of Hermogenes, the *magister equitum* of Constantius who was lynched in Constantinople in 342 when he attempted to arrest the bishop Paul (14.10.2). The emperor Jovian was the son of Varronianus, tribune of the Joviani and *comes domesticorum* (25.5.4, 8). The imperial brothers Valentinian and Valens were the sons of Gratianus, who rose to be *comes rei militaris* in Britain (30.7.2–3). And Masaucio was the son of Cretio, who commanded the troops in Africa for Constantius as *comes rei militaris per Africam* from circa 350 to 361 (26.5.14). Ammianus, it is clear, "must have had connections."[23] If all the other known *protectores domestici* of his generation were the sons of generals, then he too may have been. Whether or not Jean Gimazane was justified in suggesting, more than a hundred years ago, that the historian was the son of the Marcellinus who was *comes Orientis* in 349,[24] his instinct for Roman social norms was correct: to be a *protector domesticus* at such an early age, Ammianus must surely have belonged to a family of high status. Moreover, although subsequent writers about Ammianus have shown coolness towards Gimazane's identification of Ammianus' father,[25] several considerations (it may be noted) tell indirectly in its favor.

---

[20] On such exemptions in the early fourth century, see esp. Jones, *LRE* 69–70, 135–36, 740–41; F. Millar, *JRS* 73 (1983), 91–96.

[21] R. I. Frank, *Scholae Palatinae. The Palace Guard in the Later Roman Empire* (Papers and Monographs of the American Academy in Rome 23, 1969), 73. Frank adduces Ammianus as "the most famous example" of the sons of decurions who "formed a second group of Roman officers" (76–79), but none of the others was a *protector domesticus*, while two of Frank's alleged military officers are civilian palatine officials (*PLRE* 1.277, Eleusius; 554, Marcianus 8).

[22] Romanus and Vincentius (22.11.2) and Equitius (26.1.4).

[23] R. S. O. Tomlin, *The Roman World*, ed. J. Wacher, 1 (London / New York, 1987), 115.

[24] Gimazane, *Ammien* (1889), 24–27.

[25] A conspicuous exception was L. Dautremer, *Ammien Marcellin. Étude d'histoire littéraire* (Diss. Paris, publ. Lille, 1899), 11: "pour qu'Ammien ait été placé si jeune dans l'état-major d'un

Ammianus was Greek, but he did not come from Asia Minor, since he jeers at the customs of the area (15.7.6: Asiatici mores). He knew Antioch well and admired the city. But that does not make him a native of the city. For he lived there for a long period, probably almost twenty years from 363 or thereabouts to shortly after 380. His local knowledge is obvious and profound: for example, he alludes to the unexpected appearance of the Persian king Shapur in the early 250s while the citizens of Antioch were absorbed in the theater (25.5.3)—a story told elsewhere only in the Antiochene writers Libanius and Malalas (though Eunapius of Sardis has it in a garbled form).[26] But no amount of local knowledge could prove that the historian was a native of Antioch. Ammianus knew and admired Antioch because he lived in the city for a number of years. Similarly, Ammianus' praise of noster Hypatius for his conduct in 372 (29.2.16) reflects friendship, not community of origin: Hypatius was the brother of Constantius' second wife and a native of Thessalonica, who lived in Antioch while Ammianus resided there and then migrated to Rome when he was appointed praefectus urbi in 379 (Chapter X).

Ammianus, it appears, could speak Syriac: not only was he a personal friend of Jovinianus the satrap of Corduene, who recognized him when he was sent to Corduene on a reconnaisance mission (18.6.20−21), but also he could move around in the Mesopotamian countryside (18.8.7−13, 19.8.5−12). That might seem to support an Antiochene origin.[27] On a dispassionate assessment, however, fluency in Syriac indicates only that Ammianus came from the general area of Syria and Palestine. Does his text in any way disclose anything more precise? He reveals his origin, it may be suggested, in an idiosyncratic linguistic usage.

Ammianus uses the plural Syriae in preference to the singular Syria, and he uses it to associate Phoenicia, the Lebanon and Palestine with Antioch. The satrap Jovinianus was not, as is often stated, "sent to Syria as a hostage":[28] he was a hostage in Syriis (18.6.20). Elsewhere, Ammianus has per Syrias (26.3.2), Syriae omnes (2.10.1) and Syriarum provinciae (22.15.2). Pride in his eastern origin is obvious in Ammianus' survey of the provinces of Oriens in Book XIV:

> Next Syria spreads for a distance over a beautiful plain. This is famed for An-
> tioch, a city known to all the world, and without a rival, so rich is it in imported

général en chef en qualité de *protector doesticus*, il fallait que son père occupât un poste élevé et disposât d'une influence considérable."

[26] Libanius, *Orat.* 24.38, 60.2; Malalas 295.20−296.20 Bonn; Eunapius, *Vit. phil.* 6.5.2 (465). Eunapius trots out the story as if the episode occurred very shortly before Eustathius' embassy to Persia in 358 (Ammianus 17.5.15, 14.1).

[27] Matthews, *Ammianus* (1989), 44, 55−57.

[28] Matthews, *Ammianus* (1989), 44.

and domestic commodities; likewise for Laodicea, Apamea, and also Seleucia, most flourishing cities from their very origin.

After this comes Phoenicia, lying at the foot of Mount Libanus, a region full of charm and beauty, adorned with many great cities; among these in attractiveness and the renown of their names Tyre, Sidon and Berytus are conspicuous, and equal to these are Emesa and Damascus, founded in days long past.

The last of the Syrias is Palaestina . . . (14.8.8−9)

Ammianus' praise of Tyre, Sidon, and Berytus may reflect the pride of a man from Phoenicia. Neither Berytus nor Sidon had produced any outstanding intellectuals under the Roman Empire, although Berytus was the *patria* of Domitius Leontius, who served Constantius as praetorian prefect from 342 to 346 and would thus have been in a position to start a fellow townsman on a career.[29] From Tyre, however, had come both Domitius Ulpianus, the foremost of Roman jurists,[30] and the philosopher Porphyry, who also knew Aramaic or Syriac.[31] It may be relevant that Herculanus, on whom Ammianus bestows a gratuitously favorable notice, inherited a house at Tyre.[32] Herculanus went to Gaul in 354 to report to Constantius about the misdeeds of Gallus (14.10.2). Ammianus may have known him before they served together: the two young *protectores domestici* might even have been boyhood friends.

There may exist, moreover, an external item of evidence concerning the historian. One of a number of letters from Libanius to his former pupils Apollinaris and Gemellus in Tarsus concludes with the following two sentences:

> Please, my boys, show concern for your teacher either by inviting him to Cilicia or sending something from there. You may be persuaded to despise money without my frequent admonitions in the past by the man who bears this letter: to judge from his dress he is enlisted in the army, but in fact he is enrolled among philosophers; he has imitated Socrates despite having gainful employment—the fine Ammianus.[33]

The letter appears to have been written in 360.[34] At this date, the future historian could have taken it from Antioch, where he was (it may be assumed)

---

[29] On Leontius' prefecture, see *ZPE* 94 (1992), 251−52, 253−54: his origin is inferred from the fact that the *ordo* of Berytus, following "honorific decrees of the province of Phoenice ratified by the verdict of the emperors," honored him with a statue (*ILS* 1234).

[30] *PIR*² D 169.

[31] Porphyry, *Vita Plotini* 17.4−15.

[32] Libanius, *Ep.* 828 (363).

[33] Libanius, *Ep.* 233.4 (my translation).

[34] O. Seeck, *Die Briefe des Libanius* (*Texte und Untersuchungen* 30, 1906), 374.

stationed after the dismissal of Ursicinus. For Libanius' description fits what is known about the culture and formation of Ammianus Marcellinus.[35]

Nomenclature is no obstacle to identifying Libanius' philosophical soldier as the future historian. It is true that Priscian called the historian Marcellinus little more than a century after his death.[36] But naming practices in the fourth century were not wholly consistent. Julian's praetorian prefect, for example, is Saturninius Secundus on three inscriptions, Secundus Salutius on his first mention in Ammianus (22.3.1), Salutius on subsequent mentions in Ammianus, Salutius in the manuscripts of his treatise *On the Gods and the Universe*, Salutius, Salustius, or Sallustius in most other literary texts, and Secundus in the law codes.[37] Similar alternations of name can be documented for others in the fourth century[38] and Ammianus may not have cared to give undue prominence to a name that so clearly indicated his eastern origin after he came to Rome.

For, although the name Marcellinus is too indistinct to prove anything, Wilhelm Schulze noted long ago, in another context, both that the *cognomen* Ammianus is very rare in Italy and that all its known bearers are of Greek origin.[39] Subsequent discoveries have strengthened his observation or inference.[40] Moreover, where the origin of possessors of names beginning in Am(m)i– can be verified, it is usually Semitic, like the woman whose ossuary in Jerusalem states her name and provenance as Ammia from Scythopolis in both Greek and Hebrew.[41] It seems that no Ammia, Ammias, Ammion, or Ammianus is

---

[35] See Chapters VII, VIII, XIV: the letter was argued to refer to the historian by M. Büdinger, *Ammianus Marcellinus und die Eigenart seines Geschichtswerkes* (*Denkschriften Wien*, Phil.-hist. Cl. 44.5, 1895), 9.

[36] Priscian, *Inst. Gramm.* 9.51 (quoted in Chapter III, n. 42).

[37] *PLRE* 1.814–817, Saturninius Secundus Salutius 3, cf. J. L. Desnier, *REA* 85 (1983), 53–65, who argues that the fourth-century author took the name of the historian Sallust as a pseudonym.

[38] For example, Ammianus refers to Q. Flavius Maesius Egnatius Lollianus *signo* Mavortius as Lollianus when stating the names of the consuls of 355 (15.8.17), but as Mavortius when he appears in his narrative as praetorian prefect (16.8.5).

[39] W. Schulze, *Zur Geschichte lateinischer Eigennamen* (*Abh. Göttingen*, Phil.-hist. Kl., N.F. 5.5, 1904), 121 n. 1, citing *CIL* 9.1207 (Aeclanum); *IG* 14.1381, 1446 (Rome), to which add *CIG* 9725 (Rome).

[40] There are few men called Ammianus of any prominence before the fourth century: only an epigrammatist of the second century and Statilius Ammianus, who is attested as prefect of Egypt in 271–72: see, respectively, R. Reitzenstein, *RE* 1 (1894) 1845, Ammianus 1; G. Bastiniani, *ZPE* 17 (1975), 317, cf. J. R. Rea, *Oxyrhynchus Papyri* 40 (Oxford, 1972), 24, 82 (on *P. Oxy.* 2923). Otherwise, a search in the *Thesaurus Linguae Graecae* reveals the following approximate distribution of epigraphically attested Ammiani: (1) pre-Christian: Athens 4, Ephesus 5, Caria 5; (2) Christian: Asia Minor 11, Cyprus 1, Rome 2; (3) Jewish: 2.

[41] *CIJ* 1372 = P. Thomsen, *ZDPV* 44 (1921), 120, no. 204a, cf. H. Wuthnow, *Die semitischen Menschennamen in griechischen Inschriften und Papyri des vorderen Orients* (Diss. Tübingen, pub. Leipzig, 1930), 19–21.

to be found in Greek inscriptions before the middle Hellenistic period,[42] and of the ten women with the name Ammia listed in a recent compendium of ancient Athenians, no fewer than four are stated to have a levantine origin— one each from Antioch, Jerusalem, Samaria, and Sidon.[43]

Ammianus came from Syria or Phoenicia, his city of origin being perhaps either Tyre or Sidon. He was the son of an officer in the Roman army who achieved high rank in the early years of the reign of Constantius, he had personal connections in the military élite, and he took the first steps in what ought to have become a distinguished career.[44] Three of Ammianus' close coevals from very similar backgrounds even became emperor. Yet something went wrong with his career and the bright hopes of his youth were blighted. Why? Unlike Thucydides, who recorded both his failure to relieve Amphipolis and the fact that he was exiled for twenty years,[45] Ammianus is reticent about himself. Perhaps he was damaged by his close association with Ursicinus, who was officially blamed for the loss of Amida in 359 (20.2.2−5). Yet Ammianus served as an officer in Julian's army, which invaded Mesopotamia in 363. Perhaps, therefore, he compromised his career under Julian, as the orator Himerius, who abandoned his official chair of rhetoric in Athens in the winter of 361−362 and rushed enthusiastically to join the court of Julian, appears to have done.[46] There are good reasons for holding that Ammianus was brought up a Christian (Chapter VIII). If he became an apostate in 361−362, still more if he helped to enforce Julian's anti-Christian policies, then his way to further preferment may have been barred under Julian's Christian successors.

By the time that he wrote his history, Ammianus was a disppointed and embittered man. His use of the word *potentes* reflects the attitudes of one not accustomed to enter the portals of real power.[47] The plural *potentes* occurs four

---

[42] See P. M. Fraser and E. Matthews, *A Lexicon of Greek Personal Names*, 1. *The Aegean Islands, Cyprus, Cyrenaica* (Oxford, 1987), 31; 2. *Attica* (Oxford, 1994), 25; 3A. *Peloponnese, Sicily, Western Greece, and Southern Italy* (Oxford, 1996), 33; A. B. Tataki, *Ancient Beroea: Prosopography and Society* (Athens, 1988), 103−5.

[43] J. S. Traill, *Persons of Ancient Athens* (Toronto, 1995), 80.

[44] N. J. E. Austin, *Ammianus on Warfare: An Investigation into Ammianus' Military Knowledge* (*Collection Latomus* 165, 1979), 164−65, concludes that "Ammianus' viewpoint for the narration of military history is generally that of a member of the headquarters staff rather than of a field officer" and that "he was a staff officer attached to various commanders, and not on combat duties."

[45] Thucydides 4.105−7, 5.25.1, cf. A. W. Gomme, *Historical Commentary on Thucydides* (Oxford, 1956), 584−88.

[46] *CP* 82 (1987), 220−25.

[47] Contrast his use of *potiores* in a wide variety of favorable senses (Viansino, *Lexicon* 2.326−27).

times. One passage is neutral: Valentinian takes a decision without consulting the *potentes* (27.10.10: nullo potentium in conscientam arcani adhibito). In the other three passages, however, the connotations of the word are extremely negative. Under Constantius, the *potentes* in the palace coveted and appropriated the property of condemned persons (16.8.11), and Antoninus, who had suffered great losses through the cupidity of certain persons, ran the risk of being unjustly ruined because he railed against the *potentes* (18.5.1). Under Julian, in contrast, the *potentium tumor* was broken (30.4.1).

[VII]

THE GREEK TEMPLATE

In the final paragraph of his history, Ammianus describes himself as "a former soldier and a Greek" (31.16.9: haec ut miles quondam et Graecus . . . pro virium explicavi mensura). The tone of the words that Ammianus uses to describe himself has been a matter of some debate.[1] Are they a proud boast? And is Ammianus claiming that he has both the practical experience of affairs and the culture needed to be an authoritative historian? Or is he, as has recently been argued, "offering an apology rather than staking a claim"? And can his words be construed as "the apology of a mere soldier ("ut," in a concessive sense) to have ventured on an occupation more characteristic of civilian, even aristocratic, pursuits than of the military profession, and of a native-born Greek to have written in the Latin language"?[2]

The new interpretation is not persuasive, even if the word *ut* could mean "although" in this context. For, while any author may preface his work with an apology and protest as he proceeds that he has only a middling talent (16.1.2, 23.4.1: mediocre ingenium), a historian's epilogue ought to reflect pride in the achievement of completing a difficult task, and Ammianus' self-characterization precedes a claim that he has, to the best of his ability, avoided ever misrepresenting the truth (31.16.9: opus veritatem professum/ numquam, ut arbitror, sciens/ silentio corrumpere vel mendacio). Moreover, for Ammianus the term *Graecus* is more than an epithet assigning a man to a par-

---

[1] For a careful discussion of modern interpretations, see G. Calboli, *Festschrift für Robert Muth* (Innsbruck, 1983), 33–53.

[2] J. F. Matthews, *History and Historians* (1983), 30–31; *Ammianus* (1989), 461, cf. H. Drexler, *Ammianstudien* (1974), 179 n. 122; R. Browning, *Cambridge History of Classical Literature 2: Latin Literature*, ed. E. J. Kenney (Cambridge, 1982), 749.

ticular culture: it conveys a strong commendation. The only other singular *Graecus* in the extant books is the Augustan historian Timagenes, whom Ammianus quotes as an authority on the ethnography of Gaul. Timagenes is introduced as a Greek by both scholarly expertise and language (15.9.2: et diligentia Graecus et lingua). The order is highly significant: it is his scholarly expertise that stamps Timagenes as a Greek even more than the language in which he wrote.

Ammianus should not be measured against contemporary Roman aristocrats who dabbled in history in the reign of Theodosius.[3] He intended to evoke a very different standard of comparison. He set himself in the noble tradition of Thucydides and Polybius, historians who appealed to their own direct and indirect knowledge of contemporary events as conferring authority on what they wrote.[4] When Ammianus described his method of writing the history of his own lifetime in the preface to Book XV, he used words that he surely intended to recall Thucydides: "Using every effort to investigate the truth, I have set out, in the order of their occurrence, events which my age allowed me to see myself or to know by thorough questioning of those who took part in them" (15.1.1). And the one explicit mention of Polybius in the extant books is immensely revealing in what it implies about Ammianus himself. At the siege of Pirisabora, the emperor Julian took part in an unsuccessful attempt to force one of the gates of the city: "He himself was unhurt, but his face was suffused with a modest blush. For he had read that Scipio Aemilianus with the historian Polybius, an Arcadian from Megalopolis, and thirty soldiers, had successfully undermined a gate at Carthage by an attack of this sort." (24.2.16). Since the young Ammianus served as a soldier in Julian's Persian expedition, it seems an irresistible inference that he is here comparing his relation to his hero to that of Polybius to Scipio Aemilianus.[5] Whether the implied comparison is deliberate or unconscious, it implies that Ammianus thought of himself as a historian in the tradition of Polybius—and hence also of Thucydides.

---

[3] Such as Nicomachus Flavianus, who was permitted to dedicate his lost *Annales* to the emperor Theodosius (*ILS* 2948: annalium quos consecrari sibi a quaestore et praefecto suo voluit). Flavianus has often been postulated as an important source for both Ammianus and other writers of the late fourth century: J. Schlumberger, *Die "Epitome de Caesaribus": Untersuchungen zur heidnischen Geschichtsschreibung des 4. Jahrhunderts n. Chr.* (*Vestigia* 18, 1974); F. Paschoud, *Cinq Études sur Zosime* (Paris, 1975), 63–183 (Eunapius); *Histoire Auguste* 5.1: *Vies d'Aurélien, Tacite* (Paris, 1996), 10–12, 230–31; B. Bleckmann, *Historia* 44 (1995), 83–99 (Ammianus).

[4] F. W. Walbank, *Historical Commentary on Polybius* I (Oxford, 1957), 6–16; *Speeches in Greek Historians* (Oxford, 1965); *Polybius* (Berkeley, 1972), 32–96.

[5] Sabbah, *Méthode* (1978), 92–101, 593–600; T. D. Barnes, *Reading the Past* (1990), 67–68.

The giants of classical scholarship in Wilhelmine Germany saw the essential Greekness of Ammianus' history very clearly. In his survey of artistic prose from Gorgias to the Renaissance, Eduard Norden declared boldly that Ammianus "thinks in Greek."[6] Norden confessed that he had read little of the *Res Gestae* (only a couple of books), but he instantly recognized the author's hatred of Constantius and partiality for Julian, he found his style excessively emotional, and he illustrated its underlying Greek structures of thought by quoting the Greek equivalent of individual words such as *conducentia* (18.1.1: = *ta sumpheronta*) and by offering a Greek retroversion of whole clauses (14.6.8, 10.16).[7] The Hellenist Wilamowitz, the Latinist Friedrich Leo, and the Byzantinist Karl Krumbacher accepted that characterization wholeheartedly: in a survey of Greek and Latin language and literature, they presented Ammianus as a Greek or early Byzantine historian, not among the Latin historians of Rome.[8] Eduard Fraenkel agreed: he observed that Ammianus' use of the word *dies* reflected rules learned in the schoolroom rather than the usage of a native speaker of Latin.[9]

At a more mundane level, a series of dissertations by young scholars and *Programmschriften* by teachers in German gymnasia found a large number of Greek usages and turns of phrase when they examined Ammianus' diction and syntax. Georg Hassenstein presented his dissertation on the syntax of Ammianus at the University of Königsberg in 1877: he started from the assumption that as a Greek Ammianus could not have avoided Graecisms, which he proceeded to find especially in his free use of adjectives and participles as nouns, in apparent peculiarities in his use of the pronoun *is* and the third-person reflexive

---

[6] E. Norden, *Antike Kunstprosa*[2] (Leipzig, 1909), 648: "zwar ist dieses Gräcisieren kein beabsichtiges, sondern die natürliche Folge der Unfähigkeit des Schriftstellers, sich in korrektem Latein auszudrücken: er *denkt* griechisch." Norden expressly distinguished Ammianus' unintentional use of Greek locutions from the learned and deliberate Graecisms employed by Latin literary artists from Ennius to Apuleius and Tertullian, which are documented by E. Löfstedt, *Syntactica. Studien und Beiträge zur historischen Syntax des Lateins*, 2 (Lund, 1933), 406–31. Löfstedt, it may be observed, applied Norden's criteria to the jurist Gaius, arguing that Graecisms such as the use of *ut* followed by an indicative or by an accusative and infinitive to express purpose point to an eastern origin (431–32).

[7] Norden, *Kunstprosa*[2] (1909), 646–50. Compare the recent comment on 15.1.1 by C. W. Fornara, *Cabinet of the Muses*, ed. M. Griffith and D. J. Mastronarde (Atlanta, 1990), 166: "the sentence is structurally Greek."

[8] U. Wilamowitz-Moellendorff, *Die griechische und lateinische Literatur und Sprache*[2] (Berlin and Leipzig, 1907), 201, comparing Ammianus to Eunapius, Olympiodorus and Priscus; K. Krumbacher, ibid. 266; F. Leo, ibid. 389: "der griechischen, nicht der längst verlassenen römischen Bahn des Geschichtschreibung folgend."

[9] E. Fraenkel, *Glotta* 8 (1917), 55: "Dieser Grieche steht eben nicht inmitten des lebendigen Flusses der Sprache, er hat sein Latein in der Schule gelernt."

(including the genitive *sui* instead of the adjective *suus*), and the frequency of the indicative mood in reported speech.[10] Others soon offered confirmation. H. Ehrismann could only explain oddities in Ammianus' use of moods and tenses by the hypothesis that he was a Greek who learned Latin late.[11] Anton Reiter, a schoolteacher at Amberg, agreed with Hassenstein that Ammianus' use of the indicative in *oratio obliqua* was an authentic Graecism.[12] Hassenstein had also suggested that Ammianus' free use of the preposition *per* might be influenced by the Greek *dia*:[13] the dissertation on Ammianus' use of prepositions by Gustav Reinhardt documented the case at length.[14] And a systematic study of Ammianus' vocabulary, syntax and style by F. Liesenberg, which he seems never to have completed, found extensive Greek influence on Ammianus' vocabulary: he noted locutions such as *exnunc* (21.10.2 = *apo nun*) and *suasionis opifex* (30.4.3 = *pathous demiourgos*) and strengthened Reinhardt's interpretation of *per* as the equivalent of *dia*.[15]

Much scholarly writing on Ammianus in the second half of the twentieth century, however, even in Germany, has ignored or discounted the views of Norden, Wilamowitz, and Leo, choosing to emphasize the Roman side of Ammianus to the detriment of the Greek, and hence preventing a proper understanding of the historian. Articles with programmatic titles such as "Ammianus Marcellinus as a Roman Historian" and "Ammianus Marcellinus as a Late Antique Roman Historian" have proclaimed the historian to be fundamentally Roman rather than Greek;[16] the concluding chapter of John Matthews' large study (which seems nowhere to refer to Norden) is entitled "The Roman and the Greek," not "The Greek and the Roman";[17] and it has subsequently been argued that, although Ammianus may have been educated primarily in Greek as a boy, his knowledge of Greek literature was superficial and

---

[10] G. Hassenstein, *De syntaxi Ammiani Marcellini* (Diss. Leipzig, pub. Königsberg, 1877), 3, 8−9, 30−31, 37−38.

[11] H. Ehrismann, *De temporum et modorum usu Ammianeo* (Diss. Straßburg, 1886), 6.

[12] A. Reiter, *De Ammiani Marcellini usu orationis obliquae* (Prog. Amberg, 1887), 68−69.

[13] Hassenstein, *De syntaxi* (1877), 32.

[14] G. Reinhardt, *De praepositionum usu apud Ammianum* (Diss. Halle, pub. Cöthen, 1888), 8−45.

[15] F. Liesenberg, *Die Sprache des Ammianus Marcellinus* (Prog. Blankenburg, 1888−1890), 3.1, 2.15, 1.13, 3.11−15.

[16] Respectively, H. Tränkle, *Antike und Abendland* 11 (1962), 21−33; K. Bringmann, *Antike und Abendland* 19 (1973), 44−60.

[17] Matthews, *Ammianus* (1989), 452−72. His earlier essay on Ammianus' historical evolution held a better balance between the Greek and the Roman sides of Ammianus, concluding that Greek was "the dominant literary influence on his manner of writing" (*History and Historians* [1983], 30−41, esp. 39).

derivative, whereas he had acquired a "deep familiarity with the Latin literary tradition."[18]

Yet the best Latin philologists have never doubted that Ammianus sometimes lapses into the Graecisms characteristic of one whose first language was Greek,[19] and evidence has continued to accumulate to confirm Norden's view that he thinks in Greek. In 1962 a brief article by Wolfang Seyfarth heavily reinforced the point: discussing the phrase *exacerbantia tela* in Ammianus' story of the third-century Persian capture of Antioch (25.3.2), which earlier editors had emended in various ways, he defended the transmitted reading as "ein echter Gräzismus" and observed that Graecisms were a characteristic feature of Ammianus' Latinity.[20] The parallel of Claudian reinforces the point: as Alan Cameron trenchantly observed, neither Claudian nor Ammianus can be understood except "in terms of a Greek, not a Latin, literary tradition."[21]

The interpreter of Ammianus needs cultural sensitivity as well as the old-fashioned scholarly virtues. It is significant that the German scholar Joachim Classen stated the correct balance between "Greek and Roman in Ammianus Marcellinus' *History*" in an article composed in English while he was teaching in Nigeria[22]—and that the present writer lives in an officially bilingual country whose prime minister at the time of writing is a Francophone with an imperfect command of English. Moreover, the two studies that have decisively defined the Greekness of Ammianus were produced by scholars working in a social and intellectual milieu that made them alert to cultural diversity.

Hermann Schickinger was a teacher at the state gymnasium in the small Moravian town of Nikolsburg, on the main road from Vienna to Brünn (Brno): the town is now called Mikulov and lies just north of the Czech-Austrian border. In the late nineteenth century, its population was one quarter Jewish, an unusually high proportion for the region.[23] In the *Programm* for the acad-

---

[18] C. W. Fornara, *Historia* 41 (1992), 420–38.

[19] E. Löfstedt, *Vermischte Studien zur lateinischen Sprachkunde und Syntax* (Lund, 1936), 200, 208; Blomgren, *Quaestiones* (1937), 57, n. 1.

[20] W. Seyfarth, *Klio* 40 (1962), 63–64.

[21] Alan Cameron, *Renaissances before the Renaissance*, ed. W. Treadgold (Stanford, 1984), 46–47.

[22] C. J. Classen, *Museum Africum* 1 (1972), 39–48.

[23] V. de St. Martin, *Dictionnaire de géographie universelle* 4 (Paris, 1890), 150: "5650 habitants, 7640 avec la communauté israélite" (from the census of 1881). Jews thus comprised about 26 percent of the population of Nikolsburg (1,990 out of 7,640), even though overall they constituted only about 2 percent of the total population of Moravia and less than 5 percent of the total population of Austria-Hungary: see the figures and estimates set out in A. Nossig (ed.), *Jüdische Statistik* (Berlin, 1903), 432–52; J. Thon, *Die Juden in Oesterreich* (Berlin-Halensee, 1908), 5–9. Nineteenth-century gazetteers note the salient characteristics of Nikolsburg as its castle, its syn-

emic year 1896–1897 Schickinger published a study of "The Graecisms in Ammianus Marcellinus" in which he set out the grammatical, syntactical, and lexical usages in the historian that are Greek.[24] Although not all of the Graecisms which he detected are real proofs that Ammianus' mother tongue was Greek,[25] Schickinger had a keen eye. He noted several apparent transpositions of Greek words or expressions into Latin, such as the phrase "mother of cities" (*mater urbium*) for the metropolis of a province (21.10.2; 26.1.3) and the use of the Latin verb *docere* as if it were its Greek equivalent (16.8.10: tonstrices docuit filias = "taught his daughters to be barbers").[26] Moreover, he observed that Ammianus does not share the normal fondness of Latin historians for the historical infinitive: in Gardthausen's edition, he found a single solitary example in six hundred pages,[27] which had rightly been emended away even before he wrote (29.3.7: mandarat magistris equitum auditoribus princeps,/ ut etc.).[28] Ammianus, let it be added, does not avoid the historical infinitive because it had fallen into desuetude: it probably still survived in popular speech;[29] Claudian uses it more than forty times;[30] and Jerome employs it even in letters and lives of saints.[31] Most striking of all, the historical infinitive is common in writers contemporary with Ammianus who, like him, were strongly influenced by Sallust: the Christians "Hegesippus" and Sulpicius Severus no less than the pagans Aurelius Victor and the author of the *Epitome de Caesaribus*.[32]

---

agogues, and the high proportion of Jews: *Nuovo dizionario geografico universale* 4.1 (Venice, 1831), 201; W. G. Blackie, *Imperial Gazetteer* 2 (Edinburgh/London, 1855), 489–90; J. C. Smith, *Harper's Statistical Gazetteer of the World* (New York, 1855), 1260.

[24] H. Schickinger, *Programm des Staats-Gymnasiums in Nikolsburg* 24 (1896–97), 13–30. Schickinger's work is unfortunately absent from the bibliographies in R. Moes, *Les Hellénismes de l'époque théodosienne. Recherches sur le vocabulaire d'origine grecque chez Ammien, Claudien et l'Histoire Auguste* (Strasbourg, 1980), viii–xi; Matthews, *Ammianus* (1989), 554–60 ("Works directly relevant to Ammianus").

[25] Seyfarth, *Klio* 40 (1962), 63, n. 5. For example, Schickinger, *Programm Nikolsburg* 24 (1896–1897), 30, himself noted that the adjective *semestris* in the sense "lasting half a month" rather than "of six months' duration" already occurs in Apuleius, *Met.* 11.4.

[26] Schickinger, *Programm Nikolsburg* 24 (1896–1897), 29.

[27] Schickinger, *Programm Nikolsburg* 24 (1896–1897), 27.

[28] In favor of the pluperfect *mandarat* in place of the infinitive *mandare*, see O. Günther, *Quaestiones Ammianeae criticae* (Diss. Göttingen, 1888), 55–56, cf. H. Kallenberg, *Quaestiones grammaticae Ammianeae* (Diss. Halle, 1868), 42. In 16.11.9 and 31.9.3 *redire* and *transire* had long before been emended to *rediere* and *transiere*, respectively: on other passages where V offers a historic infinitive, see J. den Boeft, *Cognitio Gestorum* (1992), 17.

[29] J. B. Hofmann, *Die lateinische Umgangssprache*[3] (Heidelberg, 1951), 50–51.

[30] J. J. Schlicher, *CP* 10 (1915), 65–66, 73.

[31] E.g., *Ep.* 60.10.7–8 (Nepotianus' activities as a priest); *Vita Hilarionis* 10.4, 12.4, 29.8.

[32] Schlicher, *CP* 10 (1915), 71, 74.

Jan den Boeft, a Dutch scholar writing in English, has brought the insights of modern linguistic theory to bear with telling effect, for the phenomenon of bilingualism in the modern world has been much studied—indeed, in many countries it is a pressing political problem. Den Boeft shows how, although Ammianus is functionally bilingual in Greek and Latin, Greek is dominant in various ways, the most obvious (and often noted) being his use of the phrase "as we call it in Greek" (e.g., 17.7.11: quas Graece syringas appellamus; 23.6.20: transire enim diabainein dicimus Graeci).[33] Greek was Ammianus' first language. There is no way to discover at what age he learned Latin. But, although he may have been functionally bilingual, Ammianus' Latin remains awkward and always reflects the Greek substratum of his thought.

Computer analysis and modern statistical techniques have shown how greatly the clausulae employed by Ammianus differ from those of all other ancient Latin authors. In 1987 Steven Oberhelman examined the provenance of Ammianus' style by comparing the clausulae in the Res Gestae with those in more than a hundred Latin prose texts written between circa 200 and circa 450, and he concluded that Ammianus stands apart from all the other Latin writers of the period in that his clausulae do not display any of the "metrical tendencies" detectable to some extent in all of them.[34] Oberhelman identified the basis of Ammianus' prose rhythm as "the Greek accentual system that he knew from his rhetorical training": his practice was to adhere to the Greek cursus, but with a preference for accentual clausulae that replicate familiar Latin metrical clausulae, since he needed to adapt the Greek system to take account of the heavier, more spondaic nature of the Latin language, where the accent can never fall on the final syllable of any disyllabic or longer word and where long syllables and hence paroxytone accentuation preponderate.[35]

Ammianus was a Greek by language, education, and culture long before he ever entertained the idea of writing history in Latin. It is his Greek cast of mind that explains one of the most unusual and distinctive features of the Res Gestae: the large number, the variety and expansiveness, and the structural

[33] J. den Boeft, Cognitio Gestorum (1992), 9–18. On 22.9.7 (apo tou pesein quod cadere nos dicimus), see ibid. 12: it is not an exception, as is often claimed (e.g., Ensslin, Ammianus [1923], 30; Matthews, Ammianus [1989], 107), but should be translated, in conformity with other passages, "from pesein, which is our word for cadere."

[34] S. M. Oberhelman, QUCC, N.S. 27.3 (1987), 79–87. This article belongs to a series on prose rhythm in Latin prose from the second century to the sixth: S. M. Oberhelman and R. G. Hall, CP 79 (1984), 114–30; 80 (1985), 214–27; CQ, N.S. 35 (1985), 201–14; 36 (1986), 208–24; S. M. Oberhelman, CP 83 (1988), 136–49; CQ, N.S. 38 (1988), 228–42.

[35] On Ammianus' clausulae, see further Appendix 6.

prominence of formal excursus, which it is misleading (though conventional and perhaps forgivable) to call digressions.[36] The excursus in a sense provide the web for the literary and intellectual fabric of the work.

This central fact about the *Res Gestae* deserves especial emphasis because the recent Penguin translation of Ammianus omits almost all the excursus. Andrew Wallace-Hadrill confesses in his preface to Walter Hamilton's translation that the omission "leaves a slightly unbalanced impression of Ammianus' writing" and acknowledges that "the digression was an integral feature of Ammianus' approach to historical writing"; nevertheless, he justifies the omission on the grounds that the excursus are "frankly tedious to a modern reader."[37] But it misrepresents an author, no less than a composer of music, to improve his work by leaving out passages that offend the taste of a later age.[38]

Ammianus explicitly marks thirty-one passages as formal excursus (Appendix 5). They deserve to be considered as a group to the exclusion of other passages that he does not so mark explicitly, however interesting the latter may be. Ammianus writes about the mating of palm trees (24.3.12–13) and explains how midges limit the lion population in Mesopotamia: they attack the lions' eyes and drive them mad from the irritation so that they either plunge into the river and drown or else blind themselves by constant scratching (18.7.5). But since Ammianus does not mark these passages as formal excursus with the traditional formulae of transition, they should be excluded from consideration of the function of the excursus in the *Res Gestae* as a whole.

Serious Greek and Latin historians had always included digressions, most commonly geographical, but also cultural and ethnographical.[39] But Ammianus uses them on a scale unparalleled since Herodotus.[40] On the other hand, he uses another standard device for varying or enlivening a narrative very sparingly. Whereas Tacitus had used speeches frequently to analyze motives or situations, and had even included private exchanges between an emperor and his minister,[41] Ammianus includes few long speeches, all delivered on ceremonial occasions.[42] The emperor Constantius delivers formal speeches to

---

[36] E.g., A. Emmett, *History and Historians* (1983), 42–53.

[37] A. Wallace-Hadrill, *Ammianus Marcellinus* (Harmondsworth, 1986), 25.

[38] For example, the epilogue of Mozart's *Don Giovanni,* which is now rightly included in performance.

[39] P. Pédech, *La Méthode historique de Polybe* (Paris, 1964), 515–97.

[40] M. Caltabiano, *Metodologie della ricerca sulla tarda antichità,* ed. A. Garzya (Naples, 1989), 289–96.

[41] For example, Tiberius and Sejanus (*Ann.* 4.39–40) and Nero and Seneca (*Ann.* 14.53–56), where Tacitus maliciously makes the imperial pupil more philosophical than his tutor.

[42] G. B. Pighi, *I discorsi nelle Storie d'Ammiano Marcellino* (Milan, 1936), 29–30. He also lists twelve briefer utterances as "discorsi storiografici minori" (30–31).

his army when he grants peace to the Alamanni and Sarmatae Limigantes (14.10.11−16, 17.13.26−33), when he proclaims Julian Caesar (15.8.5−8, 10, 12−14), and when he is about to march against Julian in 361 (21.13.10−15). Julian addresses his army when he urges delay before the Battle of Strasbourg in 357 (16.12.9−12), when he is proclaimed Augustus in 360 (20.5.3−7), when he is about to invade Illyricum in 361 (21.5.2−8), when he is about to enter Persian territory in 363 (23.5.16−23) and at Pirisabora (24.3.3−7). And, as he lies mortally wounded, Julian delivers a philosophical discourse to his friends (25.3.15−20). Valentinian addresses the army both when he is proclaimed Augustus (26.2.6−10) and when he confers the imperial purple on his son Gratian (27.6.6−9, 12−13). Ammianus also includes three letters quoted at length. Shapur writes to Constantius in 358 (17.5.3−8) and Constantius replies (17.5.10−15), and Julian writes to Constantius after his proclamation as Augustus (20.8.5−17).

Ammianus also departs from conventional practice by entirely avoiding the familiar genre of paired speeches in which opposing generals exhort their troops and answer each other when about to enter the fray of battle. Tacitus provides the most spectacularly unreal example of the genre when he makes Agricola and Calgacus debate the merits of Roman imperialism: in what is virtually a formal *controversia*, the highland chieftain denounces Rome with a school rhetoric indistinguishable from that of the Roman general, who speaks as if he knows exactly what has just been said on the opposing Scottish mountainside.[43] Paired speeches before battle constituted a minor literary genre that was not only fictitious, but also recognized as such by the ancients.[44] As a soldier, Ammianus knew that such speeches did not occur in real life, where there was only the possibility of a few exhortatory remarks.

Ammianus' avoidance of pre-battle speeches and the overall sparsity of speeches in the *Res Gestae* contrast strikingly with the abundance of excursus. The two phenomena must surely be connected. Ammianus has made a conscious choice. Why? The conventional answer to this question is to appeal to the model of Herodotus. Like Herodotus, it is assumed, Ammianus recited his work in order to entertain: since an educated audience of the late fourth century expected excursus and judged them "as a sort of virtuoso cadenza," Ammianus was giving his hearers what they wanted—and doing so allowed him both to slow down the tempo of his narrative to place dramatic emphasis on

---

[43] Tacitus, *Agr.* 30−34, cf. R. M. Ogilvie and I. A. Richmond, *Cornelii Taciti de Vita Agricolae* (Oxford, 1967), 253−54, 265.

[44] M. H. Hansen, *Historia* 42 (1993), 161−80. This central point is not contested by C. T. H. R. Ehrhardt, *Historia* 44 (1995), 120−21.

an episode that followed an excursus and to put Roman history "in perspective" by illustrating the diversity of the empire and of the barbarians that beset it.[45] This answer may be correct in part, but it is founded on a mistaken assumption and it is incomplete. The only evidence that Ammianus recited his history is the letter of Libanius to Marcellinus in 392: if Libanius wrote that letter to another Marcellinus (Chapter VI), then there is no evidence that any part of the *Res Gestae* was recited to please an audience: on the contrary, Ammianus sets himself in the tradition of Thucydides and Polybius in implicit opposition to that of Herodotus. Comparison with Herodotus explains neither why Ammianus includes scientific excursus nor why he so often gives a learned exposition of explanatory theories for natural phenomena.[46] When he expatiates on earthquakes, eclipses, the rainbow or the plague, he is concerned to classify the phenomena and to report what seem to him the plausible explanations set out by traditional Greek wisdom. Earthquakes, he informs his readers, occur in several ways:

> They are either (1) *brasmatiae* which, arousing the earth from the bottom like a tide, propel enormous masses upwards—as in Asia Delos arose from the sea, and Thera, Anaphe, Rhodes, which used to be called Ophiusa and Pelagia in former centuries, and was once drenched in a golden shower; and Eleusis in Boeotia and Vulcanus in the Tyrrhenian Sea and several more islands; or (2) *climatiae* which rush sideways and obliquely flatten cities, buildings and mountains; or (3) *chasmatiae* which, suddenly opening up abysses with their greater motion, swallow parts of the earth, as in the Atlantic an island larger than the whole of Europe, in the Crisaean Gulf Helice and Bura, and in the Ciminian part of Italy the town of Saccumum were dragged into the gaping mouth of Erebus and are hidden in eternal darkness. Among these three types of earthquakes, *mycematiae* are heard with a threatening roar, when the elements burst their bonds and leap up of their own accord or slip back as the earth subsides. For then, of necessity, the crashing and rumbling of the earth must resound like the bellowing of bulls. (17.7.13/14)

Similarly, plagues are of three types:

> Scientists and eminent physicians tell us that infectious diseases are brought on by excess of cold or heat, or of moisture or dryness. That is why people who live in damp or marshy places suffer from coughs and ophthalmia and the like, whereas the inhabitants of hot countries are dehydrated by burning fever. . . . Others as-

[45] Wallace-Hadrill, *Ammianus* (1986), 25, cf. Matthews, *Ammianus* (1989), 462.
[46] On the literary function of the scientific excursus, see D. den Hengst, *Cognitio Gestorum* (1992), 39–46.

sert that the air, like water, can be infected by the stench of dead bodies or the like and gravely affect men's health, or at any rate that minor illnesses are caused by a sudden change of air. There are also some who say that when the atmosphere is thickened by unusually dense exhalations from the earth it blocks the body's natural vents and sometimes causes death. . . . The first type of pestilence, which causes the inhabitants of excessively dry regions to be visited by frequent fevers, is called endemic. The second, which occurs periodically and affects the sight and causes dangerous humors in the body, is epidemic. The third is plague, which also lasts only for a time, but brings death with lightning speed. (19.4.2–7)

The genre of discourse in passages such as these is not historical. Nor is it truly scientific, the product of deep enquiry or research. It is rather doxographical.[47] But the aggregation of doxographies on a multitude of varied subjects adds up to something approaching an encyclopedia.

Theodor Mommsen pointed out this unifying feature of Ammianus' excursus at the end of a long and famous paper on the historian's geographical knowledge.[48] Paradoxically, however, although Mommsen's paper is well known and his conclusions about Ammianus' geographical sources have often been quoted with approval,[49] his general remarks on the function of the excursus have had little resonance in subsequent scholarship.[50] His conclusions, therefore, deserve to be restated. Behind the separate geographical excursus divided and worked up schematically, Mommsen detected conscious intention and a deliberate plan, whereby the historian intended to weave into his history a description of the whole inhabited world. Mommsen waxed eloquent on Ammianus' deficiencies—awful carelessness, empty words concealing of lack of knowledge, a parade of erudition ineffectually veiling profound ignorance, an idle striving to know all. But he partly excused the dark shadows of Ammianus' inadequacy as the inevitable consequence of the fact that he belonged to an unhappy generation of squatters in the ruined world of a great past.[51] Mommsen's harsh and unsympathetic assessment of both Ammianus and his intellectual environment owes more to his own lifelong anticlericalism than to a correct appreciation of the historian's achievement. Moreover, he seriously underestimated Ammianus' learning. Ammianus did not crib his scientific material from encyclopedias. Rather, he gave his real, if limited,

---

[47] R. von Scala, *Festgabe zu Ehren Max Büdinger's von seinen Freunden und Schülern* (Innsbruck, 1898), 117–50.

[48] T. Mommsen, *Ges. Schr.* 7 (Berlin, 1909), 423–24.

[49] E.g., Syme, *Ammianus* (1968), 105.

[50] Observe, however, Ensslin, *Ammianus* (1923), 16; A. Solari, *Rendiconti Lincei*[8] 4 (1949), 21.

[51] Mommsen, *Ges. Schr.* 7 (1909), 423: "der Fluch jener unseligen, auch auf dem geistigen Gebiet in der Trümmerwelt einer grösseren Vergangenheit kümmerlich hausenden Generationen."

scientific, ethnographic, and philosophical knowledge the form of entries in an encyclopedia. He informed his readers about the crocodile and the hippopotamus, about comets and atoms, and even about utterly unfamiliar peoples in southern Russia—the Byzares, Sapires, Tibareni, Mossynoeci, Macrones, and Philyres (22.8.31: populi nulla nobis adsuetudine cogniti). That is a parade of knowledge for its own sake, designed more to impress than to instruct, but it is knowledge that Ammianus acquired as a result of his study of Greek ethnographical, scientific, technical, philosophical, and historical writers.

It has been conventional to belittle Ammianus' erudition. A century ago, an attempt was made to derive most of the material in most of Ammianus' excursus from a single doxographical handbook, whose author was none other than Posidonius.[52] More recently, it is argued that when Ammianus names Ptolemy as an authority on astronomy (20.3.4), he has "in all likelihood" not consulted Ptolemy directly, and that, although he may have consulted "popular Greek astronomical treatises" such as those by Cleomedes, Theon of Smyrna, and Geminus, similarities to Cicero's *De Re Publica* and Calcidius' commentary on Plato's *Timaeus* prove that his working sources were in fact Latin.[53] Hence a systematic enquiry concludes that, out of the one hundred and six passages where Ammianus names or cites a Greek writer, no more than twenty show direct knowledge of the author named or cited.[54] But it is surely improbable a priori that one who thought in Greek preferred Latin over Greek sources. Let one striking example where Ammianus' direct acquaintance with a text to which he explicitly refers has been denied be taken as a test case for his learning.

Ammianus names the philosopher Plotinus twice, both times in excursus. One mention is a mere gloss: the Alexandrian philosopher Ammonius Saccas is identified as the teacher of Plotinus (22.16.5). The other reference is more substantial:

> It is made clear by the immortal poems of Homer that it was not the gods in heaven who conversed with heroes or stood by and helped them as they fought, but the familiar spirits which belonged to them. By their signal assistance, it is said, Pythagoras, Socrates, Numa Pompilius, the elder Scipio, Marius (in the opinion of some) and Octavian, who was the first to be awarded the title of Au-

[52] R. von Scala, *Festgabe zu Ehren Max Büdinger's* (1898), 122: "eine einheitliche und zwar doxographische Weisheitsquelle"; 150: "kann diese doxographische Quelle schwerlich eine andere als Poseidonios gewesen."

[53] D. den Hengst, *Mnemosyne*[4] 39 (1986), 137.

[54] I. Lana, *Politica, cultura e religione nell'Impero romano (secoli IV–VI) tra Oriente e Occidente*, ed. F. Conca, I. Gualandri and G. Lozza (Naples, 1993), 23–40.

gustus, attained fame, as also Hermes Trismegistus, Apollonius of Tyana and Plotinus, who was bold enough to write on this esoteric subject and to demonstrate by profound reasoning from what beginnings these spirits are joined to the souls of mortals and, as it were, taking them in their bosoms protect them as long as it is allowed, and instruct them in higher truths, if they feel that they are pure and have kept themselves spotless and free from any stain of sin by associating with the body in an immaculate fashion. (21.14.5)

Ammianus here summarizes Plotinus' treatise "On Our Allotted Guardian Spirit"[55]—and the natural assumption should be that he has read the text of the treatise.[56] It may be true, as the Dutch commentators state, that this brief paraphrase is "totally inadequate," but that is not a sufficient reason for concluding that Ammianus bases it not on direct knowledge of Plotinus, but on the account that Porphyry offers in his *Life of Plotinus* of how Plotinus came to write it.[57] The most superficial acquaintance with modern scholarship ought to show how fallacious the inference from misrepresentation to ignorance can be. Moreover, all that Porphyry's *Life* says about the content of the treatise is that Plotinus "sets out to explain the differences between spirit-companions."[58] Hence the truth is probably much more complicated than has been supposed. Ammianus appears to make a perceptible effort to report Plotinus' often obscure train of thought,[59] yet the phrase *tamquam gremiis suis susceptas tuentur* seems to reflect the title of the treatise, which Porphyry, not Plotinus, gave it.[60] Furthermore, the Dutch commentators have observed a notable fact about the language that Ammianus employs in this summary of Plotinus. He uses the noun *colluvio* and the adjective *immaculatus* in a metaphorical sense. Both usages are attested elsewhere only in Christian writers: hence Ammianus transmits this brief précis of a treatise of Plotinus to his readers through a Christian filter, presumably in his own mind.

The evaluation of this passage involves a fundamental fact about Ammianus. The standard assumption of late has been that he acquired all his knowledge of Neoplatonism in Rome in the 380s.[61] But why may Ammianus not have

---

[55] Plotinus, *Ennead* 3.4.

[56] S. Eitrem, *Symb. Osl.* 22 (1942), 63.

[57] As suggested by P. Henry, *Plotin et l'Occident* (Louvain, 1934), 196–99. Henry's cautious proposal ("il se peut donc" etc.) has been elevated to a certainty by later writers.

[58] Porphyry, *Vita Plotini* 10.33–35.

[59] For a modern synopsis of this difficult treatise, see A. H. Armstrong, *Plotinus* 3 (Cambridge, Mass., 1967), 141.

[60] Porphyry, *Vita Plotini* 10.31, 25.3, cf. Henry, *Plotin* (1934), 198; P. Henry and H.-R. Schwyzer, *Plotini Opera* (Paris/Brussels, 1951), 310.

[61] Besides the Dutch commentators, note esp. J. Szidat, *Mus. Helv.* 39 (1982), 132–45; Matthews, *Ammianus* (1989), 429–30.

taken an interest in philosophy in his youth? Even if the collected edition of the *Enneads* that Porphyry completed in 300 remained unknown in the East until the last third of the fourth century, individual treatises by Plotinus certainly circulated much earlier.[62] Ammianus could have come across the treatise that he summarizes in Phoenicia or elsewhere in the Syrian region in the 340s or 350s, and he could have studied it with a pupil of Porphyry. In 360, it should be recalled, Libanius referred to an Ammianus in military service who was a philosopher underneath his uniform: he could be the future historian.[63]

[62] J. M. Rist, *Basil of Caesarea: Christian, Humanist, Ascetic*, ed. P. J. Fedwick (Toronto, 1981), 137–220.
[63] Libanius, *Ep.* 233.4.

[VIII]

CHRISTIAN LANGUAGE AND
ANTI-CHRISTIAN POLEMIC

Ammianus' eastern origin and his Greek cast of mind are very relevant to as-
sessing his religious beliefs and his treatment of Christianity. When he wrote
Graecus, what he heard inside his own mind was the Greek word *Hellen*,
which has a very different semantic range from its Latin equivalent.[1] For, although *Hellen* could indicate merely that someone was culturally Greek,[2] by
the late fourth century it often had the specific meaning of "pagan," especially
when used by anyone at all hostile to Christianity.[3] This sense of the word is
first clearly documented in Porphyry's polemic *Against the Christians*: probably writing circa 300, he complained that Origen, though "a Greek educated
in Greek learning," had deviated into "barbarian recklessness" by becoming
a Christian,[4] and represented the Christians as apostates from both Hellenism
and Judaism.[5] Eusebius of Caesarea accepted the dichotomy between Hellenism and true religion, but claimed that the traditional religions of the Roman Empire were a declension from the original pure religion of the Hebrew
patriarchs, which the coming of Christ had renewed in the Christian church.[6]

[1] G. W. Bowersock, *Hellenism in Late Antiquity* (Ann Arbor, 1990), 9–13.

[2] Alan Cameron, *Ancient World* 24 (1993), 25–29.

[3] Note Eunapius' usage in his *Lives of Philosophers and Sophists*: once certainly to designate inhabitants of Greece (6.6.2 [466]) and once possibly (6.4.7 [465]), but five times clearly meaning
non-Christian (6.5.3 [465]; 7.3.12 [477]; 10. 6. 3 [490], 6.6 [491], 8.2 [493]).

[4] Eusebius, *HE* 6.19.7 = Porphyry, *Against the Christians*, frag. 39 Harnack. On the date and
context of the work, which are controverted, see *BICS* 38 (1994), 53–65.

[5] Eusebius, *Praep. Ev.* 1.2.1–4 = Porphyry, *Against the Christians*, frag. 1 Harnack, cf. *BICS*
38 (1994), 65.

[6] Eusebius, *HE* 1.2.2–4.1; *Praep. Evan.* 7.8–8.14; *Dem. Evan.* 1.6.29–76, 7.1.80–154,
8.3.6–15; J. Sirinelli, *Les Vues historiques d'Eusèbe de Césarée durant la période prénicéenne* (Dakar,
1961); T. D. Barnes, *Constantine* (1981), 126–27, 184–85.

The emperor Julian simply reversed Eusebius' values while retaining his basic antithesis and asserted a fundamental incompatibility between Greek culture and Christianity, between Hellenism and barbarism.[7] Hence, when Ammianus described himself as *miles quondam et Graecus*, he was declaring his religious allegiance in unambiguous terms.[8]

Since Ammianus' religious beliefs are central to interpreting his history, they have by no means been neglected by modern students of the historian. Initially at least, it may seem surprising that scholars from the seventeenth century onward have attributed to Ammianus every shade of opinion within the religious spectrum—at the one extreme a Christian, a monotheist sympathetic toward Christianity, a man who genuinely respected Christianity,[9] at the other a committed and militant pagan striving to rescue something of Rome's traditional religions from the discredit attendant on Julian's catastrophic failure.[10] The center of the spectrum has of course appealed most to scholars who wish to appear to be judicious: hence Ammianus has most often been presented as a man of genuine, but broad-minded piety who accepted the doctrines of no specific religion, an adherent of a "neutral monotheism" who was neither a Christian nor a committed believer in the old gods.[11] On this majority view, Ammianus was hostile to fanaticism and excess of any sort: as a moderate and tolerant pagan, he believed strongly in religious toleration and respected Christianity, even if he sometimes criticized the conduct of individual Christians and Christian groups.[12]

[7] See the numerous passages registered in their index by J. Bidez and F. Cumont, *Imp. Caesaris Flavii Iuliani Imperatoris Epistulae Leges Poematia Fragmenta varia* (Paris/London, 1922), 302.

[8] A. Stoian, *Latomus* 25 (1967), 73–81; J. Heyen, *Latomus* 26 (1968), 191–96.

[9] For a survey of modern opinions, see Rike, *Apex Omnium* (1987), 1–5. The view of the seventeenth-century scholars Pithou and Chifflet that Ammianus was a Christian was decisively refuted by Gronovius in the introduction to his edition (Leiden, 1693), reproduced in the variorum edition of Wagner and Erfurdt (Leipzig, 1808), xlii; sympathy is detected by Demandt, *Zeitkritik* (1965), 82; a "positive evaluation of monastic asceticism" by V. Neri, *Ammiano e il cristianesimo. Religione e politica nelle "Res gestae" di Ammiano Marcellino* (Bologna, 1985), 70.

[10] Rike, *Apex Omnium* (1987), 8, 69–133. This book is criticized harshly by Matthews, who accuses Rike of "insecure technique in handling certain aspects of the text" (*Ammianus* [1989], 545, n. 10).

[11] As argued by E. Witte, *Ammianus Marcellinus quid iudicaverit de rebus divinis* (Diss. Jena, 1891), 58–59.

[12] So, for example, Syme, *Ammianus* (1968), 137–38; J. F. Matthews, *Ancient Writers*, 2 (New York, 1982), 1118; E. D. Hunt, *CQ*, N.S. 35 (1985), 186–200, strongly commended by Matthews, *Ammianus* (1989), 546, n. 22. For criticism of this view, *Reading the Past* (1990), 75–82; *CP* 88 (1993), 67–69. Hunt has attempted to reassert it in *Studia Patristica* 24 (1993), 108–13, where he admits "satirical exaggeration" in the comparison of Christians to wild beasts (22.5.2). In his book, John Matthews is deeply inconsistent: sometimes he adopts a position close to that argued here, as when he speaks of "a polemic of distortion" or of "the dismantling of apparently authentic connections" in order to minimize the role of Christians and draws attention to Ammianus' use of standard polemical techniques (*Ammianus* [1989], 435, 441, 451); yet he de-

Why has there been such a wide spectrum of views? Why have different scholars discovered such a variety of divergent *Weltanschauungen* in the same text? The reason is not that scholars have simply imported their own preconceptions into their interpretation. It is the contrary one that virtually all modern views have some foundation in Ammianus' text. Divergence arises because a simple and straightforward answer is sought, when there is a deep and irremovable inconsistency in what the historian says about Christianity.

At the conscious level, Ammianus sets out to marginalize Christianity by deliberately understating the role that Christians and Christianity played in the political history of the fourth century. The most widely acknowledged omission was noted by Norman Baynes in 1910.[13] It concerns Armenia. Ammianus offers a moderately detailed account of Roman dealings with Armenia in the reign of Valens (27.12, 29.1.1–4, 30.1–2). The Armenian historian Pʿawstos Buzand presents the conflict between King Pap and the *katholikos* Nerses as the central fact of the politics of the kingdom in the 370s: the king, who was hostile to Rome, had the pro-Roman *katholikos* murdered.[14] Ammianus never mentions Nerses or his opposition to the king, despite its relevance to the events that he describes. There is a similar, but far more serious, omission of ecclesiastical politics in the Roman Empire. Book XV introduces Athanasius as if Ammianus had never mentioned him before (15.7.7–10). Yet Athanasius' career as bishop of Alexandria from 328 to 373 (with significant interruptions and periods of exile) shows that ecclesiastical affairs were at the center of imperial politics in the reign of Constantius.[15] In 350, for example, Constantius' praetorian prefect was on his way to Egypt to arrest Athanasius when news came of the death of Constans: fearful that Egypt might transfer its allegiance to the usurper Magnentius, the emperor reversed his policy and insincerely assured the bishop of Alexandria of his undying friendship and support.[16] Ammianus also leaves out completely the ecclesiastical affairs that occupied a large amount of Constantius' time during the years for which his

---

tects genuine sympathy for captured Christian virgins and for martyrs as victims of persecution and expressly denies that Ammianus was "a polemical writer in the manner, say, of Eunapius of Sardis" (436, 445).

[13] N. H. Baynes, *EHR* 25 (1910), 625–43, reprinted in *Byzantine Studies and Other Essays* (London, 1955), 186–208. For subsequent discussion, see N. G. Garsoïan, *REArm*, N.S. 4 (1967), 297–320; Blockley, *Ammianus* (1975), 62–72; Elliott, *Ammianus* (1983), 180–82.

[14] For the relevant passages (5.1, 21–24, 30–31), see N. G. Garsoïan, *The Epic Histories attributed to Pʿawstos Buzand (Buzandaran Patmutʿiwnk)* (Cambridge, Mass., 1989), 185–87, 202–5, 210–13 (translation); 306–67, 317–19, 323–24 (commentary); 395–96 (on Nerses); 397–98 (Pap). Pʿawstos 5.1 records the installation of Pap circa 370 by Terentius and Addaeus: Ammianus names only Terentius (27.12.10).

[15] *Athanasius* (1993), 165–73.

[16] Athanasius, *Hist. Ar.* 51.4; *Apol. ad Const.* 23, cf. *Athanasius* (1993), 104–5.

account is extant. Between the summer of 353 and the spring of 360, the emperor Constantius was close at hand to supervise the conduct of several important gatherings of bishops: the Council of Arles in the winter of 353−354, the Council of Milan in the summer of 355, the small gathering of bishops that produced the so-called "dated creed" in his presence at Sirmium on 22 May 359, and the Council of Constantinople in January 360. Moreover, during the summer and autumn of 359, the emperor was deeply involved in convening, then in coercing the Councils of Ariminum and Seleucia, and finally in the complicated negotiations that produced the homoean creed on the last day of December.[17]

None of these councils earns the merest mention in Ammianus' narrative of these years. Nor does the ecclesiastical background to Julian's rebellion against Constantius. Julian was able to establish his independence of Constantius largely because western Christians rallied to his support as the only way to avoid the imposition in the West of the official homoean creed which the Council of Constantinople proclaimed in January 360.[18]

In addition, like other historians of Late Antiquity, Ammianus adopts an external stance when he writes about Christianity and the Christian church. This has normally been regarded as a mere literary convention that reveals nothing about Ammianus' attitude toward Christianity: a similar stance, using very similar language, can be seen in historians down to the sixth century, including writers such as Procopius and Agathias, who were undoubtedly Christians.[19] The argument is valid in general, but it has been given a misleading application. In contrast to Ammianus, Procopius makes his Christianity clear in several passages.[20] But when Ammianus twice glosses the word *synodus* with the phrase *ut appellant* (15.7.7; 21.16.18), he implies that one of the commonest forms of political assembly in the fourth century is an exotic rarity.

At a deeper level, however, the *Res Gestae* exhibit a feature that contradicts Ammianus' external stance toward Christianity. Any satisfactory analysis of his religious attitudes must recognize and explain the fact that Ammianus often uses Christian language and Christian modes of thought and expression without any apparent sign of self-consciousness. This important linguistic phenomenon was detected several decades ago by G. B. Pighi,[21] and is now docu-

---

[17] For these events, see, briefly, *Athanasius* (1993), 109−20, 136−51.

[18] *Athanasius* (1993), 149−51, 153−54.

[19] Alan and Averil Cameron, *CQ*, N.S. 14 (1964), 312−28.

[20] Averil Cameron, *Historia* 15 (1966), 466−82; *Procopius and the Sixth Century* (Berkeley, 1985), 33−46, 113−33.

[21] G. B. Pighi, *Studi dedicati alla memoria di Paolo Ubaldi* (Milan, 1937), 41−72; *RAC* 1 (1950), 386−94.

mented on a massive scale by the Dutch commentators (who have so far reached Book XXII). Ammianus thus uses Christian language while implicitly disparaging the importance of Christianity. What might be the explanation of this apparent contradiction? The analogy of Julian, whose writings exhibit a similar linguistic phenomenon,[22] suggests that Ammianus, too, was an apostate Christian.

Ammianus betrays the artificiality of his external stance when writing about Christianity in his use of the ordinary words, common to both Greek and Latin, for priest, bishop, and church. He uses the word *presbyter* twice in the extant part of his history. On the first occasion, he mentions, without glossing the word, a "certain man of Epirus who was a priest of the Christian religion" (29.3.4: Epirotem aliquem ritus Christiani presbyterum). In Book XXXI, however, when precisely the same phrase occurs for the second time, the word *presbyter* is glossed, for emphasis and with polemical intent. On the morning of the Battle of Adrianople, the Gothic leader Fritigern sent envoys to the emperor Valens. The embassy is described as comprising "a priest (as they themselves call them) of the Christian religion together with other humble fellows" (31.12.8: Christiani ritus presbyter, ut ipsi appellant . . . cum aliis humilibus). A few lines later Ammianus informs his readers that this same Christian priest (*idem Christianus*) was privy to the plans of Fritigern and gave Valens a secret and dishonest letter (31.12.9). That looks like guilt by association—and the association is deliberate.

The extant books use *episcopus* for "bishop" seven times,[23] but Ammianus never glosses it, though he does also use circumlocutions such as *Christianae legis antistes* (15.7.6). And he uses *ecclesia* ("church") without inhibition four times in the extant books as a word whose meaning needs no explanation.[24] In his account of the killing of Silvanus, however, Ammianus avoids the word *ecclesia* by using an apparently classical circumlocution: he states that Silvanus fled *ad conventiculum ritus Christiani* (15.5.31). This attempt at classicism fails in a most interesting way: the word *conventiculum* in the sense "place of meeting" is predominantly Christian.[25]

Ammianus sometimes unconsciously accepts Christian values as well as Christian vocabulary. In his obituary of Julian, he states at the outset that he will assess the dead emperor in terms of the four traditional cardinal virtues of the philosophers (self-control, wisdom, justice, and courage) together with the

---

[22] See G. J. M. Bartelink, *Vig. Chr.* 11 (1957), 37–48; Chapter XIII.
[23] Viansino, *Lexicon* 1.473.
[24] Viansino, *Lexicon* 1.456.
[25] *TLL* 4.844–45.

practical gifts of military skill, dignity, prosperity, and generosity (25.4.1).[26] Yet his detailed enumeration of Julian's virtues starts with the statement that the emperor was "so spectacularly and incorruptly chaste that after the loss of his wife he never tasted the pleasures of sex" (25.4.2). Despite the allusions to Plato and Bacchylides that follow, the frame of reference is Christian: Ammianus claims that not even his closest attendants ever suspected Julian of harboring any *libido* during the whole of his adult life (25.4.3).[27] A Christian standard of morality also lies behind the way in which Ammianus praises Julian for disdaining a beautiful captive girl offered to him after the storming of Maiozamalcha. As Ammianus observes, Alexander and Scipio provided the model for such a refusal.[28] But Julian refused even to look upon the captive, lest his resolve be broken by desire (24.4.27: ne frangeretur cupiditate). To avoid even lusting after a beautiful woman is a Christian more than a traditional Greek or Roman, virtue.[29]

Such Christian language and Christian assumptions are, however, overlaid with prejudicial anti-Christian vocabulary taken from the discourse of religious polemic. Since Ammianus thought in Greek, it was easy and natural for him to transpose into Latin the polemical vocabulary used against the Christians by contemporary Greek pagans. Denigration of the type employed by Ammianus can be found in the emperor Julian, the orator Libanius, Eunapius' *Lives of the Philosophers and Sophists*,[30] the historian Zosimus in that section of his history where he follows Eunapius, and Damascius' *Life of Isidore* in the sixth century.[31]

[26] On this obituary, see Drexler, *Ammianstudien* (1974), 94–136. The order in which Ammianus lists the four cardinal virtues is untraditional, but was also adopted by Mamertinus in his panegyric of Julian delivered in Constantinople on 1 January 362 (*Pan. Lat.* 3[11]). An innovation of the reign of Julian is detected by H. Gärtner, *Abh. Mainz*, Geistes- und Sozialwiss. Kl. 1968, 524 n. 1; A. Guida, *Un anonimo panegirico per l'imperatore Giuliano (Anon. Paneg. Iul. Imp.)* (Florence, 1990), 75. I have argued that the emperor praised in the fragmentary panegyric edited by Guida may be Constantine rather than Julian, and hence that the new order, which put self-control first, begins under the first Christian emperor: *Akten des 21. Internationalen Papyrologenkongresses in Berlin* 2 (Leipzig, 1997), 67–70.

[27] C. J. Classen, *Museum Africum* 1 (1972), 44–45, aptly comparing Jerome, *Commentary on Ephesians* 1.2 (*PL* 26.464).

[28] Ammianus appears to be copying Aulus Gellius, *Noctes Atticae* 7.8.1–3. Scipio's motives were political, according to Polybius 10.19.3–7; Livy 26.50, cf. H. H. Scullard, *Scipio Africanus: Soldier and Politician*[2] (London, 1970), 64.

[29] Matthew 5.28: "If a man looks on a woman with a lustful eye, he has already committed adultery with her in his heart."

[30] On the anti-Christian polemic in this work, see G. J. M. Bartelink, *Vig. Chr.* 23 (1969), 293–303. Unfortunately, he begins by contrasting Eunapius with "Ammien Marcellin, historien impartial, qui ne dénigre jamais les Chrétiens dans son œuvre historique" (293).

[31] The annotation in the excellent edition by C. Zintzen, *Damascii Vitae Isidori reliquiae* (Hildesheim, 1967), identifies many anti-Christian allusions: although Damascius provides a very full repertoire of insults, I refrain from adducing him to avoid any suspicion of anachronism.

When Ammianus applies the derogatory term "corpse" to the relics of the martyr Babylas, he seems to be echoing a specific passage of Julian. The *Misopogon* speaks of the "corpse of Daphne" and "the shrine of the corpse" in a tone and a context that make it clear that Julian is referring to the shrine and the relics of the martyr Babylas.[32] Ammianus refers to the same relics in the same way: after fire destroyed the shrine of Apollo at Daphne in October 362, Julian decided to remove "the bodies buried nearby" (22.12.8: circumhumata corpora statuit exinde referri). Except for introducing a generalizing plural, Ammianus repeats Julian's statement that he had removed "the corpse of Daphne": he had read the *Misopogon* (22.14.2) and the phrase stuck in his mind.[33]

Both Christians and pagans derided the places of worship of the other group as tombs. The Christian apologists of the second and third centuries called temples tombs;[34] in the fourth century, pagans reversed the taunt and called Christian churches tombs,[35] and the emperor Theodosius denounced the conventicles of the Manichees as "tombs of deadly mysteries."[36] Both polemical meanings of the word *sepulchrum* can be found in Ammianus. He reports that, when bishop George looked at the temple of the Tyche of Alexandria, he exclaimed "How long will this tomb stand?" (22.11.7: quam diu sepulchrum hoc stabit?). Ammianus uses the term *in propria persona* to associate Christianity with cowardice and military incompetence. Sabinianus, who had replaced the historian's commanding officer and friend Ursicinus as *magister militum per Orientem* with overall responsibility for the defense of the eastern frontier, was (he alleges) lazy and inefficient.[37] He "was leading a life of dissolute luxury among the cemeteries of Edessa, secure, I suppose, in the belief

---

[32] Julian, *Misopogon* 361bc. Libanius' monody on the burning of the temple of Apollo at Daphne, composed immediately after the fire on 22 October 362, calls the martyr's remains "some corpse" (*Orat.* 60.5).

[33] Saints are also ridiculed as *nekroi* in Julian, *Gal.*, frags. 43.26, 48.7, 61.2, 81.4−5 Masaracchia (where the "fresh corpses" are contrasted with "the ancient corpse," i.e., Christ), cf. R. Asmus, *Woch. kl. Phil.* 24 (1907), 152. The same taunt occurs at the end of Julian's attack on the "uneducated cynics," where D. A. Russell, *CR*, N.S. 15 (1965), 43, convincingly conjectured "*philonekron* = corpse-loving" as an epithet applied to "the life of wretched women" (*Orat.* 9[6], 203c2). The designation *nekros* was applied to Jesus by Celsus: Origen, *Contra Celsum* 3.41, 43; 7.68, cf. P. de Labriolle, *La Réaction païenne. La polémique antichrétienne du Ier au VIe siècle* (Paris, 1934), 415.

[34] G. W. Clarke, *The "Octavius" of Minucius Felix* (*Ancient Christian Writers* 39, 1974), 210−11. The Alexandrian epigrammatist Palladas parodied Christian rhetoric circa 400 by equating the pagan gods with dead men: Alan Cameron, *JRS* 55 (1965), 23−28.

[35] Julian, *Orat.* 7, 228c; *Ep.* 84a, 429d; *Misopogon* 344a, 357c, 361a; *Gal.*, frags. 79.12, 81, 82 Masaracchia; Eunapius, *Vit. phil.* 6.11.8, 10 (472).

[36] *CTh* 16.5.7 (8 May 381): consueta feralium mysteriorum sepulchra.

[37] Sabinianus has usually been taken to be a civilian who did not belong to the officer cadre from which *magistri militum* were usually drawn: so, most explicitly, A. Demandt, *Chiron* 10

that the dead were in no position to disturb the peace" (18.7.7). This dismissive passage contains two polemical phrases: the *Edessena sepulchra* among which Sabinianus wasted his time are the martyrs' churches outside the city that the pilgrim Egeria saw some twenty-five years later,[38] and in Ammianus *vita remissior* is not merely characteristic of Christians, it is virtually coded language for the religion itself.[39]

In his letter to the people of Bostra, Julian defined Christians as "those who have turned away from the gods to corpses and relics."[40] Following his lead, Ammianus calls Christians "atheists" and "criminals," a usage that some recent students have failed to recognize in the historian. Ammianus describes a reign of the emperor Julian in which there are no Christian martyrs, in which no Christian is punished for his religion (Chapter V). Yet he does mention one prominent martyr by name: he is Artemius, whose extant passion, though composed centuries later, draws so heavily on the lost ecclesiastical history of Philostorgius that it is an important historical source for the middle of the fourth century.[41] Artemius had brought to Constantinople the relics of Timothy in 356 and of Andrew and Luke in 357, and after his death he came to be revered as a martyr in the imperial capital.[42] In Egypt, however, Artemius was not remembered with respect or affection. He became *dux Aegypti* in the late 350s and in this capacity harassed the supporters of Athanasius, occupied the Serapeum, and used troops against the populace of Alexandria, thus making himself detested by both Christians and pagans.[43] Artemius was tried and executed at Antioch in October 362.[44]

(1980), 611; J. Szidat, *Historia* 40 (1991), 494–500. However, the crucial phrase is transmitted by V as *victus quidem senex*: although Seyfarth prints *cultus* (Heraeus), Bentley's *unctus* is surely preferable—and carries no implications about Sabinianus' status. For all that Ammianus says, he may have had a long (if undistinguished) military career before 359: see R. P. C. Blockley, *East Roman Foreign Policy. Formation and Conduct from Diocletian to Anastasius* (Leeds, 1992), 180, n. 54, who argues that Jerome, *Vita Malchi* 11, indicates that Sabinianus was probably *dux Mesopotamiae* in the 330s.

[38] *Itinerarium Egeriae* 19.4, cf. P. Maraval, *Lieux saints et pèlerinages d'Orient* (Paris, 1985), 350–52.

[39] Compare *solutioris vitae mollities*, which seems to refer to the conversion of Constantine (31.5.14, cf. Chapter XIV).

[40] Julian, *Ep.* 114, 438c.

[41] The full text is edited by B. Kotter, *Die Shriften des Johannes von Damaskos* 5 (*Patristische Texte und Studien* 29, 1988), 202–45.

[42] *Passio Artemii* 16–18; Zonaras 13.11.28, cf. *Descr. cons.* 356, 357.1 (where Artemius is not named): on his cult, see now S. M. C. Lieu, *From Constantine to Julian: Pagan and Byzantine Views*, ed. S. Lieu and D. Montserrat (London, 1996), 213–23.

[43] For Artemius' career, see, briefly, *PLRE* 1.102, Artemius 2; for a full treatment, J. Dummer, *AfP* 21 (1971), 121–44.

[44] The place is stated as Daphne by *Passio Artemii* 67: on the date, see Appendix 7.

Ammianus heartily approved and presented Artemius as a notorious criminal who was accused by the people of Alexandria and tried and condemned to death "for a mass of outrageous crimes" (22.11.1). The tendentious phrase *atrocium criminum moles* refers to Artemius' actions as a subordinate loyally carrying out the religious policies of Constantius. Theodoretus supplies the charge that Ammianus omits: Artemius was beheaded and his property confiscated because he had destroyed idols in Egypt under Constantius.[45] Ammianus voices sentiments very similar to those Eunapius later expressed: the Egyptian monks at Canopus "collected the bones and skulls of criminals who had been put to death for numerous crimes, men whom the law courts of the city had condemned to punishment."[46]

When he expresses explicit opinions about Christianity and Christian behavior, Ammianus assiduously tries to appear to deliver a balanced verdict. That does not entail, as has so often been maintained, that he had a realistic and even-handed attitude.[47] Similar apparently balanced verdicts abound in Gibbon, who often employs formal balance to sharpen the rhetorical force of his denigration of Christianity.[48] Ammianus, too, had mastered the art of "grave and deliberate irony." The best illustration of his skill in deploying the technique is his discussion of the secret interview that the bishop of Bezabde was alleged to have had with the Persian king Shapur shortly before his city was taken by storm:

> The bishop incurred a suspicion, which in my opinion was ill-founded, though it obtained wide currency, that in a secret meeting he had informed Shapur which parts of the city-walls he should attack as weak on the inside and thus vulnerable. This story was subsequently rendered plausible by the fact that after his visit the enemy siege-engines began deliberately to batter the places which were insecure and crumbling through decay, with great shouts of triumph as if the men who directed them were aware of conditions inside the city. (20.7.9)

What is the overall effect of this passage? It is a serious misreading of Ammianus to argue that Ammianus "defends the bishop of Bezabde against unjust suspicions" or that he had no intention to "incriminate him on a charge of

---

[45] Theodoretus, *HE* 3.18.2.

[46] Eunapius, *Vit. phil.* 6.11.8 (472).

[47] Matthews, *Ammianus* (1989), 450, claims that "his criticism was reserved for cases and circumstances in which it was undeniably justified."

[48] For example, the otiose and malicious parenthesis in the following footnote: "Apollonius of Tyana was born about the same time as Jesus Christ. His life (that of the former) is related in so fabulous a manner by his disciples, that we are at a loss to discover whether he was a sage, an impostor, or a fanatic" (*Decline and Fall* 1.305 n. 70 [B] = 1. 315 n. 63 [W]).

treachery."[49] Writing a generation later in a different part of the world, the historian could simply have omitted a rumor that he disbelieved or considered undeserving of mention. Ammianus chose to include the story because he had learned from Tacitus how to use rumors to suggest disreputable conduct or a dishonest motive while taking no authorial responsibility for the dubious information thus conveyed.[50] The passage is a "progressive insinuation," where Ammianus lets the inherent plausibility of the rumor and its confirmation by the subsequent course of events outweigh his initial (and insincere) disclaimer.[51] Ammianus could neither know nor report what the bishop actually said to Shapur; yet he states very clearly that after the interview the Persian king attacked the defenses of Bezabde where they were weak and could be breached. In Ammianus' opinion, Christians were intrinsically unpatriotic.

The key text that best reveals Ammianus' bias is his analysis of the ecclesiastical policies of Constantius in the obituary of the emperor at the end of Book XXI:

> Confusing the plain and simple Christian religion with the superstition of an old woman, and more interested in complicated enquiries than in settling disputes wisely, he aroused very many quarrels which he fed with verbal argument as they spread widely, so that, with hordes of bishops scurrying hither and thither on public mounts to attend what they call synods, his attempts to force every rite to conform to his whim only succeeded in hamstringing the post service. (21.16.18)

This passage used to be paraded as proof of Ammianus' perceptiveness.[52] In fact, it is a tissue of absurdities, but absurdities that echo Christian complaints about Constantius' interference in ecclesiastical affairs. After Constantius was dead, it was convenient for Christians to blame him for the constant quarrels of bishops and the frequent synods of his reign. For blaming Constantius disguised the unpalatable fact that between 335 and 351 no fewer that ten councils of eastern bishops had either condemned Athanasius, Marcellus of Ancyra, and other worthy bishops or implicitly impugned the creed of the "ecumenical" Council of Nicaea in 325 or both.[53] The theological controversy that dominated these years had begun while Licinius still ruled the East, and the

---

[49] So, respectively, Matthews, *Ancient Writers* 2 (1982), 1118; Hunt, *CQ*, N.S. 35 (1985), 196.

[50] On Tacitus' use of rumor and innuendo, see esp. I. S. Ryberg, *TAPA* 73 (1942), 383–404; R. Syme, *Tacitus* (Oxford, 1958), 314–16.

[51] Sabbah, *Méthode* (1978), 414.

[52] Matthews, *Ancient Writers* 2 (1982), 1118; Hunt, *CQ*, N.S. 35 (1985), 186. In his book, Matthews is markedly more cautious and distances himself from Ammianus' verdict (*Ammianus* [1989], 263, 438, 449).

[53] For the details, see *Athanasius* (1993), 19–120.

dispute over whether Athanasius was the rightful bishop of Alexandria had begun with his election in 328.[54] How could Constantius have started controversies that began when he was an infant and had raged for nearly twenty years before he was able to intervene in any way?

So far from attempting to impose his own wishes, as Ammianus alleges, Constantius refrained from intervening personally in the theological debates for more than twenty years. Admittedly, after 353, he attempted to secure western acceptance of the decisions of the eastern Council of Sirmium of 351. But he played no part in formulating the doctrines set out in the synodical letter of that council. It was only in frustration that he intervened directly in 359 by convening the separate eastern and western Councils of Seleucia and Ariminum to ratify a creed drawn up in his presence, on the twenty-second anniversary of the death of his father. And the result of these councils and the negotiations that followed them was not doctrinal complexity, but extreme doctrinal simplification: the homoean creed laid down merely that God the Son is like the Father, but carefully omitted to specify in what sense or senses Father and Son are alike.[55] Moreover, Valerio Neri has now shown that Ammianus' complaint that Constantius could not distinguish between an *absoluta et simplex religio* and an *anilis superstitio* and his phrase *scrutando perplexius* express a verdict which any catholic Christian of the reign of Theodosius could wholeheartedly accept.[56]

The satirical quality of Ammianus' assessment of Constantius comes out clearly in his allegation that throngs of bishops scurrying to and fro hamstrung the *cursus publicus* (21.16.18). Most modern discussions have failed to ask two obvious questions that are relevant to evaluating this remark: how many people used the *cursus publicus* regularly? and how many bishops used it on special occasions? The system was enormous and available for anyone on official business:[57] it must therefore have been used every year by several thousand governors, officials, soldiers, *agentes in rebus*, and private citizens with influence. But most councils of bishops were small gatherings of the bishops of a single province or of a group of neighboring provinces. Even in the reign of Constantius, most councils were small affairs with predominantly local attendance. Despite the high numbers (well into the hundreds) bandied about by ecclesiastical historians, ancient and modern, the Councils of Arles in 353–354 and Milan in 355 were both attended by no more than about thirty bishops.[58]

---

[54] *Constantine* (1981), 201–7, 230–42; *Athanasius* (1993), 14–25.
[55] *Athanasius* (1993), 136–51.
[56] V. Neri, *Cognitio Gestorum* (1992), 59–65.
[57] Jones, *LRE* 830–34.
[58] *Athanasius* (1993), 115, 117, 275–77, n. 45–47.

Between 337 and 361 there were only two dates at which more than one hundred bishops gathered together in a single city.[59] The first was in 343, when ninety western and seventy six eastern bishops assembled in Serdica, although they never all met together as a single council.[60] It is significant that the eastern bishops voiced exactly the same complaint that Ammianus repeats—that the *cursus publicus* was "being worn out and reduced to nothing."[61] The second occasion was in 359, when four hundred western bishops were compelled to spend several months in Ariminum under the watchful eye of the praetorian prefect Taurus,[62] and one hundred and sixty eastern bishops met at Seleucia in Cilicia under the supervision of the *comites* Bassidius Lauricius and Leonas.[63] During the summer of 359 Ammianus traveled post-haste with Ursicinus from Samosata across Asia Minor and into Europe, then in the reverse direction from the River Hebrus back to Mesopotamia (18.4.7, 6.5, 8). A suspicion thus inevitably arises that his complaint about "crowds of bishops" reflects the personal irritation of a man in a hurry who arrived at a *mansio* only to find that bishops had taken all the fresh horses that his party needed to continue their urgent journey.[64] If that suspicion is well founded, then Ammianus' remark, which has impressed so many for its perceptiveness, represents a misleading generalization of a single occurrence, exaggeration based on personal inconvenience—the procedure of a satirist like Juvenal rather than a historian.[65]

Christian language, prejudicial vocabulary, explicit polemic, and satire do not exhaust the variety of material relevant to Ammianus' attitude toward Christianity. There is also covert polemic against Christianity, and it is a pervasive feature of the *Res Gestae*. The detection of hidden polemic involves an obvious danger: the eager exegete is likely to find what he seeks whether it is really there or not. That Ammianus makes such covert attacks on Christianity can be established only by providing cogent examples. An acute enquiry has discovered covert anti-Christian polemic in a passage where Ammianus de-

---

[59] *Athanasius* (1993), 71–81.

[60] The precise numbers on each side are deduced from Athanasius, *Hist. Ar.* 15.3; Socrates, *HE* 2.20.5. Lists survive, albeit incomplete, of the bishops who subscribed the eastern and western synodical letters: *CSEL* 65.74–78 (73 eastern bishops); *CSEL* 65.132–39; *EOMIA* 1.545–59 (61 and 59 western bishops respectively), cf. *Athanasius* (1993), 260, n. 10–12.

[61] *CSEL* 65.64.24–25: cursusque ipse publicus attritus ad nihilum deducitur.

[62] Sulpicius Severus, *Chron.* 2.41–44.

[63] For the number, see Athanasius, *Syn.* 12.1; Socrates, *HE* 2.39.5; on the role played by Lauricius and Leonas, *Athanasius* (1993), 146–48.

[64] *Reading the Past* (1990), 80.

[65] On the personal elements in the poet, see still G. Highet, *Juvenal the Satirist. A Study* (Oxford, 1954), exaggerated in detail, but instinctively correct in principle.

scribes the state of the eastern armies before Julian reformed them in the winter of 361–362.[66] The soldiers of Constantius were soft, corrupt, and addicted to luxury: they slept on soft beds, their drinking goblets weighed more than their swords, and they recited effeminate ditties instead of martial hurrahs (22.4.6: cum miles cantilenas meditaretur pro iubilo molliores etc.).[67] Ammianus alludes (it seems) to the recitation of prayers by soldiers, a practice instituted by Constantine.[68] There is something analogous in Libanius and Zosimus: the latter alleges that the three hundred and sixty men whom Constantius gave Julian when he sent him to Gaul (that is, part of the scholae palatinae as his bodyguard) knew only how to pray, the former that when Constantius removed the best of Julian's bodyguard in 360, he left him soldiers capable of nothing else than praying.[69] All three authors thus equate Christian prayer with military incompetence.

The end of Book XIX repays close examination as an exercise in disguised anti-Christian polemic. What editors print as the last two chapters comprises one substantial episode narrated at length (19.12.1–18) and two quasi-annalistic notices (19.12.19–20, 19.13). The placing of these three items is significant: Book XIX concludes a hexad, and these notices immediately precede the proclamation of Julian as Augustus.

Paul "the Chain," whom Ammianus had introduced once before (14.5.6), is introduced again as tartareus ille notarius, an expert in the arts of bloodshed who did not shrink from fraud to ruin the innocent. An opportunity for villainy arose from a trivial incident. The remote oracle of the god Besa in Upper Egypt was normally consulted by submitting questions in writing, which were retained in the shrine after the god had answered them. Someone sent some of these papers to Constantius. In a rage, the emperor sent Paul to search out those who had submitted the offensive questions, arrest them, and bring them to trial before Modestus, the comes Orientis (who normally resided in Antioch). Paul carried out his assignment, and the trials were held at Scythopolis in Palestine. Ammianus explains that Scythopolis was chosen because it was both remote and mid-way between Antioch and Alexandria, from where many of the accused came (19.12.1–8).[70] By secretior, it has been suggested,

---

[66] D. Woods, JTS, N.S. 49 (1998), 145–48.

[67] Despite TLL 3.285–86, cantilenae has a clearly derogatory sense here, whereas iubilum occurs predominantly in Christian texts (TLL 7.2.588–89).

[68] Eusebius, VC 4.19–20.

[69] Zosimus 3.3.2 (quoting a lost letter of Julian himself); Libanius, Orat. 18.94, cf. Ammianus 20.4.3.

[70] On the trials, which Ammianus describes at some length (12.9–18), and their political background, see J. Straub, Heidnische Geschichtsapologetik in der christlichen Spätantike. Untersuchungen über Zeit und Tendenz der Historia Augusta (Bonn, 1963), 63–74; H. Funke, JAC 10 (1967), 151–65; R. von Haehling, JAC 21 (1978), 74–101.

Ammianus "presumably means that it was distant from centres of pagan influence."[71] More relevant in the present context is the demonstrable fact that Ammianus has left out the principal reason for Paul's journey to Alexandria. Two local sources record that Paul arrived in the city on 23 June 359, published an imperial edict in favor of George, whom the Council of Sirmium in 351 had appointed bishop of Alexandria in place of Athanasius, and used force to cow Athanasius' supporters.[72]

The first of the two brief notices that follow resembles an annalistic notice from Livy in both content and language (19.12.19–20). At Daphne "that pleasant and splendid suburb of Antioch" was born a child with two mouths, two sets of teeth, a beard, four eyes and two very small ears. Ammianus interprets the birth of such a deformed child as a warning that the state was being deformed: such portents, he explains, often indicate the future, but "since they are not expiated publicly as in the days of the ancients, they pass without anyone hearing or knowing of them."[73] This lament comes from the heart: Ammianus believed in the validity of all the traditional forms of divination (Chapters V, XIV). He then proceeds, in a passage unfortunately omitted in the Penguin translation, to record a renewal of raiding by the Isaurians (19.13.1). As a result, he continues:

> To quieten them by force or persuasion Lauricius was sent as governor with the added rank of *comes*, a man with understanding of civil affairs, who corrected many things with threats rather than severity, so effectively that though he held the province for a long time nothing happened which might be deemed worthy of notice.[74] (19.13.2)

This, the very last sentence of Book XIX, is oddly over-emphatic. Together with the *comes* Leonas, Bassidius Lauricius presided over the Council of Seleucia in late September 359:[75] he was a *praeses* of Isauria who probably received the rank of *comes* precisely for the purpose of supervising the council,[76] since

---

[71] J. Binns, *Ascetics and Ambassadors of Christ. The Monasteries of Palestine 314–631* (Oxford, 1994), 134.

[72] *Historia acephala* 2.5 Martin; *Festal Index* 29.

[73] The extant books of Livy have no double birth of this sort, but they record three births of an infant of indeterminate sex as prodigies requiring expiation (27.3.5, 27.11.4, 31.12.6).

[74] I accept Seyfarth's interpretation of *animadversione dignum* as "bemerkenswert": in the Budé edition, G. Sabbah translates "qui justifiât une répression."

[75] Epiphanius, *Panarion* 73.25; Socrates, *HE* 2.39–40; Sozomenus, *HE* 4.22.

[76] An inscription records that Bassidius Lauricius restored a fort which had long been occupied by *latrones*, garrisoned it, and named it Antiochia, stating his title and rank as *v. c., com(es) et praeses* (ILS 740). The combination of *comes* and *praeses* is anomalous: R. Scharf, *EA* 16 (199), 147–51.

it seems to follow from Ammianus that he was appointed governor in 359 when the council was about to take place. The assertion that nothing worthy of note happened in his province while he was governor can hardly be an innocent misapprehension.

Even Ammianus' geographical excursus are sometimes subtly polemical. The excursus on the shores of Thrace and the Black Sea contains an implicit denial of the importance of Constantine's new Christian city on the Bosporus: "the left bank (sc. of the Propontis) is overlooked by the port of Athyras, Selymbria, Constantinople, the ancient Byzantium, an Athenian colony, and the promontory of Ceras" (22.8.8). Fourth-century Constantinople was much more than "the ancient Byzantium" with which Ammianus here equates it.[77] In reality, it more than matched contemporary Antioch, which he praised as "a city known to the world, with which no other could compete in abounding with both imported and home-grown supplies" (14.7.8). Moreover, Ammianus' praise of Antioch and other cities in the Syrian region when he describes the provinces of Oriens in Book XIV culminates in a most remarkable and effective covert insult to Christianity:

> The last of the Syrias is Palestine, extending over a great extent of territory and abounding in cultivated and well-kept lands; it also has some splendid cities, none of which yields to any of the others, but they rival one another, as it were, by plumb-line. These are Caesarea, which Herodes built in honor of the emperor Octavianus, Eleutheropolis, and Neapolis, along with Ascalon and Gaza, built in a former age. In these districts, no navigable river is anywhere to be seen, but in numerous places natural warm springs gush forth, adapted to many medicinal uses. But these regions also met with a like fate, being formed into a province by Pompey, after he had defeated the Jews and taken Jerusalem, and left to the jurisdiction of a governor. (14.8.11–12)

Ammianus' message could hardly be clearer.[78] The significant cities of fourth century Palestine are Caesarea, Eleutheropolis, Neapolis, Ascalon, and Gaza. He excludes from the list Jerusalem, which Constantine had turned into a rich, monumental city crowded with resident ascetics and visiting pilgrims,[79]

---

[77] G. Dagron, *Naissance d'une capitale. Constantinople et ses institutions de 330 à 451* (Paris, 1974), 13–74, 119–46, 213–60, 297–314, 367–453.

[78] G. Stemberger, *Juden und Christen im Heiligen Land. Palästina unter Konstantin und Theodosius* (Munich, 1987), 156–57.

[79] E. D. Hunt, *Holy Land Pilgrimage in the Later Roman Empire, A.D. 312–410* (Oxford, 1982), 6–27, 128–79; P. M. L. Walker, *Holy City, Holy Places? Christian Attitudes to Jerusalem and the Holy Land in the Fourth Century* (Oxford, 1990), 199–308.

and which was already, when Ammianus wrote, challenging Caesarea for ecclesiastical primacy in the Roman province of Palestine.[80] Ammianus deliberately closed his eyes to the importance of contemporary Jerusalem, just as he closed his eyes to the central role that Christianity played in the politics, society, and culture of the Roman Empire after Constantine.

[80] The political conflict between the sees of Jerusalem and Caesarea went back to circa 325, when Macarius, the bishop of Jerusalem, discovered what was believed to be the wood of the cross on which Jesus was crucified: Z. Rubin, *Jerusalem Cathedra* 2 (1982), 79–105.

[IX]

THINGS SEEN AND THINGS READ

Ammianus' geographical and ethnographical excursus combine three very different types of material.[1] The framework usually comes from either official lists of Roman provinces or lists of peoples and places outside Roman territory that he may have found in Ptolemy's *Geography*.[2] He added historical notices from Festus' *Breviarium*, drew on Solinus and Greek topographical works for particular sections, and used Sallust and Livy where they provided relevant material.[3] Ammianus also sometimes drew on his own recollection of what he had seen or heard. Hence the description *visa vel lecta* that he applies to the content of his account of the coasts of Thrace, the Hellespont, and the Black Sea (22.8.1).

The balance between *visa* and *lecta* varies from one excursus to another. The lost discussion of the *situs Africae* (cf. 29.5.18) is likely to have been bookish and Sallustian, for Ammianus had read the *Bellum Jugurthinum*, but probably never set foot in Roman Africa. And the excursus on the Huns apppears to be almost entirely a tissue of ethnographical commonplaces that owes nothing to

---

[1] On the quality of these excursus and Ammianus' geographical knowledge, see now G. A. Sundwall, *AJP* 117 (1996), 619–643.

[2] Ammianus names Ptolemy with Eratosthenes, Hecataeus "aliique huiusmodi cognitionum minutissimi sciscitatores" as asserting that the shape of the coast of the Black Sea is like a Scythian bow, which is certainly untrue of Ptolemy (22.8.10). For Ammianus' use of Ptolemy for oriental geography, see M. Schuffner, *Ammianus Marcellinus in rerum gestarum libris quae de sedibus ac moribus complurium gentium scripserit* (Prog. Meiningen, 1877), 14–17; T. Mommsen, *Gesammelte Schriften* 7 (Berlin, 1909), 402–9; L. Dilleman, *Syria* 38 (1961), 135–42. It is denied by M. F. A. Brok, *Mnemosyne*[4] 28 (1975), 47–56.

[3] Mommsen, *Ges. Schr.* 7 (1909), 393–425. For an attempt to distinguish between what Ammianus took from written sources and what he added to them, A. Malotet, *De Ammiani Marcellini digressionibus quae ad externas gentes pertineant* (Diss. Paris, 1898), 1–46.

close observation and hence possesses little historical value.[4] The excursus on the Black Sea, which may have been intended to challenge comparison with Sallust's famous digression on the *situs Ponti*,[5] is a mosaic put together from very diverse sources, mainly and perhaps exclusively Greek.[6] The intellectual level is closer to that of a periplus (such as the *Periplus Maris Erythraei*) than to serious scientific geography, and the Dutch commentators rightly doubt whether anything in it draws on personal observation, except when Ammianus writes about the Bosporus and its surrounds, which he had visited. Ammianus' account of the provinces of Oriens, by contrast, though repeating phrases from Festus' *Breviarium* of 370,[7] reveals significant facts about how this eastern believer in the traditional gods viewed the post-Constantinian Roman Empire in which he lived (Chapter VIII).

The balance between what Ammianus had seen and what he had read is perhaps most evenly held in his excursus on Gaul. The successive investigations of Victor Gardthausen in 1873, Theodor Mommsen in 1881, and Walter Sontheimer in 1926, together with the evaluation of their findings by P. de Jonge in his commentary on Book XV, have identified with some precision the varied elements that this excursus amalgamates.[8] Nevertheless, it will be worth reviewing their conclusions and asking again what Ammianus has added from his own experience.

Ammianus marks the importance of his excursus on Gaul by quoting a famous passage of "the bard of Mantua" where Virgil marks the transition from the "Odyssey" of the Trojans in the first six books to the "Iliad" of the second half of the *Aeneid*, and he quotes more than a line with the words partly transposed in order to avoid the full metrical pattern of hexameter verse in prose.[9] Ammianus names Timagenes as his principal authority for the origin of the

[4] C. King, *AJAH* 12 (1987, publ. 1995), 77–95 (with reference to earlier, mostly much more favorable analyses). In contrast, what Ammianus says in his narrative about the Sarmatians and Quadi seems to be based on accurate and reliable observation: U.-B. Dittrich, *Die Beziehungen Roms zu den Sarmaten und Quaden im vierten Jahrhundert n. Chr. (nach der Darstellung des Ammianus Marcellinus)* (Diss. Bonn, 1984).

[5] Rufius Festus, *Ora maritima*, 36–37: inclytam descriptionem. B. Maurenbrecher, *C. Sallustii Crispi Historiarum reliquiae* (Leipzig, 1891), 134–38, reconstructed its outline from Pomponius Mela, *Chorographia* 1.99–2.15; Pliny, *Nat. Hist.* 4.75–91, 6.1–22; Valerius Flaccus, *Argonautica* 4.714–32; Ammianus 22.8.4–48. The Dutch commentators acidly note that "only the odd phrase in Ammianus' resembles the validly attested fragments."

[6] I. Gualandri, *Parola del Passato* 23 (1968), 211.

[7] Mommsen, *Ges. Schr.* 7 (1909), 396–400.

[8] V. Gardthausen, *Jahrb. für class. Phil.*, Supp. 6 (1873), 509–56; T. Mommsen, *Hermes* 16 (1881), 602–36 = *Ges. Schr.*, (1909), 393–425; W. Sontheimer, *Klio* 20 (1926), 19–53.

[9] 15.9.1: ut Mantuanus vates praedixit excelsus, opus moveo maius/ maiorque mihi rerum nascitur ordo (quoting *Aen.* 7.44–45: maior rerum mihi nascitur ordo,/ maius opus moveo).

Gauls: he commends him as a Greek in both scholarship and language, who collected information from a wide range of earlier books and gave accurate information about matters on which his predecessors possessed only inaccurate opinions (15.9.2). Ammianus promises to relate the same facts as Timagenes "clearly and plainly," and both the structure and much of the content of the excursus reflect the fact that his main authority was writing in the reign of Augustus.[10]

Ammianus took from Timagenes both the ethnography of Gaul (15.9) and much of what he says about the Alps (15.10). The provenance of this material is clear,[11] and Ammianus was fully aware that Gallic society had changed over the course of four centuries: he carefully uses the aorist tense when he talks about the three categories of men who represented learning and culture among the ancient Gauls (15.9.8). Comparison with the historian Diodorus Siculus and the geographer Strabo makes it clear that both they and Timagenes here reproduced the classification and in part the language of Posidonius.[12] All three Augustan writers named the poets and composers of sacred hymns among the Gauls as *bardi*, the philosophic druids, and a third category, for whose Celtic name Ammianus may provide the best guidance, corrupt though the transmitted text obviously is: "euhagis vero scrutantes †serviani† et sublimia naturae pandere conantur."[13] Diodorus describes these men as seers who practice divination by watching birds and through sacrifices, whereas Strabo states that they perform sacred duties and investigate nature and claims to give their Celtic name.[14] The form in which the name was stated by Timagenes has been a matter of erudite discussion, and the truth can only be divined by conjecture: nevertheless, it seems now to be agreed by competent judges that Ammianus repeats the Greek word *euageis* from Timagenes, who attempted to reproduce the Celtic term, whereas the *ouateis* offered by the manuscripts of Strabo sounds uncomfortably reminiscent of the Latin word *vates* (bard, poet).[15]

---

[10] Seneca, *De Ira* 2.23.4–8; *Suda* T 588 (4.549 Adler) = *FGrH* 88 T 2, 1.

[11] F. Jacoby prints Ammianus 15.9.2–8, 10.9, 12.1–4 as *FGrH* 88 F 1, 14, 15.

[12] Diodorus 5.25–32 = *FGrH* 87 F 116 = Posidonius, frag. 169 Theiler, cf. J. Malitz, *Die Historien des Poseidonios* (*Zetemata* 79, 1983), 196, n. 217.

[13] I print the readings of V: Seyfarth accepts the emendation *euages* for *euhagis* and registers a plethora of modern conjectures for *serviani*, which he rightly obelizes.

[14] Diodorus 5.31.2–3; Strabo 4.4.4 (197C).

[15] W. Aly, *Strabonis Geographica, 4: Strabon von Amaseia. Untersuchungen über Text, Aufbau und Quellen der Geographie* (Bonn, 1957), 456–59, cf. E. Bickel, *Rh. Mus.*, N.F. 87 (1938), 195–201, 217–20; *Festschrift für August Oxé* (Darmstadt, 1938), 164–66. Aly argues that *euagis* accurately reproduces what both Posidonius and Timagenes wrote and that Strabo found the word already deformed in his written source: given the state of his text (the Vatican palimpsest is not available for Book IV), it might be preferable to emend the transmitted *ouateis* to *ouageis* in Strabo.

Also from Timagenes must derive the surprising prominence given to King Cottius when Ammianus writes about the Alpes Cottiae (15.10.2–8). Together with the inscription on the triumphal arch that Cottius erected at Segusio,[16] Ammianus provides the greater part of what is known about him.[17] Cottius was hardly of much interest to anyone in the fourth century, but Ammianus had seen his tomb close to the city walls of Segusio: he notes that Cottius was received into friendship by Octavian, built roads to aid Alpine travelers, governed justly, bequeathed permanent peace to his tribe, and still received cultic devotions in 355 (15.10.2, 7).

What other literary sources did Ammianus use when writing about Gaul? He had read Sallust, he uses a Sallustian phrase when he mentions the people of Saguntum,[18] and he names Sallust at the end of the excursus (15.12.5–6). But there is no good reason to imagine that he derived any of the material in the excursus from Sallust.[19] Sallust's *Histories* did not contain a digression on Gaul, for which his narrative of the 70s B.C. provided no appropriate opportunity. The passage that Ammianus quotes is known to come from Sallust's preface, which observed that, within ten years, Caesar had conquered the whole of Gaul except what was too boggy to be accessible.[20]

Mommsen derived part of what Ammianus says about tribes, rivers, and the original provinces into which the Romans divided Gaul from Caesar's *Gallic War* (15.11.1–5).[21] That hypothesis is unnecessary. For Ammianus can have taken what Caesarian material there may be in the excursus (if indeed there is any) from a later author, who himself used Caesar, conceivably the lost portion of Livy.[22] Sontheimer compared what Ammianus says about Hannibal's route over the Alps (15.10.11) with Polybius and Livy and argued that the three historians all depend, directly or indirectly, on two early and somewhat discrepant accounts: Polybius (he held) used one of these versions and Ammianus the other, while Livy conflated the two.[23] That could be true: if so, the two early or primary accounts were presumably those of the Roman Fabius

---

[16] *CIL* 5.7231 = *ILS* 94. Dessau reprints the text of Mommsen, who verified readings from ground level with the aid of a telescope: for the first edition based on close inspection, see E. Ferrero, *L'arc d'Auguste à Susa* (Turin, 1901), 30, with Planches XIV–XVII.

[17] *PIR*² J 274.

[18] 15.10.10: Saguntinis memorabilibus aerumnis et fide. Ammianus is copying Sallust, *Hist.* 2.64 M: Saguntini fide atque aerumnis incliti prae mortalibus.

[19] Mommsen, *Ges. Schr.* 7 (1909), 394, 400.

[20] 15.12.6: omnes Gallias, nisi qua paludibus inviae fuere. The model is Sallust, *Hist.* 1.11M: omni Gallia . . . , nisi qua paludibus invia fuit, perdomita.

[21] Mommsen, *Ges. Schr.* (1909), 411, n. 1.

[22] Gardthausen, *Jahrb. für class. Phil.*, Supp. 6 (1873), 550.

[23] Sontheimer, *Klio* 20 (1926), 28–53.

Pictor and Silenus.[24] But what was Ammianus' immediate source? Sontheimer identified it as "an ancient annalistic account" and named its author as Claudius Quadrigarius.[25] That is flatly impossible: although Livy used Quadrigarius extensively, no one shows direct acquaintance with his text after Aulus Gellius, who is the source of most of the apparent quotations of Quadrigarius in Late Antiquity.[26] Gardthausen and Mommsen more plausibly identifed Livy as the source of Ammianus' information about Hannibal.[27]

Ammianus also employed nonliterary written sources. He had before him either a list of the provinces and cities of Gaul very similar to the extant, though later, *Notitia Galliarum* or, more probably, a map or maps of Gaul from the middle of the fourth century: as de Jonge observed, he will presumably have used maps for his own journeys in the 350s. For the provincial divisions are correct for 355, the date where Ammianus places the excursus, not for the time of writing.[28] Moreover, Ammianus notes that distances in Gaul are measured not in miles, but in *leugae* (15.11.17), which were about one and a half Roman miles (2.2 kilometers), a practice that began under Septimius Severus.[29]

Whatever his written sources were or may have been, Ammianus draws on his own memories of his journey over the Alps in 355.[30] He emphasizes that he reports what inhabitants of the region tell all travelers and has seen confirmatory inscriptions (15.9.6).[31] He has also imposed form and order on the varied material that he incorporates. If he has reproduced or used a written list of Gallic cities, he has made a personal selection of which cities to record, and he adds comments of his own. He notes the ancient grandeur of the walls of Autun (15.11.11) and that Aventicum is deserted, its buildings half-ruined (15.11.12).

When Ammianus writes about the passes over the Alps, he writes as one who has himself stood at the top of a mountain pass and admired the view he describes: "From the top of this Italian slope a plateau extends for seven miles as far as the post named after Mars; from there another loftier height, difficult to surmount, reaches to the peak of Matrona, so called from an accident to a

---

[24] P. G. Walsh, *T. Livi ab urbe condita liber XXI* (London, 1973), 38. For Fabius and Silenus, *FGrH* 809; 175.

[25] Sontheimer, *Klio* 20 (1926), 49, 53.

[26] H. Peter, *Historicorum Romanorum Reliquiae* 1² (Leipzig, 1904), cccii–cccciii; L. Holford-Strevens, *Aulus Gellius* (London, 1988), 179–80, 184–85.

[27] Gardthausen, *Jahrb. für class. Phil.*, Supp. 6 (1873), 553–56; Mommsen, *Ges. Schr.* 7 (1909), 411, n. 1.

[28] *New Empire* (1982), 217–18.

[29] G. Walser, *Epigraphica* 31 (1969), 84–103.

[30] G. M. Woloch, *Arctos* 26 (1992), 137–40.

[31] G. M. Woloch, *Arctos* 27 (1993), 149–53, attributes Ammianus' apparent mistakes mainly to a fallible memory and misleading maps.

noble lady. After that a steep but easier route lies open to the fort of Brigantia"
(15.10.6). The references to the *statio* named after Mars and the fort Brigantia
subtly indicate the context in which Ammianus crossed the Alps: he had traveled from Milan to Cologne when he helped to assassinate Silvanus in 355
(15.5.17–31). A more personal and more revealing recollection surfaces in the
passage where Ammianus describes the character of the Gauls:

> Almost all Gauls are of imposing stature, fair-skinned, with reddish hair, fearsome
> because of their savage eyes, eager to quarrel and excessively insolent. For, not
> even a whole group of foreigners can stand up to a single one of them if, in the
> course of a dispute, he summons his grey-eyed wife, who is much stronger than
> he is, especially when, with swollen neck and gnashing teeth, she swings her enor-
> mous snow-white arms and begins to deliver a rain of punches mixed with kicks,
> like missiles launched by the twisted strings of a catapult. (15.12.1)

Ammianus had doubtless read about the physical strength of Gallic women in
Timagenes, since Diodorus observes that they are not merely as large as their
menfolk, but their match when it comes to blows.[32] But the phrase *globus pere-
grinorum* surely hints, if only unconsciously, at a personal experience. It evokes
a dispute in a tavern—Ammianus and his fellow officers pitted against an inn-
keeper and his fearsome wife, who is depicted with a satirical intensity worthy of Juvenal.[33]

The passages that draw on personal recollection in the excursus on Gaul encourage a search for similar passages elsewhere in the *Res Gestae* in which Ammianus may indirectly reveal something significant about himself. The historian had seen much during his long and varied life. He gives an unforgettable
account of his adventures in 359 when he was besieged in Amida and escaped
with difficulty when the Persians stormed the city (18.6–19.9).[34] Two passages
in this account are unintentionally revealing. As Ammianus and his companions hurried to take refuge in Amida in 359, they found a soldier in hiding in
the woods of Meiacarire and brought him before Ursicinus:

> Suspicion was aroused by the inconsistent answers that he gave in his fright, and
> finally threats extracted from him the whole truth. He told us that he was born

[32] Diodorus 5.32.2.

[33] On the viscerally visual nature of Juvenal's poetical imagination, see R. Jenkyns, *Three
Classical Poets. Sappho, Catullus and Juvenal* (London, 1982), 174–221.

[34] On the gripping quality (and literary artifice) of these personal reminiscences, see Rosen,
Studien (1970), 51–68; Bitter, *Kampfschilderungen* (1976), 12–56; Matthews, *Ammianus* (1989),
57–65.

at Paris in Gaul: when serving in a cavalry regiment, he had fled into exile in
Persia because he feared punishment for an offence he once committed. After
that, when he had proved the excellence of his character by acquiring a wife and
raising children, he was sent to our territory as a spy and often brought back reliable information. On the present occasion he had been sent by Tamsapor and
Nohodares, grandees who commanded raiding parties, and was returning to report what he had learned. After he then added what he knew of operations on
the other side, he was killed. (18.6.16)

Killing at close quarters and being killed were a normal part of life for an officer
like Ammianus, who had spent a whole night in 359 pressed against a corpse:

> Here we stood motionless until the sun rose, mixed with Persians who were striv-
> ing with equal effort to reach higher ground with us. We were packed together
> so tightly that the bodies of the dead propped up by the press could not find the
> space to fall anywhere, and a soldier in front of me, whose head had been split
> into two equal halves by a powerful sword-stroke, was hemmed in on all sides
> and stood upright like the stump of a tree. (18.8.12)

Such experiences can hardly fail to mark a man unless he is unusually insensitive. The fourth century was a brutal age, and the historian was capable of
brutality: indeed, one student of Ammianus has argued that the cruel world
in which he lived so brutalized the historian that he became insensitive to human suffering.[35]

Despite the obvious danger that the exegete may read into Ammianus' text
what is not really there, another passage requires consideration in this context:

> The people of Egypt are for the most part swarthy and dark, rather gloomy, lean
> and with a dried-up look, easily roused to excited gestures, quarrelsome and most
> persistent in pursuing a debt. Among them a man blushes who cannot exhibit
> many scars on his body incurred by refusing to pay taxes. And it has not yet been
> possible to devise a torture harsh enough to compel an obstinate robber from
> that region even to state his name against his will. (22.16.23)

As in his description of the muscular women of Gaul, Ammianus is surely drawing on his own experience. He writes as one who has tortured, or supervised

---

[35] Blockley, *Ammianus* (1975), 156: "as he passes through various adventures, he is totally
alone—no friendship, no real relationship at all, no feeling."

the torture of, an Egyptian who refused even to reveal his name. Ammianus may have enjoyed inflicting pain on others. For much in his narrative has a palpably sadistic quality.

The problem of the relation between erudition and observation in Ammianus, between book learning and the reporting of fact is posed most acutely by his account of an eclipse of the sun in Book XX, which immediately precedes the proclamation of Julian as Augustus:

> At the same time, throughout the regions of the East the sky was seen veiled in a dark mist, and the stars shone through it continuously from the first dawning of the day until noon. And there was added to these terrors the fact that, since the light of heaven was covered with its globe hidden from the sight of the earth, the fearful minds of men thought that the sun had been eclipsed for longer than usual. (20.3.1)

It has long been recognized that this passage is highly problematical: at the most obvious and elementary level, anyone who has observed a total eclipse of the sun knows that it lasts but a very few minutes in any one place. Although Szidat and the Dutch commentators have diligently investigated the sources of the excursus on astronomy that follows this report (20.3.2–12),[36] they have unfortunately failed to set out the full extent of the problems inherent in the report itself. These were duly noted by Max Büdinger, who drew an alarming conclusion: the reader and the researcher who wish to use Ammianus as a repository of facts ought to be warned that either he has uncritically repeated erroneous information or else he is indulging his imagination.[37] The latter is the correct explanation of three serious difficulties in what Ammianus says about the eclipse of 360.

The first concerns the date. Ammianus unambiguously dates the eclipse he describes to the late winter or spring of the year. It follows the cashiering of Ursicinus for the loss of Amida in 359, even though the real responsibility (Ammianus asserts) lay with the stubbornly lazy Sabinianus (20.2), and it precedes the proclamation of Julian as Augustus while he was still in winter-quarters in Paris (20.4, cf. 1.1). Now there were two solar eclipses in 360: one occurred on 4 March, at the date indicated by Ammianus, but was visible only in the

---

[36] Also D. den Hengst, *Mnemosyne*[4] 39 (1986), 136–41.

[37] M. Büdinger, *Ammianus Marcellinus und die Eigenart seines Geschichtswerkes* (*Denkschriften Wien*, Phil.-hist. Cl. 44.5, 1895), 40.

southern hemisphere; the other, to which it has always been assumed that Ammianus referred, occurred on 28 August.[38]

The second difficulty is that Ammianus misstates the nature of the eclipse. Modern astronomers distinguish between total eclipses of the sun, when the interposed disk of the moon totally obscures that of the sun, leaving only the solar corona visible to the observer on earth, and annular eclipses, when the moon, being further away from the earth, does not totally block out the direct light of the sun, but leaves a rim or ring of the sun's disk visible throughout. (Some eclipses are total at some places on the earth's surface, annular at others.) The distinction was known to ancient astronomers too: although Ptolemy effectively denied that annular eclipses could occur at all,[39] the Neoplatonist Proclus states the distinction clearly and reports that Sosigenes, the teacher of Alexander of Aphrodisias, observed one, whose date can be fixed as 4 September 164.[40] The solar eclipse of 28 August 360 was an annular eclipse, not a total eclipse at any place on the surface of the globe. Hence Ammianus cannot be reporting what anyone actually observed in 360 anywhere in the northern hemisphere.

The third difficulty was stated with exemplary clarity by Julius Zech in a Leipzig prize essay of 1853: the eclipse was probably not visible at all in Roman territory.[41] Although neither of the two recent commentaries on Book XX cites Zech's rather rare work directly, the basic facts are not in dispute: in Oppolzer's standard canon of eclipses, the sunrise point for the eclipse of 28 August 360 was at a longitude of about 54 degrees east of the Greenwich meridian and the midday point was about 124 degrees east, that is, the path of annularity began at sunrise somewhere to the east of Teheran and the eclipse was visible at midday in China.[42]

---

[38] T. von Oppolzer, *Canon der Finsternisse* (*Denkschriften Wien*, Math.-naturwiss. Cl. 52, 1887), 150–51: Blatt Nr. 75 = *Canon of Eclipses*, trans. O. Gingerich (New York, 1962), 150–51: Chart 75.

The criticisms of Oppolzer voiced by J. Meeus, C. C. Grosjean, and W. Vanderleen, *Canon of Solar Eclipses* (Oxford, 1966), 33–39, do not make any difference to the point at issue here: in their charts for eclipses between 1898 and 2161 (Charts 1–24), the beginnings and ends of eclipses are identical with Oppolzer's (*Canon* [1962], Charts 149–60).

[39] Ptolemy, *Almagest* 5.14 (1.417 Heiberg), cf. G. J. Toomer, *Ptolemy's Almagest* (London, 1984), 252, n. 53.

[40] Proclus, *Hypotyposis* 1.19–20, 4.98 (10.13–23, 130.16–23 Manitius), cf. O. Neugebauer, *History of Ancient Mathematical Astronomy* 1 (Berlin, 1975), 104, n. 4.

[41] J. Zech, *Astronomische Untersuchungen über die wichtigeren Finsternisse* (Leipzig, 1853), 38, 53–55.

[42] Oppolzer, *Canon der Finsternisse* (1887), 150–51: Blatt Nr. 75 = *Canon of Eclipses* (1962), 150–51: Chart 75.

Nearly fifty years after Zech, Oppolzer's pupil Friedrich Ginzel devised an apologetic strategy designed to save Ammianus' credit. He argued that the most easterly Roman troops, who were in the vicinity of Nisibis in 360, may have seen a small partial eclipse at sunrise and that this was combined with reports that later arrived from Persia that there the sun had been completely darkened and stars observed to come out.[43] Otto Seeck grasped the straw offered by Ginzel without appreciating the real difficulty: he postulated that Ammianus based his "description" of the eclipse on a written source that drew on the report of an eyewitness who had seen the eclipse in the Persian Empire.[44] Although this theory became canonical,[45] and Ginzel's explanation has been hailed as probably definitive,[46] it plainly will not do. First, Ammianus always uses the phrase *Eoi tractus* to designate the eastern parts of the Roman Empire, not territory still further east (cf. 28.1.1; 30.2.9, 4.8).[47] Second, he states emphatically that the stars were visible for hours on end, from dawn to midday. In fact, even if some of the planets and the brightest stars may have been briefly visible during the eclipse of 28 August 360, the sky was never anywhere dark enough for "the stars" to be visible at any time. Ammianus' gross and crass misstatements about the date, nature, and duration of the eclipse of 360 show that what he says is no kind of factual "report" at all.

What is the explanation? It must be sought, not through *Quellenforschung*, but in the historian's imagination. Ammianus was in a position to know that there were two solar eclipses in 360, whether or not anyone in the Roman world saw either of them. For ancient astronomers could predict both solar and lunar eclipses accurately: the Stoic interlocutor in Cicero's *De Natura Deorum* boasts that the exact dates and extent are known and predicted for all fu-

[43] F. K. Ginzel, *Spezieller Kanon der Sonnen- und Mondfinsternisse für das Ländergebiet der klassischen Altertumswissenschaften und den Zeitraum von 900 vor Chr. bis 600 nach Chr.* (Berlin, 1899), 212–13.

[44] O. Seeck, *Hermes* 41 (1906), 537–38: "so genau und mit so reichem Detail geschildert . . . , wie es nur ein Augenzeuge dieser unheimlichen Erscheinung konnte . . . Die Beobachtungen, die er mitteilt, konnte man nur tief im Inneren des Perserreiches machen"; *Regesten* (1919), 208: "Die Schilderung bei Amm. 20.3.1 muss aus dem Perserreiche stammen."

[45] Hence the confident dismissal of the problems by A. Demandt, *Abh. Mainz*, Geistes- und Sozialwiss. Kl. 1970, 501: "beheben sich die Schwierigkeiten . . . , wenn wir einen Beobachtungsort in Mittelpersien annehmen."

[46] D. J. Schove, *Chronology of Eclipses and Comets A.D. 1–1000* (Woodbridge, 1984), 58. The successive discussions by R. R. Newton, *Ancient Astronomical Observations and the Accelerations of the Earth and the Moon* (Baltimore, 1970), 118; *Medieval Chronicles and the Rotation of the Earth* (Baltimore and London, 1972), 537; *The Moon's Acceleration and its Physical Origins*, 1 (Baltimore, 1979), 385–86, are second-hand and disregard the problems raised by Zech: nevertheless, Newton feels compelled to conclude that "this record remains a mystery" (469).

[47] Similarly *orbis Eous* and *partes Eoae*: see the passages listed by Viansino, *Lexicon* 1.472.

ture time;[48] Marinus records that during Proclus' lifetime *hemerographoi* predicted an eclipse that occurred a year after the philosopher's death;[49] and Ammianus' contemporary, the Alexandrian astronomer Theon, used the partial solar eclipse of 16 June 364 to illustrate how observation confirmed the calculation of Ptolemy's *Handy Tables*.[50]

Ammianus reproduces a standard literary account of a total eclipse, which is an imaginative reconstruction, not a report derived from observation.[51] The eclipse has a clear function in Ammianus' narrative, for it intervenes between the fall of Ursicinus and the ascent of Julian. Hence it has been argued that, although the context may be false, the historian can be pardoned for following a literary convention whereby solar and lunar eclipses accompany dramatic reversals of fortune, important battles, and the deaths of rulers.[52]

In such cases, accurate chronology is often disregarded in order to synchronize celestial and terrestrial events. The Battle of Zama in 202 B.C., in which Scipio defeated Hannibal and won Mediterranean hegemony for Rome, was preceded by an eclipse of the sun according to Zonaras, presumably repeating Cassius Dio, and followed by an eclipse according to Livy: for astronomical reasons, Livy's eclipse, which he includes among the prodigies of the consular year 202/1 B.C., must be that of 6 May 203, Zonaras' that of 19 October 202.[53] Eunapius, the contemporary of Ammianus, produced a solar eclipse during the Battle of the Frigidus on 5–6 September 394:[54] presumably he simply transferred the total eclipse of the sun on 20 November 393, which two chronicles register under the correct consular year,[55] to a date at which no eclipse can possibly have occurred.[56] The passing of rulers, too, was

---

[48] Cicero, *ND* 2.153: soli enim ex animantibus nos astrorum ortus obitus cursusque cognovimus, ab hominum genere finitus est dies mensis annus, defectiones solis et lunae cognitae praedictaeque in omne posterum tempus, quae quantae quando futurae sint.

[49] Marinus, *Vita Procli* 37. L-S-J[9] 771, which cites only this passage for *hemerographos*, misleadingly glosses as "one who keeps a diary." The word seems to occur elsewhere only in Olympiodorus' commentary on Aristotle's *Meteora* 342 b 33 (ed. W. Stüve, *Commentaria in Aristotelem Graeca* 12.2 [Berlin, 1900], 50.21), where *hemerographoi* seek an explanation for the phases of the planet Mercury.

[50] A. Tihon, *Bulletin de l'Institut historique belge de Rome* 46–47 (1976–1977), 35–79.

[51] F. Boll, *RE* 6 (1909), 2349–50: "mehr schematisch als aus Beobachtung," an annular eclipse described as if it were a total eclipse; 2363: "mancherlei Übertreibungen."

[52] A. Demandt, *Abh. Mainz*, Geistes- und Sozialwiss. Kl. 1970, 495–507.

[53] Zonaras 9.14; Livy 30.38.8: Cumis orbis minui visus est et pluit lapideo imbri, cf. F. K. Ginzel, *Handbuch der mathematischen und technischen Chronologie*, 2 (Leipzig, 1911), 217, 529.

[54] Zosimus 4.58.3.

[55] *Chr. min.* 1.299; 2.63, cf. Ginzel, *Kanon* (1899), 273–74; Boll, *RE* 6 (1909), 2363.

[56] The nearest new moon appeared near midnight during the night of 12–13 September: even the Elder Pliny could state clearly that a solar eclipse can occur only on either the first or the last day of a lunar month (*Nat. Hist.* 2.13).

announced in the heavens: according to Dio, the death of Augustus was fore-told by a solar eclipse, even though the only solar eclipse to which he can re-fer occurred on 15 February A.D. 17, two and a half years after Augustus died.[57] Similarly, the evangelist Luke, who expressly puts himself in the tradition of Greek historiography, produces an eclipse of the sun while Jesus hung on the cross.[58] The corresponding passages of Mark and Matthew merely have a mys-terious darkness, whose cause may be meteorological.[59] Origen knew (and the pious held it to his discredit) that no solar eclipse can have occurred dur-ing the crucifixion, since the gospels state the day as 14 or 15 Nisan, when the moon was on the opposite side of the earth from the sun.[60]

The plea that Ammianus merely repeats a commonplace fails to exculpate an author who parades his technical knowledge of astronomy in the excursus that immediately follows the notice of the eclipse. The historian could have discovered from Ptolemy, whom he names (20.3.4), how to verify the correct date,[61] or he could have consulted a list of actual and predicted eclipses pro-duced by a competent astronomer or professional astrologer.[62] The hypothe-sis that perhaps best explains what Ammianus has written is that he knew from the calculations of others that a total eclipse occurred on 4 March 360: since this eclipse was visible only in the southern hemisphere, the whole of his "re-port" is imaginative fiction.

---

[57] Dio 56.29.2–3, cf. Ginzel, *Handbuch*, 2 (1911), 531.

[58] Luke 1.1, 23.44.

[59] Mark 15.33; Matthew 27.45.

[60] Origen, *Comm. ser.* 134 (*PG* 13.1782 = E. Klostermann and U. Treu, *Origenes Werke* 11.2² [*GCS*, 1976], 274–78); Demandt, *Abh. Mainz*, Geistes- und Sozialwiss. Kl. 1970, 482–84.

[61] Besides compiling his *Handy Tables*, Ptolemy devoted Book VI of the *Almagest* to eclipses: Toomer, *Ptolemy's Almagest* (1984), 275–320.

[62] Three papyri relating to the prediction of eclipses (*P. Oxy.* 4137, 4138, 4138a) are to be published by A. Jones, *Astronomical Papyri from Oxyrhynchus* (*Memoirs of the American Philosophi-cal Society*, forthcoming): the first has a list of predicted lunar eclipses, including eclipses of A.D. 56–57, the other two deal with the prediction of eclipses in general.

[X]

ENEMIES, ANIMALS, AND STEREOTYPES

Ammianus discloses his likes and dislikes of individuals with unusual frankness and directness.[1] When he held a strong opinion of someone, he could express this opinion in vivid and unforgettable language that often evokes a precise visual image. Thus his account of the arrest of Peter Valvomeres strikes the reader as remarkable above all for its palpable visual qualities (Chapter II). Peter was "a very tall, red-haired man towering above the rest" who replied to the urban prefect's question with truculence, was tortured and released, but later executed for raping a virgin of good birth (15.7.4−5). Many other individuals receive an equally sharp delineation from Ammianus, even if, like Peter Valvomeres, they appear in his narrative only once and briefly. Ammianus usually delivers himself of a firm moral verdict on their conduct or character; and when he condemns, as he does in the majority of cases, he often employs animal imagery to reinforce his verdict.

An excellent example of the sharp characterization of a historical actor who makes a single brief appearance in the *Res Gestae* is Ammianus' presentation of Mercurius, the "Count of Dreams" (*comes somniorum*), who pursued those who had supported the usurpation of Magnentius. Mercurius would frequently insinuate himself into dinner parties and other gatherings "like a fierce dog which conceals its savage disposition by wagging its tail": he used "his poisonous skill" to turn reports of dreams into confessions of crimes that he then carried to the credulous emperor (15.3.5). Similar vignettes introduce many other characters who either appear once in a particular episode that

---

[1] For an anthology of Ammianus' portraits and an analysis of the "categories of asessment" that he employs, see Drexler, *Ammianstudien* (1974), 38−65, 13−19.

Ammianus develops at length or play a part in his main narrative. Book XXVIII describes a series of trials for adultery and magic in Rome, in which Maximinus of Sopianae played a large role. He is introduced as follows:

> Maximinus . . . was born in the utmost obscurity at Sopianae, a town in Valeria. His father was a clerk in the governor's office who was descended from the Carpi whom Diocletian transferred to Pannonia after they had been expelled from their original home.[2] After a modicum of education in liberal studies, an ignoble career as a defense lawyer, and administering Corsica and also Sardinia, Maximinus became governor of Tuscia. From this he was promoted to take charge of the grain supply of Rome, but still retained his provincial governorship because his successor was delayed en route for a long period.
>
> At the start, he conducted himself cautiously out of three considerations. First, there resounded in his ears the prediction of his father, who knew extremely well what the flight and song of significant birds might portend, to the effect that he would reach a high position of state, but then perish by the executioner's sword. Next, having acquired a man from Sardinia who was very skilled in raising evil spirits and eliciting prognostications from the dead and whom he later craftily deceived and killed, so a rumor circulated, he was milder and more amenable as long as this man was alive, for fear of being betrayed. Lastly, while he was still worming his way through inferior posts like a snake lurking underground, he was not yet strong enough to cause the deaths of important people. (28.1.5−7)

The unfairness of this characterization leaps off the page. What has not always been sufficiently realized is that Maximinus' successful career was not unusual for a man of his generation: it reflected the excellence of his education and his talents as a lawyer, both of which Ammianus denigrates, probably unjustly and certainly as a result of a prejudice with a personal basis.[3] Ammianus repeats his description of Maximinus as a "serpent" twice more in his account of the trials at Rome (28.1.33, 41). Other human serpents in the *Res Gestae* are the tyrannical Caesar Gallus (14.7.13), the odious pair Daniel and Barzimeres, who slandered Pap the king of Armenia to Valens (30.1.16−17), the Roman mob confronting the prefect Leontius (15.7.4), and Isaurian brigands (19.13.1). There is a certain repetitiveness about these comparisons to animals. For example, Ammianus detested Arbitio as much as Maximinus, and hence he uses identical language. Arbitio appears in Book XIV as an ardent intriguer among groups of fickle courtiers who wished to destroy the Caesar Gallus

[2] Apparently in 296: *Phoenix* 30 (1976), 176, 187.
[3] J. Szidat, *Historia* 44 (1995), 481−86.

(14.11.2). In Book XV, as he plots against Ursicinus, he is described as an excessively powerful man who was very skilled in entrapping honest men in fatal snares: he was like a snake lurking underground (again *subterraneus serpens*) that watches from its hidden hole for individual passers-by and suddenly attacks them (15.2.4). Such characterizations consistently indicate the historian's dislikes, and they usually give voice to a deep personal animosity, as when Ammianus speaks of lawyers following the scent like Spartan or Cretan hounds until they reach their lairs (30.4.8).[4]

Analysis of Ammianus' use of animal comparisons and similes produces some significant conclusions.[5] Although the soldiers of two legions recently transferred from Gaul bellow like wild beasts when they cannot make their way out of the besieged city of Amida (19.5.2) and Valentinian conducts himself like a *sagax bestia* when he investigates the corrupt administration of the praetorian prefect Probus (30.5.10), Ammianus' animal comparisons usually have a highly negative connotation.[6] When Valentinian fell ill in 367, there was talk of Rusticus Julianus, the *magister memoriae*, as a possible successor, a man eager for human blood like beasts, as he showed when he became proconsul of Africa (27.6.1).[7] The future usurper Procopius hid himself awaiting an opportunity to seize power "like a beast of prey who will jump forth as soon as he sees something that can be caught" (26.6.10). Almost the same words are applied to Valentinus, a native of Valeria in Pannonia, an arrogant fellow, the brother of the wife of Maximinus, "that deadly *vicarius* and later prefect" (Ammianus alludes obliquely to the trials in Rome, which he had just described): exiled to Britain for a serious crime, the evil beast, unable to endure inactivity, plotted against Theodosius, who justifiably had him executed (28.3.4 – 6). Leo, who assisted Maximinus in Rome, was just as bad as his superior: he was "a grave-robbing brigand from Pannonia, slobbering cruelty with an animal grin and no less thirsty for human blood" (28.1.12).

Groups and nations are also compared to wild animals. Both the Isaurian bandits who raided peaceful provinces in 353 and the Germans who were

---

[4] Blockley, *Ammianus* (1975), 183, lists a total of fifty-three passages that use "animal images."

[5] T. E. J. Wiedemann, *Past Perspectives. Studies in Greek and Roman Historical Writing*, ed. I. S. Moxon, J. D. Smart, and A. J. Woodman (Cambridge, 1986), 189–201, cf. Blockley, *Ammianus* (1975), 183–84.

[6] For a list of examples of "savagery and madness," see R. Seager, *Ammianus Marcellinus: Seven Studies in His Language and Thought* (Columbia, Miss., 1986), 54–58.

[7] Julianus' proconsulate is firmly dated to the biennium 371–373: *Phoenix* 39 (1985), 150, 273. Hence the pluperfect *ut ostenderat* has a future reference and an aorist meaning.

about to invade Gaul in 357 were like wild beasts driven by hunger (14.2.2,[8] 16.5.17), and Ammianus states that the bodies of the Huns were so prodigiously deformed and twisted that one would think that they must be two-legged beasts (31.2.2). The Saraceni of the desert were in the habit of swooping down like hawks from afar whenever they espied prey, seizing it and darting away at once (14.4.1). Similarly, the African desert tribe of the Austoriani, arrogant because of success, swooped down upon the unfortunate Tripolitanians during the reign of Valentinian "like fierce birds of prey roused to greater frenzy by the stimulus of blood" (28.6.13): apart from substituting *bestiae* for *rapaces alites*, Ammianus applies virtually the same phrase to the triumphant Goths in 378, who had defeated Valens and were about to attack the city of Adrianople (31.15.2: ut bestiae sanguinis irritamento atrocius efferatae).

Although the historian tends to regard barbarians as at least half bestial by nature, he does not apply animal similes indiscriminately to all non-Romans.[9] Thus he never calls the Persians *bestiae* in his own voice, although he does allow a Roman emperor and the Persian king to trade animal insults. Julian parades starving Persian prisoners before his troops to improve their morale and calls them "ugly she-goats disfigured with filth" (24.8.1): that passage is matched by a letter of Shapur to Constantius that implicitly compares Romans to wild beasts (24.2.8). Christians, however, are not merely bestial, they are worse than animals. Julian invited Christian bishops who disagreed with one another and their congregations, who were also rent by schism, into the imperial palace and urged them to put their quarrels aside and allow everyone complete freedom of religion. He did this so that, as freedom increased their internal dissensions, he would never in future need to fear a united church, since he knew that no wild beasts are so hostile to humans as the majority of Christians are to one another (22.5.4). Specific proof of the general charge comes in Book XXVII. When Viventius was prefect, the see of Rome fell vacant. A contest ensued between Damasus and Ursinus, who both had a passionate ambition to seize the position of bishop that surpassed human bounds. The fighting between their supporters forced Viventius to withdraw to a villa outside the city and left one hundred and thirty-seven corpses in the Basilica of Sicininus on a single day (27.3.12–13). The slaughter (if not Ammianus' precise total for the number of dead) is confirmed by a contemporary document.[10]

---

[8] The word *bestiae*, absent in both V and Seyfarth's text, should be added before *fame*, as Valesius proposed: Ammianus is quoting Cicero, *Pro Cluentio* 67: ut etiam bestiae fame monitae plerumque ad eum locum ubi pastae sunt aliquando revertantur.

[9] Wiedemann, *Past Perspectives* (1986), 196–201.

[10] The writer of the account of *Quae gesta sunt inter Liberium et Felicem episcopos* (*Collectio Avellana* 1) alleges that the supporters of Damasus invaded a basilica and killed 160 on the spot and

As a vehicle for conveying his opinion of individuals, Ammianus uses racial or cultural stereotypes as well as animal comparisons. The *locus classicus* for such stereotyping in a serious historian is Cassius Dio on Caracalla, the son of Septimius Severus and Julia Domna, who was born at Lyon: "Antoninus belonged to three races, and he possessed none of their virtues at all, but combined in himself all their vices: the fickleness, cowardice and recklessness of Gaul, the harshness and cruelty of Africa, and the slyness of Syria, from whence he came on his mother's side."[11] Ammianus is never so explicit. Yet regional and national characteristics were a staple of ancient astrology and physiognomonics,[12] and reasoning and prejudices similar to those of Dio lie behind many of his delineations of character. The government of Valentinian was largely an administration of men from Pannonia, who were regarded as irretrievably uncouth and uncultured.[13] Ammianus notes that it was Pannonian officers who carried Valentinian's election as Augustus in 364 and that the new emperor gave Pannonians preferment (26.1.5, 5.3). One of Valentinian's earliest appointments was Ursacius as *magister officiorum*: he was a crude Dalmatian, a cruel and irascible man (26.4.4, 5.7). The phrase *Delmatae crudo* reflects a cultural stereotype that was doubtless prevalent in Rome.[14] But what of Pannonians whom Ammianus for personal reasons admired? His presentation of Viventius, who belongs to this category, is subtle. Viventius is introduced in Book XXVI as a native of Siscia, which happens to be a town in Pannonia, but Ammianus here suppresses any mention of his ethnic origin as a Pannonian (26.4.4). Viventius reappears later in Book XXVII as *praefectus urbi*, and Ammianus takes the opportunity to repudiate the stereotype explicitly by commending him as "an upright and wise Pannonian, under whose quiet and peaceful administration there was general plenty" (27.3.11). The phrase *integer et prudens Pannonius* was surely intended to sound paradoxical.

In a text as poorly transmitted as that of Ammianus, geographical names, like numerals,[15] are particularly vulnerable to corruption. Hence the historian's

---

wounded many others, some of whom later died—without suffering any losses themselves (*CSEL* 35.3.18–21).

[11] Dio 78(77).6.1a (3.379.17–380.3 Boissevain). Maurice devoted Book XIV of his *Strategikon* to the "Characteristics and Tactics of Various Peoples" (trans. G. T. Dennis [Philadelphia, 1984], 113–20).

[12] T. Barton, *Ancient Astrology* (London/New York, 1994), 179–85.

[13] Alföldi, *Conflict* (1952), 13–27; Matthews, *Aristocracies* (1975), 32–55.

[14] Alföldi, *Conflict* (1952), 96–124, a chapter with the title "The Late Classical Ideal of Culture in Conflict with the Illyrian Military Spirit."

[15] On corrupt numerals (and names of months) in Ammianus, see Appendix 7; on the lamentable state in which his text has been transmitted, Appendix 1.

presentation of character as partly dependent on geographical origin cannot be documented properly. Two examples will illustrate how the condition in which the text of the *Res Gestae* has survived clouds an exact understanding of Ammianus' presentation of individuals.

In Book XV, Paul "the Chain" is introduced as "a native of Spain, with a smooth inscrutable face and an extraordinary capacity for scenting hidden perils" (14.5.1). The paradosis has *ortus in Hispania glaber quidam*, and Richard Bentley emended to *coluber quidam* ("a certain serpent").[16] Clark printed Bentley's emendation, but Seyfarth rightly reinstates the transmitted reading.[17] In Book XV, however, according to the manuscripts and editors, Paul and Mercurius are said to be instigators of evil in the state, the one a Persian, the other from Dacia (15.3.4: hic origine Persa, ille natus in Dacia). In his critical apparatus, Clark registered his own emendation of *Dacia* to *Baetica* to bring this passage into conformity with the earlier one, since the *Passion of Artemius*, drawing on the lost ecclesiastical history of Philostorgius, confirms that Paul was indeed a Spaniard.[18] The emendation seems eminently reasonable. Yet the transmitted *in Dacia* is printed by all editors of Ammianus, including Clark himself. What is significant is that no one would ever have questioned the reading *in Dacia*, had not the earlier passage and evidence external to Ammianus stated that Paul's origin was Spain, not Dacia. The fact that the reading *in Dacia* must be wrong unless Ammianus has contradicted himself suggests caution in dealing with other geographical names in his text.[19]

According to one fifteenth-century manuscript and Bentley, firmly supported by Adolf Kiessling,[20] the *quaestor* Montius, who was lynched in Antioch in 354, was "an African, but inclined to mildness" (14.7.12: Afer quidem, sed ad lenitatem propensior), unlike most of his compatriots who were notorious for their cruelty.[21] But the ninth-century manuscript, which is here the sole independent witness to the text, has *afen*, and Seyfarth prints the emendation *acer*, which he attributes to Gronovius and which the recent English translators accept. With this emendation, Ammianus characterizes Montius as "a man of excitable disposition, but not given to extremes," which seems too

---

[16] Bentley's conjecture, in the margin of his copy of Gronovius' edition (Leiden, 1693), was reported by K. Zangemeister, *Rhein. Mus.*, N.F. 33 (1878), 470.

[17] In favor of *glaber*, L. Karau and I. Ulmann, *Klio* 48 (1967), 234–35.

[18] *Passio Artemii* 21 = Philostorgius, *HE* 7.6a–7a.

[19] It is relevant here that all seven personal names in 28.4.6 are indisputably corrupt (Appendix 1).

[20] A. Kiessling, *Jahrb. für class. Phil.* 103 (1871), 499; Zangemeister, *Rhein. Mus.*, N.F. 33 (1878), 471.

[21] See, Dio 78(77).6.1a (quoted at n. 11); *HA, Sev.* 13.8: horum igitur tantorum ac tam illustrium virorum . . . interfector ab Afris ut deus habetur.

tame for a writer who is usually so pointed and incisive. Moreover, there is evidence outside Ammianus that Montius' origin must be sought in the Greek East. The *quaestor* should probably be identifed with the cultivated "Montius, best of proconsuls" to whom Libanius dedicated his hypotheses of Demosthenes' orations, and whom he clearly implies to be a Greek speaker who also has an enviable command of Latin.[22] The friend of Libanius was related to, perhaps even the father of, Calliopius who entered the Senate of Constantinople before 360.[23] It could be, therefore, that the transmitted *afen* conceals an eastern provincial or ethnic designation: Montius could, for example, have been a Paphlagonian, like the philosopher and orator Themistius.[24] For Paphlagonians had been a butt for literary ridicule ever since Aristophanes put the Athenian politician Cleon on the stage as a Paphlagonian slave.[25]

The origin of the historian's attitude toward a specific individual can often be discovered in or deduced from his text. Even though two are missing in a large lacuna in Book XXIX (Appendix 8), the *praefecti urbis* who are registered in the extant text of the *Res Gestae* provide an appropriate sample for estimating how far personal and religious bias, which often may have been only semiconscious or even subconscious, hovers behind Ammianus' verdicts on individuals.[26]

Either personal knowledge or an instinctive sympathy for pagans (sometimes both) can be discerned behind most of the favorable protraits in this group. Leontius was an easterner and a Christian.[27] Constantius appointed him prefect in 355 to enforce his religious policies in Rome, specifically to coerce the recalcitrant bishop Liberius (15.7.6–10).[28] Leontius had come to Antioch as *quaestor sacri palatii* of Gallus while Ammianus was there (14.11.4). He may well be the son of Domitius Leontius, the praetorian prefect of Constantius in the early 340s, who probably came from Berytus, and may have aided Ammianus' career (Chapter VI). A sympathetic assessment of his character introduces his prefecture. Leontius showed himself an excellent judge, who "heard cases promptly and decided them impartially, and he was of a

---

[22] R. Förster, *Libanii Opera omnia* 8 (Leipzig, 1905), 600, cf. *PLRE* 1.535.

[23] Libanius, *Ep.* 220, 214, cf. O. Seeck, *Die Briefe des Libanius* (*Texte und Untersuchungen* 30, 1906), 99; *PLRE* 1.174–75.

[24] Vanderspoel, *Themistius* (1995), 31–38.

[25] Aristophanes, *Knights* 2 etc.; Lucian, *Alexander* 9, 17, 45; Libanius, *Orat.* 1.85 ("three Paphlagonians, brothers in everything—character, ignorance, insolence and corpulence"); Palladas, *Anth. Pal.* 11.340, where "the Paphlagonian" means "Cleon" and perhaps designates Themistius.

[26] For full details of the careers of the prefects, see Chastagnol, *Fastes* (1962), 139–93, with the modifications noted in Chapter IV and Appendix 8.

[27] Epiphanius, *Panarion* 71.1.1–5, cf. *L'Église et l'empire au IVᵉ siècle* (*Entretiens sur l'Antiquité Classique* 34, 1989), 314–15.

[28] *Phoenix* 46 (1992), 256–61.

kindly nature, though some thought him severe and too much inclined to condemn in order to preserve his authority" (15.7.1).

Ampelius, too, was personally known to Ammianus before he became *praefectus urbis* under Valentinian. The notice of his prefecture reviews his long career. A native of Antioch, Ampelius had been *magister officiorum* and had held two proconsulates (28.4.3): inscriptions and the Theodosian Code identify the proconsulates as those of Achaea in 359–360 and of Africa in 364–365.[29] He was a pleasure seeker who, although capable of occasional severity, preferred to court popularity: he decreed that taverns should not open nor cooked food be sold before the fourth hour of the day, but allowed himself to be persuaded not to enforce it (28.4.4).

Viventius, who is commended as an "honest and wise Pannonian" when he became *praefectus urbi* in 365 (27.3.11), had previously, as *quaestor sacri palatii* in 364, conducted an examination of friends of the emperor Julian who had been accused of using secret magic to make Valentinian and Valens ill (26.4.4). The honesty that Ammianus praises must have helped to produce the favorable outcome that he records: not a shred of evidence was found for the existence of a plot.[30]

Julian's appointees, Maximus and Apronianus, naturally receive a favorable presentation. Julian appointed Maximus at Naissus in the autumn of 361 in preference to Symmachus, who was his senior, because he was the son of the sister of Vulcacius Rufinus: in his term the food supply was abundant and the formerly frequent riots of the populace ceased (21.12.24). Apronianus was appointed in Antioch in January 363 (23.1.4). On his journey to Rome he lost an eye through illness: blaming this loss on sorcery, he took stern measures against poisoners and sorcerers. He was an honest and severe prefect, under whom there was such a steady abundance of supplies that, contrary to normal custom, no one even muttered a complaint (26.3.1–3, 6).

Equally favorable is the presentation of *praefecti urbis* who were demonstratively pagan. Under Tertullus there was a shortage of grain that provoked serious riots. But the shortage was not Tertullus' fault, and he solved the problem: because the arrival of the grain fleet from Africa was delayed by adverse winds and rough seas, he went to Ostia and sacrificed to Castor and Pollux, at which the storm subsided, the ships sailed into port, and the granaries were filled (19.10). Symmachus, who succeeded Apronianus in 364, was a man of outstanding learning and modesty: during his prefecture, the holy city enjoyed unusual peace and plenty, and he restored a magnificent and solid bridge. Un-

---

[29] *PLRE* 1.56–57, Ampelius 3; T. D. Barnes, *Phoenix* 39 (1985), 152, 273; *CP* 82 (1987), 215–16; M. Heil, *ZPE* 108 (1995), 162–65.

[30] On this episode, see now T. M. Banchich, *Historia* (forthcoming).

fortunately, the people did not show proper gratitude: some years later (probably in 375) they burned down his beautiful house in Trastevere (27.3.3−4). Praetextatus also distinguished himself as prefect. His many acts of honesty and uprightness, for which he had been famous since his youth, earned him the unusual distinction of being feared by the citizens without losing their affection. His support of truth and justice quieted the riots caused by Christian quarrels, and his exile of Ursinus, the rival of Damasus, produced profound peace.

Praetextatus was a scrupulously impartial judge, and he took a number of salutary measures: he removed projecting galleries, he standardized weights to ensure fair dealing, and he demolished the walls of private houses that had encroached on adjoining temples (27.9.8−10). Claudius, the last *praefectus urbi* to be registered in the *Res Gestae*, was also a zealous pagan: he was a *quindecimvir sacris faciundis* and he appears to have performed a taurobolium as prefect.[31] Ammianus notes that his prefecture was marked by a flood of the River Tiber. But no riots ensued and Claudius restored many old buildings, among them the Porticus Boni Eventus close to the temple of the same deity (29.6.17−19).

It may be significant that Ammianus makes no explicit allusion to the paganism of either Symmachus or Praetextatus, which stands on record elsewhere.[32] In 384, shortly before Ammianus wrote, Symmachus' son, the orator Symmachus, had led an embassy to the young Valentinian in Milan, which vainly requested the restoration of the Altar of Victory in the senate-house,[33] and Praetextatus had died in December as consul designate for 385.[34]

In contrast to these *praefecti urbis*, two noble prefects receive a distinctly hostile presentation. Ammianus introduces Memmius Vitrasius Orfitus, who was prefect twice (from December 353 to summer 355 and again from spring 357 to spring 359), as a man who conducted himself insolently as if his power were greater than it really was, and he stresses that frequent and serious riots marked his prefecture (14.6.1). Orfitus could doubtless trace his ancestry back to the Antonine aristocracy:[35] more relevant to his long tenure of the urban prefecture is the fact, which Ammianus does not mention, that Orfitus appears to

[31] *ILS* 4147 (Rome, dated 19 July 374).

[32] Symmachus was a *pontifex maior* and a *quindecimvir sacris faciundis* (*ILS* 1257), whereas Praetextatus held many priesthoods (*ILS* 1259) and was later remembered as *sacrorum omnium praesul* (Macrobius, *Sat.* 1.17.1).

[33] On this famous episode, see Matthews, *Aristocracies* (1975), 203−11; N. B. McLynn, *Ambrose of Milan. Church and Court in a Christian Capital* (Berkeley, 1994), 151−52, 166−68.

[34] Symmachus, *Rel.* 12.4.

[35] As possible consular ancestors in the second century, note C. Memmius Fidus Iulius Albus, cos. suff. 191 or 192 (*PIR*² M 462), M. Gavius Orfitus, cos. ord. 165 (*PIR*² G 105), and T. Pomponius Proculus Vitrasius Pollio, cos. II 176, who married into the Antonine dynasty (*PIR*¹ P 558). Chastagnol, *Fastes* (1962), 140, makes Orfitus a *novus homo*.

have married into the imperial family.[36] His predecessor in the management of political affairs in Rome after the usurpation of Magnentius was another imperial relative, Naeratius Cerealis, the uncle of Gallus Caesar.[37]

The picture of C. Ceionius Rufius Volusianus *signo* Lampadius, urban prefect in 365–366, is particularly hostile (27.3.5–10). Ammianus begins with a stinging denunciation: he was so vain that he was upset if he was not praised for his unique skill in spitting. Although Ammianus admits that Lampadius was "sometimes strict and honest," the rest of his notice is equally hostile. The most obvious manifestation of Lampadius' vanity, according to the historian, was that as prefect he put his name on public buildings throughout the city claiming to have built rather than restored them. Moreover, frequent riots compelled him to withdraw to the Milvian Bridge, and he tried to avoid paying for the materials used in his construction and repair of buildings. Ammianus digresses to bring up a foolish act of spectacular liberality that showed Volusianus' contempt for the people of Rome. When he was praetor long before, presumably late in the reign of Constantine, he summoned some poverty-stricken beggars from the Vatican and gave them great wealth. The parallel complaint of Eunapius, who alleges that Constantine wasted public money on useless buildings that soon collapsed,[38] suggests that these beggars from the Vatican are Christian clerics who received a large donation for the great new church dedicated to Saint Peter.[39] Volusianus' wife Caecinia Lolliana is known to have been a priestess of Isis, and their son commemorated his *taurobolium* in a dedication to Cybele and Attis on 23 May 390.[40] Yet that does not exclude the possibility that the prefect had been a Christian under Constantine, when it would have helped his career.[41]

Whether or not Ammianus' intense dislike of Volusianus had a religious dimension, it certainly had a personal basis. Ten years before Volusianus became *praefectus urbi*, he had been praetorian prefect in Gaul, a fact to which Ammi-

---

[36] *From Eusebius to Augustine* (Aldershot, 1994), VII. 11, n. 7; *JRS* 85 (1995), 144; Alan Cameron, *JRA* 9 (1996), 295–301.

[37] Ammianus' obituary of Gallus notes that Cerialis was his uncle (14.11.27): his prefecture, which ran from 26 September 352 to 8 December 353 (*Chr. min.* 1.67) will have been registered in the lost Book XIII.

[38] Zosimus 2.32.1.

[39] The church was under construction in the 330s: see C. Piétri, *Roma Christiana: Recherches sur l'église de Rome, son organisation, sa politique, son idéologie, de Miltiade à Sixte III (311–440)* (Rome, 1976), 51–64; T. D. Barnes, *Constantine* (1981), 310, n. 61.

[40] *CIL* 6.512 = *ILS* 4154. On the role of Lampadius and his family in the late-fourth-century revival of the *taurobolium*, see N. McLynn, *Phoenix* 50 (1996), 326–28, who appears to assume that Ammianus alludes to the Vatican Phrygianum, not to St. Peter's.

[41] Constantine's preference for Christians in the highest offices is documented in *JRS* 85 (1995), 136–47.

anus draws explicit attention when introducing his urban prefecture (27.3.5: ex praefecto praetorio). During his tenure of this earlier office, according to Ammianus, there were rumors that he, together with Eusebius, the former *comes rei privatae*, and Aedesius, the former *magister memoriae*, had suborned the *actuarius* Dynamius to forge the letter that caused the unfortunate Silvanus to rebel (15.5.3: subornatore et conscio, ut iactavere rumores incerti, Lampadio praefecto praetorio etc.). Ammianus presents Silvanus as a plain soldier and an honest man unable to cope with the intrigues at the court of Constantius, just like Ursicinus, who also had been cheated of the just reward of his untiring labors (15.5.28). The fact that Ammianus was committed to hostility toward the enemies of Silvanus and Ursicinus must be relevant to his treatment of Volusianus.

The longest and most detailed portrait of an individual other than an emperor is that of Sex. Petronius Probus, four times praetorian prefect and consul in 371, who had died very recently at the time of writing (27.11).[42] Probus was a Christian of noble lineage, whose father and paternal grandfather had both been ordinary consuls (in 341 and 322, respectively).[43] Shortly after holding the ordinary consulate himself in 371 (not recorded by Ammianus), Probus married the great heiress Anicia Faltonia Proba, thus becoming by default the head of the clan of the Anicii: hence he was not only *nobilitatis culmen*, but more specifically *Anicianae domus culmen*, a man whose power Ausonius proclaimed in 374 to be greater than that of anyone except the three reigning Augusti.[44]

Probus, who came from Verona, was lauded in his lifetime by the grateful inhabitants of the province Venetia and Histria for his learning, eloquence, skillful administration, moderation and devotion to the welfare of those whom he governed.[45] And after his death, Claudian's panegyric on his young sons, who held the ordinary consulate together in 395, secured his reputation for posterity.[46] In the chorus of praise for Probus, there are only two dissenting voices. One is Jerome, whose *Chronicle* noted that as prefect of Illyricum in 372 Probus "destroyed the provinces which he governed by the most unfair

[42] For Probus' career, see *PLRE* 1.736–40, Probus 5; Alan Cameron, *JRS* 75 (1985), 164–82; on the date of his death, J. F. Matthews, *Historia* 16 (1967), 388; *Ammianus* (1989), 22, 480 n. 27; T. D. Barnes, *AJP* 111 (1990), 418; on Ammianus' portrait of him, W. Seyfarth, *Klio* 52 (1970), 411–25; Drexler, *Ammianstudien* (1974), 65–78; M. B. McCoy, *Ancient World* 11 (1985), 101–6.

[43] Averil Cameron, *The Later Roman Empire A.D. 284–430* (Cambridge, Mass., 1993), 73, bizarrely turns Probus into a "pagan aristocrat" so that she can argue that Ammianus was "relatively unconcerned about religious matters, capable of being equally scathing about pagans and Christians alike."

[44] *ILS* 1265, 1267; Ausonius, *Ep.* 16.2.16–18.

[45] *ILS* 1265 (Verona).

[46] Excellently edited and elucidated by W. Taegert, *Claudius Claudianus: Panegyricus dictus Olybrio et Probino consulibus* (Zetemata 85, 1988), cf. *AJP* 111 (1990), 414–19.

exaction of tribute before they were devastated by the barbarians."[47] The other is Ammianus, who introduces Probus at great length on his appointment as praetorian prefect of Illyricum to replace Vulcacius Rufinus, who died in office in 368:

> Probus was known for his high birth, political influence and vast riches to the Roman world, in almost every part of which he owned widely scattered estates. (I refrain from expressing an opinion on whether they were acquired honestly or not.)[48] Some as it were double Fortune, as the poets depict her, carried him on her swift wings and displayed him now as a doer of good who promoted friends to high office, but sometimes as a dangerous schemer who wrought harm because of bloodthirsty grudges. Although he enjoyed enormous power as long as he lived, by bestowing gifts and holding one office after another without interruption, he was alternately timid towards those who resisted and haughty towards the timid,[49] so that when he felt confident, he hectored in the elevated style of tragedy but, whenever he was fearful, he surpassed any comic actor in his groveling. And just as the race of fishes cannot breathe for long on dry ground, so he began to droop without the prefectures which he was compelled to hold by the quarrels of his countless dependents who were always engaged in crime because of their immense greed and who immersed their master in public life so that they might achieve their multifarious ends with impunity. (27.11.1–3)

Ammianus barely conceals his hatred of Probus. He questions whether his vast inherited wealth (*patrimonia sparsa*) was honestly acquired or not: the phrase *non iudicioli est nostri* might sound judicious, but it raises gratuitous suspicions. Out of office Probus was like a fish out of water gasping its life away; in office, he lavished benefits on his criminally rapacious dependents. Ammianus could trust his readers to identify the *familiae ingentes* of Probus as the Christian Anicii, whom he had blamed for the corruption that permeated the body politic in

[47] Jerome, *Chronicle* 246[f] Helm. Some manuscripts substitute the name of Equitius, consul in 374, who was *magister militum* in Illyricum while Probus was prefect (*PLRE* 1.282, Equitius 2), for that of Probus himself: the change is both deliberate and from a contemporary hand, though perhaps not from Jerome himself, cf. T. Mommsen, *Ges. Schr.* 7 (Berlin, 1909), 604–05.

[48] The precise nuance of the words *iuste an secus non est iudicioli nostri* is hard to define. Rolfe's "whether justly or unjustly is not a question for my humble opinion" certainly comes closer than Hamilton's "whether they were honestly come by or not is not for a man like me to say." But it substitutes a cliché for the preternaturally rare *iudiciolum*, for which *TLL* 7.2.606 registers only this passage and the *Fragmentum Bobiense de nomine et praenomine* (H. Keil, *Grammatici Latini*, 5 [Leipzig, 1868], 561.36: absurde meo iudiciolo).

[49] The transmitted text reads: "interdum timidus ad audaces, contra timidos celsior" (27.11.2). Since Ammianus is describing the typical behavior of an arrogant bully, some correlative to *interdum* (e.g., *modo*) probably needs to be supplied before *contra*, cf. *TLL* 7.2181.

his own day (16.8.13). Ammianus mentions Probus himself only to besmirch his name.[50] On the one hand, he omits Probus' role in the proclamation of the infant Valentinian in 375 (30.10.5).[51] On the other, he emphasizes his role in the torture and execution of Faustinus, the nephew of Viventius, the "honest and wise Pannonian" (27.3.11), which he regarded as unjust (30.5.11–12: Probo spectante negotium).[52]

Against this background, it must be suspected that, like so much else in the *Res Gestae*, Ammianus' portrait of Q. Clodius Hermogenianus Olybrius is subtly and deliberately polemical. His prefecture, Ammianus acknowledges, was quiet and peaceful (28.4.1–2). Olybrius was humane, concerned lest any word or act of his be found harsh. He checked slander, pruned the profits of the treasury, distinguished between right and wrong, and performed his duties capably and with mildness. These good qualities, however, were overshadowed by one grave fault, which, though harmless in itself, was discreditable in the holder of a high office. Olybrius enjoyed luxury and devoted himself almost entirely to the stage and to love affairs, though not of a criminal or incestuous nature. Since Olybrius was known to be a Christian,[53] his *luxus* is likely to represent for Ammianus the *truphe* with which Greek-speaking pagans taunted Christians (Chapters VIII, XIV).

---

[50] Seyfarth, *Klio* 52 (1970), 421–25.

[51] Rufinus, *HE* 11.15, records Probus' role. It was illegal, and usually treasonable, to proclaim a new emperor without consulting any of the surviving members of the imperial college: J. Straub, *Vom Herrscherideal in der Spätantike* (Berlin, 1939), 18–20; *Studien zur Historia Augusta* (*Dissertationes Bernenses* 1.4, 1952), 144–45.

[52] On this passage, see J. Moreau, *Annuaire de l'Institut de Philologie et d'Histoire orientales* 13 (1953), 423–31; W. Seyfarth, *Klio* 46 (1975), 374–78.

[53] *Collectio Avellana* 8–10 (*CSEL* 35.50–52); Prudentius, *Contra Symmachum* 1.554–557—a passage perhaps written c. 385, cf. T. D. Barnes and R. W. Westall, *Phoenix* 45 (1991), 58–61.

[XI]

EMPRESSES AND EUNUCHS

The *Res Gestae* move entirely in a man's world, and their author held entirely conventional views about the place of women in it and about how they ought to behave. Modern studies have reconstructed the historian's picture of women and analyzed their political role, and one is promised on their social and moral significance.[1] The result is distressingly predictable. Ammianus' attitudes toward women are so conventional for his time that they reveal little or nothing about him as an individual. Yet something interesting may emerge if it is asked which women he chooses to include and which to omit in a definable category. For, just as with the male characters in his history (Chapters X, XII, XIII), Ammianus reveals his personal likes and dislikes without inhibition when dealing with the wives of emperors.

Constantina, a daughter of Constantine and the wife of the Caesar Gallus, is introduced at the start of Book XIV, where Ammianus describes Gallus' behavior as emperor in Antioch.[2] The historian speaks of her with undisguised hostility as one who incited her husband to cruelty and excess. Previously married by Constantine to his nephew Hannibalianus,[3] she had the swollen pride of one born into the imperial family: she was a "Fury in mortal form, incessantly adding fuel to her husband's rage, and as thirsty as he for human blood" (14.1.2). Hence the obstinacy of Gallus was increased by the influence

---

[1] L. Jacob-Karau, *Das Bild der Frau in den "Res Gestae" des Ammianus Marcellinus* (Diss. Berlin, 1971); G. Sabbah, *Cognitio Gestorum* (1992), 91–105.

[2] On the political importance of Constantina, especially in the crisis provoked by the usurpation of Magnentius in 350, see B. Bleckmann, *Chiron* 24 (1994), 29–68.

[3] The marriage is also recorded in *Exc. Val.* 1.35; Philostorgius, *HE* 3.22.

of the empress,[4] who was pushing her husband headlong to destruction, although she ought to have tried "by feminine mildness and sensible advice to bring him back to the way of truth and humanity" (14.1.8).

After the opening chapter of Book XIV, Constantina disappears from Ammianus' narrative until she dies of a sudden fever in Bithynia while traveling to the court of Constantius in the hope of mollifying him (14.11.6). But she reappears after her death in a significant context. According to Ammianus, Constantina was so deeply implicated in the misgovernment of her husband that, when Gallus was interrogated after his deposition, he claimed that he had killed most of his victims at her insistence. Ammianus disallows the plea with reference to a story about Alexander the Great, who refused to kill an innocent man at the urging of his mother (14.11.22). But Alexander and his mother provide no real parallel, even by opposition. At the back of Ammianus' mind, it may be suspected, lie two biblical images. The most famous occasion when a man blamed his wife for his own transgression occurred in the Garden of Eden: when questioned by God, Adam blamed Eve with the excuse that he had disobeyed him because the woman offered him the fruit of the tree.[5] But the words of Alexander's reply to Olympias ("ask for another reward, my good mother; no favor can equal the life of a man") evoke rather the execution of John the Baptist to please Herodias.[6]

Eusebia was the second, or more probably the third, wife of Constantius.[7] She makes a number of significant appearances in the *Res Gestae*.[8] After the fall of Gallus she protected Julian (15.2.8), then opposed a proposal to send him to Gaul without the rank of Caesar (15.8.3). Later, because of her own sterility, she induced Julian's wife to drink a potion that ensured that she would miscarry whenever she conceived (16.10.18). Constantius renamed the diocese of Pontus in her honor in 358 (17.7.7). She was the object of jealousy from the wife of Barbatio, who feared that if her husband became emperor he would abandon her for Eusebia who was a woman of outstanding physical beauty (18.3.2). Finally, in the context of Constantius' subsequent marriage

[4] Here, as elsewhere when speaking of Constantina (14.1.3, 9.3) and Eusebia (15.2.8, 8.3, 16.10.18, 18.3.2), Ammianus uses *regina* as the Latin equivalent of *basilissa*, which had long been the normal Greek word for "empress."

[5] Gen. 3.12.

[6] Mark 6.14–29; Matthew 14.1–12.

[7] *PLRE* 1.300–301. Constantius' first wife, whom he married in 335, was a daughter of Julius Constantius, who was assassinated in 337 (Eusebius, *VC* 4.49; Athanasius, *Hist. Ar.* 69.1; Julian, *Ep. ad Ath.* 272d): since an emperor needed heirs, it is unlikely that he remained unmarried for about fifteen years until his marriage to Eusebia circa 352 (Julian, *Orat.* 3, 109ab, 110d).

[8] The differing depictions of Eusebia in ancient writers are compared by N. Aujoulat, *Byzantion* 53 (1983), 78–103, 421–52.

to Faustina, Ammianus notes the death of Eusebia, "the sister of the ex-consuls Eusebius and Hypatius, a woman of outstanding beauty and excellence of character, whose kindness of heart was unaffected by her high rank," who had rescued Julian from danger before he was proclaimed Caesar (21.5.3).

Eusebia was not only the protector of Julian, but also the sister of the man who was later Ammianus' friend and patron. Hypatius was (it seems) the son of Eusebius, a general who held the ordinary consulate in 347, but died before Constantius married his daughter.[9] Hypatius and his brother Eusebius, now the emperor's brothers-in-law, were ordinary consuls together in 359.[10] A dozen years later, while living in Antioch, the brothers were condemned for treason and exiled, though later pardoned. Ammianus praises Hypatius most warmly:

> Among all these my friend Hypatius (*noster Hypatius*) stood out, who deserves praise for his youthful vigor and noble virtues. He was a man of calm and cool judgement, whose honorable and mild character never deviated from the upright. He added glory to the splendor of his ancestors and himself conferred honor on his descendants by his admirable actions in two prefectures. (29.2.16)

When Hypatius was appointed prefect of the city of Rome during the difficult winter of 378–379, he was still in Antioch.[11] But he must have gone to Rome to hold office, and, after a visit to Constantinople in 381,[12] perhaps to pay his respects to Theodosius, he became praetorian prefect of Italy and Illyricum in 382–383.[13] It was surely his friend Hypatius who encouraged Ammianus to come to Rome and who introduced him to Roman society:[14] in what has always been regarded as a transparent piece of autobiography (14.6.19), Ammianus reveals that he was initially welcomed, but then scorned, presumably because he could not win social acceptance for himself, although he was the protégé of an eastern *nobilis*. Ammianus' praise of Eusebia is due to his friendship with her brother as much as to her help of Julian when he was under suspicion in 354–355.

---

[9] *PLRE* 1. 307–8, Eusebius 39.

[10] For their careers, see *PLRE* 1.306–7, Eusebius 40; 448–49, Hypatius 4. However, Ammianus' description of them as *patriciatus columina* (29.2.9) does not suffice to prove that they were created *patricii*.

[11] Libanius, *Orat.* 1.79–80. He is attested in office on 5 April 379 (*CTh* 11.36.26).

[12] Gregory of Nazianzus, *Ep.* 96.

[13] For the evidence relating to this prefecture, see *PLRE* 1.449: it is securely attested from 9 December 382 (*CTh* 11.16.15) to 28 May 383 (*CTh* 2.19.5).

[14] S. Jannacone, *Ammiano Marcellino. Profilo storico-critico* (Naples, 1970), 25. Ammianus could in theory have come to Rome with Hypatius in 378–79 and accompanied him on his visit to Constantinople in 381.

In contrast, the wife of Ammianus' hero Julian receives no praise at all. A few days after his proclamation on 6 November 355, the new Caesar received Helena "the sister of Constantius" in marriage (15.8.18). In 357 Helena went to Rome, where she suffered a miscarriage, having previously given birth in Gaul to a son whom the midwife (so it was alleged) had been bribed to kill by cutting the umbilical cord (16.10.18–19). In 360, when Helena died, Julian sent her body to be buried on the Via Nomentana just outside Rome next to her sister Constantina (21.1.5). That is the sum of what Ammianus has to say about Helena, but he notes that after her death Julian never had sexual relations with any other woman (25.4.2).[15]

Ammianus' account of the year 361 registers Constantius' marriage to Faustina after the death of Eusebia (21.6.4). Moreover, by the time the emperor left Antioch in November, Ammianus notes, his new wife was pregnant: the daughter born after his death subsequently married Gratian (21.16.5). Ammianus never alludes to the wife of either Jovian or Valens, although he names the father-in-law and the infant son of both.[16] Charito and Domnica exerted no political influence, and the name of Jovian's wife is first attested in writers of the ninth century.[17] But Ammianus records the attempt of Procopius in 365 to use the posthumous child of Constantius to lend a spurious legitimacy to his usurpation.[18] Since the widowed Faustina and her infant daughter happened to be in Constantinople, the usurper carried the child, then three years old, in his arms as he proclaimed his kinship to Constantius and Julian (26.7.10, 9.3). As soon as Constantia reached puberty, she was married to Gratian: Ammianus notes the marriage only because the bride was almost captured by barbarians as she was being taken to Gaul for her wedding (29.6.7).

Valentinian is unique among Christian emperors of Rome in that he married for a second time while his first wife was still alive. Christian writers found that embarrassing, and Valentinian's first wife is named by only four authors of late antiquity, who form a very motley collection. Three late chronicles (John Malalas, the Paschal Chronicle, and John of Nikiu) call Valentinian's first wife Marina and allege that she was banished for participating in a fraud-

[15] Julian refers several times in the *Misopogon* to sleeping alone and to his lack of interest in sex (340c, 345cd, 348d, 367b). On Ammianus' praise of his *castitas*, see Chapter VIII, at nn. 26–29.

[16] Lucillianus, whom Jovian appointed *magister equitum et peditum* (25.8.9, 10.11, cf. *PLRE* 1.517–18), and Varronianus, consul with his father in 364 (25.10.11, 17); and Petronius, whom Valens made a *patricius* (26.6.7–9, *PLRE* 1.690–91), and Valentinianus, nicknamed Galates, who was born in 366, consul in 369 and died in 371 (*PLRE* 1.381).

[17] Nicephorus, *Chronicon compendiosum* 104.14 de Boor, translated by Anastasius Bibliothecarius, *Chronographia tripertita* 47.6 de Boor. Domnica, in contrast, is named by the ecclesiastical historians of the fifth century (*PLRE* 1.265).

[18] On Procopius' desperate search for legitimacy, see N. J. E. Austin, *Rivista storica dell'antichità* 2 (1972), 187–94.

ulent property deal.[19] The story looks like an attempt to exculpate Valentinian from any blame attached to discarding her, although it could contain elements of truth. For the ecclesiastical historian Socrates, writing about 440, calls Valentinian's first wife Severa and offers a very different version of why Valentinian married Justina "even though his former wife Severa was still alive." Valentinian (he reports) fell in love with Justina after Severa introduced her to her husband, then married her without expelling Severa from the palace. Moreover, he issued a law, which he published in every city, allowing anyone who wished to have two lawful wives.[20]

The late chronicles have usually been preferred to Socrates and his version of events dismissed as unbelievable.[21] But Socrates does not say that Valentinian issued a law permitting bigamy, as has sometimes been assumed:[22] he not only fails to say that Valentinian's law allowed a man to marry two women at the same time, but he also explicitly calls Severa the emperor's "former wife." What Socrates says is that Valentinian issued a legal ruling that permitted him (and incidentally others) to remarry after divorce.[23] On general grounds, Socrates deserves preference over much later writers. Moreover, the legal bar to his marriage to Justina that Valentinian needed to remove can be identified.[24]

There was no impediment to the marriage on the bride's side. Justina was the daughter of one Justus, who had governed Picenum under Constantius.[25] She has been convincingly identified as a descendant of Constantine,[26] and she had been married to Magnentius as a young girl, so that she had been a widow since 353.[27] Valentinian may have been more interested in her imper-

[19] Malalas 341.1–7 Bonn; *Chronicon Paschale* 559.7–13 Bonn; John of Nikiu, *Chronicle*, trans. R. H. Charles, p. 82.

[20] Socrates, *HE* 4.31.13–17, repeated by Jordanes, *Rom.* 310.

[21] O. Seeck, *Geschichte des Untergangs der antiken Welt* 5 (Berlin, 1913), 431; W. Ensslin, *RE* 14 (1930), 1756–57; A. Nagl, *RE* 7A (1948), 2148. D. Woods, *Ancient Society* 26 (1995), 281–82, 288, n. 53, conjectures that Valentinian may have met Justina at the court of Magnentius. Unfortunately, his argument that Valentinian served under Magnentius, but salvaged his career by a timely defection to Constantius rests on the false assumption that Martin of Tours also served under Magentius because he left the army "by about August 356 at the latest" (282, 284–88): for the correct chronology of Martin's military career (enlistment under Constantius autumn 352, discharge autumn 357), see *Anal. Boll.* 114 (1996), 25–32.

[22] As by Theophanes 56.23–31 de Boor.

[23] A. D. Manfredini, *Atti dell'Accademia Romanistica Costantiniana* 8 (Perugia, 1990), 522–28; A. Arjava, *Women and Law in Late Antiquity* (Oxford, 1996), 180, n. 70.

[24] A similar dispensation allowed Justinian to marry the former stage performer Theodora, who was technically *infamis*: *CJ* 5.4.23 (520–23); Procopius, *Anecdota* 9.51, cf. D. Daube, *Catholic University of America Law Review* 16 (1966–67), 380–89.

[25] Socrates, *HE* 4.31.11–12.

[26] *New Empire* (1982), 44.

[27] Zosimus 4.19.1, 43.1, cf. *PLRE* 1.488–89.

ial pedigree than her beauty or sexual allure, and the recent precedent of Constantina, who had been married first to Hannibalianus (who was killed in 337), then to Gallus in 351 (14.1.2), indicates that her status as a widow did not constitute a legal impediment to her remarriage.

Socrates clearly implies that it was Valentinian's first marriage that constituted the impediment to his union with Justina. How could that be? Unfortunately, the section of the Theodosian Code in which the title *De Repudiis* occurs has not survived in full, and the *Breviarium* of Alaric preserves no law on divorce between a constitution that Constantine addressed to his praetorian prefect Ablabius in 331 and one of Honorius that modified it in 421.[28] Constantine's law is very relevant to Valentinian. Constantine ruled in 331 that a man could divorce his wife only for adultery, sorcery, or procuring, and that a woman could divorce her husband only for murder, sorcery, or robbery of tombs, not for drunkenness, gambling, or whoring. A man who divorced a wife who was not guilty of any of the three specified offenses could not remarry: if he did, the discarded wife could enter his house and seize all the dowry of the second wife to compensate for the wrong done to her.[29] The law, it appears, said nothing about divorce by mutual consent, which continued to be valid without restriction until the sixth century.[30] But the empress Severa was doubtless reluctant to agree to a divorce that entailed the loss of her social position. It follows that Valentinian needed to extend the grounds for nonconsensual divorce to accommodate himself.

The writer known as Ambrosiaster complains that an edict of Julian gave women the power to divorce their husbands that they had previously lacked, with the result that they were now (in the 380s) divorcing their husbands every day.[31] Before Valentinian, therefore, Julian had relaxed the restrictions on divorce that Constantine had introduced, but Ambrosiaster's generalized complaint does little to clarify exactly how he modified the law of 331 and does not exclude the possibility that Jovian partly reinstated Constantine's law after Julian had repealed it or that Julian allowed women as well as men to divorce their spouses for sexual infidelity. Now Augustine refers to a secular law (*lex huius saeculi*) which freely allowed remarriage after divorce (*interveniente repudio*).[32] It seems hard to deny the relevance of this observation, which im-

---

[28] *CTh* 3.16.1–2.

[29] *CTh* 3.16.1. The unusual vocabulary of this law suggests that it may have been drafted by Ablabius himself: J. Evans Grubbs, *Law and Family in Late Antiquity. The Emperor Constantine's Marriage Legislation* (Oxford, 1995), 253–60.

[30] R. S. Bagnall, *Florilegium Columbanum*, ed. K.-L. Selig and R. Somerville (New York, 1987), 41–61; A. Arjava, *Arctos* 22 (1988), 5–21; *Women and Law* (1996), 167–92.

[31] *Quaestiones de vetere et novo testamento* 115.12 (*CSEL* 50.322).

[32] Augustine, *De nuptiis et concupiscentia* 1.10.11 (*PL* 44.420 = *CSEL* 42.223).

plies that Valentinian extended the possible grounds of divorce precisely to allow him to discard his first wife and then to remarry.[33]

Ammianus nowhere names or alludes to Valentinian's first wife, even though another source attributes the proclamation of Gratian as Augustus on 24 August 367 to the insistence of the emperor's mother-in-law, whose name is unknown, and of his wife, who was the mother of his eight-year-old son.[34] He mentions Justina twice, neither time as significant in her own right. Constantianus, who was ambushed and killed in Gaul circa 369, is identified as the brother of Cerealis and Justina (28.2.10). And when Valentinian died suddenly and unexpectedly in November 375, his four-year-old son was summoned to the imperial purple from the villa called Murocincta where he was lodging with his mother (30.10.4). The obituary of Valentinian, however, praises his private life in a way that conveys an oblique and oddly emphatic reference to the emperor's two marriages: "he was entirely chaste in his personal life, both inside and outside the palace; he kept himself unspotted by any taint of immoral desires; he avoided impurity" (30.9.2). This is strong praise for an emperor whom Ammianus criticizes robustly for cruelty, greed, jealousy, and paranoia (30.8).[35] The contrast throws Ammianus' praise of his private life into stronger relief. Moreover, there appears to be a polemical edge in what Ammianus says. He asserts what contemporary Christians would emphatically have denied, had they ventured to express an opinion on Valentinian's change of wives.[36] He surely intended to contradict Christian preachers and moralists who condemned divorce and remarriage.

Tacitus emphasized the baleful influence that powerful imperial women exercised, or were believed to exercise, as mothers, wives, and mistresses.[37] What reader of the *Annales* can forget Livia and her incessant scheming to secure the succession for her son Tiberius? Or the elder Agrippina, fiercely loyal to her

---

[33] Manfredini, *Atti dell'Accademia Romanistica Costantiniana* 8 (1990), 526–28.

[34] *Epitome* 45.4. The dates of Gratian's birth (19 April 359) and proclamation are known from *Descr. cons.* 359.1, 367.2; Socrates, *HE* 4.11.3.

[35] On Ammianus' depiction of Valentinian, see the sceptical assessment by F. Paschoud, *Cognitio Gestorum* (1992), 67–84, who dismisses as a malicious invention the story that the emperor kept two man-eating bears called Gold-dust and Innocence (29.3.9).

[36] Several fourth-century church councils either prohibit or express severe disapproval of remarriage after divorce while the first spouse is alive: Iliberris, Canons 9, 10 (c. 300); 314 Arles, Canon 10; Neocaesarea, Canon 7 (314–25); Laodicea, Canon 1 (341–81); 374 Valentia, Canon 1. The last council, which met during the reign of Valentinian, excludes *digami aut internuptarum mariti* (i.e., men who marry for a second time and men who marry divorced women) from admission to the clergy, regardless of whether the second marriage occurred before or after they became Christians (*Chronica Galliae A. 314*, ed. C. Munier [*CCL* 148.38–39]).

[37] On women in the extant books of the *Histories*, where empresses play no role, see A. J. Marshall, *Ancient Society* 15–17 (1984–86), 167–84.

dead husband Germanicus? Equally vivid are Tacitus' portraits of the wanton Messalina who manipulated the doting Claudius at will, of the younger Agrippina who could control her uncle and husband Claudius but not her petulant son, and of the lascivious and importunate Poppaea Sabina who impelled Nero to kill his mother, then his wife. The only empress in Ammianus' extant books who comes close to these as a character is Constantina, the wife of Gallus. Baleful influence was exercised at the court of Constantius not by Eusebia, but by the court eunuchs, especially Eusebius, whose power prompts the wittiest epigram in Ammianus' extant text: "Eusebius, the *praepositus sacri cubiculi*, with whom, if the truth should be told, Constantius had great influence" (18.4.3: Eusebi . . . apud quem, si vere dici debeat, multa Constantius potuit). The reversal of roles is worthy of Tacitus, who consistently makes Claudius act and speak as a freedman while his powerful freedmen act as if each of them was emperor and treat their imperial master as an inferior.[38] But Ammianus' emphasis on the power of eunuchs reflects historical reality. For it is precisely in the reign of Constantius that eunuchs begin to appear in our sources as wielders of significant power at the imperial court.[39]

Eunuchs were of course no novelty in the fourth century. Individual eunuchs had achieved notoriety at the court of Nero; many other emperors had eunuchs in their service at court; and imperial mistresses like Queen Berenice, the mistress of Titus, and Panthea, the Ephesian mistress of Lucius Verus, paraded eunuchs in their retinues.[40] But not even the most hostile sources allege that eunuchs wielded undue power at the courts of Diocletian and Constantine, a charge that would undoubtedly have been made if it had had any basis in fact.[41] Moreover, although late writers invented fictitious *praepositi sacri cubiculi* for Constantine, the first securely attested holder of the title is Eusebius, who is not validly attested in this office before the death of Constantine.[42] The very real political role of Eusebius and other eunuchs under Con-

---

[38] S. Dickison, *Latomus* 36 (1977), 634–47.

[39] For known court eunuchs from Persian times down to circa 500, see P. Guyot, *Eunuchen als Sklaven und Freigelassene in der griechisch-römischen Antike* (Stuttgarter Beiträge zur Geschichte und Politik 14, 1980), 181–233; H. Scholten, *Der Eunuch in Kaisernähe. Zur politischen und sozialer Bedeutung des praepositus sacri cubiculi im 4. und 5. Jahrhundert n. Chr.* (Prismata. Beiträge zur Altertumswissenschaft 5, 1995), 205–51.

[40] *Epitome* 10.7; Lucian, *Imagines* 10.

[41] On the resentment provoked by powerful eunuchs, see K. Hopkins, *PCPS* 189 (1963), 62–80; J. Long, *Claudian's "In Eutropium," Or, How, When, and Why to Slander a Eunuch* (Chapel Hill, 1996), 65–146. The prominent eunuchs at the court of Diocletian were Christians: hence they are presented favorably by Lactantius, *Mort. Pers.* 15.2; Eusebius, *HE* 8.1.3–4, 6.5.

[42] Scholten, *Der Eunuch* (1995), 19–27, 212–13, cf. Guyot, *Eunuchen* (1980), 130, 199–201. As Scholten sees, the only late evidence that deserves any consideration at all is the statement in the *Liber Pontificalis* 34.14 that Constantine donated to the church of Rome a *massa Festi praepositi sacri cubiculi* in the territory of Praeneste (*PLRE* 1.334, Festus 2: not stigmatized).

stantius is documented most clearly in ecclesiastical affairs. In 339, near the beginning of the reign, the eunuch Arsacius accompanied Philagrius when Constantius appointed him prefect of Egypt and dispatched him from court to install Gregory as bishop of Alexandria in place of Athanasius, while in 355 Eusebius himself came to Rome to attempt to persuade the bishop Liberius to subscribe to the decisions of the Council of Sirmium.[43]

Ammianus blamed Eusebius more than anyone else for Ursicinus' disappointments and dismissal. He unleashes a torrent of abuse on Eusebius and the "multitude of eunuchs at the court of Constantius" (14.6.17).[44] Yet he makes an exception for Eutherius, the *praepositus sacri cubiculi* of Julian, whom the Caesar sent to the court of Constantius to defend him against slander and intrigue (17.7.2) and who lived long enough for Ammianus to meet and converse with him as a respected figure in Rome (16.7.7: ut subinde Romam secedens ibique fixo domicilio consenescens . . . colatur a cunctis ordinibus et ametur). Eutherius was unlike other eunuchs. Just as roses grow among thorns and some wild beasts can be tamed, so Eutherius was honest despite being castrated as an infant, sold into slavery, and brought up in the palace: his only predecessor, the only worthy eunuch known to history was Menophilus, who served King Mithridates of Pontus (16.7.9–10). It may be relevant that Eutherius was a pagan.[45]

Ammianus records Eutherius' mission to Constantius in 360, his subsequent retirement, and his recall to his court by Julian in late 361 (20.8.19, 9.1–4, 16.7.6). The extant text does not mention two other prominent eunuchs who were Christians. It is impossible to be certain whether or not Ammianus recorded Mardonius, the tutor who took charge of Julian in 338, in one of the lost books.[46] But he appears to have made a conscious choice to omit the Mardonius who was *praepositus sacri cubiculi* of Valens. This Mardonius is known to history only because he played an important role in bringing the head of John the Baptist to Constantinople.[47]

---

[43] Athanasius, *Hist. Ar.* 10.1, 35.4–40.3; Theodoretus, *HE* 2.16, cf. *Athanasius* (1993), 118, 130, 276 n. 56. Eusebius' other interventions in ecclesiastical politics are listed in *PLRE* 1.202–03, Eusebius 11. Ammianus alludes to Liberius' refusal to acquiesce in the condemnation of Athanasius: in this context, however, he makes no mention of Eusebius' journey to Rome to put political pressure on the bishop (16.7.6–10).

[44] The word *spado* occurs in nine other passages in Books XIV–XXI (Viansino, *Lexicon* 2.592).

[45] Julian, *Ep.* 29.

[46] Guyot, *Eunuchen* (1980), 215 no. 67.

[47] Sozomenus, *HE* 7.21.2–3, cf. Guyot, *Eunuchen* (1980), 215 no. 68.

[XII]

TYRANNY AND INCOMPETENCE

Three emperors of whom Ammianus disapproved serve as foils to his hero Julian in Books XIV–XXV. Gallus had been appointed Caesar in 351 and sent to Antioch: Book XIV recounts his actions from the summer of 353 to his recall and execution in the following year. Constantius had been Augustus since 337: he appointed Gallus and Julian successively as Caesars, and he shares Ammianus' main narrative with the latter from the winter of 355–356 until his death on 3 November 361 (Books XVI–XXI). Jovian succeeded Julian and ruled for less than eight months (27 June 363 to 16–17 February 364): Ammianus presents his brief reign as a dismal epilogue to that of his glorious predecessor. The historian approaches the depiction of each of these three emperors with a firm idea of his attainments and character which dominates his narrative virtually throughout.

Gallus

Ammianus' treatment of Gallus is inevitably ambiguous.[1] Constantius appointed Gallus Caesar in March 351 to forestall usurpation in the East while he campaigned against Magnentius, whom he was not able to defeat completely until the summer of 353.[2] But Constantius intended Gallus to be a mere figurehead. Real power was vested in Thalassius, the praetorian prefect

---

[1] On Ammianus' portrait of Gallus, see esp. Thompson, *Ammianus* (1947), 56–71; R. P. C. Blockley, *Latomus* 31 (1972), 433–44, 461–68; H. Tränkle, *Mus. Helv.* 33 (1976), 162–79; Elliott, *Ammianus* (1983), 15–21.

[2] See, briefly, *Athanasius* (1993), 105–6.

of Gallus, and the *quaestor* Montius, newly given the title *patricius*.[3] Constantius appointed all the other officials who surrounded the Caesar. Constantius expected Gallus to behave like Lucius Verus two centuries earlier, who enjoyed the circus and sensual pleasures, but entrusted conduct of the Parthian war to his generals.[4] At first, Gallus probably showed proper subservience: it is significant that the Palestinian Talmud has several stories about Ursicinus in Galilee during the Jewish rebellion of 351–352, but nothing whatever about Gallus.[5]

By the summer of 353, however, where the extant narrative of the *Res Gestae* opens, Gallus had begun to assert himself—to appalling effect. It is not necessary here to analyze his dealings with the local senate of Antioch in attempting to put grain on the market when it was scarce.[6] Let it merely be noted that famines are now known never to be the consequence of poor harvests alone, but result from specific actions of individuals and groups, in particular hoarding and profiteering, or even from deliberate government policy.[7] It will suffice to observe that all the ancient sources, with one solitary and surprising exception,[8] assert that Gallus' conduct was intolerable and that he had to be removed from office after he attempted to arrest, then connived at the lynching of Montius and Domitianus, the successor of Thalassius, who had died in office. Gallus had committed high treason: he was recalled, deposed, tried, and executed. Ammianus does not deny or mitigate the criminality of Gallus' behavior, which he describes at length (14.1, 7, 9). Yet the Caesar was the half-brother of Julian and a victim of Constantius. Hence Ammianus' attitude toward him could not avoid a certain degree of ambiguity.

In his *Letter to the Athenians*, in which he bitterly denounced Constantius as a murderer of his kinsmen, Julian argued that, even though Gallus had shown himself unfit to rule, he did not deserve to die: his death was the result of envy on the part of his cousin and the hatred and intrigues of the eunuch Eusebius.[9]

---

[3] Philostorgius, *HE* 3.26ᵃ = *Passio Artemii* 12.

[4] *HA, Verus* 6.7–7.10, cf. *JRS* 57 (1967), 70–72; A. R. Birley, *Marcus Aurelius: A Biography*[2] (London, 1987), 123–31, 141–47.

[5] J. Geiger, *LCM* 4 (1979), 77, cf. Appendix 3, n. 4.

[6] On which, see Matthews, *Ammianus* (1989), 406–8.

[7] For the former in twentieth-century India, see A. K. Sen, *Poverty and Famines. An Essay on Entitlement and Deprivation* (Oxford, 1981), 52–153; for the latter in the Ukraine in 1921–22 and 1932–33, R. Conquest, *The Harvest of Sorrow: Soviet Collectivization and the Terror-Famine* (London, 1986), esp. 43–57, 225–307.

[8] Jerome, *Chronicle* 239ᶜ Helm: Gallus Caesar sollicitatus a Constantio patrueli, cui in suspicionem ob egregiam indolem venerat, Histriae occiditur. An earlier entry had noted "nonnulli nobilium Antiochiae a Gallo interfecti" (238ᵍ).

[9] Julian, *Ep. ad Ath.* 270c–71a, 272a–d.

Ammianus takes the same view as Julian. He presents Gallus as a tyrant, as different from his younger brother Julian as Domitian was from his older brother Titus (14.11.28), and his obituary of Gallus invokes traditional villains like Dionysius of Syracuse, Eunus and Spartacus who led slave insurrections, and Viriathus the bandit who led Lusitanian resistance against Rome in the middle of the second century B.C. as similar examples of men who were corrupted by sudden power (14.11.29–34). Ammianus applies some of his favorite animal imagery to Gallus, whose ferocity did not abate even after many executions: on the contrary, "like a lion who has tasted human flesh," he sought other prey (14.9.9). Moreover, Ammianus concedes, more explicitly than Julian,[10] that power had turned the Caesar's head and that he may have been contemplating rebellion: it seemed likely, he notes, that Gallus would challenge the Augustus who had appointed him Caesar as soon as the opportunity offered (14.1.1).[11]

On the other hand, as a victim of Constantius, the executed Caesar merited pity and sympathy. For he was ruined not merely by his own ineptitude but also by the treachery and perjury of others. One of the offenders was Thalassius, who failed to calm Gallus down with sage advice: instead, he drove him into rages by openly opposing him and exaggerated his vices in the frequent reports that he submitted to Constantius (14.1.10).[12] As a result Constantius finally decided to remove the knotty obstacle in his way—at least, that is what Ammianus probably said, but the transmitted text is corrupt and needs to be emended (14.11.1).[13] It was resolved to remove Gallus from power by persuading him to leave Antioch. The difficult task was entrusted to Scudilo, tribune of the Scutarii, who came and persuaded Gallus to accompany him back to the court of Constantius (14.11.11). When they reached Poetovio in Noricum, the *comes* Barbatio and Apodemius, an *agens in rebus*, appeared with carefully selected soldiers. Gallus was stripped of his imperial dress, clothed in the tunic and military cloak of an ordinary soldier, then taken to Istria, where he was questioned: a report was sent to Constantius, who decreed a sentence of death, whereupon Gallus was beheaded like a common brigand (14.11.19–21, 23).

---

[10] Julian, *Ep. ad Ath.* 272bc.

[11] In 14.1.1[b] the word *etiamtum* appears to be misplaced: the logic of the passage indicates that it belongs with the phrase *ausurus hostilia* (see Appendix 1, at n. 20).

[12] Ammianus later names the prefect's son, also called Thalassius, as one who plotted against Gallus (22.9.16).

[13] Seyfarth accepts a Renaissance conjecture for the *vox nihili odiem* in V and prints *tamquam nodum et odium difficillimum*. But both palaeography and comparable passages tell heavily in favor of emending to *obicem*: R. Unger, *De Ammiani Marcellini locis controversis epistula critica* (Neustrelitz, 1868), 3; Viansino, *Lexicon* 2.183.

Ammianus regarded the part that Scudilo and Barbatio played in these politically necessary and legally correct proceedings as criminal acts which ought to be punished:

> While Gallus was brought down by his own cruel actions, not long afterwards both the men were cut off by painful deaths who by their flattering, lies, and cajolery had led him into a fatal trap, guilty though he was. Scudilo was attacked by an abscess of the liver and died vomiting up his lungs; Barbatio, who had already for a long period been inventing false charges against Gallus, was accused by a whispering campaign of having higher ambitions than being *magister peditum* and condemned, thus by his unlamented death making reparation with his soul to the shade of the Caesar whom his treachery had destroyed. (14.11.24)

Apodemius was almost as guilty. In 362 he was dragged out of retirement and burned alive with Paul "the Chain" (22.3.11). Ammianus smugly notes that he had described Apodemius' mad eagerness to destroy Gallus and Silvanus: he thus met the fate he deserved.

Constantius

Constantius was a cautious, conscientious, and not unsuccessful ruler.[14] Yet Ammianus presents him as an incompetent, malevolent, and vicious tyrant. When he dies, Ammianus follows his invariable practice of offering an assessment of the dead ruler in a formal obituary. He arranges his obituary of Constantius as a list of his good qualities (21.16.1−7) followed by an analysis of his vices (21.16.8−18), with a brief epilogue on his physical appearance (21.16.19). The analysis of Constantius' vices reads like a bill of impeachment more than the dispassionate assessment of a historian. Six main charges are leveled against the dead emperor. The first, developed at the greatest length and with all the resources of rhetoric that an orator could have mustered, is that Constantius was a tyrant. Whenever a case of treason was suspected, Ammianus alleges, Constantius' endless investigations showed a cruelty that easily surpassed that of Caligula, Domitian, and Commodus, "whose barbarity he emulated at the start of his reign by destroying root and branch all who were connected with him by blood and birth" (21.16.8).[15] The exaggeration is obvious: "all" would

---

[14] Jones, *LRE* 116−18. On his cultural attainments, which Ammianus also disparages (21.16.4), see H. C. Teitler, *Cognitio Gestorum* (1992), 117−22.

[15] Ammianus had earlier alleged that Constantius detested the doers of brave deeds in exactly the same way as Domitian had (15.5.35).

include Constantius' cousins Gallus and Julian, who survived the bloodbath of 337, even though their older brother did not.[16] Nor is Constantius' real role in these dynastic killings in fact clear: on balance, it seems most probable that the military high command acted on its own initiative and that Eutropius was correct to state that Constantius acquiesced in the murders rather than ordered them (except for the praetorian prefect Ablabius).[17]

Ammianus proceeds by comparing Constantius to a notoriously unsuccessful emperor of the third century: he was more savage than Gallienus, because, whereas Gallienus was confronted by several genuine usurpers and sometimes acted mildly, he employed torture to obtain apparent proof of invented or doubtful accusations (21.16.10). Gallienus may not deserve his evil reputation as an incompetent ruler, but it was firmly established before the end of the third century.[18] Constantius was the antithesis of Marcus Aurelius: Ammianus reminds his readers that Marcus destroyed without reading them the letters that those who secretly supported his rebellion had written to Avidius Cassius. In short, Constantius disregarded the lessons inculcated by Cicero in his condemnation of Julius Caesar and by Heraclitus long ago: true glory requires a man to subdue his angry and savage impulses (21.16.11–14).

Book XVI had already invoked one of the most amusing tyrant stories from the ancient world:

> Constantius always expected to be attacked, just like Dionysius the famous Sicilian tyrant, who because of the same fault taught his daughters to be barbers so that he did not need to entrust his throat to anyone outside the family for shaving. Dionysius also surrounded the little building in which he was accustomed to sleep with a deep ditch and constructed a collapsible bridge over it: he dismantled the planks and pins, and took them with him when he went to sleep, and reassembled them at daybreak when he wished to come out. (16.8.10)[19]

Of the five other charges that Ammianus lays to the discredit of Constantius in his obituary, that relating to the Christian church has been discussed in another context (Chapter VIII). The remaining four allege military incompe-

---

[16] Julian, *Ep. ad Ath.* 270d. His name is unknown, but his mother Galla was the sister of Vulcacius Rufinus, cos. 347, and Naeratius Cerialis, cos. 358 (*PLRE* 1.382, Galla 1).

[17] Eutropius, *Brev.* 10.9.1. Eunapius, *Vit. phil.* 6.3.8–13 (464), places the death of Ablabius some time after Constantius dismissed him from office. For a recent (and speculative) discussion of the purge of 337, see M. di Maio and D. H. W. Arnold, *Byzantion* 62 (1992), 158–211.

[18] *Pan Lat.* 8(5).10.1–3 (delivered on 1 March 297).

[19] Ammianus takes the story from Cicero, *Tusc. Disp.* 5.58, cf. H. Hagendahl, *Studia Ammianea* (Diss. Uppsala, 1921), 81–82.

tence, vanity, weak-mindedness, and oppression. They may be considered in reverse order.

First, Constantius allowed his officials to exact taxes with rapacity and he crushed the provinces with a multiplicity of dues and imposts (21.16.17). In this the emperor merely conforms to his stereotype as a bad emperor: in the Greco-Roman world, a good ruler always reduced taxes, whereas a ruler who increased them was by definition a tyrant.[20] Counterexamples were simply denied, so that what purport to be statements of fact are often merely reflections of approval or disapproval. Did Constantine raise or lower taxes? The answer depended on the prejudice of the reporter. According to Eusebius, he lowered taxes; according to the hostile Zosimus, he devised new taxes that were both cruel and ruinous to his subjects.[21] Such ancient modes of thought, it may be observed in passing, are not yet entirely dead.

Second, Constantius was excessively influenced by his wives, shrill eunuchs, and court officials who flattered him (21.16.16). The truth behind this allegation, to judge from Ammianus' narrative and indications in Athanasius and the ecclesiastical historians, is that Constantius not only regulated access to his person carefully, but also took all important decisions after secret discussions with a chosen group of trusted advisers, as all emperors had always done.[22] This group included some generals, especially Arbitio, who was honored with the ordinary consulate in 355, but it excluded and was hostile to Ursicinus. Ammianus reflects contemporary resentments to which Aurelius Victor gave expression during the emperor's lifetime. Victor's concluding verdict on Constantius was that, although there might be nothing finer than the emperor himself, there was nothing more frightening than most of his servants.[23]

Third, Constantius was so vain that he erected triumphal arches in Gaul and Pannonia on the ruin of the provinces to advertise his successes (21.16.15).[24] This charge has specific reference to the defeats of Magnentius and their commemoration: it repeats the charge made in Book XVI that Constantius' visit to Rome in 357 celebrated without mentioning it a triumph won by the

[20] H. Kloft, *Liberalitas Principis. Herkunft und Bedeutung. Studien zur Principatsideologie* (Cologne, 136–57. For the stereotype of bad emperors levying excessive taxes, see Lactantius, *Mort. Pers.* 22–23; (Galerius); Eusebius, *HE* 10.8.12; *VC* 1.55 (Licinius).

[21] Eusebius, *VC* 4.2–4; Zosimus 2.38.2–4.

[22] On the role of the imperial *consilium* before it was institutionalized as the *consistorium*, see J. A. Crook, *Consilium Principis* (Oxford, 1953); F. Millar, *The Emperor in the Roman World* (*31 B.C.–A.D. 337*) (London, 1977), 94–97, 119–22, 234–38, 268–72. Ammianus notes Constantius' consultation of the *consistorium* five times in Books XV and XVI, but nowhere else (15.5.5, 18; 16.5.11, 7.2, 8.7).

[23] Victor, *Caes.* 42.25.

[24] Ammianus' complaints may in part reflect contemporary criticism of Constantius: M. Caltabiano, *Studi de antichità in memoria di C. Gatti* (Milan, 1987), 37–46.

spilling of Roman blood (16.10.1: absque nomine). But the official occasion of the visit to Rome was the emperor's thirty-fifth year of rule (admittedly celebrated a little early),[25] although his visit inevitably recalled his father's entry into Rome after the Battle of the Milvian Bridge. The hexameter inscription on the base of the obelisk that he erected in the Circus Maximus (16.10.17, cf. 17.4.12–23) duly spoke of triumphs, the recovery of the whole world, and the death of the *tyrannus*.[26] Ammianus also intends a general complaint. For, at several points in his narrative, he has presented Constantius as boastful and arrogant. His exaggeration sometimes verges on the ludicrous. Constantius' reaction to Julian's victory at Strasbourg stands in an emphatic position, at the very end of Book XVI, concluding a triad and interrupting Julian's campaign of 357, which continues in Book XVII. According to Ammianus, he was induced by flattering courtiers to make false claims in imperial edicts that he alone had fought, defeated, and concluded a treaty with the kings whom Julian had defeated while he was far away (16.12.69). What lies behind this accusation is imperial collegiality. When Constantius wrote a letter or issued an edict from November 355 onward, he did so both in his own name and in that of his junior colleague, and it was standard practice in the fourth century for one emperor both to speak in the name of the whole imperial college and to claim joint credit for victories.[27] Hence a letter written by Constantine to his imperial colleague Maximinus from Rome in November 312 can be described by Eusebius as a "most perfect law on behalf of Christianity" issued by both Constantine and Licinius jointly.[28] In the late 350s, Constantius was merely following well-established convention when he used the first-person plural to speak of victories won in the field by his junior colleague.

The most serious charge that Ammianus levels against the emperor is incompetence in defending the empire: although he suffered damaging defeats

---

[25] *RIC* 8.277 Rome 296–98; 335 Aquileia 210, 211; 376 Siscia 357–59; 388–89 Sirmium 55–64; *Descr. cons.* 357.2, cf. R. W. Burgess, *NC* 148 (1988), 83–84; J. Long, *ANSNM* 33 (1988), 114–16. The latter unfortunately follows the consensus of scholarship in accepting Mommsen's emendation of *edidit xxxv* in the *Descriptio consulum* to *edidit vicennalia*, which cannot be correct: since Constantius' *dies imperii* was 8 November 324, he celebrated his *vicennalia* in 343–344 (cf. *RIC* 8. 513–14, Antioch 22, 24, 25, 27, 30, 31, 35, 36) and his *tricennalia* in late 353, as Ammianus noted (14.5.1, cf. Appendix 7).

[26] *ILS* 736.

[27] Most obviously in shared victory titles: for the well-documented case of the successive colleges of emperors between 285 and 337, see *Phoenix* 30 (1976), 174–93; *New Empire* (1982), 27, 254–58: Tables 4–8. An inscription from Sirmium of 354 gives Constantius the victory titles *Germanicus maximus, Alamannicus maximus, Gothicus maximus, Adiabenicus maximus* (*ILS* 732): the first two must reflect victories won in the field by his brother Constans.

[28] Eusebius, *HE* 9.9.12, 9a.12, cf. Lactantius, *Mort. Pers.* 44.11. On the necessity of identifying the two, see *New Empire* (1982), 67–68.

against external enemies, Constantius took pride on his successes in civil wars and covered himself "with the hideous gore which poured from the internal wounds of the state" (21.16.15). Constantius' political skill is beyond doubt or dispute, and he could draw upon a large fund of loyalty to the Constantinian dynasty, which played a significant role in denying Magnentius control of Illyricum in 350.[29] What is in dispute is whether Constantius defended the imperial frontiers successfully. Both in the obituary and in the preceding narrative, Ammianus firmly denies it: although fortune kept a watchful eye on the emperor in civil strife, he asserts, his foreign wars usually ended in disaster (14.10.16), and in 361 he was as eager to march against Julian as he had always been to take the offensive in civil wars (21.15.1).[30]

This charge, too, relies on a stereotype, modern as well as ancient, that can seriously mislead. What makes for a successful commander or general? The obvious, but false, answer is that a successful commander is one who wins battles. The truer, if less obvious, answer is that military success has two aspects: one is the winning of wars, not battles, the other successful resistance to superior opponents. The denial of overwhelming victory to a stronger opponent on the battlefield has often turned apparent defeat into victory in the political arena. On both the eastern and northern frontiers, Constantius was compelled to adopt a primarily defensive policy. Despite occasional victories in the field, his policy was on the whole unspectacular, even inglorious. Judged by the appropriate criteria, however, it proved to be successful, against the newly aggressive King Shapur no less than on the lower and middle Danube.

In the East, it took Persia a full generation to recover from the crushing defeat of 298 and the peace dictated by Diocletian and Galerius.[31] But when Persia recovered, she was bent on revenge. In the 330s Shapur began a long and determined attempt to recover lost territory in Mesopotamia and lost influence in Armenia. Constantine responded by planning an invasion of Persia to install a Roman nominee as ruler in Ctesiphon.[32] But when Constantine died suddenly and unexpectedly in 337, Shapur was able to take the initiative, invade Roman territory, and besiege Nisibis.[33] Constantius, who was occupied with internal politics during the summer and autumn of 337, was

[29] B. Bleckmann, *Chiron* 24 (1994), 42–49.

[30] The passages in which Ammianus discusses the eastern frontier policy of Constantius are conveniently summarized by R. Seager, *CQ*, N.S. (1997), 253–59.

[31] On the treaty of 298, see E. Winter, *The Eastern Frontier of the Roman Empire*, ed. D. H. French and C. S. Lightfoot (*BAR*, Int. Ser. 553, 1989), 555–71 (with full bibliography).

[32] *JRS* 75 (1985), 126–36.

[33] *JRS* 75 (1985), 132–33: for confirmation that Shapur's first siege of Nisibis must be dated to 337 (not 338), see R. W. Burgess, *Continuatio Antiochiensis Eusebii: An Antiochene Continuation of Eusebius' Chronici Canones* (forthcoming), no. xx.

thus forced on the defensive. To resist Shapur, he built a number of forts in northern Mesopotamia to serve as hard points of defense: Ammianus notes both his fortification of Amida, previously a very small town, and his refoundation of Antoninopolis as a strongly fortified city with the name Constantia (18.9.1–2),[34] while archaeology has revealed a fort apparently unknown to our literary sources.[35]

Constantius' defensive strategy entailed annual expeditions but few large battles. A decade after his death, Festus summarizes the result. Apart from frontier skirmishes, there were nine serious battles during his reign: Constantius was personally in command at only two, the other seven were waged by his generals.[36] Once the Romans squandered the chance of a smashing successs through indiscipline (i.e., after the Battle of Singara in 344).[37] Nisibis was besieged three times (in 337, 346, and 350), but it neither surrendered nor succumbed to Persian assault.[38] Amida was captured in 359, Bezabde in 360. But the sieges cost Shapur dearly: Festus observes that his losses were always heavier than those of the defenders, and the narrative of Ammianus shows how the long siege of Amida (which lasted seventy-three days and was believed to have cost Shapur thirty thousand dead) blunted the impetus of an invasion for which all the vast resources of the Persian empire had been mobilized (19.1–9).[39] In 361, Shapur was prevented from crossing the Tigris: Ammianus attributes this, not to defensive measures taken by Constantius, but to unfavorable omens (21.13.2).[40]

Constantius' defensive achievement should be put in a long-term perspective. Many Parthian and Persian invasions had penetrated into the Roman province of Syria, one of them under the Antonines, and Antioch itself was captured and sacked in both 252 and 540.[41] Constantius' strategy achieved its main aim: given the very real limitations of Roman power, the loss of two or

[34] Ammianus states that Constantius fortified Amida and Constantia *Caesar etiamtum*, which seems to imply a date before 9 September 337 (19.9.1), but the correct date is 349–350: see Burgess, *Continuatio Antiochiensis* nos. 47, 48.

[35] C. S. Lightfoot, *The Eastern Frontier of the Roman Empire*, ed. D. H. French and C. S. Lightfoot (*BAR*, Int. Ser. 553, 1989), 285–94.

[36] Festus, *Brev.* 27.

[37] Libanius, *Orat.* 59.99–120; Julian, *Orat.* 1, 22d–25b. The date must be 344, not 348: Burgess, *Continuatio Antiochiensis*, no. 38, cf. Athanasius (1993), 220, 312, n. 19.

[38] On the third siege, which soon acquired mythical dimensions and inspired the novelist Heliodorus, see esp. C. S. Lightfoot, *Historia* 37 (1988), 105–25; G. W. Bowersock, *Fiction as History: Nero to Julian* (Berkeley, 1994), 153–55.

[39] On Ammianus' account, see R. P. C. Blockley, *Phoenix* 42 (1988), 245–60.

[40] On Ammianus' unfairness here, see R. P. C. Blockley, *Studies in Latin Literature and Roman History* 5 (*Collection Latomus* 206, 1989), 465–88.

[41] G. Downey, *History of Antioch in Syria from Seleucus to the Arab Conquest* (Princeton, 1961), 226, 252–59, 533–46.

three frontier fortresses did not amount to defeat or even to failure.[42] Real and symbolic success are often very different: as the Syriac poet Ephrem observed, the Persians had been trying to take Nisibis for thirty years before the city was surrendered to the Persians in 363.[43]

Constantius' achievement on the northern frontiers is far harder to assess. Ammianus omits a campaign that Constantius conducted in Raetia in 356 as part of a combined strategy to rid Gaul of its invaders: although his narrative of 357 refers back to Constantius' presence in Raetia acting in concert with Julian "in the previous year" (16.12.16), his account of Constantius' movements in 356 records no such campaign. In that year, even though Ammianus once calls the court of Constantius *castra Augusti* (16.8.1), his text nowhere states explicitly that Constantius ever left Milan. It must be acknowledged, however, that the textual transmission of the *Res Gestae* is such that a campaign could possibly have been lost in an undetected lacuna (Appendix 1).

Where Julian is not involved, Ammianus is capable of seeing merit and virtue in Constantius' generalship, and Joachim Szidat has drawn attention to a most peculiar phenomenon.[44] Despite his repeated condemnations, despite the general tenor of his narrative, Ammianus on one occasion presents Constantius as a model commander who displays the standard qualities of a good general (17.12–13). In his Sarmatian campaign of 358, the emperor surprises the enemy by the speed of his march; he shows clemency to defeated foes; he negotiates prudently; he campaigns successfully; his soldiers salute him as invincible; he returns to Sirmium in triumph over foreign foes. Ammianus praises the happy outcome of this campaign warmly and commends the emperor for successfully achieving both the great tasks that he had undertaken (17.13.34). Whatever the reason (which has not been fully elucidated), Ammianus here shows an appreciation of Constantius that contrasts markedly with his depiction of him elsewhere as a textbook tyrant.

Jovian

Ammianus' verdict on Jovian is simple: he was never really emperor at all. Jovian is introduced briefly in the last paragraph of Book XXI, when he escorts

---

[42] For appreciations of Constantius' military achievement, see B. H. Warmington, *Limes. Akten des XI. Internationalen Limeskongresses (Székesfehérvar, 30.8.–6.9. 1976),* ed. J. Fitz (Budapest, 1977), 509–20; R. C. Blockley, *East Roman Frontier Policy. Formation and Conduct from Diocletian to Anastasius* (Leeds, 1992), 12–24, 175–82.

[43] Ephrem, *Contra Iulianum* 3.3 (ed. E. Beck, *CSCO* 175 = Scr. syri 78 [1957], 82). In an earlier poem Ephrem had noted a visit of Constantius to his city (*Carmina Nisibena* 13.4 [ed. E. Beck, *CSCO* 218 = Syri 92 (1961), 35]).

[44] J. Szidat, *Historia* 21 (1972), 712–20.

the body of Constantius from Cilicia to Constantinople. Ammianus does not content himself with registering the bare fact, which is highly significant in itself, since it probably implies that Jovian was related to the deceased emperor. If that inference is correct, then Jovian was presumably a relative either of Faustina, whom Constantius married in 361, but about whose origin, family, or connections nothing whatever is known,[45] or of the wife whom it should be presumed that Constantius married shortly after 337.[46] Ammianus presents the journey as an omen:

> The body of the dead emperor was washed and placed in a coffin, and Jovian, who was then a *protector domesticus*, was ordered to escort it in royal state to Constantinople to be buried next to his family. As Jovian was sitting in the vehicle which carried the remains, samples of the soldiers' rations (which they call "tastes") were presented to him and the animals of the post service were paraded before him, as is normally done with emperors, and the throngs grew larger as he proceeded. These and other similar things foretold that imperial power would come to this same Jovian, though only in an empty and shadowy form as befitted the director of a funeral procession. (21.16.21)

The last clause ("imperium cassum et umbratile ut ministro rerum funebrium portendebant") is not a disparaging comment on Jovian's role in 361: rather, it looks forward to 363, when the Roman army brought the body of Julian back to Roman soil and Julian's relative Procopius was deputed to escort it to Tarsus for burial (25.9.12).

When Julian was killed, the Roman army was deep in Persian territory and the generals needed a new commander who could extricate the expeditionary force from danger. Ammianus gives the fullest surviving account of their deliberations. It has usually been treated as a fair and accurate account, since Ammianus was there and perhaps participated in the deliberations. However, Raban von Haehling, developing some brief remarks of his teacher Johannes Straub, has demonstrated how utterly tendentious, and hence how unreliable, his account in fact is.[47] According to Ammianus, there were two parties in the high command, those who had served under Constantius and the generals who came east from Gaul with Julian. Although each group wanted to elect

---

[45] *PLRE* 1.326.

[46] On Constantius' marriages, see Chapter XI, n. 7.

[47] R. von Haehling, *Bonner Festgabe Johannes Straub zum 65. Geburtstag am 18 October 1977 dargebracht*, ed. A. Lippold and and N. Himmelmann (Bonn, 1977), 347–58, cf. J. Straub, *Vom Herrscherideal in der Spätantike* (Berlin, 1939), 11–14, 22–25. Readers of Straub's book should not miss the deferential quotations from *Mein Kampf* on the first page of the introduction (1) and from a speech of Adolf Hitler (232–33 n. 340).

one of their own number as emperor, the praetorian prefect Salutius (who was not a career soldier) emerged as a compromise candidate acceptable to all.[48] But he refused the purple on grounds of age and ill health. A soldier of high rank thereupon upbraided him:[49] "What would you be doing if the emperor had entrusted you with the conduct of the war in his absence, as has often happened? Would you not have put everything else aside and be trying to rescue the army from the misfortunes which press upon it? Do the same now: and if we are allowed to see [Roman] Mesopotamia, the united votes of both armies will then proclaim a legitimate emperor" (25.5.3). The stage thus set, Ammianus can proceed with the farce of an election in which Jovian conforms to the stereotype of the usurper or tyrant.[50]

Jovian is elected, in Ammianus' account, not by universal consent or acclamation, as a genuine emperor would have been, but by the hasty action of a few (25.5.4–9). He did not possess any of the outstanding virtues required; he was merely "a passable candidate" who owed more to his father's achievements than his own (*paternis meritis mediocriter commendabilis*).[51] He did not make the traditional and obligatory show of reluctance, but donned the imperial purple eagerly and in a hurry. He emerged from his tent suddenly, not in the slow and stately manner expected of an emperor, and his appearance did not provoke the outburst of joy that would have confirmed his legitimacy. On the contrary, the army rejoiced when they believed, briefly and erroneously, that Julian might have recovered from his wound; when they saw Jovian in the imperial purple, all broke into tears of lamentation. The standard bearer of the Joviani was an enemy of the new emperor: in fear for his life, therefore, he deserted to the Persians and informed the Persian king that the adversary whom he feared was dead and that in his place "an unruly throng of camp-followers had proclaimed the obscure, lethargic and effeminate Jovian, who was still a mere *protector*, as pseudo-emperor."[52] Ammianus reinforces this slanted presentation with an authorial comment: "If some scrupulous lover of legality

---

[48] Before Constantius recalled him from Gaul in 358–59, Salutius had been *praeses* of Aquitanica, *magister memoriae*, proconsul of Africa and *quaestor*, i.e., presumably *quaestor sacri palatii* of Julian (*ILS* 754: Ancyra, cf. *PLRE* 1.814–15). Eunapius placed the offer of the purple to Salutius, not after the death of Julian in 363, but after that of Jovian in 364 (Zosimus 3.36.1). On the latter occasion, Ammianus presents Valentinian as the first choice of the *potestatum civilium militiaeque rectores* (26.1.3–5), and his version has always been preferred to that of Zosimus: V. Neri, *Rivista Storica dell'Antichità* 15 (1985), 153–82. But the traditional assumption that Ammianus is always closer to the truth than Zosimus is mistaken (Chapters XIII n. 92; XIV).

[49] In favor of identifying this *honoratior aliquis miles* as Ammianus himself, see C. Brakman, *Mnemosyne*[2] 47 (1919), 108–09, who adduces the telling parallel of Xenophon, *Anabasis* 2.4.16.

[50] Von Haehling, *Festgabe Straub* (1977), 354–55.

[51] R. I. Frank, *AJP* 88 (1969), 309–18, mistakenly denies the evaluative force of the adjective.

[52] On this episode, where Ammianus has suppressed relevant facts, see Chapter V, at nn. 32–33.

denounces this action taken at the last gasp as rash, he might more justly blame sailors who, when they have lost their captain who knew how to steer the ship and the winds and sea are raging, entrust command and the helm to one of their number chosen at random" (25.5.7). The passage to which Ammianus here alludes (and virtually quotes) is famous and familiar. He evokes the sixth book of Plato's *Republic*, where Socrates compares the expertise of the true philosopher to a pilot confronted with an ignorant and unruly crew each of whom claims the right to steer the ship even though he has never learned the art of navigation.[53] Jovian (Ammianus implies) totally lacked the skills needed to be emperor.

Ammianus' account is palpably unfair. Nevertheless, despite these distortions, it might still be argued that Ammianus has not seriously misrepresented the course of events, and in fact his account has traditionally been preferred, with some modifications, to the very different accounts in the ecclesiastical historians, who present Jovian as a reluctant emperor until the army declared itself Christian.[54] This version has seemed not only suspicious in itself, but also incompatible with the traditional picture of the Christianization of the Roman Empire in the fourth century and the assumption that the Roman army cared little for religion.[55] However, Constantine carried through something that may legitimately be called a reformation affecting all levels of society, and from 312 in the West, from 324 in the East until late 361, the emperor's official standard was the Christian labarum.[56] Moreover, Julian's attempt to reinstate traditional religion produced disaffection in the army and imperial guard (Chapter V), and the version of the ecclesiastical historians is confirmed by the pagan historian Zosimus, who reproduces from Eunapius the fact that Ammianus most emphatically denies, that Jovian was chosen emperor by common consent.[57] Furthermore, according to Zosimus, the praetorian prefect Salutius was elected emperor on a later occasion, after the death of Jovian:[58] it appears to follow that Ammianus has wilfully transferred this attempt to make Salutius emperor from February 364 to June 363 in order to discredit Jovian.

Ammianus' assessment of Jovian as a mediocrity was accepted by all modern historians of the fourth century until very recently.[59] However, a long es-

---

[53] Plato, *Rep.* 488a7–e2: quoted by Cicero, *De Officiis* 1.87.

[54] Socrates, *HE* 3.22.1–5; Theodoretus, *HE* 4.1.4–2.1; Sozomenus, *HE* 6.3.1.

[55] Thus Jones, *LRE* 138, 3.25, n. 1, follows Ammianus without even mentioning the alternative version.

[56] *Constantine* (1981), 43–53, 208–12, 245–60; *From Eusebius to Augustine* (1994), nos. V, VII, IX; *Athanasius* (1993), 165–79.

[57] Zosimus 3.30.1.

[58] Zosimus 3.36.1.

[59] E.g., Jones, *LRE* 138: "a nonentity, Jovian, a genial and popular young man of a little over thirty."

say by Gerhard Wirth has now rehabilitated his reputation as a competent emperor.[60] Wirth's favorable verdict is valid also for Jovian's ecclesiastical policies: he promoted peace and concord within the church, supported the Council of Antioch in 363, which reaffirmed the Nicene creed of 325, and gave Athanasius the imperial recognition he sought.[61] Jovian was a large and cheerful man; although a Christian, he enjoyed wine and lovemaking (25.10.15), and he knew that his main task was to pacify an empire that Julian had brought to the brink of civil war.[62] Against Ammianus' condemnation must be set the panegyric that Themistius delivered in the emperor's presence on New Year's Day 364. A panegyrist is constrained to praise. Yet his choice of what to praise may be highly revealing and significant. Themistius praises Jovian for rescuing philosophy and restoring it to the imperial palace.[63] That assertion embodies an assessment of both Jovian and Julian very different from what can be found in the pages of Ammianus. Where was philosophy, Themistius' listeners must have asked themselves, while Julian ruled? They can hardly have been unaware that the philosophers Priscus and Maximus of Ephesus accompanied Julian on the Persian expedition and were present when the emperor died after delivering a philosophical discourse on the immortality of the soul (25.2.15−23) in conscious and deliberate imitation of the Socrates of Plato's *Phaedo*.[64]

[60] G. Wirth, *Vivarium. Festschrift Theodor Klauser zum 90. Geburtstag* (*JAC*, Ergänzungsband 11, 1984), 353−84.

[61] *Athanasius* (1993), 159−61.

[62] On the true effect of Julian's policies, which has often been denied, see Bowersock, *Julian* (1978), 91−105.

[63] Themistius, *Orat.* 5, 63c, cf. Vanderspoel, *Themistius* (1995), 135−54.

[64] The presence of Priscus and Maximus is also recorded by Libanius, *Orat.* 18.272, cf. D. Scheda, *Historia* 15 (1966), 380−83.

[XIII]

THE NEW ACHILLES

O brightest eye of your race, you who have become for your family exactly what your ancestor Helios has often been for you! For of this fine pair, the one, like the morning star at dawn, has risen with you who illumine the great thrones, imitating your bright rays with his reflected lights; while the other, shining forth from the herd of young men like some high-spirited bull that leads the herd has leapt in the meadows of the Muses like a young horse full of divine spirit who holds his neck high, and has imitated the young man in Homer, the son of Thetis, having become a good speaker of words and doer of deeds.[1]

This fragment of a speech by Himerius, quoted by Photius out of context for its rhetorical allure, is of the highest historical significance. The three men praised are easily identified. The brightest eye of his race, the sun who illumines the great thrones is Constantius. The others are Gallus and Julian. Gallus has risen like the morning star: that is to say, he has been proclaimed Caesar—and this passage could come from a speech delivered at his proclamation in Sirmium on 1 March 351.[2] Whether or not that was in fact the occasion on which Himerius spoke, and whether Julian was present or not, no orator could have uttered such words after the fall of Gallus.[3] Already before he became Caesar, therefore, Julian was being compared to Achilles, a good speaker of words and doer of deeds, although Himerius' comparison of him to a high-spirited bull and a bucking horse inevitably suggest an impetuosity that could lead to ruin.

---

[1] Himerius, frag. I.6 (249–50 Colonna), quoting *Iliad* 9.443.
[2] *CP* 82 (1987), 209.
[3] J. Bidez, *La Vie de l'empereur Julien* (Paris, 1930), 95.

Julian, who was steeped in Homer from an early age,[4] accepted the comparison to Achilles and employed it in the daring and subversive opening of his third oration, which he composed in the winter of 358–359.[5] In form, and largely in content, the speech is a panegyric of Constantius that partly reiterates and embellishes Julian's earlier conventional (and straightforward) panegyric of the emperor.[6] Yet it reveals so much about Julian's real state of mind that it is most improbable that he sent the finished speech to Constantius. Julian protests that the Battle of Strasbourg has not changed his attitude toward Constantius, but he fails to conceal the fact that he was already beginning to contemplate rebellion.[7] Although the Homeric allusions are ultimately transformed into praise of Constantius, the comparison that opens the work carries an unmistakably hostile implication. Constantius and Julian are quarreling like Agamemnon and the hero of the *Iliad*:

> Achilles, as the poem tells us, when his wrath was kindled and he quarreled with the king, let fall from his two hands his spear and shield and, stringing his harp and lyre, he sang and chanted the deeds of the demi-gods. He made this his pastime during his inactivity, choosing extremely wisely in this. For to provoke the hatred and anger of the king was excessively rash and violent. . . . [Yet] the author of the tale tells us that Agamemnon also did not behave to his general with either moderation or tact, but used threats, then inflicted a real insult by depriving Achilles of his prize of valor.[8]

Then, after a few sentences summarising Homer, Julian draws the moral of the story, making its relevance to his own situation very clear:

> Here I think that <Homer> uses the heroes whom he sets before us like types in a tragedy in order to teach us that kings ought never to inflict insults, nor use their power indiscriminately, nor be carried away by anger like a bold horse rush-

---

[4] P. Athanassiadi-Fowden, *Julian and Hellenism. An Intellectual Biography* (Oxford, 1981), 14–22, 27–29.

[5] Julian refers to his Batavian campaign of 358 (*Orat.* 3[2], 56b, cf. Ammianus 17.8.3–5), but Rome and Persia are still at peace (66d–67a).

[6] Julian, *Orat.* 1 conforms to the prescriptions for a *basilikos logos* in the rhetorical handbook attributed to Menander: W. C. Cave (Wright), *The Emperor Julian's Relation to the New Sophistic and Neo-Platonism, with a Study of His Style* (Diss. Chicago, pub. London, 1896), 26–29; C. Gladis, *De Themistii Libanii Juliani in Constantium orationibus* (Diss. Breslau, 1907), 20–29; I. Tantillo, *La prima orazione di Giuliano a Costanzo* (Rome, 1997), 16–31, who argues convincingly that Julian composed the speech for Constantius' visit to Rome in 357 (36–50).

[7] Bowersock, *Julian* (1978), 43–44; Athanassiadi-Fowden, *Julian* (1981), 63–66.

[8] Julian, *Orat.* 3(2), 49c–50a. My translations from Julian are based on the Loeb version by Wilmer Cave Wright (London/Cambridge, Mass., 1913).

ing along without bridle or rider, and to advise generals not to resent the contempt of a king, but to endure his censures with self-control and serenity, so that the life of both may not be filled with remorse.[9]

The very first sentence of the speech is very revealing in another way, too. Julian explicitly invokes Achilles, who in his wrath put aside spear and shield to praise the deeds of the demi-gods, just as in his winter quarters the Caesar has turned aside from war to praise Constantius. At a deeper level, however, Julian's language evokes a still more provocative comparison.

Achilles took up his *psalterion* and his *cithara*. Now Julian never uses the word *psalterion* elsewhere, and the combination of *psalterion* and *cithara* is found nowhere in Greek literature except in the Septuagint and in authors who are quoting from or alluding to the Greek Bible.[10] Julian had read both the Old and the New Testament either entire or at least in large part.[11] Moreover, his allusion is probably a very precise one. The phrase "psaltery and harp" occurs in a passage that appears in two psalms attributed to King David.[12] The heading to the earlier of the two psalms in which it occurs states that David composed the poem while he was hiding in the cave to escape king Saul. Although the headings are neither original nor authentic, they were accepted as accurate and authoritative by Christians of the fourth century, who used them as hermeneutical guides for interpreting the text.[13] If Julian subconsciously thought of himself as David pitted against Saul, the implications were dangerous—and treasonable. Moreover, whether deliberately or not, several passages of the speech reveal its author to be a pagan and a Neoplatonist who believed that the true ruler should be the prophet and servant of "the king of the gods."[14]

Unlike Saul, Constantius died in his bed. His last act was one of ultimate statesmanship: he named Julian his heir and successor. Ammianus subtly calls

[9] Julian, *Orat.* 3(2), 50bc.

[10] E.g., Josephus, *AJ* 1.64, in reference to Genesis 4.21. In that passage, however, the Hebrew text has כנור ועוגב, i.e., "harp and pipe" (NEB): in the passage from the Psalms adduced here (n. 12), the Hebrew has הנבל וכנור, where both nouns do indeed refer to stringed instruments.

[11] See the quotations, allusions, and parallels noted by R. Asmus, *Julians Galiläerschrift im Zusammenhang mit seinen übrigen Werken* (Prog. Freiburg i. B., 1904), 8–39; E. Masaracchia, *Giuliano Imperatore: Contra Galilaeos* (1990), 349–51, 377–79, 389–91.

[12] Psalm 57 (56). 7–11 = 108 (107). 1–5.

[13] Gregory of Nyssa wrote a whole treatise *In Inscriptiones Psalmorum*, ed. J. McDonough, *Gregorii Nysseni Opera* 5 (Leiden, 1962), 1–175. For fourth-century application of the heading of Psalm 57(56) to exegesis of the psalm, see Eusebius, *PG* 23.501–08; Athanasius, *PG* 27.257–61; Gregory of Nyssa, *Insc. Ps.* 2.14 (154.15—158.21).

[14] *Orat.* 3(2), 90a, cf. J. Bidez, *L'Empereur Julien: Oeuvres complètes* 1.1 (Paris, 1932), 113–15, who detected pagan notions of ritual purity and Neoplatonic ideas of the great chain of being in the speech (70d–71a, 80a–c, 81d, 82d–83a, 90bc).

this disinterested and patriotic act into question by representing it as merely an uncertain rumor (22.15.2, 5). As a result, many modern historians of the fourth century, including the most critical, have dismissed the rumor as baseless.[15] But that is to place too much trust in a biased historian. The dying Constantius decided to prevent civil war. What wiser action could he take before facing his creator? Ammianus' denial (for that is what his words convey) is an extreme example of his partisanship for Julian, although paradoxically also of his independence of judgment. Once Constantius was safely dead, Julian dropped the overt hostility that he displayed in the summer and autumn of 361 and saluted him as "the blessed Constantius."[16] For to continue to denounce him as a tyant would have cast doubt on the legitimacy of both his initial appointment as emperor and the dying Constantius' conferral on him of the title of Augustus.

Libanius employed comparison to Achilles to characterize Julian's treament by Constantius both while he was in Antioch in 362 and after his death.[17] As a skilled orator, Libanius knew how to quote Homer for his own purposes. After Julian left Antioch in anger at the city, he composed a plea for reconciliation: everyone (he stated) was talking about the Persian expedition, not about the Trojan War or Alexander, but the wrath of Achilles needed urgently to be assuaged.[18]

Explicit comparison to Achilles was always a double-edged compliment to an emperor who was impetuous and prone to anger. Hence it plays a negligible part in Julian's conception of himself as Augustus, in his propaganda while he ruled and in retrospective panegyrics after he died. Yet implicit evocation of Achilles often lurks beneath the surface of Ammianus' text. When he reached Ctesiphon, Julian drew up his battle line *secundum Homericam dispositionem* and there ensued a display of valor comparable to the combats of Hector, the bravery of Achilles and the crowning glories of the Persian wars of the early fifth century B.C. (23.6.9–14). Ammianus' obituary commences by stating that Julian was "vir profecto heroicis connumerandus ingeniis, claritudine rerum et coalita maiestate conspicuus" (25.4.1). The Latin conveys much more than "Julian must be reckoned a man of heroic stature, conspicuous for his glorious deeds and his innate majesty" (as Hamilton and Wallace-Hadrill render

---

[15] Bowersock, *Julian* (1978), 65.

[16] Julian, *Epp.* 33, 389d–390a; 40 (45.27 Bidez-Cumont); 59, 443b: contrast *Ep. ad Ath.*. 270c–274b, where Julian depicts him as a murderer. However, official canonization as *divus Constantius* is neither celebrated on the Roman imperial coinage nor, apparently, attested by any inscription.

[17] Libanius, *Orat.* 12.49, 73; 13.6; 18.66, cf. 32.

[18] Libanius, *Orat.* 15.1, 8, 31–35.

it). Ammianus is not using a dead metaphor: he means that Julian belongs with the *heroica ingenia*, the heroes of great talent.[19] He is thinking primarily of Achilles, whose glorious deeds ultimately failed to bring him success because of a fatal weakness. The concealed image of Achilles, it may be suggested, underlies the whole of Ammianus' account of Julian. After the public ceremony at which he was proclaimed Caesar on 6 November 355, Ammianus' Julian goes with Constantius to the palace in Milan constantly whispering to himself a line of the *Iliad*: "wrapped in death's purple by all-powerful fate."[20] Seven and a half years later, as Julian willfully disregards the warnings sent by the gods as he marches into Mesopotamia, his blindness and folly are those of a tragic hero.[21]

Julian himself proclaimed two famous rulers as his principal models. They are Alexander and Marcus Aurelius. Julian names them together at the start of his letter to Themistius, which he probably wrote in 356,[22] and the same pairing is implicit in the *Caesars*, which he composed in Antioch in December 362. This work offers an assessment of Roman emperors from Julius Caesar to Constantine and his sons. Julian selected the literary form of a dialogue describing a banquet that Romulus gave for the gods to celebrate the Saturnalia. This allowed him both to omit emperors whom he did not wish to discuss and to introduce Alexander as one of the competitors for the title of best emperor.[23] The winner of the contest is Marcus Aurelius, who receives the majority of the gods' votes in a secret ballot.[24] However, after the Roman emperors have been welcomed and seated, but before the competition commences, Heracles insists that Alexander be invited as superior to all of them,[25] which might seem to suggest that he is superior to Marcus. For Heracles had a special meaning for Julian, who proclaimed that he was the savior of the world

---

[19] Apart from using *heroici versus* of the poems of the Gallic *bardi* (15.9.8), Ammianus restricts the epithet *heroicus* to mythical heroes in general (28.4.12) or to individuals like Mopsus (14.8.3) and the heroes who fought at Troy (22.8.3).

[20] *Iliad* 2.104.

[21] Rosen, *Studien* (1970), 149–78, cf. G. Wirth, *Julianus Apostata* (1978), 455–07.

[22] Julian, *Ep. ad Them.* 253a. For the hypothesis that Julian composed most of the letter in 356, but completed and sent it for his own political advantage between the spring of 360 and November 361, see T. D. Barnes and J. Vanderspoel, *GRBS* 22 (1981), 187–89. Further arguments for dating the composition of the letter to the winter of 355–356 are produced by R. Smith, *Julian's Gods: Religion and Philosophy in the Thought and Action of Julian the Apostate* (London/New York, 1995), 27–29. S. Bradbury, *GRBS* 28 (1987), 235–51, argues that Julian wrote the whole letter then, including its final page (266c–267b).

[23] G. W. Bowersock, *YCS* 27 (1982), 159–72.

[24] Julian, *Caes.* 335c.

[25] Julian, *Caes.* 316bc.

and that he walked on water as though it were the dry land.[26] Since the time of Dio Chrysostom, who assimilated Trajan to him, Heracles had stood as a model for Roman emperors, who imitated their divine avatar by strenuous and unceasing efforts to better the lot of mankind:[27] hence the short-lived dynasty of Herculian emperors in the days of Diocletian.[28] But there is an unusual warmth and an unusual polemical edge to what Julian says about Heracles, whom he makes the son of Athena, a virgin mother on the model of Mary, the mother of God.[29] Julian goes on, however, to emphasize Alexander's cruelty, drunkenness and lack of self-control: Alexander could not, therefore, serve as his exemplar except on the actual field of battle.[30]

After Julian's death, comparison with Alexander, like comparison with Achilles, became a double-edged compliment. Like Alexander, Julian won glorious victories in war and died young. But, whereas Alexander had defeated the Persian king and conquered the Achaemenid Empire, Julian failed and perished at the head of an army in retreat. Ammianus distracts his readers from this damaging comparison by a series of other comparisons to great generals of Greece and Rome.

Book XVI opens with a miniature panegyric of the new Caesar. He was a second Titus in wisdom,[31] most like Trajan in his military successes, clement like Antoninus Pius, and "in his striving after truth and perfection the equal of Marcus Aurelius, on whom he endavoured to model his own actions and character" (16.1.4). Later, as he prepares for war against Persia, Julian encounters criticism, but no more lets himself be deflected from his purpose than Hercules did when assailed by the Pygmies or the wild Lindian Thiodamas (22.12.4). In the course of his narrative, Ammianus compares Julian to a wide range of historical exemplars. The earliest in time is the Athenian general Cimon who, despite his victory over the Persians at the River Eurymedon, was—a lacuna has presumably removed a reference to his ostracism (17.11.3).

---

[26] Julian, *Orat.* 7, 219d (from Julian's attack on the Cynic Heraclius, composed in Constantinople in the winter of 361–362).

[27] R. Hoïstad, *Cynic Hero and Cynic King. Studies in the Cynic Conception of Man* (Uppsala, 1948), 50–73; C. P. Jones, *The World of Dio Chrysostom* (Cambridge, Mass., 1978), 116–20.

[28] Maximian (285–305), Constantius (293–306), Severus (305–07) and Constantine, until he abruptly dropped the title after his conversion (*New Empire* [1982], 24, cf. Lactantius, *Mort. Pers.* 52.3).

[29] Julian, *Orat.* 7, 220a, cf. *Orat.* 5, 166ab. The assimilation of Heracles to Jesus was acutely noted by Asmus, *Julians Galiläerschrift* (1904), 34–35.

[30] Julian, *Caes.* 321c, 330c–331c. On Julian's necessarily ambiguous attitude toward Alexander, see now R. J. Lane Fox, *CQ*, N.S. 47 (1997), 247–52.

[31] Although Titus' high reputation was ensured by the praises of both Tacitus and Suetonius, Julian disapproved and presented him as a promiscuous playboy: *Caes.* 311a, cf. J. F. Gilliam, *AJP* 88 (1967), 203–8; Bowersock, *YCS* 27 (1982), 167.

Next in time is the Theban commander Epaminondas who was fatally wounded in 362 B.C. at the Battle of Mantinea (25.3.8). When Ammianus compares Julian to Alexander the Great, it is not for victories in battle. Like Alexander, Julian divided the night into three equal parts for rest, for business, and for the Muses, but unlike Alexander he needed no artificial devices to prevent him from falling asleep (16.5.4). And like Alexander and many other skilled generals, Julian sent ahead a few troops spread out to create the impression that they formed a large army (21.8.3). Alexander and Scipio both declined to touch beautiful captive girls who were offered to them for their pleasure. So, too, did Julian, who avoided even lusting after them.[32] Scipio Aemilianus is invoked twice. He was accused of sleepiness, although his vigilance destroyed two most powerful cities (17.11.3). And he acted bravely, with Polybius at his side, during the siege of Carthage (24.2.16–17). Even Sulla is brought in. During the Battle of Strasbourg, Julian imitated Sulla, who, when deserted by his men in battle against Archelaus, strode forward, seized the standard, and advanced against the enemy (16.12.41). Like Julian, Pompey was unfairly criticized, despite his bravery and patriotism, even though only two utterly trivial complaints could be brought against him (17.11.4). And Julius Caesar provided a model for writing in a tent during the night (25.2.3).

This list contains some unexpected names. From Sallust onward, Sulla was remembered more for slaughtering his political opponents than for his victories over the enemies of Rome.[33] So, too, was Marius, whose victory over the Cimbri and Teutones Ammianus attributes to unnamed "excellent generals" (31.5.12: per duces amplissimos superati). Ammianus names Marius twice. One mention is conventional and unfavorable: Marius and Cinna allowed the plebs of Rome to loot the houses of the proscribed (30.8.9). The other is most surprising and relates to Julian. Ammianus includes both men among the select company of famous Romans who had genii familiares (21.14.5): three of the other names are predictable (king Numa, the elder Scipio and Augustus), but the inclusion of Marius is puzzling. Despite the valiant efforts of the Dutch commentators, the precise inpiration of Ammianus' list is uncertain. But the passage reinforces the comparisons of Julian to famous generals, which set Julian as a military commander in a long and noble tradition, both Greek and Roman.

---

[32] On the implications of this observation, see Chapter VIII, at nn. 26–29.

[33] Sallust, Cat. 5.6, 11.4–5, 28.4, 37.9, 51.32–34; Hist. 3.49.9 Maurenbrecher. When Virgil lists victorious Roman generals, he includes Marius, but not Sulla (Georgics 2.169–70). For Sulla as an exemplum of cruelty: Pliny, Nat. Hist. 7.137; Suetonius, Tib. 59.2; Pan. Lat. 12(9).20.4, 21.1; 2(12).46.1; Claudian, Ruf. 1.263. In view of his reputation, the emendation Sullas in Pan. Lat. 2(12).7.4 must be regarded as questionable.

Ammianus structures his narrative of Julian's actions as emperor in four main chronological sections. Julian is proclaimed Caesar by Constantius and sent to Gaul in Book XV, which closes with a long excursus on Gaul designed to emphasize the importance of Julian's arrival in Gaul (Chapter IX). Four books then cover Julian's actions as Caesar in Gaul from his arrival in the winter of 355–356 to his return to his winter quarters in Paris after the campaign of 359–360 (XVI–XIX). The next two books describe Julian's proclamation as Augustus early in 360, his subsequent dealings with Constantius, and his seizure of the Balkans in the summer of 361 (XX–XXI). Book XXII describes Julian as sole Augustus in Constantinople, crossing Asia Minor and in Antioch: it covers the period from Constantius' death on 3 November 361 (22.1.1, 2.1) to December 362 (cf. 23.1.1). Then an elaborate (and significant) series of notices tied to the Kalends of January 363 (23.1) introduces Julian's ill-fated Persian expedition (Chapter V). The expedition itself, with the reign of Jovian added as a mere footnote or epilogue to that of Julian (Chapter XII), occupies a full triad of books (XXIII–XXV). Within this narrative structure, Ammianus includes both formal excursus and extensive discussion of Julian's political, administrative and religious reforms.

If the historian's presentation of Julian is to be assessed at all adequately, analysis must concentrate on those aspects of it where independent evidence exists and where significant inferences can be made.[34] Three topics are here chosen for detailed consideration where both external and internal criteria are available. They do not include Julian's administrative reforms, which are likely always to remain matters of controversy.[35] For the administrative history of the Roman Empire contains many obscurites that will probably never be elucidated because the type of archival material used by historians of more recent periods is too often lacking. In the case of Julian there are two additional

[34] For an elegant general assessment of Ammianus' depiction of Julian, see J. Fontaine, *L'Empereur Julien. De l'histoire à la légende, 331–1715* (Paris, 1978), 31–65.

[35] For discussion of these, see W. Ensslin, *Klio* 18 (1923), 104–99; R. Andreotti, *Nuova Rivista Storica* 14 (1930), 342–83; Bowersock, *Julian* (1978), 71–78; Athanassiadi-Fowden, *Julian* (1981), 96–120; Elliott, *Ammianus* (1983), 104–21; Pack, *Städte und Steuern* (1986), 57–300; Matthews, *Ammianus* (1989), 104–13.

Ammianus' account of Julian's actions in response to the food shortage in Antioch (22.13.4–14.2) has been scrutinized with especial intensity: see P. de Jonge, *Mnemosyne*[4] 1 (1948), 238–45; G. Downey, *Studies in Roman Social and Economic History in Honor of A. C. Johnson* (Princeton, 1951), 312–21; P. Petit, *Libanius et la vie municipale à Antioche au IVe siècle après J.-C.* (Paris, 1955), 109–18; J. H. W. G. Liebeschuetz, *Antioch: City and Imperial Administration in the Later Roman Empire* (Oxford, 1972), 127–31; Pack, *Städte und Steuern* (1986), 301–377; P. Garnsey, *Famine and Food Supply in the Graeco-Roman World. Responses to Risk and Crisis* (Cambridge, 1988), 247–48; Matthews, *Ammianus* (1989), 408–13.

difficulties. First, the full text of most of the original documents enacting his administrative reforms is lost: hence their precise purport must be deduced either from brief and potentially misleading extracts in the Theodosian Code or from partisan, biased, and partial reports of authors whose main aim is either to praise or to blame. Hence there is, for example, serious uncertainty whether Julian's law that prohibited Christians from teaching forbade Christians from all teaching, even in private houses, as is implied by both Ammianus, who deprecates the law (22.10.7, 25.4.20) and Christian writers,[36] or applied only to the holders of municipal chairs, whose appointment is the subject of the extract preserved in the Theodosian Code.[37] Second, the general tenor of all the literary sources, favorable and hostile, Christian and pagan alike, is to emphasize a contrast between the administrative policies of Julian and Constantius even where the primary documents prove basic continuity.[38]

Julian in Gaul

When Constantius proclaimed Julian Caesar and sent him to Gaul, he intended him (like Gallus) to be the figurehead of an administration appointed by and obedient to himself.[39] In 356, Julian and Constantius acted in tandem: the Caesar advanced through Gaul to the Upper Rhine, then sped north to relieve Cologne (16.2–4), while the Augustus pinned the Alamanni down by advancing through Raetia. But Ammianus has obscured the cooperation of the two emperors operating in different theaters of war: his narrative of the campaigning season of 356, at least in the form in which it survived the Middle Ages, omits any mention of Constantius, although his account of the next year refers to it (16.12.15–16).

---

[36] The evidence is collected by J. Bidez and F. Cumont, *Imp. Caesaris Flavii Claudii Iuliani Epistulae Leges Poematia Fragmenta varia* (Paris/London, 1922), 69–75 no. 61.

[37] *CTh* 13.3.5, cf. T. M. Banchich, *JHS* 107 (1987), 164–65; *Ancient World* 24 (1993), 5–14.

[38] W. A. Goffart, *CP* 65 (1970), 145–51. However, *CTh* 2.29.1 shows that Julian radically changed the rules pertaining to payment for lobbying at court (*suffragium*): T. D. Barnes, *CP* 69 (1974), 288–91; *Phoenix* 39 (1985), 371–72.

[39] Julian, *Ep. ad Ath.* 277d–280c, cf. R. P. C. Blockley, *Latomus* 31 (1972), 445–55. Julian's claim that Constantius gave him real command over the Gallic army in spring 357 (278d) is contradicted by Ammianus (16.12.14). The praetorian prefects in Gaul, Honoratus (355–357) and Florentius (357–360), were appointed by Constantius and took their orders from him rather than from Julian: the former had been *comes Orientis* under Gallus and became the first *praefectus urbis Constantinopolitanae* in 359, while the latter operated independently of Julian, whom he felt entitled to disobey, and fled to Constantius as soon as Julian was proclaimed Augustus (*PLRE* 1.438–39, Honoratus 2; 365, Florentius 10).

In 357, too, Julian was supposed to cooperate with the army of Constantius, which was under the command of the *magister peditum* Barbatio, not of the Augustus himself (16.11).[40] It was in this year that Julian won the smashing victory near Strasbourg that was (and is) the basis of his reputation as a good general. Ammianus gives a long and detailed account of the battle that uses every literary trick and rhetorical device at his disposal to enhance Julian's glory (16.12). Literary analysis has effectively brought out its two main features.[41] First, Ammianus throughout contrasts the confidence, arrogance, and ferocity of the barbarians with Julian's calm resoluteness and his divine support: the *caelitis dei favor* and a *salutaris genius* help to bring the battle about (16.12.13); a standard bearer utters the exhortation "Follow, Caesar, the guidance of your lucky star: you are Fortune's darling" (16.12.18); and the *propitiati numinis arbitrium* aids the Romans (16.12.52). Second, the Roman victory at Strasbourg in Book XVI forms a diptych with the Roman defeat at Adrianople in Book XXXI. For in 378 the Goths display the virtues that the Romans had shown in 357 while the Romans of 378 have acquired the vices of Chnodomarius and his Alamanni.[42]

Ammianus nevertheless provides the fullest and most reliable account of the Battle of Strasbourg. The Germans had been crossing the Rhine for three days and the Roman army had encamped twenty-one miles from their entrenchment. After his infantry had advanced slowly from dawn to midday, Julian advised caution: Ammianus provides him with a speech in which he proposes that his tired troops halt, rest, refresh themselves, and attack the following day (16.12.9–12). When the troops clamor to fight, the decision to do so is taken by the *celsae potestates* and the praetorian prefect Florentius—that is, by the men whom Constantius had appointed to conduct the campaign with Julian as their titular commander. Ammianus reports the reason urged by Florentius, who argued that, although fighting always involved some risk, battle must be joined while conditions were favorable and while the barbarians were in one mass. If they dispersed, an unmatched opportunity would be lost, and the Roman troops, who were impetuous by nature, might mutiny if they felt that an inevitable victory had been snatched from their grasp (16.12.14). Had Julian really been in command, and had his plan been put into effect, there would have been no glorious victory at Strasbourg, where Roman tactics were to

---

[40] Ammianus denigrates Barbatio unfairly: Rosen, *Studien* (1970), 84–95; Elliott, *Ammianus* (1983), 76–79.

[41] Rosen, *Studien* (1970), 95–131; Bitter, *Kampfschilderungen* (1976), 56–101; R. P. C. Blockley, *Phoenix* 31 (1977), 218–31.

[42] Blockley, *Phoenix* 31 (1977), 224–28, cf. G. B. Pighi, *Nuovi studi ammianei* (Milan, 1936), 61–127.

push the largely unprepared Germans into the River Rhine and the marshes along its western bank.[43]

The victory thus belonged to others. But Julian soon claimed the credit that was at the time assigned to Constantius, and he began to use "his" victory as justification for acting with a greater degree of independence. Julian understood the importance of propaganda: he wrote his own account of the Battle of Strasbourg.[44] It has heavily influenced all extant accounts, including that of Ammianus, who had read it (16.5.7). The historian, however, had access to information independent of Julian through his contacts in the high command of the Roman imperial army.[45] His knowledge of the discussion by Julian and his advisers over whether to attack the Germans before they finished crossing the Rhine must come from fellow-officers who had been there and was presumably acquired shortly after the battle. Thus, despite his panegyrical tone and presentation, Ammianus undermines Julian's claim to credit for the victory by exposing Julian's version of the battle as misleading on the crucial issues of strategy and tactics[46]—which calls his reputation as a good general into doubt. Moreover, the subversive detail that Ammianus supplies both confirms his claim to have questioned participants in historical events (15.1.1) and implies that he was contemplating a history of his own time long before 378.

After the campaign of 357, Julian turned his attention to the Lower Rhine, where he prosecuted war with less enthusiasm. He was emancipating himself from the tutelage of Constantius' appointees and beginning to contemplate a challenge for supreme power. A classic analysis of his strategy established long ago that Julian stopped serious campaigning after 358 to prepare cleverly and covertly for the proclamation as Augustus that occurred in Paris in the early months of 360.[47] The argument inevitably relies heavily on Ammianus' detailed account of Julian's campaigns in 358 and 359 (17.8−10, 18.1−2), though rejecting his interpretation of the actions he narrates.

Ammianus presents Julian throughout as a consistently loyal subordinate who was taken by surprise when his troops unexpectedly proclaimed him Augustus and compelled him to agree to accept the title against his wishes (20.4.16: assentire coactus est). The letters and speeches that Julian composed as Caesar

---

[43] On the site and course of the battle, see esp. G. A. Crump, *Ammianus Marcellinus as a Military Historian* (*Historia Einzelschriften* 27, 1975), 85−89; Matthews, *Ammianus* (1989), 296−300; H. Elton, *Warfare in Roman Europe, A.D. 350−425* (Oxford, 1996), 250−56.

[44] Eunapius, frag. 9 Müller = 17 Blockley: other allusions are collected by Bidez and Cumont, *Iuliani Epistulae Leges* (1922), 212−13 no. 160.

[45] Crump, *Ammianus* (1975), 20.

[46] Matthews, *Ammianus* (1989), 91−92.

[47] I. Müller-Seidl, *HZ* 180 (1955), 225−44. There is a good diagrammatic map of Julian's campaigns in Matthews, *Ammianus* (1989), 82: Map 2.

reveal aspirations and ambitions that the historian has suppressed. By invoking Achilles openly and King David unconsciously, the second panegyric on Constantius lays bare a deep resentment and reveals dangerous hopes.[48] In a letter to the doctor Oribasius, the Caesar spoke more freely still. He described a dream whose political meaning is transparent. Julian saw a very tall tree bending over to the ground under its own weight and height and beside it a small shoot growing out of its roots. He feared for the safety of the young plant, and when he drew nearer he saw the large tree falling to the ground. The small tree was still standing; its roots remained in the earth; and an unknown person advised the dreamer not to fear for its safety. Julian commented disingenuously: "God knows what this means."[49]

Julian was thus already thinking or dreaming of declaring himself the equal of Constantius as early as the winter of 358–359.[50] A year later he was ready for usurpation. The fall of Amida in the late summer of 359 had damaged Constantius' prestige, and his request that Julian send some of his best troops to reinforce the eastern frontier provided an occasion too good to miss.[51] According to the official story, which Julian circulated in the letters he wrote to Greek cities in 361, Constantius was preparing to remove Julian from power out of jealousy over his successes. Hence he wrote him insulting letters and gave orders for the transfer of Caesar's best troops from Gaul to the East. The troops were distressed at the prospect. When an anonymous letter was circulated accusing Constantius of betraying Gaul, those around Julian, who were all loyal to Constantius, urged him to dispatch the troops at once. Julian assembled the men in Paris. The night before their departure they unexpectedly surrounded the palace shouting. Julian prayed to Zeus, who gave him a sign that that he should not oppose their will. Finally, although he continued to decline their salutation as Augustus and to refuse the diadem, he allowed a soldier to place his collar on his head, after which he returned to the palace groaning in his heart.[52]

This version of events was false, and contemporaries knew it to be false.[53]

[48] Above, pp. 144–45. According to Ammianus, Julian was saluted Augustus by his victorious troops immediately after the Battle of Strasbourg in 357, but swore on oath that he would never take the title (16.12.64).

[49] Julian, *Ep.* 10.

[50] Bowersock, *Julian* (1978), 17; J. F. Drinkwater, *Studies in Latin Literature and Roman History* 3 (*Collection Latomus* 180, 1983), 370–75.

[51] On the background to this request, whose consequences Constantius cannot have foreseen, see Drinkwater, *Studies in Latin Literature* 3 (1983), 376–78.

[52] Julian, *Ep. ad Ath.* 282–85; cf. Libanius, *Orat.* 18.95–105; Zosimus 3.9.1–3.

[53] Müller-Seidl, *HZ* 180 (1955), 241–44; K. Rosen, *Acta Classica* 12 (1969), 121–49; Bowersock, *Julian* (1978), 46–54, whose analysis of the episode is not invalidated by the minor flaws detected in it by R. S. O. Tomlin, *Phoenix* 34 (1980), 266–70.

When the praetorian prefect Mamertinus, who had been in Gaul at the time, delivered a *gratiarum actio* for his ordinary consulate on 1 January 362 in Constantinople, he passed quickly and with evident embarrassment over his benefactor's proclamation as Augustus. To this obligatory topic he allotted only a few vague, general, and tendentious remarks. Could Julian (he asked rhetorically) have surrendered Roman cities to the enemy just to avoid offending his cousin?[54]

More than twenty years later, Ammianus did not need to be so coy. Moreover, Eunapius had probably already presented Julian as a justified rebel against tyranny. For his later *Lives of the Philosophers*, composed in 399, states that Julian "summoned the hierophant from Greece, and after performing with his aid certain rites known to them alone, he was emboldened to abolish the tyranny of Constantius."[55] Eunapius is presumably speaking of Julian's actions after his proclamation at Paris, which he probably depicted as the spontaneous elevation of an unwilling Augustus.[56] Although Ammianus adds details not reported elsewhere, such as the name of the *hastatus* of the Petulantes who placed on Julian's head the *torques* that he was wearing as bearer of the dragon standard (20.4.18: Maurus nomine quidam), he adheres closely to the official version of his proclamation as Augustus that Julian circulated in 360 and 361 by depicting an unsuspecting innocent who yielded to extreme necessity and pressing danger (20.4–6). Yet he concurs with Zosimus in including something that conclusively proves Julian's complicity in the proclamation: after he had addressed the troops in the outskirts of the city, but before they surrounded the palace, he entertained his officers to dinner (20.4.13).[57] They lamented their lot—and presumably decided to do something about it.

Julian's Religion

For six years as Caesar and then as Augustus, Julian comported himself as a Christian, even though he had been converted from the Christianity of his

[54] *Pan. Lat.* 3(11).5.2.

[55] Eunapius, *Vit. phil.* 7.3.7 (476). He names Oribasius of Pergamum and the African Euhemerus as his accomplices: Bowersock, *Julian* (1978), 50. For disproof of the existence of a "pagan underground" in the East covertly aiding Julian before November 361, see Drinkwater, *Studies in Latin Literature* 3 (1983), 348–60.

[56] D. F. Buck, *AHB* 7 (1993), 73–80.

[57] On the damning implications of this dinner party, see Bowersock, *Julian* (1978), 49–51. Zosimus 3.9 has a parallel, but less detailed, account.

upbringing to paganism in 351.[58] At first he enforced Constantius' ecclesiastical policies in Gaul, sending Hilary of Poitiers into exile in Asia Minor in 356 after he had been condemned by the Council of Baeterrae.[59] After he was proclaimed Augustus, however, Julian began to support Constantius' ecclesiastical opponents and allowed the "Catholic" bishops of Gaul to hold a council in Paris during 360.[60] The death of Constantius removed all external constraints, and he commenced open avowal of paganism at once.[61] It may, or may not, be significant that Ammianus delays the moment of change, which occurred in Naissus, until Julian has entered Constantinople (22.5.1–2).

Julian's religious policies as sole emperor are clear, at least in outline.[62] He defined the purpose of his religious reforms as the preservation of traditional religion.[63] Yet Julian was a neopagan rather than an restorer of authentic traditional religion. When he described what a city ought to be, he offered a peculiar mixture of the ancient city and a puritanical ideal. A happy city, on Julian's definition, was one

> full of many shrines and many secret rites, with countless holy priests within its walls dwelling in holy enclosures. For the sake of this, I mean keeping everything in the city pure, they have expelled what is superfluous, sordid, and vicious from the city—public baths, brothels, shops, and everything of that sort without exception.[64]

Julian's ideal pagan city observes Christian standards of purity. For Julian's paganism was not of the original, earthy variety: it was a puritanical and ascetic neopaganism that owed a great deal to Christianity and was therefore markedly untraditional.[65] A perceptive analysis of Julian's personality, which firmly re-

---

[58] Julian, *Ep.* 111, 434d.

[59] Hilary, *CSEL* 65.198.5–15, cf. *Vig. Chr.* 46 (1992), 129–40; *Athanasius* (1993), 141, 171; P. Smulders, *Hilary of Poitiers' Preface to his "Opus Historicum"* (Leiden, 1995), 119–31.

[60] *CSEL* 65.43–46, cf. *Athanasius* (1993), 153–54.

[61] Julian, *Ep.* 26, 415c, informs the philosopher Maximus that he is openly worshipping the gods and has sacrificed many hecatombs of oxen, apparently while still in Naissus (cf. 415a).

[62] J. Bidez, *Vie de Julien* (1930), 219–35, 261–76, 291–315; Bowersock, *Julian* (1978), 79–83; T. D. Barnes, *Athanasius* (1993), 153–55. The present discussion deliberately eschews any attempt to define the precise intellectual nature of Julian's paganism.

[63] Julian, *Ep.* 89, 453bc.

[64] Julian, *Orat.* 6, 186d.

[65] H. Koch, *Revue belge de philologie et d'histoire* 6 (1927), 123–46; 7 (1928), 49–82, 511–50, 1363–85.

For a conspicuous example of Julian's ignorance of authentic tradition in a different area, see V. A. Maxfield, *The Military Decorations of the Roman Army* (London, 1981), 248–51. Julian decorated those who showed the greatest bravery in the capture of Maozamalcha with *obsidionales coronae* in old-fashioned style (24.4.24: veterum more), and before Ctesiphon he decorated sol-

jects the quasi-hagiographical approach of much modern writing about the emperor, recognizes his fanaticism and classifies him as a "revolutionary ascetic."[66] Ammianus acknowledges but plays down the fanaticism, and he seriously misrepresents both Julian's religious policies and his religious beliefs. Ammianus gives his readers a reign of Julian in which no Christian suffered for his faith (Chapter V), he declines to record his attempt to found a neo-pagan counterchurch, and he completely omits two central elements of the emperor's personal creed: theurgy and Mithraism.

Julian had embraced Iamblichus' version of Platonism wholeheartedly, and he regarded this Neoplatonist heir of a long philosophical tradition, from whom he had learned his philosophy, as an equal of the great founder of the school. For Julian, Plato was of course a great philosopher, but Iamblichus of Chalcis was by no means inferior to him in genius: Iamblichus was a glorious hero, divine, and the friend of God.[67] Iamblichus accepted the authority of the so-called Chaldaean Oracles, which were associated with Julianus the Chaldaean and his son Julianus the Theurgist, who had revealed them to the world in the reign of Marcus Aurelius.[68] Iamblichus integrated the Chaldaean Oracles into his philosophical system, so that the practice of theurgy became central to it: although he presented his system as the logical development of classical Greek philosophical thought, he transformed what had been primar-

---

diers with *navales coronae et civicae et castrenses* (24.6.15). Such decorations had fallen completely out of use circa 200, so that Julian's revival was an act of conscious antiquarianism. But he made a significant mistake. Aulus Gellius, who has a chapter on *coronae militares*, defines the *corona obsidonalis* as one given by a besieged city to the general who has liberated it by lifting the siege and states that Q. Fabius Maximus received one for rescuing Rome from Hannibal (*Noctes Atticae*, 5.6.8–10).

[66] Bowersock, *Julian* (1978), 12–20. The merits of this brief, but incisive, study were sadly underestimated by J. F. Matthews, *TLS* 3 November 1978, 1283, who failed to see that neither its brevity nor some minor factual errors invalidate its analysis of Julian's tortured psyche: for a juster appreciation, see F. Paschoud, *REL* 58 (1980), 117–23.

[67] Julian, *Orat.* 4, 158cd, cf. 150d. On Iamblichus, see now the collection of essays edited by H. J. Blumenthal and E. G. Clark, *The Divine Iamblichus. Philosopher and Man of Gods* (London, 1993), with the review article by P. Athanassiadi, *JRS* 85 (1995), 244–50.

[68] *Suda* I 433, 434 (2.641–42 Adler). It is possible that Porphyry incorporated some of the Chaldean Oracles in his youthful *Philosophy from Oracles*, viz., frags. 219–25 des Places, which are quoted from Porphyry in Eusebius, *Praep. Ev.* 5.8.4–7, 9.1., 12.1. However, their provenance is disputed by E. R. Dodds, *HTR* 54 (1961), 264–67. Porphyry later questioned the authority of the Chaldean Oracles in a work that may have had the composite title "On the return of the Soul, in Reply to the Writings of Julian the Chaldean." However, although the direction of the change in Porphyry's opinions is clear (J. Bidez, *Vie de Porphyre le philosophe néoplatonicien* [Ghent/Leipzig, 1913], 88–97), it is normally assumed that two separate works are in question: A. Smith, *Porphyrii Philosophi Fragmenta* (Leipzig, 1993), 319–50 (frags. 283–302), 435–40 (frags. 362–68).

ily a philosophy with mystical overtones into something closer to a religion with both a theology and cult acts.[69]

Julian saw himself as a disciple of Iamblichus, but he gave a unique and individual twist to his teachings by combining theurgy with Mithraism in a novel blend of personal mysticism.[70] In his *Hymn to the Mother of the Gods*, composed at Pessinus in 362, he vaunts his participation in the Mithraic mysteries and claims Julian the Chaldaean as a Mithraist:

> And if I should also touch on the secret teaching of the mysteries which the Chaldean revealed in divine frenzy concerning the God of the Seven Rays, lifting up the souls of men through him, I should be saying what is incomprehensible, indeed completely incomprehensible to the common herd, but well known to the blessed theurgists.[71]

Julian practiced a conscious syncretism which integrated Roman tradition into his Iamblichan philosophical and religious thought world. At the army camp in Carnuntum in 308, the former emperor Diocletian, the senior reigning emperor Galerius, and the newly proclaimed Augustus Licinius had restored a shrine of the Deus Sol Invictus Mithras whom they saluted as the sustainer of their imperial rule.[72] Julian went much further. The *Hymn to King Helios*, which Julian addressed to his praetorian prefect Salutius, envisages Helios as a Neoplatonic triad: the sun is transcendental and as such indistinguishable from the Good in the intelligible world; the sun is identical with Mithras and the ruler of the intellectual gods; and the visible sun illumines the physical world.[73] The worship of Mithras and the quadriennial games of Sol

---

[69] On this development, see E. R. Dodds, *The Greeks and the Irrational* (Berkeley, 1951), 283–311; H. Lewy, *Chaldean Oracles and Theurgy: Mysticism, Magic and Platonism in the Later Roman Empire* (Cairo, 1956; photographic reprint with corrigenda and extensive addenda, ed. M. Tardieu, Paris, 1978); F. W. Cremer, *Die chaldäischen Orakel und Jamblich de mysteriis* (Diss. Cologne, 1967; publ. Meisenheim am Glan, 1969); R. T. Wallis, *Neoplatonism* (London, 1972), 100–10, 118–23; A. Smith, *Porphyry's Place in the Neoplatonic Tradition. A Study in Post-Plotinian Neoplatonism* (The Hague, 1974), 83–141; B. Nasemann, *Theurgie und Philosophie in Jamblichs De mysteriis* (Diss. Cologne, 1989; pub. Stuttgart, 1991); B. E. Pearson, *Neoplatonism and Gnosticism*, ed. R. T. Wallis and J. Bregman (Albany, 1992), 253–75; G. Shaw, *Theurgy and the Soul. The Neoplatonism of Iamblichus* (University Park, Pa., 1995), 16, 61–242.

[70] On the importance of Mithraism in Julian's thought, see Athanassiadi-Fowden, *Julian* (1981), 38–41, 113–14, 133–35, 153, 197–98. It is denied by Smith, *Julian's Gods* (1995), who attempts to demonstrate that Julian was at heart a traditional polytheist.

[71] Julian, *Orat.* 5, 172d–173a.

[72] *ILS* 657: d. S. i. M. fautori imperii sui Iovii et Herculii religiosissimi Augusti et Caesares sacrarium restituerunt. For the political context, see, briefly, *Constantine* (1981), 32.

[73] Julian, *Orat.* 4(10), 132c–133c, cf. P. Athanassiadi-Fowden, *JTS*, N.S. 28 (1977), 360–71.

Invictus may be recent (the *solis agon* was instituted by Aurelian in 274),[74] but Julian claims that the Romans have worshipped the sun since the days of King Numa.[75] Julian names Mithras only once in the *Hymn* and only once elsewhere.[76] Such reticence was required of a Mithraist by the secret nature of the cult, which was less a religion than an ancient version of freemasonry for soldiers and government servants.[77] Nevertheless, the equation of Mithras with Helios was fundamental to Julian's religious beliefs, as the other passage that names Mithras makes clear. In the concluding paragraph of the *Caesars*, Hermes informs Julian that he has granted him knowledge of his father Mithras and adds the following injunction: "Keep his commandments, securing for yourself a secure stern-cable and mooring during your lifetime, and making with good hopes a guardian god who will be favorable to you when you need to depart from here."[78]

There is independent confirmation of the importance of Mithras for Julian. The sophist Himerius, a native of Bithynia, had been teaching in Athens as the holder of an official chair of rhetoric since circa 353. When he heard of Julian's successful advance to Naissus, he abruptly left Athens, attached himself to the imperial court, and eagerly took part in a celebration of the mysteries of Mithras in the Mithraeum which Julian constructed in the imperial palace in Constantinople.[79] Himerius proclaimed the fact in an address to the city that was also a panegyric of the emperor. It opens as follows:

> Having purified our soul to Helios-Mithras already by the aid of the gods in the company of an emperor who is a friend of the gods, come now! let us light up a speech rather than a lantern to the emperor and the city! A law of Athens orders the mystic initiates to carry light and handfuls of grain to Eleusis as tokens of civilised life. For our mystic initiates let a speech be presented as a thank-offering, if indeed Apollo is, as I think, identical with Helios, and speeches are the children of Apollo.[80]

An issue of bronze coins from most of the imperial mints except Rome combines the reverse legend *Securitas rei pub(licae)* with a bull and two stars (some-

---

[74] *Chr. min.* 1.148; Jerome, *Chronicle* 223[b] Helm, cf. E. Cizek, *L'empereur Aurélien et son temps* (Paris, 1994), 178–82.

[75] Julian, *Orat.* 4(10), 155a–156b.

[76] Julian, *Orat.* 4(10), 155b; *Caes.* 336c.

[77] For Mithraism as a club, see R. L. Beck, *Voluntary Associations in the Roman World*, ed. J. S. Kloppenborg and S. G. Wilson (London/New York, 1996), 176–85. Its affinites with freemasonry were noted by N. Swerdlow, *CP* 86 (1991), 48, 62–63.

[78] Julian, *Caes.* 336c.

[79] Libanius, *Orat.* 18.127, cf. *CP* 82 (1987), 221–22.

[80] Himerius, *Orat.* 41.1.

times also an eagle).[81] The type has never been convincingly explained.[82] But two stars associated with a bull ineluctably suggest Cautes and Cautopates, the helpers of Mithras, who were associated with the stars Aldebaran and Antares,[83] and there can be no doubt of the centrality of Mithras in Julian's mind, despite both his reticence and the silence of Ammianus.[84]

Like the rites of Mithras, theurgy was practiced in secret, not in public. Julian engaged in theurgy with the assistance of his philosophical mentor and guide, Maximus of Ephesus, who accompanied the Persian expedition and was present when the emperor died (25.3.23).[85] Ammianus' treatment of Julian's relationship with Maximus is idiosyncratic. He presents Maximus as a genuine philosopher, not as the arrogant charlatan depicted in Eunapius' *Lives of the Philosophers*, who took advantage of an unsuspecting Julian.[86] But he criticizes the emperor sharply for excessive display of his friendship for him. One day, when he was he was hearing legal cases, it was reported that Maximus had arrived from Asia. The emperor leapt up in undignified haste, ran out, kissed Maximus, and brought him back with him into court. Ammianus condemns this "untimely ostentation" that showed Julian up as "excessively anxious for empty glory" (22.7.3). Ammianus knew that Julian had been converted in 351, since he makes him pray secretly to Mercury, that is, to Hermes, whom Julian often invokes as the god of eloquence and his protector,[87] shortly after his arrival in Gaul (16.5.5). But he so deeply disapproved of Julian's blend of paganism that he ridiculed the emperor's religion.

---

[81] *RIC* 8.195 Lyons, 236–38; 229 Arles, 313–23; 337 Aquileia, 242–43; 380 Siscia 411–13, 417–19; 392 Sirmium, 105–07; 423 Thessalonica, 222–26; 438 Heraclea, 101–04; 462–63 Constantinople, 161–64; 483–84 Nicomedia, 118–22; 500 Cyzicus, 125–28; 532 Antioch, 216–18. Julian, *Mis.* 355d, alludes to the Antiochenes' mockery of his coinage: Socrates, *HE* 3.17.5–6, states that it was this issue that they ridiculed. It is also mentioned by Ephrem, *Contra Iulianum* 1.16–19.

[82] J. P. C. Kent, *RIC* 8 (1981), 47. Ephrem, *Contra Iulianum* 1.16–19 (ed. E. Beck, *CSCO* 174 = Syr. 78 [1957], 74–75: English translation by K. E. McVey, *Ephrem the Syrian: Hymns* [New York, 1989], 231–32) inveighs against the bull coinage and compares the bull on the coins to the golden calf of Exodus 32.1–35: Bowersock, *Julian* (1978), 104, deduces that "the meaning of Julian's strange new coinage was quite unknown even then."

[83] R. Beck, *Journal of Mithraic Studies* 2 (1977), 6–8.

[84] The contrary is confidently asserted by R. Turcan, *Mithra et le mithraicisme* (Paris, 1993), 118: "rien, ni dans ses discours ni dans son monnayage ou sa politique, ne comporte le moindre indice probant de mithraicisme." He appears not to mention Himerius.

[85] On whom, see *PLRE* 1.583–84, Maximus 21.

[86] Eunapius, *Vit. phil.* 7.4.1–4 (477).

[87] Julian, *Orat.* 4, 132a; 6, 182c; 7, 225b, 230c–231a, 232d, 234b, 237c: in the *Caesars*, Hermes is named as the author's informant (307a), who has also given him knowledge of Mithras (336c, quoted above, p. 159).

Ammianus belonged in the philosophical tradition of Porphyry (Chapters VII, XIV), who was intellectually opposed to Iamblichus on many issues.[88] The two philosophers perhaps differed most sharply over the issue of animal sacrifice. Porphyry condemned it roundly as irrational in his *Letter to Anebo*; Iamblichus replied to him under the pseudonym of Abammon, using the scholarly genre of "problems and solutions" to pose objections one by one and answer them in the tone of a master correcting a wayward pupil.[89] Ammianus fastened on this aspect of Julian's religion:

> He drenched the altars with the abundant blood of sacrificial victims with excessive frequency. On several occasions he sacrificed a hundred bulls at a time, countless flocks of varied livestock and white birds sought afar by land and sea. As a result, almost every day soldiers, who gorged themselves uncontrollably with meat till their bellies were distended and they were demoralised by their craving for drink, were carried to their quarters on the shoulders of passers-by through the streets from public temples where they indulged in wild parties which ought to have been punished rather than permitted. (22.12.6)

Ammianus proceeds to complain about the unparalleled expense that Julian's religiosity entailed and that divination was practiced by many who had no genuine expertise in interpreting oracles, inspecting entrails, or understanding the

[88] For the deep disagreement between the two philosophers over basic issues, see H. D. Saffrey, *Philomathes: Studies and Essays in the Humanities in Memory of Philip Merlan* (The Hague, 1971), 227–39: Smith, *Porphyry's Place* (1974), xvii–xviii, 81–141. A long tradition makes Iamblichus a pupil of Porphyry and Porphyry "the historical and ideological mediator between Plotinus and Iamblichus": B. D. Larsen, *Jamblique de Chalcis. Exégète et philosophe* (Diss. Aarhus, 1970: pub. Aarhus, 1972), 36–40; J. Dillon, *Iamblichi Chalcidensis in Platonis Commentariorum Fragmenta* (*Philosophia Antiqua* 23, 1973), 8–11; Shaw, *Theurgy* (1995), 2–3, 12–13. But it is highly doubtful whether Iamblichus ever studied with Porphyry, as is stated by Eunapius, *Vit. phil.* 5.1.2–3, (458). The profound intellectual divergences between the two men are noted by G. Mau, *RE* 9 (1916), 645; H.-I. Marrou, *The Conflict between Paganism and Christianity in the Fourth Century*, ed. A. Momigliano (Oxford, 1963), 132–33; Smith, *Porphyry's Place* (1974), xvii–xviii. And Iamblichus, who had a son who was married by 300 (Porphyry, *Vita Plotini* 9.3–5), must have been born before 250, probably c. 242–243: J. Bidez, *REG* 32 (1919), 32 ("né vers 250 au plus tard"); Alan Cameron, *Hermes* 96 (1968), 374–76, so that he was only ten to fifteen years younger than Porphyry. Accordingly, since Iamblichus is not known ever to have left Syria, it is probable that, if he studied with Porphyry, he did so, not "at Rome" (as *PLRE* 1.450; T. D. Barnes, *GRBS* 19 [1978], 105), but before the latter went to Rome in 263 and met Plotinus.

[89] Both the conventional title *De Mysteriis*, bestowed on it by Marsilio Ficino, and the conventional division into ten books are seriously misleading: M. Sicherl, *Die Handschriften, Ausgaben und Übersetzungen von Iamblichus De Mysteriis. Eine kritisch-historische Studie* (*Texte und Untersuchungen* 62, 1957); *BZ* 53 (1960), 9; Saffrey, *Philomathes* (1971), 227–39; *Divine Iamblichus* (1993), 144–58.

flight of birds (22.12.7). Subsequently, Ammianus' obituary of Julian delivers a verdict on his religion that both mocks and condemns:

> He was too devoted to divination, so that he seemed in this respect to rival the emperor Hadrian. He was superstitious rather than a genuine observer of religious rites, and he sacrificed innumerable animals regardless of expense, so that it was reckoned that, if he had returned from Parthia, there would soon have been a dearth of cattle. He resembled the famous Caesar Marcus, about whom we are told that the following was said:
>
> > Greetings to Marcus from the oxen white.
> > We're done for if you win another fight.
> >
> > (25.4.17)

Julian was *superstitiosus magis quam sacrorum legitimus observator*: Ammianus believed that he perverted traditional religion as badly as Constantius perverted Christianity. Yet he filters out Julian's Mithraism, his devotion to Helios, and his practice of theurgy. Instead, he emphasizes traditional forms of divination, such as *haruspicina* and augury (21.2.4, 22.1.1–2), notes that *haruspices* accompanied Julian on the Persian expedition (23.5.10, 25.27–28), and states repeatedly that Julian ignored the warnings that the gods gave him as he marched into Mesopotamia (23.2.7, 3.3, 5.6, etc.).[90] At the time, in contrast, Julian had written to Libanius from Hierapolis to inform him that all the omens had so far been propitious.[91]

The Persian Expedition

Much has been written about Ammianus' detailed account of Julian's invasion of Mesopotamia, and especially about what written sources he may have used.[92] The present exposition, therefore, can concentrate on Julian's strategy,

[90] On these omens and portents, see W. Liebeschuetz, *Roma Renascens*, ed. M. Wissemann (Frankfurt, 1988), 198–213. D. Conduché, *Latomus* 24 (1965), 364–79, argues that the adverse omens reflect contemporary disapproval of Julian's plans voiced by officers serving on the expedition.

[91] Julian, *Ep.* 98, 399d, 401b.

[92] For a critical survey of both the problems and the solutions offered by modern scholarship, see M. F. A. Brok, *Die perzische expeditie van Keizer Julians volgens Ammianus Marcellinus* (Groningen, 1959); F. Paschoud, *Zosime: Histoire Nouvelle* 1 (Paris, 1971), xliii–lvii; 2.1 (Paris, 1979), xii–xix, 100–227. Among recent discussions, note E. Bliembach, *Libanius Oratio 18 (Epitaphios): Kommentar (§§ 111–308)* (Diss. Würzburg, 1976), 129–225; Bowersock, *Julian* (1978), 106–19; Elliott, *Ammianus* (1983), 122–34; Matthews, *Ammianus* (1989), 130–83; C. W. Fornara, *JHS* 111 (1991), 1–15; *AJAH* 10 (1985, publ. 1994), 28–40. R. T. Ridley, *His-*

which has often been misunderstood and which Ammianus misrepresents. Ammianus states that Julian took care that no rumor of his march preceded him, so that he might seize Babylonia before he was detected (23.2.7: ut . . . improvisus Assyrios occuparet). Modern students of the campaign usually assume that Julian looked to Alexander the Great not only as his hero, but also as his model.[93] Some have even asserted that he regarded himself "as a reincarnation of Alexander."[94] Hence they have supposed that his strategy must have been one of strategic surprise—to march rapidly on Ctesiphon and take it by storm before Shapur, diverted by a second Roman army in northern Mesopotamia, could return to defend his capital.[95] Julian failed and thus revealed that he was "no second Alexander."[96] But strategic surprise, in the sense of mounting an unexpected invasion against an unprepared foe, was impossible in ancient conditions,[97] and few leaders in history (with the conspicuous exception of Josef Stalin in 1941) have shut their eyes and ears to obvious signs of an impending invasion. When Julian arrived in Antioch on 18 or 19 July 362 (22.9.15),[98] it soon became obvious that he was preparing to invade Persia. Shapur knew what Julian intended and sent an embassy to Antioch to try to avert the impending invasion. Libanius refers to its arrival in a speech delivered on 1 January 363, and after Julian was dead, he lamented his brusque refusal to negotiate.[99] Ammianus omits both the embassy and Julian's display of obstinacy. He also omits the fact, on casual attestation in a letter of Libanius, that Julian hoped to replace Shapur with Hormisdas.[100]

---

toria 22 (1973), 317–30, demonstrated that the account in Zosimus 3.13–30, despite manifold shortcomings, is in important respects superior to that of Ammianus.

[93] N. H. Baynes, Byzantine Studies and Other Essays (London, 1955), 346–67.

[94] Athanassiadi-Fowden, Julian (1981), 193, repeating verbatim the allegation of Socrates, HE 3.21.7.

[95] W. E. Kaegi, Athenaeum, N. S. 59 (1981), 209–13.

[96] B. Strauss and J. Ober, The Anatomy of Error: Ancient Military Disasters and Their Lessons for Modern Strategists (New York, 1990), 216–43, a perceptive and penetrating essay, despite being mistaken on this point.

[97] A. D. Lee, The Eastern Frontier of the Roman Empire, ed. D. H. French and C. S. Lightfoot (BAR, Supp. Ser. 553, 1989), 257–65; Information and Frontiers. Roman Foreign Relations in Late Antiquity (Cambridge, 1993), 112–28, 149–61.

[98] As interpreted by F. Cumont, Syria 8 (1927), 339–40, whose inference is confirmed by Jerome's commentary on Ezekiel (3.8.13, 14 [PL 25.82–83 = CCL 75.99]). Older editions of Jerome misguidedly emended the transmitted Iulio mense to Iunio: from this false emendation derives the erroneous date of June for Julian's arrival in Seeck, Regesten (1919), 210, repeated in Matthews, Ammianus (1989), 540, n. 13, although his text has the correct month (409).

[99] Libanius, Orat. 12.76–77; 17.19; 18.164–65.

[100] Libanius, Ep. 1402.3. Ammianus records several actions by Hormisdas as a general during the Persian expedition (24.1.2, 1.8, 2.4, 2.11, cf. Zosimus 3.15.4–6, 18.1, 23.4, 29.2).

The only strategic surprise that Julian could achieve was the precise route of invasion. However, his range of options was very limited: there was no possibility of a sudden breakthrough in a lightly defended sector of the sort that the German tank divisions achieved in France in 1940. Julian must advance either down the Euphrates or close to the Tigris. His plan was to keep Shapur guessing by advancing to Carrhae before splitting his forces. Ammianus notes that he went from Antioch to Hierapolis "by the usual route" (23.2.6), then to Carrhae: Julian wrote to Libanius from Hierapolis describing his reception in Litarba, a village of Chalcis, Beroea, and Batnae on the way there.[101]

The main expeditionary force then swung south, crossed the Euphrates, and marched downriver along its right bank in tandem with the fleet. What did Julian intend to do with this fleet after the outward march? This is the *crux interpretationis* for understanding his strategy. Ammianus goes badly wrong, and he is dutifully followed by most modern writers. Ammianus was puzzled by Julian's destruction of the fleet in front of Ctesiphon: he depicts it as an outright error that Julian tried too late to rectify (24.7.4–6). In reality, Julian must have intended to destroy his fleet as soon as it ceased to be useful and became an encumbrance.[102] Julian advanced down the Euphrates, used the Naarmalcha canal to cross to Ctesiphon, planning to return to Roman territory by the end of the campaigning season (23.2.5). His intended return route was along the left or northern bank of the Tigris, then through the foothills of the Zagros Mountains, where he expected to find sufficient supplies of food.[103] He could not take a fleet either up the Tigris (it flowed too strongly) or away from the river into the foothills: therefore, because he must either abandon his boats to the enemy or destroy them, his chosen strategy dictated their destruction.

Did Julian intend to capture Ctesiphon? Probably not: he had neither a large enough army nor adequate siege equipment to take the city by storm— and a long siege was unimaginable. If he had a rational strategy, it was rather to menace Ctesiphon, thereby compelling Shapur to come to its rescue. Julian surely intended to fight Shapur in pitched battle, in which the Romans had

---

[101] Julian, *Ep.* 98, cf. Zosimus 3.12.1–2. On his route, see F. Cumont, *Études syriennes* (Paris, 1917), 1–33, who noted that the absence of any mention of the famous shrine of Atargatis indicates that a Christian copyist has omitted an important part of the letter (23–24).

[102] The destruction is presented as a planned and deliberate action by Libanius, *Orat.* 18.261–63; Zosimus 3.26.2–3. N. J. E. Austin, *Athenaeum*, N.S. 50 (1972), 301–9, plausibly suggests that Ammianus' narrative combines two different and partly contradictory versions of Julian's actions at Ctesiphon—that of the high command and that of officers and men who were not privy to their deliberations and decisions.

[103] Lee, *Information* (1993), 87–89.

often prevailed over Persian forces. He would have his back to Ctesiphon, but he would be protected from attack in the rear by the river. Shapur frustrated this plan by declining to march quickly to the relief of his capital. Instead, he remained in northern Mesopotamia and dealt with the army under Procopius and Sebastianus, who were instructed to join Arsaces, the king of Armenia (23.3.5, cf. 2.2), and to advance through Corduene to facilitate Julian's withdrawal to Roman territory. Libanius complained that Arsaces played Julian false and that Procopius and Sebastianus failed to carry out their orders because of personal quarrels with each other.[104] Military action by Shapur is an equipollent explanation. Unfortunately, Ammianus' account of the activities of this army, whatever it was, is lost in a lacuna (24.7.3).

A rational strategy can be discerned behind Julian's actions when they are matched with maps of Mesopotamia.[105] After advancing down the Euphrates, he planned to return up the northern bank of the Tigris. But, if rational, his strategy was excessively optimistic, and Shapur countered it effectively. Although Ammianus was with the army, he failed to understand Julian's strategy—or that his generals had retrospectively foisted on his dead hero responsibility for a catastrophe that could still have been avoided at the time of his death. For disaster followed on their decision to attempt a shorter and more direct route back to Roman Mesopotamia rather than following the longer, but safer, route north of the Tigris into the foothills of the Zagros Mountains, where Julian expected to procure adequate supplies of food and water. Shapur starved the Roman army into submission only after the death of Julian.

A generation later, Ammianus could not recapture the genuine atmosphere of the late summer and autumn of 363, when Jovian's subjects genuinely welcomed his accession as emperor (Chapter XII). The imperial coinage celebrated the safe return of most of the expeditionary force that Julian had led into Persia as if it were a Roman victory won by the new Augustus.[106] And Jovian was saluted by the Syriac poet Ephrem for bringing solace to the afflicted and terrifying their oppressors.[107]

---

[104] Libanius, *Orat.* 18.260.

[105] Ridley, *Historia* 22 (1973), 317–30, cf. M. A. Beek, *Atlas of Mesopotamia*, trans. D. R. Welsh (London/Edinburgh, 1962), 48 (physical map and soil types); *Atlas of the Middle East*, ed. M. Brawer (New York/London, 1988), 82 (agriculture in modern Iraq).

[106] K. Ehling, *Klio* 78 (1996), 186–91.

[107] Ephrem, *Carmina Nisibena* 21.14, 21–23 (ed. E. Beck, *CSCO* 218 = Syri 92 [1961], 57, 58–59, with a German translation in *CSCO* 219 = Syri 93 [1961], 70, 72–73). Ephrem appears to be writing before he realized that Jovian had agreed to surrender Nisibis to the Persians (Beck, ibid. iii–iv).

[XIV]

PAST, PRESENT, AND FUTURE

An officer and a gentleman is not normally expected to be deeply versed or profoundly interested in philosophy. By the same token, however, imprecision or inconsistency does not prove that such a man's apparent interest in philosophy is merely superficial or second-hand, as has been assumed in most modern discussions of Ammianus' thought world and his "religious and moral universe."[1] Ammianus' philosophical views (so it is normally held) are not the product of independent reflection, for they derive from handbooks, from popularized Neoplatonism, from Cornelius Labeo: the historian had never read any Plotinus or Porphyry in the original Greek, but knew them only through the translations or adaptations by Nicomachus Flavianus.[2] Such assumptions have never been proved and ought to be rejected. John Matthews, to his credit, has broken with scholarly tradition: he argues that Ammianus' allusion to Plotinus "suggests more careful reflection on certain issues" and treats Ammianus' "Neoplatonic learning" as something that he acquired for himself.[3] But it is R. L. Rike who has provided the proof that Ammianus has a personal creed that is the product, not of borrowed learning, intellectual confusion, or apathy, but of conscious decision and the exercise of thought.[4]

---

[1] P.-M. Camus, *Ammien Marcellin. Témoin des courants culturels et religieux à la fin du IVe siècle* (Paris, 1967), 266: "l'historien est resté sur le seuil de la philosophie sans y pénétrer réellement." Camus' book is a remarkable achievement: he wrote it at the age of twenty-three, but was killed in a traffic accident on 18 August 1964 before he could amplify and deepen his researches: they would (I suspect) have led him to conclusions very similar to my own.

[2] For such belittling of Ammianus' erudition, see Chapter VII, at nn. 51–61.

[3] Matthews, *Ammianus* (1989), 434–35.

[4] Rike, *Apex Omnium* (1987), 8–36. His conclusions are rejected by Matthews, *Ammianus* (1989), 545, n. 10.

Ammianus has a fundamentally consistent metaphysical scheme, which he applies to his evaluation of historical events and historical actions. The two crucial passages occur in the obituary of the Caesar Gallus in Book XIV and the excursus on divination in Book XXI. Both passages present a divine hierarchy or triad. In the first, the just celestial godhead (*superni numinis aequitas*) watches over events, while subordinate to it Adrasteia or Nemesis, whom the ancient theologians depicted as the daughter of Justice, administers the fates and elements (14.11.25–26). In the second, an omnipresent force of undiminished vigor, Jupiter, shares with men the gifts of divination, while Themis, whom the ancient theologians made his bedfellow, presides over those powers and publishes the decrees fixed by fate (21.1.8).

These two hierarchies are not only related, but are in fact similar and complementary: they are "two aspects of a single theological scheme, which the historian first describes from the viewpoint of *aequitas*, the descent of Fate upon men, then from that of *benignitas*, the religious and intellectual ascent of men to the gods through a generously shared knowledge of divine will."[5] In both passages, Ammianus carefully aligns himself with the *theologi veteres*: he belongs to an ancient and noble tradition, and he did not intend to say anything new or original. The second passage is the key to Ammianus' philosophical viewpoint. What he says about Themis and *tetheimena* is strikingly similar to a passage of Porphyry known only because Eusebius' *Preparation for the Gospel* quotes it.[6] Recent exegetes assume that Ammianus cannot have read Porphyry: hence Joachim Szidat posits an intermediary as his direct source,[7] while the Dutch commentators observe that "Porphyry was a polymath who gathered his data from many sources, which may also have been accessible to Ammianus." The latter observation may be factually correct. But it ignores something both startling and relevant about the word *tethimena* in the text of Ammianus. In the corpus of Greek literature, the perfect participle passive of the Greek verb *tithemi* occurs just over one hundred times, but has the meaning "fixed decrees of fate" only in this one passage of Porphyry quoted by Eusebius.[8] It is probable, therefore, that Ammianus knew Porphyry directly[9], and there is no good reason to deny that he read him in the original Greek (Chapter VII).

---

[5] Rike, *Apex Omnium* (1987), 15.

[6] Eusebius, *PE* 3.11.14 = Porphyry, frag. 358.34–37, Smith = *De cultu simulacrorum*, frag. 7, p. 10* Bidez.

[7] J. Szidat, *Mus. Helv.* 39 (1982), 136–44. From similarities between Servius and Macrobius, he infers that Ammianus knew Porphyry only through his western interpreters.

[8] I rely on a search in the Thesaurus Linguae Graecae.

[9] For other points of similarity, see Szidat, *Mus. Helv.* 39 (1982), 139–45.

Ammianus puts before his readers' eyes a Roman Empire in which, despite everything, the old religion is still alive.[10] At the shrine of Mopsus in Cilicia cures are still performed: "his heroic *manes* cure a variety of diseases" (14.8.3). That is not merely an antiquarian observation: in his panegyric on Theodorus, Gregory of Nyssa claims that the martyr is now in heaven "seeking from God on our behalf what will benefit us" and that he has made the church at Euchaita a place of healing for various diseases.[11] An Apis bull was found in Egypt in 362. Ammianus describes its distinctive markings (a crescent moon on the right flank) and the customs attending its discovery as if they still persisted with undiminished vigor: an Apis bull is brought to Memphis, "a city famous for the frequent visits of the god Aesculapius" and "the inhabitants of those parts believe" that the finding of an Apis bull "portends a good harvest and various other blessings" (22.14.6–8).

One episode at Rome is especially significant. When Tertullus was *praefectus urbi*, a severe shortage of food threatened. Riots ensued, in which the prefect was frequently mobbed by menacing crowds, even though it was obvious that he could do nothing about the rough weather at sea and contrary winds that were holding up the grain fleet. Finally, in despair, a weeping Tertullus produced his small sons and addressed the rioters in tears:

> "Look at your fellow-citizens, who will share your fate—may the gods in heaven avert the omen!—unless a happier fortune shines upon us. So, if you think that no disaster can happen if they are put out of the way, here they are at your disposal." Soothed by this pitiful speech, the mob, which is inclined to clemency by its very nature, fell silent, and calmly awaited their future lot. Soon afterwards, at the wish of the divine power which has attended Rome from its cradle and guaranteed that it will be eternal, while Tertullus was sacrificing in the temple of Castor and Pollux at Ostia, the sea became smooth and the wind changed to a light southerly breeze: the ships entered harbour under full sail and replenished the warehouses with grain. (19.10.3–4)

Whether this story is true or not does not matter. The significant fact is that Ammianus chose to include something that has been construed as an aretal-

---

[10] P. Brown, *Authority and the Sacred: Aspects of the Christianisation of the Roman World* (Cambridge, 1995), 32: Ammianus failed or refused to see "the writing on the wall for a whole, non-Christian way of life and worship."

[11] Gregory of Nyssa, *De sancto Theodoro*, ed. J. P. Cavarnos, *Gregorii Nysseni Opera* (Leiden, 1990), 69.23–24 (*PG* 46.745).

ogy of Castor and Pollux.[12] It is a story that fits the well-known pattern of divine response to sacrifice or prayer. Ammianus included it because he firmly believed that the gods intervene actively in human affairs.

Ammianus held that ancient learning was not yet dead despite its decadence. When he digresses on earthquakes, he appeals to the *veteres* who approached closer to the truth than "our common ignorance" or the writers about physics who always disagree with one another (17.7.9: haec nostra vulgaris inscitia . . . sempiterna . . . physicorum iurgia). The tradition to which Ammianus regarded himself as heir went back beyond Greco-Roman antiquity to ancient Egypt before the alphabet was invented: he commends hieroglyphics and he quotes Hermapion's Greek translation of those on the obelisk in the Circus Maximus, in which the Sun gives King Rameses dominion over all the earth and salutes him as Apollo and Ares (17.14.17–23). In Ammianus' own day, ancient learning continued to flourish, at least in Alexandria:

> Although most, including those whom I have mentioned, flourished long ago, even now various branches of learning are not silent in the city. For the teachers of different disciplines still somehow stay alive; hidden truth is brought to light by the geometer's rule; among them music has not wholly dried up nor harmony relapsed into silence; some, though not many, still keep warm the study of the movements of the earth and the stars; there are others who are skilled in arithmetic; and in addition to these a few are skilled in the science which reveals the ways of the fates. The study of medicine too, whose assistance is often needed in this life of ours, which is neither frugal nor sober, advances daily, so that for a doctor merely to say that he was trained in Alexandria is sufficient recommendation of his skill. (22.16.17–18)

Ammianus appears to allude to the mathematician Pappus and to Theon, the father of Hypatia, who composed arithmetical and mathematical works, a commentary on Ptolemy's *Almagest*, and much else besides, including a treatise on divination.[13] Phrase after phrase either states or implies a sad decline in the ancient tradition—*quodam modo; nondum . . . penitus exaruit; apud quosdam licet raros; pauci.* The one exception is Alexandrian medicine, which appears to have flourished more in Ammianus' day than it had in the third century.[14]

[12] J. Vogt, *Abh. Mainz*, Geistes- und sozialwiss. Kl. 1963, 814.

[13] *Suda* Π 265, Θ 205 (4.26, 2.702 Adler). On Pappus and Theon, see esp. A. Jones, *Pappus of Alexandria: Book 7 of the Collection* (*Sources in the History of Mathematics and the Physical Sciences* 8, 1986), 1.1–15.

[14] V. Nutton, *Clio Medica* 7 (1972), 165–76.

Ancient learning was especially valid and relevant where it provided an insight into the divine order of things, that is, in divination. Ammianus introduces an excursus on divination to defend his hero Julian against the *malevoli* who accused him of practicing the black arts to discover the future. The historian protests that it is legitimate for a wise man to master this important branch of learning:

> The spirit that rules the elements inasmuch as they are eternal bodies and is always and everywhere active in foreseeing events shares with us the gifts of divination through our pursuit of various disciplines, and the powers of reality, when they are propitiated by diverse rites, supply words of prophecy to mortals as if from the veins of never-failing springs. Over these the divine power Themis is said to preside, who is so named because she makes known beforehand what is ordained by the fixed decrees of deadly fate (which in Greek are called *tethimena*) and to whom the ancient theologians assigned a place in the bed and on the throne of Jove, the life-giving force.
>
> Auguries and auspices are not collected by the will of birds, who have no knowledge of the future. (Not even a total fool would assert that.) On the contrary, God directs the flight of birds, so that the noise from their beaks or the movement of their wings, whether violent or gentle, may show the future in advance. For, by these arts too, the gracious deity loves to reveal impending events, either because men deserve to know or because he is touched by affection for them.
>
> In the same way those who inspect the prophetic entrails of animals know the course of events from the countless shapes which they take. The discoverer of this discipline, a man called Tages, according to fable, was seen to spring suddenly out of the ground somewhere in Etruria.
>
> Coming events are also revealed when men's hearts are on fire and utter divine words. For the sun, which is the mind of the universe, as natural philosophers say, sends out our minds from itself like sparks: when it kindles them into flame, it makes them aware of the future. Hence the Sibyls often say that they burn with great flames rushing violently through them. Much is also signified by the sound of voices and signs which we encounter, as well as by thunder, lightning and thunderbolts and equally by the tracks of meteors. (21.1.8–11)

This excursus has a clearly articulated logical structure. First comes the cosmological basis of divination. Then its four domains, divided between the artificial (augury and *haruspicina*) and the natural (prophecies and dreams). Finally, Ammianus defends divination against scepticism. He carefully combines Roman and Greek methods of predicting the future, invoking Tages and the

Sibyls and quoting Aristotle and Cicero.[15] There is no mention here, however, of astrology. The reason cannot be that Ammianus denied its validity, which he asserts elsewhere (23.6.25),[16] but because in this sphere he accepted complete determinism. If our fate can be completely predicted from the position of the stars at our birth, knowledge of our horoscope can be of no practical use. The types of divination that Ammianus discusses relate rather to divine warnings that allow the individual some scope for freedom of action within a framework immutably laid down by Themis.

Ammianus seems to be inconsistent here. But so (it may be argued) are all determinists, like the disciples of Karl Marx who strove, plotted, even died endeavoring to bring about a revolution that their creed proclaimed to be inevitable even if they never lifted a finger.[17] For, if all our actions are determined by fate, heredity, or any other pervasive forces beyond our control, or predestined by God, then it makes no sense to exercise choice, since freedom of the will is mere illusion, our apparent choices due to no act of our will. But none of us can avoid conducting our lives on the assumption that we do in fact make choices. The compatibilist position espoused by Ammianus had a long and respectable pedigree in Greek philosophy.[18]

"The future is dark, the present burdensome; only the past, dead and finished, bears contemplation." Ammianus would heartily have agreed with this verdict of a modern practitioner of the historian's art.[19] Growing up in the newly Christian Roman Empire, Ammianus could not avoid contemplating the course of human history. The dominant ideology of his youth was Christian triumphalism. In his *Chronicle*, in his *Ecclesiastical History*, in his *General Elementary Introduction*, in his vast double polemic against Porphyry, the *Preparation for the Gospel* and the *Demonstration of the Gospel*, and in his more popular

---

[15] On the different types of divination practiced in the Greco-Roman world, see still A. Bouché-Leclercq, *Histoire de la Divination dans l'Antiquité* 1 (Paris, 1879), 111–374; 2 (1882), 1–317. Discussion of this excursus has too often concentrated on identifying its hypothetical written sources: e.g., Ensslin, *Ammianus* (1923), 83–96.

[16] Ensslin, *Ammianus* (1923), 77–82. A. Bouché-Leclercq, *L'Astrologie grecque* (Paris, 1899), 570, adduced Juvenal as a precedent and possible model for Ammianus' ridicule of Roman aristocrats who consult the stars before going out to dine or to bathe (28.4.24).

[17] For three classic modern discussions of the problem, see K. Popper, *The Open Society and Its Enemies* (London, 1945), chap. XXII; I. Berlin, *Historical Inevitability* (London, 1954); E. H. Carr, *What Is History?* (London, 1961), 85–93.

[18] R. Sorabji, *Necessity, Cause and Blame: Perspectives on Aristotle's Theory* (Ithaca, 1980), traces it back through the Stoics to Aristotle.

[19] G. R. Elton, *The Practice of History* (Sydney, 1967), 1. When that writer turns to questions of appropriate size and scale, he notes that "some 500-page books turn out on further inspection to be inflated articles" (123).

Theophany, Eusebius of Caesarea set out an idiosyncratic view of history. Christianity, so Eusebius maintained, was the primeval religion of the human race, identical with the religion of the patriarchs of the Old Testament, from which the traditional religions of the Greco-Roman world were mere off-shoots or declensions. Divine providence had prepared the world for the coming of Christ by means of the temporary dispensation of Judaism and had then ensured the worldly success of Christ's church, which constituted a race or nation of a unique type with a special relationship to God.[20]

Even in Eusebius' day, few Christians can have accepted his theories about religion in the Old Testament. No contemporary Christian, however, doubted the central propositions of his overall view of human history: God had sent his Son to save men, and divine providence either guided or intervened in human history to produce the success of the Christian church. In the East, the church's victory was very recent when Ammianus was born, less than ten years after Constantine defeated "the last of the persecutors." Christians had come to power in the cities of the East through war and violence, as the regime of Licinius first harassed the church, then collapsed when Constantine invaded his territory. In the revolutionary situation that existed in 324–325 the new master of the East acted decisively to establish Christianity as the official religion of the Roman Empire.[21] Christianization proceeded apace after 325. Constantine confiscated the treasures laid up in temples over the centuries and used the proceeds to finance an enormous program of church building throughout the East, but especially in Palestine and above all in Jerusalem.[22] Under Constantine, few cults or temples were suppressed by imperial action, but bishops began to attack shrines and temples with increasing freedom as time passed.[23] The brief reign of Julian suddenly interrupted the process, and Christians in the reigns of Jovian and Valens showed more restraint than under Constantius. But with the accession of Theodosius in 379, the suppression of pagan cults recommenced in earnest. Now it was not merely bishops and monks attacking local cults: the praetorian prefect Cynegius toured the East twice (in 384–386 and again in 388), encouraging and supervising the demolition of temples.[24] In 391, the Serapeum in Alexandria succumbed,

---

[20] For a full exposition, see J. Sirinelli, *Les Vues historiques d'Eusèbe de Césarée durant la période prénicéenne* (Dakar, 1961); more briefly, T. D. Barnes, *Constantine* (1981), 126–36, 179–88.

[21] For this interpretation, which is by no means universally shared, see *Constantine* (1981), 208–12, 245–60; *From Eusebius to Augustine: Selected Papers* (Aldershot, 1994), nos. IV–IX, all composed with the modern parallel of Iran after the fall of the Shah and the return of Ayatollah Khomeini very much in mind.

[22] *Constantine* (1981), 247–50.

[23] G. Fowden, *JTS*, N.S. 29 (1978), 53–78.

[24] Matthews, *Aristocracies* (1975), 140–45.

which Ammianus had recently advertised as one of the wonders of the world (22.16.12).[25]

Against this background, any pagan of the later fourth century needed to formulate a coherent interpretation of history if he wished to challenge the dominant ideology. Julian adumbrated one in his *Caesars* by placing personified Luxury and Wantonness next to the Jesus who welcomed seducers, murderers, the sacrilegious, and infamous, including Constantine.[26] Eunapius soon developed these hints into an interpretation of the fourth century in which Rome was strong and successful until the conversion of Constantine, who refused to celebrate the Secular Games when they fell due in 314 and then totally weakened, demoralized and corrupted the Roman Empire. The original text of Eunapius' history is lost except for sporadic fragments, but Zosimus who wrote at the start of the sixth century faithfully reproduced his views (and often his words) in the central section of his history: hence Eunapius could with some plausibility be styled "the first historian of Rome's fall."[27] If the first edition of Eunapius' history ended with the Battle of Adrianople (as seems probable),[28] then Ammianus could consult it, and he may well have Eunapius in mind when he complains that those who are ignorant of ancient times (*antiquitatum ignari*) allege that the defeat of Valens in 378 was the darkest moment in Rome's history (31.5.11).

Although he was Greek, Ammianus took the whole history of Rome from its founding by Romulus within his purview. At the start of his excursus on Rome in Book XIV, he states his belief in the eternity of Rome and compares the history of the city to a human life (14.6.3–5). In its infancy and childhood, a period of three hundred years, the Roman people waged local wars. In adolescence it expanded beyond Italy; in manhood it conquered the world. Then, when it was verging on old age and able to triumph sometimes through reputation alone, it retired (*ad tranquilliora vitae discessit*).[29] Accordingly, the city

---

[25] The date is certain, despite recent attempts to argue for 392 (*CP* 88 [1993], 61–62).

[26] Julian, *Caes.* 336a, cf. *Ep.* 89, 453c.

[27] W. A. Goffart, *AHR* 76 (1971), 412–41, applied the sobriquet to Zosimus, but every single one of his proof texts comes from the Eunapian section of Zosimus (1.47–5.26).

[28] Eunapius produced two editions of his history, one before he wrote his *Lives of the Philosophers and Sophists* in 399 and one that ended in 404 and was used by Zosimus.
The traditional date of the first edition (circa 395) is ably defended by F. Paschoud, *Bonner Historia-Augusta-Colloquium 1977–1978* (Bonn, 1980), 146–62; *Bonner Historia-Augusta-Colloquium 1982–1983* (Bonn, 1985), 253–84; *Zosime* 3.2 (Paris, 1989), 90–91. In favor of an earlier terminus, see *CP* 71 (1976), 265–67; *The Sources of the Historia Augusta* (*Collection Latomus* 155, 1978), 114–23; *Constantine* (1981), 403, n. 5; T. S. Banchich, *GRBS* 27 (1986), 319–24. A. Baker, *GRBS* 29 (1988), 389–402, argues that the "new edition" that Photius inspected was a bowdlerized version by a later hand, not one of the two authentic editions.

[29] Ammianus uses the phrase *tranquilliora vitae* only once elsewhere, to refer to the death, not the retirement, of Varronianus, the father of Jovian (25.5.4).

behaved as a rich parent who is thrifty and wise behaves to his children: it ceded control of its estate to the emperors so that they could administer it (*Caesaribus tamquam liberis suis regenda patrimonii iura permisit*).[30]

Very similar comparisons survive in three other Latin authors besides Ammianus: Florus and Lactantius, who wrote before Ammianus, and the *Historia Augusta* after him.[31] This *Lebensaltervergleich* has been much discussed.[32] But much of the discussion has been misguided as far as Ammianus is concerned. For Ammianus, who echoes him verbally, took the idea from Florus, who seems in turn to have adapted Seneca.[33] Moreover, the evidence of Cicero establishes the equation "old age equals weakness"[34]—which some exegetes of Ammianus have doubted.[35] It follows that Ammianus' message is a pessimistic one. Florus asserted that under the emperor Trajan, in whose reign he was probably writing, the Roman Empire had bestirred itself to action and that, contrary to the expectation of all, its old age was revived as if it had regained

[30] Despite the consensus of modern editors, the paragraph should end with these words: the next sentence, which refers to the cessation of popular elections and the Senate as reflecting the prestige of Rome (14.6.6), belongs with what follows and introduces the long denunciation of the vices of contemporary Rome (14.6.7–26); it does not conclude the comparison of Rome's history with four stages in a human life. Similarly, the next two paragraphs should be 14.6.9–10 and 11–14 (not 9–11 and 12–14), and 14.6.18–20 should form a single paragraph (not two, as in Seyfarth's text).

[31] Florus, pr. 4–8; Lactantius, *Div. Inst.* 7.15.14–16; *HA, Carus* 2–3. The Seneca whom Lactantius quotes is usually assumed to be the Elder Seneca, who died in 39.

[32] See esp. R. Häussler, *Hermes* 92 (1964), 313–41; Demandt, *Zeitkritik* (1965), 118–42; *Metaphern für Geschichte: Sprachbilder und Gleichnisse im historisch-politischen Denken* (Munich, 1978), 37–45; *Gymnasium* 87 (1980), 178–89. The latter argues that Ammianus depicts the old age of Rome as the apogee of the city, a state of eternal, unaltering prosperity from which all elements of decadence have disappeared (*Metaphern* [1978], 39).

[33] H. Finke, *Ammianus Marcellinus und seine Quellen zur Geschichte der römische Republik* (Diss. Heidelberg, 1904), 38–40; Drexler, *Ammianstudien* (1974), 155–65.

[34] Drexler, *Ammianstudien* (1974), 160–62, adducing Cicero, *Ad Quintum fratrem* 2.13.5; *De re publica* 1.58, 2.3, 2.21, 3.34.

[35] So J. F. Matthews, *The Inheritance of Historiography* (Exeter, 1986), 22: "Ammianus is not talking, as a cursory reading might suggest, of a decline but of a rejuvenation of Rome in the persons and office of the emperors; it is through their efforts in conducting wars in the name of Rome (*nomine solo aliquotiens vincens*) that Rome will live—or conquer: *victura*—as long as there are men." This interpretation fails to respect the order of the text: Ammianus attributes the victories won *nomine solo* to the late prime of the Roman people, before it ceded control to the emperors. Moreover, the phrase *victura dum erunt homines Roma* does not contain a pun on two meanings of the future participle *victura*. For it occurs at the very beginning of the excursus before any mention of victories: it means simply "Rome will live as long as the human race." But in what sense will Rome live on? Even if Ammianus is not using *vivere* in this and a later passage (26.1.14: victura cum saeculis Roma) metaphorically, as Ennius had in his famous funerary epigram (*Varia* 18 Vahlen: volito vivus per ora virum), it need mean no more than "exist" or "live on in an increasingly squalid existence": the passage is correctly interpreted by G. B. Conte, *History of Latin Literature*, trans. J. Solodow (Princeton, 1994), 649.

its youth.[36] Ammianus has removed the optimistic conclusion of his immediate model. It must be a deliberate choice.

Ammianus refers to the heroes of Republican Rome in many passages, but usually as examples of behavior or in geographical excursus.[37] When Julian, about to invade Persia, invokes M. Curtius, Mucius Scaevola, and the noble Decii (23.5.19), these are standard *exempla* of patriotism and devotion to Rome, whose function is primarily rhetorical. There appears to be only one passage in the *Res Gestae* that offers serious reflections on the course of Roman history over the centuries, but it is a passage of immense significance. Ammianus compares the disaster of Adrianople to earlier Roman disasters, both Republican and imperial:[38]

> Those who are ignorant of ancient times say that this was the darkest disaster which ever fell upon the state, but they are led astray because they are overwhelmed by their horror at recent disasters. A review of earlier or even quite recent history will show that such melancholy events have often happened.
>
> The Teutones and Cimbri from the furthest shores of the Ocean suddenly flooded into Italy, but after they had inflicted enormous defeats on the Roman state, they were overcome by our excellent generals in their last battles, and they learned from their destruction root and branch in their last trials what martial power can achieve when combined with good judgement. Again, when Marcus ruled the empire, the mad fury of discordant tribes acting as one, after the clangor of vast wars, after the sufferings of cities which were captured and sacked, paid the penalty for killing a governor <. . .> and only a tiny part of their number were left unscathed.[39] But after calamitous losses the situation was restored in due

---

[36] Florus I pr. 8. The main clause reads: a Caesare Augusto in saeculum nostrum haud multo minus anni ducenti, quibus consenuit atque decoxit. Hence it is normally deduced that Florus was writing circa 135: see, e.g., P. Jal, *Florus: Oeuvres* I (Paris, 1967), lxix–cxi. But a date under Trajan seems historically more plausible. Accordingly, I would reconstruct Florus' chronological schema as follows: (1) *prima aetas sub regibus* = *infantia* lasting 250 years; (2) *adulescentia* of 250 years from 509 to 264 B. C.; (3) *maturitas* of 200 years *quibus totum orbem pacavit* plus the reign of Augustus; (4) nearly 100 years of senility between Augustus and Trajan (emending *ducenti* to *centum*).

[37] The passages are conveniently collected and discussed by Finke, *Ammianus Marcellinus* (1904), 60–91.

[38] On the intellectual context of this passage, see N. Lenski, *TAPA* 127 (1997), 129–68, who collects and discusses the contemporary reactions to the Battle of Adrianople that survive. In his official panegyrics of Theodosius, Themistius first minimized, then magnified the effects of the Roman defeat; Libanius and Jerome succumbed to despair when they heard news of the disaster; and Ambrose indulged in apocalyptic musings about the end of the world.

[39] The text printed by Seyfarth is defective in both logic and grammar, and what I offer is not a real translation: the fact that *eorum* refers to the *gentes* whom Marcus defeated leads me to posit a lacuna.

course. The reason was that the old, sober morality had not yet been infected by the effeminacy of a laxer way of life, and that there was no craving for ostentatious banquets and ill-gotten gain: high and low agreeing with one another with unanimous enthusiasm hastened towards a glorious death for the state as if <striving to reach> some calm and peaceful harbor.

Although the hordes of Scythian tribes, who invaded by bursting through the Bosporus and the shores of the Propontis with two thousand ships, wrought bitter massacres by land and sea, they lost the greatest part of their number and retreated. The two emperors Decius, father and son, fell fighting against the barbarians; the cities of Pamphylia were besieged, many islands laid waste, and the whole of Macedonia set on fire; a vast throng besieged Thessalonica and Cyzicus for a long time; Anchialus was taken, and at the same period Nicopolis, which the emperor Trajan founded as a memorial of his victory over the Dacians. After much cruel slaughter had been received and inflicted, Philippopolis was destroyed with one hundred thousand, unless the histories lie, butchered within its walls. Foreign foes roamed freely over Epirus, Thessaly, and the whole of Greece. But after the glorious leader Claudius had been made emperor and then carried off by a noble death, they were driven out by Aurelian, an energetic man and a severe avenger of injuries, and remained silent and immobile for long ages, except that on rare later occasions bands of robbers raided areas near to them—and were killed. (31.5.11–17)

What is the great change to which Ammianus here alludes? and when did it occur? The answer to these questions is easy. For Ammianus transposes the vocabulary of denigration used by Julian, Libanius, and Eunapius from Greek into Latin (Chapter VIII). His *solutioris vitae mollities* corresponds to the Luxury and Wantonness whom Julian depicted as the boon companions of Jesus as he extended pardon to murderers and adulterers.[40] Ammianus blames the decline of the Roman Empire on Christians and Christianity in a manner very similar to Eunapius,[41] though with greater intellectual sophistication. Ammianus asserts that *sobria vetustas* has been destroyed by Christianity, which is intrinsically corrupt. This connection emerges most clearly in Ammianus' comments on Julian's reform of the palace after the death of Constantius:

> The greater part of them [sc. the *palatini* of Constantius] had grown widely such a seedbed of all the vices that they corrupted the state by their depraved lusts and harmed many more by their bad example than by the impunity with which they

[40] Julian, *Caes.* 329a, 336a.

[41] Zosimus 2.14.2 (failure to celebrate the Ludi Saeculares in 314), 2.30–38 (Constantine's innovations). Zosimus sums up Constantine's achievement as the defiling of the state (2.39.1).

offended. Some of them, who had grown fat on the plunder of temples and smelled out profit at every opportunity, had been raised at a bound from grinding poverty to enormous wealth: becoming habituated always to appropriate the property of others, they bribed, robbed, and squandered without restraint of any kind. Hence there sprouted in abundance the seeds of a laxer way of life (*fluxioris vitae initia*) and perjury; there was no regard for reputation, and an insane pride polluted its credit through the criminal pursuit of gain. At the same time, gluttony grew and reckless expenditure on banquets: triumphs in battle were replaced by triumphs at table, there was lavish use of silk and the art of textiles was enhanced, the kitchen became the object of ever keener attention, and pretentious sites for luxurious houses were sought out—sites so large that if Cincinnatus had possessed so much farmland, he would have forfeited the glory of poverty after his dictatorship. (22.4.2−5)

The plunder of temples was not merely an operation of private enterprise: Constantine had sent special commissioners to tour every eastern province and confiscate temple treasures and ornaments, including (it is reported) doors made of precious metals.[42]

Diocletian and Constantine have often been regarded as polar opposites.[43] That was the opinion of everyone in the fourth century, whether Christian or pagan, and an eloquent modern restatement contrasted Diocletian as "the last and most radical defender of the Roman ideology of restoration" with Constantine, the revolutionary who broke with all existing traditions and abandoned everything Roman.[44] Yet recent research has discovered a basic continuity of administration and administrative reform that, even if it began in 284, proceeded along essentially the same lines after 305, 312, 324, and 337. One example will aptly illustrate. Zosimus saw the establishment of regional praetorian prefectures as a sudden and deleterious innovation by Constantine[45]—which some modern historians of Rome used to transfer to Diocletian.[46] In fact, the regional prefectures of the late fourth century came into ex-

---

[42] Eusebius, *Panegyric of Constantine* 8.1−7; *VC* 3.54−58, cf. *L'Église et l'empire au IVe siècle* (*Entretiens sur l'Antiquité Classique* 34, 1989), 322−33.

[43] For a survey of ancient opinions, see N. Baglivi, *Orpheus*, N.S. 12 (1991), 429−91. M. T. W. Arnheim gives successive chapters of his study of *The Senatorial Aristocracy of the Later Roman Empire* (Oxford, 1972) the titles "Diocletian, Hammer of the Aristocracy" and "Constantine the Reformer" (39−73).

[44] A. Schenk von Stauffenberg, *Das Imperium und die Völkerwanderung* (Munich, 1948), 108−11.

[45] Zosimus 2.33.1−2.

[46] Most influentially, O. Seeck, *Rhein. Mus.*, N.F. 69 (1914), 1−39. Epigraphical discoveries long ago rendered this view untenable (*New Empire* [1982], 123−39).

istence gradually in a process that lasted several decades. There were regional prefects in Africa under Constantine, but only as a temporary measure; the lasting transformation of the prefecture began in the West in 343, spread to the East in 354, and was not completed before the 360s.[47] Historians now speak rather of "the new empire of Diocletian and Constantine" and of "the political, social and economic evolution of the Roman world from Diocletian to Julian."[48]

Constantine was not the indiscriminate disturber of ancient laws and traditional custom whom Ammianus makes Julian denounce (21.10.8: novator turbatorque priscarum legum et moris antiquitus recepti). His radical innovations were largely confined to the religious sphere, but here they were fundamental and far-reaching. Although there was no "Constantinian revolution," as some have incautiously imagined, there was a "Constantinian reformation"—with all that that phrase implies.[49]

Unfortunately, Ammianus' account of the reigns of Diocletian and Constantine has perished with the rest of the first half of his history. The few explicit references to Diocletian in the extant books reveal little about the historian's attitude.[50] He knows that Diocletian settled Carpi in Pannonia (28.1.5)[51] and that the Caesar Galerius walked on foot in front of the chariot of the Augustus when the two entered Antioch: like other writers of the fourth century, he construes this as a deliberate humiliation rather than a symbolic gesture of subordination (14.11.10).[52] He repeats the canard that Diocletian was the first emperor to introduce the ceremony of *adoratio* (15.5.18).[53] It is true that it was Diocletian who made *adoratio* a normal part of court ceremonial, obligatory for imperial relatives as well as officials.[54] But Ammianus'

---

[47] *Bonner Historia-Augusta-Colloquium, 1984–1985* (1987), 13–23; *ZPE* 94 (1992), 249–60. On the still obscure question of the number and function of praetorian prefects in the early years of the fourth century, see *JRA* 9 (1996), 546–48.

[48] A. Chastagnol, *L'Évolution politique, sociale et économique du monde romain de Dioclétien à Julien: La mise en place du régime du Bas-Empire (284–363)* (Paris, 1982): the title of my *New Empire* (1982) was chosen in implicit homage to Gibbon, *Decline and Fall*, Chapter XIII (1.383 [B] = 1.390 [W]).

[49] *From Eusebius to Augustine* (1994), nos. V, VIII, IX.

[50] S. A. Stertz, *Studies in Latin Literature and Roman History* 2 (*Collection Latomus* 168, 1980), 511–12, argues that Ammianus gives a negative picture of Diocletian, while himself happily conflating Maximian and Galerius.

[51] For proof that it was Diocletian and not, as often assumed, Galerius, see *Phoenix* 30 (1976), 187.

[52] As argued by W. Seston, *REA* 42 (1940), 515–19, cf. J. W. Eadie, *The Breviarium of Festus* (London, 1967), 146–48.

[53] Also Victor, *Caes.* 39.2–4; Eutropius, *Brev.* 9.26; Jerome, *Chronicle* 226[c] Helm. All three authors derive the story from the lost "Kaisergeschichte."

[54] Lactantius, *Mort.Pers.* 18.9, makes it clear that Maxentius was expected to "adore" both his father, the Augustus Maximian, and his father-in-law, the Caesar Galerius, cf. A. Alföldi, *Die monarchische Repräsentation im römischen Kaiserreiche* (Darmstadt, 1970), 25–118.

moral indignation reveals a significant gap in his Latin reading: had he read Suetonius, he would have discovered that L. Vitellius performed *adoratio* of Caligula.[55] And when he invokes Diocletian in 285 as the most recent precedent for Julian's sharing of the ordinary consulate of 363 with a private citizen, he either forgets or ignores the fact that Maximian did so in 288, three years after Diocletian (Chapter V).

It is nevertheless clear that for Ammianus, the reign of Diocletian belonged to Rome's glorious and ancient past. He reveals this significant assumption obliquely in a passage criticizing Constantius for entering Rome in triumph in 357 as if all the enemies of the Empire had been laid low and as if he were coming to close the Temple of Janus. According to Ammianus, Constantius never defeated any foreign tribe either himself or through his generals, and he never appeared in person in the thick of battle. He preferred empty ceremonial, ignorant perhaps of the personal courage shown by some earlier emperors: one entrusted himself to a small fishing-boat at the height of a raging storm, another vowed to sacrifice his life for the state, and a third had personally made his way into the enemy's camp with some common soldiers (16.10.1–3). The three emperors whom the degenerate Constantius failed to emulate are easily identified. Caesar's attempt to cross the Adriatic in a fishing-boat at night was a famous episode even before Lucan wrote it up.[56] Two other pagan writers of the fourth century depict the death of Claudius in 270 as a formal *devotio*.[57] And it was Galerius who reconnoitred the camp of Narses during his Armenian campaign of 297.[58] Christians had a very different opinion of Galerius as the main instigator of the "Great Persecution":[59] by calling Galerius glorious and heroic, even though he does not name him, Ammianus marked a sharp break between Rome's heroic past, which lasted until the reign of Diocletian, and the corrupt and degenerate empire of Constantine and his Christian successors.

Ammianus took it as proven fact that "Constantine was the first to whet the appetite of his courtiers, but it was Constantius who fattened them with the marrow of the provinces." For under Constantius the leading men of the state

[55] Suetonius, *Vitellius* 2.5: primus C. Caesarem adorare ut deum instituit. The passage was duly adduced by Alföldi, *Repräsentation* (1970), 39.

[56] Lucan 5.504–677, cf. Valerius Maximus, *Mem.* 9.8.2; Pluarch, *Caes.* 38; Florus 2.35–37; Appian, *BC* 2.57; Dio 41.46.

[57] Victor, *Caes.* 34.2–3; *Epitome* 34.3.

[58] Eutropius, *Brev.* 9.25.1; Festus, *Brev.* 25, cf. N. J. E. Austin and N. B. Rankov, *"Exploratio." Military and Political Intelligence in the Roman World from the Second Punic War to the Battle of Adrianople* (New York, 1995), 62–63.

[59] Lactantius and Eusebius consistently depict Galerius as the moving force behind the anti-Christian legislation of Diocletian: in favor of accepting their testimony, see now *Usurpationen in der Spätantike* (*Historia Einzelschriften* 111, 1996), 99–109.

were consumed by a boundless lust for wealth and totally disregarded justice and right. Ammianus names the worst and most prominent offenders in a lacunose passage: Rufinus the praetorian prefect,[60] Arbitio the master of cavalry, the grand chamberlain . . . , the quaestor [. . .]nus,[61] and in Rome the family of the Anicii, whose contemporary descendants rival their forebears in their inability to rest content even with much greater possessions (16.8.12−13).[62] Ammianus sees a process of corruption rather than the sudden change denounced by the Greek historians Eunapius and Zosimus. He blames Constantine for starting it and Constantius for carrying it much further. But in this passage, whatever he may have said in the lost books, he concentrates his odium on the leading Christian family in Rome. The Anicii had risen to prominence with an African supporter of Septimius Severus, and they were to play an important historical role in the fifth and sixth centuries.[63] When Ammianus was composing his *Res Gestae*, the *culmen Aniciorum* was the great Sextus Petronius Probus, consul in 371 and four times praetorian prefect, who had married into the clan, and to whom Ammianus devoted a long and hostile character sketch (Chapter X). Ammianus makes it clear that he regarded Christians as thoroughly corrupt in every way.

The emperor Julian was of central importance to Ammianus. But he, no less than Constantine, belonged to a past that was dead. Could Julian have reversed the changes in Roman society that had occurred under Constantine and his sons? On the one hand, Ammianus has so constructed his narrative of the Persian expedition as to lead readers to infer that Julian could have avoided disaster if he had heeded the long series of omens and portents that the gods sent to warn him: for example, the Sibylline books forbade the emperor to set

[60] Vulcacius Rufinus, consul in 347 and maternal uncle to the Caesar Gallus (14.11.27), was a *pontifex maior* (*ILS* 1237) and hence a pagan (*PLRE* 1.782−3): Ammianus later praises him as "omni ex parte perfectus," although he never let slip an opportunity to enrich himself if he thought that he might remain undetected (27.7.2).

[61] V has a lacuna of 19 letters between *praepositusque cubiclui laps* and *anus quaestor:* the latter cannot be identified (*PLRE* 1.997, -anus), and Eusebius, whose name is often supplied (as in the Penguin translation), is not attested as *praepositus sacri cubiculi* before the death of Constantine (Chapter XI, at n. 42).

[62] Elsewhere Ammianus makes Julian denounce Constantine as a subversive innovator (21.10.8) and holds him responsible for the defeat of Julian's Persian expedition (25.4.23). But eleven other references to Constantine seem to be neutral (14.1.2, 14.11.20, 14.11.27, 15.5.19, 15.5.33, 15.13.2, 16.7.5, 17.4.13, 21.12.25, 25.3.23, 26.6.14).

[63] On Q. Anicius Faustus, cos. suff. circa 198, see A. R. Birley, *The African Emperor Septimius Severus*[2] (London, 1988), 143−44, 147, 151−52; for his descendants in the third century, see M. Corbier, *Epigrafia e ordine senatorio* (*Tituli* 5, 1982, pub. 1984) 740−41; for Anicii in the fourth, fifth, and sixth centuries, *PLRE* 1.1133: Stemma 7; 2.1309: Stemma 3. The family came from Uzappa in Africa Proconsularis, as did the Memmii (cf. Chapter X, n. 37).

foot outside Roman territory during the consular year 363 (23.1.7).[64] On the other hand, Julian disregarded the prudent advice of Sallustius, the praetorian prefect of Gaul, to postpone his invasion of Persia until the gods signified their approval "because no human strength or virtue has ever availed to forestall what has been ordained by the decree of destiny" (23.5.5: quod praescripsit fatalis ordo). Yet the obituary of Julian argues that moral responsibility for his failure rested with Constantine. For it was Constantine, Ammianus argues, who started the long war against Persia as a result of believing the lies of Metrodorus. Hence the long series of disasters under Constantius—Roman armies cut down, units captured, cities destroyed, fortresses seized or demolished, the provinces exhausted by the burdens imposed on them, with the Persians claiming Roman territory up to the shores of the Propontis. In the West, the insolent Germans were on the point of breaking through the Alps to ravage Italy, while the provincials were in panic until Julian, sent to Gaul as a Caesar only in name, retrieved the situation with miraculous rapidity. It was with the same eagerness to restore the East that he attacked the Persians, whom he would have conquered, "had his plans and glorious deeds been consonant with the decrees of heaven" (25.4.23–26).

After the death of Julian, the Roman Empire was a different place.[65] The Alamanni recovered from the losses and damage inflicted by Julian and became a permanent threat to the Gallic frontier (27.1.1). The Persian king not only imposed a shameful treaty on Jovian, but did not even respect its terms and pursued his designs on Armenia, with no small success (27.12.1). There was constant trouble on the Danube, where the admission of the Goths to Roman territory in 376 led inexorably to the defeat of Valens in 378. Even Valentinian, though endowed with virtues that Ammianus celebrates in his obituary (30.7), had deleterious vices: he was cruel, he allowed greed to reach unparalleled heights (30.8), and, despite his reputation as a careful commander, he could act with foolish recklessness in the field (27.10.1–11).[66] In Ammianus' eyes, the salient features of the society in which he lived after 363 were disorder, repression, and corruption.

After Book XXVI Ammianus abandons a connected year-by-year narration of events centered on the activities of the eastern and western emperors each campaigning season and each winter (Chapter IV). Books XXVII to XXX have a more thematic arrangement and a looser chronology: Valens'

---

[64] On the omens of January 363, see Chapter V.

[65] On "il 'dopo Giuliano,'" see now N. Baglivi, *Ammianea* (Catania, 1995), 177–243.

[66] On the damaging implications of this passage, where Ammianus seems to be deliberately undermining Valentinian's own favorable depiction of his actions, see Sabbah, *Methode* (1978), 209; R. Seager, *Papers of the Leeds International Latin Seminar* 9 (1996), 191–96.

three Gothic campaigns of 367–369 are grouped together in a single chapter (27.5), and there is room for dispute over what date Ammianus indicates for the campaign of the elder Theodosius in Britain (27.8, 28.3).[67] The historian also has a thesis to argue. He narrates in some detail, and thereby emphasizes, episodes such as the havoc caused in Rome by Maximinus (28.1) and in Antioch by a treasonable seance (29.1–2),[68] the miseries of Tripolitania caused by nomadic raids, and the corrupt conduct of the *comes Africae* Romanus (28.6).[69] Ammianus gives especial prominence to the campaigns of the elder Theodosius, whom he praises warmly several times: he is introduced as a man known for his military successes (27.8.3: officiis Martiis felicissime cognitus), he bears a heroic name (28.3.1: dux nominis inclyti),[70] he is a magnificent leader of armies (28.6.26: ductor exercituum ille magnificus), and he is compared to Domitius Corbulo and Lusius Quietus, the generals of Nero and Trajan (29.5.4). Yet the fact that Theodosius needed to campaign in Britain (27.8, 28.3), in Raetia (28.5.15, 29.4.5), and in Africa (28.6.26, 29.5.4–56) shows the prevalence of disorder[71]—and Firmus the Moor rebelled because Romanus dishonestly used his influence at court to turn Valentinian against him (29.5.2).

In Ammianus' eyes, the disaster of 378, to which he devotes his last book, was the product of greed and corruption. Valens admitted the Goths into the Roman Empire because he wished to reinforce his army while enriching his treasury by commuting the obligations of his subjects to provide recruits into cash payments (31.4.3–4). The Goths became hostile because of the sinister greed of the two generals Lupicinus and Maximus, who supervised their crossing of the Danube. Predictably, there was insufficient food on hand in Thrace to feed the Goths. Hence "these loathsome generals" collected all the dogs that they could find and demanded a slave in exchange for each dog: among those enslaved for food were some Gothic nobles (31.4.11). And finally,

[67] R. S. O. Tomlin, *Britannia* (1974), 303–09, puts the campaigns in 367 and 368, R. P. C. Blockley, *Britannia* (1980), 223–26, in 368 and 369.

[68] On 28.1, see Appendix 9; on 29.1–2, W. Seyfarth, *Klio* 46 (1965), 381–382; H. Funke, *JAC* 10 (1967), 165–70; Elliott, *Ammianus* (1983), 154–58; T. Zawadski, *Labor Omnibus Unus. Gerold Walser zum 70. Geburtstag dargebracht von Freunden, Kollegen und Schülern*, ed. H. E. Herzig and R. Frei-Stolba (Wiesbaden, 1989), 274–87.

[69] On the career of Romanus, see B. H. Warmington, *BZ* 49 (1954), 55–64. That Ammianus' negative portrait of him is highly biased is demonstrated by A. Demandt, *Byzantion* 38 (1968), 354–60. The allegation that Romanus demanded no fewer than 4,000 camels before he would help Lepcis (28.6.5) ought to have aroused suspicion long ago.

[70] Ammianus styles two other men *dux inclytus*, viz., Scipio (23.5.20) and Epaminondas (25.2.8).

[71] On these campaigns, see A. Demandt, *Afrika und Rom in der Antike*, ed. H.-J. Diesner, H. Barth and H.-D. Zimmermann (Halle, 1968), 277–92; *Hermes* 100 (1972), 81–113; J. Matthews, *Aspects of the Notitia Dignitatum* (*BAR*, Supplementary Series 15, 1976), 157–86; *Ammianus* (1989), 367–76.

on 9 August 378, Valens made the catastrophic decision to fight rather than to wait for the arrival of the western emperor Gratian, who was hastening to reinforce him, because of his own obstinacy and the flattery of his courtiers, who urged him not to share with his nephew a victory already as good as won (31.12.7).[72]

The last six books of Ammianus construct a subtle and complex argument to prove that the weakness of the Roman Empire after 378 was caused by the corruption that began with Constantine, flourished under Constantius, and reached a peak under Valentinian and Valens, when it infected not just the emperors and their *proximi* but the whole administration of the empire. The times were out of joint, but that is Ammianus' historical thesis, not objective reporting.[73] It is bad historical method to use Ammianus' narrative as if it constituted straightforward evidence that corruption so increased in the later fourth century that it became a major cause of the "decline of the Roman Empire."[74] Moralists have always tended to depict their own age as more degenerate than that of their parents.[75] Such conventional opinions are not always false, for some governments are truly corrupt, even when measured by the normally lax standards that prevail in political life.[76] Yet a general charge of corruption needs to be illustrated by specific and convincing examples, even though, in the nature of the case, documentary proof will usually be unobtainable. For in any age corruption is more likely to be the characteristic of specific structures of power than to represent the temper of a whole society.

Ammianus respected convention by stopping his consecutive narrative of western events at the death of Valentinian in November 375 and his consecutive narrative of eastern events at the death of Valens in August 378. For he knew the cardinal rule of imperial historiography, that history could only be written about dead emperors since the living expected (and deserved) to re-

---

[72] Ammianus' account of the battle has often been discussed: among recent studies, note N. J. E. Austin, *Acta Classica* 15 (1972), 77–83; T. S. Burns, *Historia* 22 (1973), 336–45; Bitter, *Kampfschilderungen* (1976), 102–18; Matthews, *Ammianus* (1989), 296–301; M. P. Speidel, *Klio* 78 (1996), 434–37; Austin and Rankov, *Exploratio* (1995), 241–43. R. S. O. Tomlin, *The Roman World*, ed. J. Wacher 1 (London / New York, 1987), 118, aptly observes that Ammianus' narrative "ekes out some vital facts with masses of 'colour.'"

[73] On the demonstrable dangers of trusting partisan statements by contemporaries, see J. H. Hexter, *Reappraisals in History* (Evanston, Ill., 1961), 119–22, 153–61.

[74] As does R. MacMullen, *Corruption and the Decline of Rome* (London / New Haven, 1988), 146–47, cf. the classic analysis of "corruption and its antidote, terrorism" in the fourth century by Alföldi, *Conflict* (1952), 28–47.

[75] As so often, Horace gives classic expression to a banal sentiment: aetas parentum peior avis tulit/ nos nequiores, mox daturos/ progeniem vitiosiorem (*Odes* 3.6.46–48).

[76] For a striking and well-documented example, see S. Cameron, *On the Take: Crime, Corruption and Greed in the Mulroney Years*[2] (Toronto, 1995).

ceive panegyric. Hence, in his farewell to his readers in his last paragraph, he invites younger and abler men to continue the story—in panegyrical style (31.16.9: maiores stili).[77] Although Gratian was safely dead, his activities as western emperor, with the exception of military campaigns relevant to eastern affairs (31.10, 11.6, 12.4, 7), could not be described without describing the embarrassing execution of the elder Theodosius, the father of the ruling emperor, at Carthage in the winter of 375–376.[78] Ammianus, therefore, concluded Book XXX with the proclamation of the younger Valentinian as Augustus at Aquincum on 22 November 375 (30.10.5)[79] and devoted his final book to events connected with the Battle of Adrianople. The emperor Theodosius himself comes into the narrative once as a young man, where he receives a conventional compliment (29.6.15: princeps postea perspectissimus). Yet the close of Ammianus' work confirms Erich Auerbach's diagnosis that "his manner of writing history nowhere displays anything redeeming, nowhere anything that points to a better future."[80] For the final paragraph discloses a deep underlying pessimism that gives the lie to those who glibly speak of "the fundamental optimism of Ammianus."[81]

A brief postscript to the Battle of Adrianople hints at what Ammianus expected of the future. First, Ammianus describes how the Goths unsuccessfully raided Constantinople, were repulsed by Saracen troops, and dispersed over the Danubian provinces (31.16.3–7). He then turns to another episode:

> During these days, Julius, master of the soldiers beyond the Taurus, distinguished himself by a swift and salutary deed. Learning of the disasters in Thrace, he sent secret letters to the commanders, who were all Romans, an unusual thing

---

[77] Demandt, *Zeitkritik* (1965), 61–62. Similar statements are made in similar contexts by Eutropius, *Brev.* 10.18.3; Jerome, *Chronicle* 7.3–7 Helm. It was conventional for panegyrists to declare themselves unequal to their great theme: Libanius, *Orat.* 11.6, cf. R. Helm, *Rh. Mus.*, N.F. 76 (1927), 305–6. The commonplace is parodied in *HA, Quad. Tyr.* 15.10.

[78] Jerome, *Chronicle* 248 c Helm, has the execution as the first item under the twelfth year of Valens (i.e., 376), and he registers the slaughter of 30,000 Alamanni near Strasbourg by the army of Gratian in the following year (248 f).

[79] The date and place are certified by *Descr. cons.* 375.3; Socrates, *HE* 4.31.7. On this proclamation, see recently G. de Bonfils, *Ammiano Marcellino e l'imperatore* (Bari, 1986), 36–47; J. Szidat, *Historia Testis*, ed. M. Piérart and O. Curty (Fribourg, 1989), 175–88. Ammianus' emphatic statement that the infant was "imperator legitime declaratus" (30.10.5) confirms that he was writing before the death of Valentinian II (15 May 392): J. Straub, *Vom Herrscherideal in der Spätantike* (Berlin, 1939), 19, 220 n. 122; Alan Cameron, *JRS* 61 (1971), 261.

[80] *Mimesis* (1953), 59–60 (quoted and discussed in Chapter II).

[81] C. P. T. Naudé, *Gnomon* 41 (1969), 484. Matthews turns the historian into a historical optimist whom he explicitly compares to Olympiodorus of Thebes (*Ammianus* [1989], 472, cf. *Aristocracies* [1975], 382–86). That seems also to be a mistaken estimate of Olympiodorus: A. Gillett, *Traditio* 48 (1993), 1–29.

at this present period, and gave orders that the Goths who had been received earlier and dispersed in various cities and fortresses were to be collected without
arousing their suspicions outside the walls in the expectation of receiving the pay
that they had been promised and all were to be killed on one and the same day
as if the signal for battle had been given. When this wise plan was carried out without fuss or delay, the provinces of the East were rescued from great perils. (31.16.8)

Eunapius and Zosimus have a version of the same events that differs from Ammianus in three crucial respects: first, they place it in the spring of 379, after the
accession of Theodosius, not in the autumn of 378; second, they report that
the Goths were causing widespread damage in Asia Minor; and third, they explicitly identify the Goths who rioted and were killed as teenage hostages surrendered to the Roman authorities in 376.[82] Now a homily of Gregory of
Nyssa refers to an attack by "Scythians" on the shrine of Theodorus at Euchaita on the Black Sea, which it dates to the Julian year 379.[83] Since the first
two particulars in the account of Eunapius and Zosimus are thus confirmed
by contemporaneous evidence, a cogent case has recently been made for believing them against Ammianus on the third too.[84] At the very least, it appears
to be undeniable that Ammianus has knowingly transposed an episode that
occurred in the spring of 379 to the immediate aftermath of the Battle of
Adrianople in the autumn of 378. Moreover, nothing in Ammianus' text explicitly contradicts Eunapius' statement that the Goths slaughtered on the orders of Julius were mainly unarmed young men. Ammianus' presentation must
thus be pronounced to be deliberately misleading. That is a disturbing conclusion on at least two levels. First, it disproves the claim that immediately follows and on which so many modern interpretations of Ammianus are based—
that the historian has never knowingly distorted the truth. Second, it reveals
how Ammianus believed that "the barbarian crisis" should be tackled. Like
Synesius a few years later,[85] Ammianus believed that Goths on Roman soil
were a plague that could be eradicated only by the most drastic measures. He

---

[82] Eunapius, frag. 42 Müller = 42 Blockley; Zosimus 4.26.

[83] Gregory of Nyssa, *De sancto Theodoro* 61.15–62.2 Cavarnos. Since Gregory was speaking
on 7 February 380, his reference to "the year which has passed" (61.16) establishes 379 as the
year in which the raid occurred: see C. Zuckerman, *Travaux et Mémoires* 11 (1991), 480, 482–
84. The argument rests indirectly on the assumption that Basil of Caesarea died on 1 January 379:
for proof that this date, which has recently been challenged, must be correct, see *Studia Patristica*
29 (1997), 6–13. Another homily of Gregory records a raid by "Scythians" on Comana, but
gives no indication of the date (*De Baptismo* [*PG* 46.424]).

[84] Zuckerman, *Travaux et Mémoires* 11 (1991), 479–86.

[85] Synesius, *De Regno*, which is conveniently summarized by Alan Cameron and J. Long,
Barbarians and Politics at the Court of Arcadius (Berkeley, 1993), 103–6, cf. A. Garzya, *Il mandarino
e il quotidiano. Saggi sulla letteratura tardoantica e bizantina* (Naples, 1983), 171–98.

marks the didactic import of the episode that he narrates. The *efficacia* of Julius was *salutaris*, he devised a *consilium prudens*: no reader could miss or mistake the lesson being imparted.[86] Ammianus recommended massacre as politically expedient—and even, if necessary, genocide.

[86] S. Elbern, *Hermes* 115 (1987), 106. On the didactic nature of Book XXXI as a whole, see K. Rosen, *Cognitio Gestorum* (1992), 85–90.

[XV]

TACITUS, AMMIANUS, AND MACAULAY

Ammianus and Tacitus both wrote history in a way that can be described as dramatic. Yet they write history, depict the actors in the historical drama that they narrate, and represent reality in very different ways. It is worth the effort, therefore, to attempt to analyze how precisely, or in what precise sense, each of these two historians is dramatic. For important studies of both historians have obscured the individual genius of each by assimilating it to that of the other. Edmond Courbaud began his classic book on the artistic procedures of Tacitus by quoting Racine's paradoxical opinion that Tacitus was "the greatest painter of antiquity,"[1] then analyzed the *Histories* in visual terms that would have been more appropriate for Ammianus: Tacitus (Corbaud asserted) divided every book into a series of tableaux and always subordinated narrative to the tableau, because it was the composition of tableaux that gave him artistic satisfaction.[2] On the other side, it has been claimed that Ammianus presents the confrontation between the urban prefect Leontius and Peter Valvomeres "almost like a scene from a play" with "the contrasting emotions and postures" leading to a "dialogue between the central characters" resolved by "ritual violence."[3]

---

[1] In the second preface to his *Britannicus*: Racine, *Théâtre complet*, ed. M. Rat (Paris, 1960), 236.

[2] E. Courbaud, *Les Procédés d'art de Tacite dans les "Histoires"* (Paris, 1918), x, 28, 66, 96, 120, 121, 130, 161. Two specific examples of Courbaud's method: he analyzes *Hist.* 3.10 as "un exemple caractéristique," where "deux tableaux dans un même chapitre sont encadrés par trois fragments de récit" (125–27), and he finds in Tacitus, as in Racine, a strong preoccupation with describing gesture (134).

[3] J. F. Matthews, *Homo Viator. Classical Essays for John Bramble* (Bristol/Oak Park, 1987), 279. Also *Ammianus* (1989), 460: "his descriptions of persons and situations resembling (sometimes by deliberate choice of language) scenes from a play or masque."

In fact, it is Ammianus who concentrates on the visual aspect of an event and narrates it as a series of tableaux, Tacitus who presents an episode as a series of scenes from a play in which the historical actors display emotions that issue in action. Johann Wilhelm Süvern seems to have been the first to suggest that Tacitus deliberately imitated tragic form both in the overall structure of the *Annals* and *Histories* and in his presentation of individual episodes.[4] But it was a famous address by Friedrich Leo in 1895 that placed the idea at the center of learned discussions of Tacitus as a literary artist. Leo provocatively asserted that Tacitus was more a poet than a historian in the same way as Plato was more a poet than a philosopher, then analysed Tacitus' presentation of the emperors Tiberius, Nero, Galba, Otho, and Vitellius as tragedies. Leo meant this in a strong, virtually literal sense, not a weak metaphorical one. He divided the tragedy of Tiberius into five acts: the first is dominated by the heroic figure of Germanicus, the second by the avenging of his death; in the third act the evil Sejanus enters and prepares the ruin of Tiberius' only son and the family of the dead Germanicus; the climax of the drama comes in the fourth act with the fall of Sejanus; there follows the horrible end of the lonely tyrant, unrolling quickly, like the fifth act of one of Shakespeare's histories.[5]

Leo's analysis soon became a cliché of Tacitean scholarship. Pieter Everts argued that the structure of various episodes was dramatic in a formal sense: he analyzed Tacitus' accounts of the mutiny in Pannonia in 14 and of Germanicus' campaign in Germany in 16 as dramas in five acts, of the mutiny on the Rhine in 14 and the march of Caecina back to safety in 15 as dramas in four acts, and of the plot and punishment of Scribonius Libo as a tragedy in three acts.[6] Similarly, Kenneth Quinn divided Tacitus' account of the murder of Agrippina into four distinct scenes and an epilogue.[7] In more general terms, Leo's pupil Eduard Fraenkel contended that Tacitus' narrative comprises a series of scenes structurally linked together as if forming a drama;[8] Clarence Mendell that the only artistic unity in the *Annals* is its dramatic construction;[9] Einar Löfstedt that Tacitus is a "tragic poet" whose style and technique were shaped

---

[4] J. W. Süvern, *Abh. Berlin*, Hist.-phil. Kl. 1822–23, 95–96, 107, 121.

[5] F. Leo, *Tacitus*, ed. V. Pöschl (Darmstadt, 1969), 13–14.

[6] P. S. Everts, *De Taciti historiae conscribendae ratione* (Diss. Utrecht, publ. Kerkrade, 1926): respectively, *Ann.* 1.16–30, 2.8–22, 1.31–44, 1.63–58, 2.27–31.

[7] K. Quinn, *Latin Explorations: Critical Studies in Roman Literature* (London, 1963), 115, 123 (on *Ann.* 14.1–9).

[8] E. Fraenkel, *Kleine Beiträge zur klassischen Philologie* 2 (Rome, 1960), 329: "die reifste Kunst des Tacitus in szenenhaftem Aufbau gipfelt."

[9] C. W. Mendell, *YCS* 5 (1935), 53: "he accepted the annalistic form as a framework but gave it the semblance of unity by means of dramatic technique."

by the fact that he "occupied himself with the composition of tragic poetry in his youth." [10]

Leo's analysis has not commended itself to all recent students of Tacitus: it has been pronounced "too schematic" and Tacitus' technique has been defined as "pictorial-dramatic," more indebted to rhetoric and rhetorical historiography than to drama. [11] That is to miss a central aspect of the way in which Tacitus depicts historical reality. Margarete Billerbeck has rightly protested and reasserted the validity of Leo's approach: division into five acts can be seen even in such a minor episode as the murder of his mistress by the tribune Octavius Sagitta, [12] and Tacitus habitually uses a variety of dramatic devices, including the heightening of expectation, emotional death scenes, and sudden reversals. [13] In the present context, it suffices to show how Tacitus presents two important episodes in the *Annals* as a series of separate acts or scenes and how he signals transitions carefully, if often only implicitly, by indicating a change of scene or setting—a feature of Tacitus' narrative technique that editors too often obscure by making their paragraph divisions coincide with the misleading chapter divisions introduced in the Renaissance. [14]

The first book of the *Annals* begins with a rapid sketch of Roman history, a brief author's preface, and an analysis of the political situation at the end of the reign of Augustus. [15] Tacitus then narrates the accession of Tiberius as a drama in five acts. [16] The first covers the final illness and death of the old emperor: there was a rumour that he had visited his exiled grandson Agrippa Pos-

[10] E. Löfstedt, *Roman Literary Portraits*, trans. P. M. Fraser (Oxford, 1958), 153.

[11] F. R. D. Goodyear, *The Annals of Tacitus, Books 1–6* 1 (Cambridge, 1972), 195; A. J. Woodman, *Rhetoric in Classical Historiography. Four Studies* (London and Sydney, 1988), 160–96. Unfortunately, the latter scholar has often treated Tacitus as a novelist who invents freely, not a historian interested in discovering the truth: thus his analysis of Tacitus' account of the collapse of the amphitheatre at Fidenae under Tiberius reaches the astounding conclusion that the historian had at his disposal "no more source material than is provided by Suetonius" (A. J. Woodman, *CQ*, N.S. 22 [1972], 156), ignoring totally the fact that Tacitus refers to and paraphrases the *senatus consultum* condemning the contractor Atilius, who is otherwise unknown (*Ann.* 4.62.1–63.3, cf. *PIR*² A 1293).

[12] Tacitus, *Ann.* 13.44.

[13] M. Billerbeck, *ANRW* 2.33.4 (1991), 2752–71. On the theatricality of Tacitean death scenes, see also R. Barthes, *A Barthes Reader*, ed. S. Sontag (New York, 1982), 162–66; A. Malissard, *Theater und Gesellschaft im Imperium Romanum*, ed. J. Blänsdorf (Tübingen, 1990), 213–22. Billerbeck's approach is now adopted by Tony Woodman in his illustration of how Tacitus portrays the Pisonian conspiracy in *Ann.* 15.49–74 as belonging to "a world of unreality" (*Tacitus and the Tacitean Tradition*, ed. T. J. Luce and A. J. Woodman [Princeton, 1993], 104–12).

[14] For instances of the same phenomenon in Ammianus, see Chapter IV.

[15] Tacitus, *Ann.* 1.1.1–2 + 1.3 + 2–5.

[16] Tacitus, *Ann.* 1.5–15 = 1.5 + 6 + 7.1–8.5 + 8.6–10.7 + 10.8–15. On the need to begin new paragraphs at 1.3, 8.6, and 10.8, see Goodyear, *Annals* 1, 88, 151, 169.

tumus and was intending to restore him, but he fell seriously ill and died, and Tiberius immediately seized power. The second act presents the killing of Agrippa Postumus and the reaction of Tiberius and his mother. The scene moves to Rome for the third act, in which oaths of loyalty are taken to the new emperor, who summons the Senate, which meets and discusses arrangements for the funeral of Augustus. The fourth act is set on the day of the funeral: Tacitus evokes the sentiments of those who could recall the burial of Julius Caesar, alludes briefly to the *Res Gestae Divi Augusti*, and offers his verdict on Augustus in the form of the opinions for and against him that men of wisdom expressed on the occasion. Finally, the Senate meets: it consecrates the deceased emperor as Divus Augustus, discusses the legal powers of Tiberius (it would be anachronistic to call it his constitutional position), and settles various other matters.[17]

The episode of the "marriage" of Messalina to her young lover C. Silius (which was in reality no such thing)[18] has a similar structure. (1) Tacitus begins with a prologue that vouches for the truth of the story, however far-fetched it may appear to be, then analyzes the situation by imagining a debate among the imperial freedmen, who felt themselves imperiled by the empress's new amour.[19] (2) Despite the hesitations of Callistus and Pallas, Narcissus decides to act: he persuades a concubine to reveal his wife's infidelity to Claudius while he is at Ostia and confirms the truth of all she says, after which Claudius consults his *consilium*. (3) In Rome Messalina and Silius continue their wild orgy until news arrives that Claudius is returning to the city, whereupon Messalina sets out to meet him, taking a Vestal virgin with her. (4) Claudius returns to Rome: Narcissus prevents Messalina from gaining access to him, shows him the house of Silius, and takes him to the camp of the praetorian

[17] Tacitus marks the main transitions in *Ann.* 1.5–15 carefully: (1) 5.1: haec atque talia agitantibus gravescere valetudo Augusti; (2) 6.1: primum facinus novi principatus; (3) 7.1: at Romae, after which new paragraphs should begin at 7.5 (sed defuncto Augusto) and 8.1 (nihil primo senatus die); (4) 8.6 (die funeris), with new paragraphs at 9.3 (at apud prudentes) and 10.1 (dicebatur contra); (5) 10.8: ceterum sepultura more perfecta templum et caelestes religiones decernuntur, i.e., in the Senate on 17 September 14. It ruins the articulation of the text to divide 8.6–9.2 into two paragraphs, as Goodyear does. The subsequent Teubner edition of H. Heubner (1983) faithfully follows the conventional chapter divisions (which are of renaissance origin) and begins new paragraphs at 9.1, but not at 8.6 or 9.3, and at 11.1 instead of 10.8.

[18] B. Levick, *Claudius* (London, 1990), 64–67, cf. J. Colin, *Les Études classiques* 24 (1956), 25–39.

[19] Tacitus, *Ann.* 11.27–28. After the action proper commences (29.1), changes of scene are marked by the following phrases: at Messalina (31.2, where Heubner correctly begins a new paragraph); trepidabatur nihilo minus a Caesare (33.1); interim Messalina (37.1). Reparagraphing is also necessary in the final chapter of the book: although the traditional chapter division occurs immediately before Messalina's death, the logical break surely comes after it with the transition from the suppression of the "conspiracy" to its aftermath (38.1[b]: corpus matri concessum).

guard, where he authorizes the execution of all the alleged plotters except two. (5) Messalina seeks out her mother and is killed in her house. By way of epilogue Tacitus describes the reaction of Claudius, the condemnation of Messalina by the Senate, and the honors voted to Narcissus. In this episode, as in his account of the accession of Tiberius, Tacitus breaks his narrative into separate and clearly defined sections, each of which begins with an initial phrase indicating a change of place or temporal progression. The technique is dramatic: Tacitus uses modes of presentation and expression familiar to him from the recitation drama that flourished in the first century.[20] Hence, when he describes the mutiny of the praetorians under Otho, Tacitus focuses his readers' attention on the mutinous soldiers and their motives, passing quickly over the decisive confrontation between the emperor and the mutineers.[21]

Ammianus' method of narrating similar episodes is vastly different: as with the arrest of Peter Valvomeres (Chapter II), it is the decisive confrontation itself that he chooses to emphasize. The two historians also differ vastly in their presentation of physical detail and in their readiness to use ordinary vocabulary for everyday things. Tacitus maintains a highly elevated tone throughout. Tiberius was bald and had a blotchy face, but Tacitus avoids the vulgar word *calvus*: the emperor had a "summit denuded of hair."[22] The emperor Vitellius was a glutton who gorged himself like a pig: Tacitus avoids the normal Latin word for pig, for which he substitutes a periphrasis of extreme preciosity: "lazy animals which lie down and go to sleep if you offer them food."[23]

Ammianus has no such stylistic inhibitions. He uses colloquialisms and words whose stylistic overtones are far from elevated, such as *crapulentus* (29.5.54),[24] *palpamentum* (27.12.6),[25] *suctus* (31.6.7),[26] and *vomito* (14.11.24).[27] The stylistic gulf that separates the two historians is perhaps most obvious in their treatment of spitting. Ammianus can say straightforwardly that when Constantius

[20] On Tacitus' relation to recitation drama, see *HSCP* 90 (1986), 232–44.

[21] Tacitus, *Hist.* 1.82.1, cf. H. Heubner, *Studien zur Darstellungskunst des Tacitus (Hist. I,12–II,51)* (Würzburg, 1935), 23–24; E. Hohl, *Klio* 32 (1939), 307–24. Comparison with Plutarch, *Otho* 3.6–11, shows that the emphasis is Tacitus' own.

[22] Tacitus, *Ann.* 4.57.2: nudus capillo vertex, ulcerosa facies et plerumque medicaminibus interstincta, cf. R. Syme, *Tacitus* (Oxford, 1958), 343.

[23] Tacitus, *Hist.* 3.36.1: umbraculis hortorum abditus, ut ignavia animalia, quibus si cibum suggeras, iacent torpentque, praeterita instantia futura pari oblivione dimiserat. Tacitus uses the word *sus* twice: once in registering Jewish abstention from pork (*Hist.* 5.4.2: sue abstinent), once in the notice of a prodigy in 62, which he doubtless transcribed from the Elder Pliny (*Ann.* 12.64.1: suis fetum editum, cui accipitrum ungues inessent).

[24] On the form of the adjective, see Blomgren, *Quaestiones* (1937), 119–20: all the derivatives of *crapula* appear to be vulgar or biblical (*TLL* 4.1098).

[25] The word occurs nowhere else, but its cognates are non-literary (*TLL* 10.160).

[26] *OLD* 1889 cites only Varro and the Elder Pliny.

[27] *OLD* 2103 cites only Seneca, *Epp.* 18.4, 108.37; Suetonius, *Vit.* 13.1.

entered Rome no one saw him spit or wipe his mouth or nose (16.10.10),[28] and he uses both the verb *spuo* in three other passages (21.16.7; 23.6.80; 27.3.5) and the noun *sputamen* (14.9.6). When Tacitus described Nero performing on stage with a lyre, he avoided the normal Latin words for spit and saliva: the emperor wipes his face with the garment that he was wearing "so that no emanations from his mouth or nose were seen."[29] Another linguistic difference between the two historians is equally significant.[30] As far as he can, Tacitus avoids official terminology and the technical terms for administrative posts.[31] Ammianus in contrast has no objection to using bureaucratic and official phraseology.[32]

How much does Ammianus owe to Tacitus? The question has received greatly divergent answers. Long lists of borrowings and imitations have been produced,[33] and Ammianus has been saluted as "the heir of Tacitus, in every sense."[34] Yet it must be doubted whether it is illuminating to regard Ammianus as the successor of Tacitus in any real sense:[35] the world about which Ammianus writes had undergone a profound transformation, his historical techniques and methods of presentation are vastly different from those of Tac-

[28] Ammianus' words "nec spuens aut os aut nasum tergens aut fricans" appear to echo Xenophon, *Cyropaedeia* 8.1.42, 8.8: see C. J. Classen, *Rh. Mus.*, N.F. 131 (1988), 177–81.

[29] Tacitus, *Ann.* 16.4.3: ingreditur theatrum, cunctis citharae legibus obtemperans, ne fessus resideret, ne sudorem nisi ea, quam indutui gerebat, veste detergeret, ut nulla oris aut narium excrementa viserentur. I avoid the obvious English translation of *excrementa* in order to preserve Tacitus' elevated stylistic level: he uses the word elsewhere of the blind man who came in quest of healing and asked Vespasian "ut genas et oculorum orbes dignaretur respergere oris excremento" (*Hist.* 4.81.1). A similar avoidance of vulgar words is evident at *Ann.* 11.32.3: "vehiculo quo purgamenta hortorum excipiuntur."

[30] For archaisms, often with a colloquial flavor, in Ammianus, see H. Fesser, *Sprachliche Beobachtungen zu Ammianus Marcellinus* (Diss. Breslau, 1932), 29–61. Tacitus wrote before archaism became fashionable under Hadrian.

[31] Thus, although *legati* of provinces are frequent in his text, none is ever styled *legatus Augusti*, *legatus pro praetore* or *legatus Augusti pro praetore*, as they normally are on inscriptions (H. Dessau, *ILS* 3.1, pp. 368–82).

[32] For some examples, see A. Helttula, *Studia in honorem Iiro Kajanto* (*Arctos*, Supplement 2, 1985), 41–56; *Studies on the Latin Accusative Absolute* (*Commentationes Humanarum Litterarum* 81, 1987), 46–47, 105–11. The topic merits a systematic investigation (*CP* 88 [1993], 66).

[33] H. Wirz, *Philologus* 36 (1877), 634–35; Fesser, *Beobachtungen* (1932), 23–27; G. B. A. Fletcher, *Rev. phil.* 63 (1937), 390–92; Rosen, *Ammianus* (1982), 95–96.

[34] Syme, *Tacitus* (1958), 503, n. 8, cf. *Ammianus* (1968), 129. On this issue at least, Arnaldo Momigliano was in complete agreement with his arch-enemy: he opined that Ammianus "continues Tacitus as the *Historia Augusta* continues Suetonius" (*Essays in Ancient and Modern Historiography* [Oxford, 1977], 131).

[35] D. Flach, *Historia* 32 (1973), 333–50; L. E. Wilshire, *CJ* 68 (1972–73), 221–27; R. P. C. Blockley, *Latomus* 32 (1973), 63–78; I. Borszák, *Acta Antiqua* 24 (1976), 357–68; Matthews, *Ammianus* (1989), 32, 456, 468, 482–83, n. 35, 549, n. 4, 550, n. 11; G. W. Bowersock, *JRS* 80 (1990), 246.

itus, his style is characterized by opulence and abundance where Tacitus strives for terse brevity,[36] and he stands in the Greek rather than the Latin tradition of historiography (Chapters VII, IX).[37] Moreover, many of the alleged imitations of Tacitus will not withstand critical scrutiny.[38] A careful assessment is needed, therefore, of the true nature and real extent of Ammianus' debt to Tacitus.

There can be no doubt that Ammianus had read widely and deeply in Latin. The *Res Gestae* quote Cicero many times, not infrequently from works that are now lost, and long lists of convincing verbal echoes have been compiled.[39] Throughout his work, Ammianus repeats and adapts phrases from other Latin authors, above all Terence, Sallust, Virgil, Livy, and the antiquarian Aulus Gellius.[40] In addition, echoes of a wide variety of other Latin authors can be documented, including the prose writers Valerius Maximus, Curtius Rufus, Seneca, Florus, and Apuleius, and the poets Horace, Ovid, Lucan, Valerius Flaccus, and Silius Italicus.[41] Indeed, so pervasive are echoes of earlier Latin writers that possible allusions must always be considered when emending corrupt or supplementing lacunose passages.[42]

[36] H. Hagendahl, *Eranos* 22 (1924), 161–216: he defines the three main traits of Ammianus' style as "color poeticus, variatio, abundantia."

[37] For comparison of Ammianus' "narrative sentence" to that of other Latin historians, see A. Debru, *Rev. phil.*[3] 66 (1992), 267–87.

[38] For example, W. Richter, *Historia* 23 (1974), 366–67, confidently claims that 31.7.16 (reliqua peremptorum corpora dirae volucres consumpserunt/ assuetae illo tempore cadaveribus pasci,/ ut indicant nunc usque albentes ossibus campi) cannot reflect Ammianus' personal inspection of the battlefield at Ad Salices because the passage copies what Tacitus says about the remains of the slaughtered legions of Quintilius Varus (*Ann.* 1.61.2: medio campi albentia ossa, ut fugerant, ut restiterant, disiecta vel aggerata). In fact, Ammianus is closer to the model that he and Tacitus have independently imitated: sanguine adhuc campique ingentes ossibus albent (Vergil, *Aen.* 12.35).

[39] H. Michael, *De Ammiani Marcellini studiis Ciceronianis* (Diss. Breslau, 1874); G. B. A. Fletcher, *Rev. phil.*[3] 11 (1937), 377–81. However, the three derivations alleged by Wirz, *Philologus* 36 (1877), 633, are not persuasive.

[40] See the passages adduced by Valesius on 25.4.14, 22; M. Hertz, *De Ammiani Marcellini studiis Sallustianis dissertatio* (Breslau, 1874); *Hermes* 8 (1874), 265 n. 1, 271, 275–302; Wirz, *Philologus* 36 (1877), 628–35; H. Finke, *Ammianus Marcellinus und seine Quellen zur Geschichte der römischen Republik* (Diss. Heidelberg, 1904), 10–14, 20–30; H. Hagendahl, *Studia Ammianea* (Diss. Uppsala, 1921), 1–14; Fesser, *Beobachtungen* (1932), 3–23; Fletcher, *Rev. phil.*,[3] 11 (1937), 377, 382–86, 390–93; *Ut pictura poesis* (Leiden, 1955), 85–86; Bitter, *Kampfschilderungen* (1976), 208–10; C. W. Fornara, *Historia* 41 (1992), 427–38.

[41] Hertz, *Hermes* 8 (1874), 272–73; E. Schneider, *Quaestiones Ammianeae* (Diss. Berlin, 1879), 12–13, 34–35, 38; C. Weyman, *Sb. München*, Phil. u. hist. Cl. 1893.2 (1894), 361; Finke, *Ammianus* (1904), 15–20, 30–40; E. Bickel, *Gött. Gel. Anz.* 180 (1918), 282–92; H. Hagendahl, *Studia Ammianea* (Diss. Uppsala, 1921), 15; Fletcher, *Rev. phil.*,[3] 11 (1937), 383, 386–89; Bitter, *Kampfschilderungen* (1976), 208–9.

[42] C. Brakman, *Ammianea et Annaeana* (Leiden, 1909), 1, 15–16; Hagendahl, *Studia* (1921), 13–14.

On general grounds, therefore, it is probable that Ammianus read Tacitus. One certain borrowing will constitute proof positive, and two separate echoes of the same passage of Tacitus have been identified, which are clearly intended to be significant and consequently must be deliberate.[43] Tacitus opens the second book of his *Histories* with a striking expression:

struebat iam fortuna in diversa parte terrarum initia causasque imperio.[44]

Ammianus repeats Tacitus' phrasing very closely in the opening words of Book XXII:

dum haec in diversa parte terrarum fortunae struunt volubiles casus. (22.1.1)

Tacitus then proceeded to describe the journey of Titus, the son of Vespasian, who was on his way to Rome in the hope of being adopted as Galba's heir. At Corinth Titus received news that Galba was dead and deliberated whether to continue to Rome and risk becoming a hostage in the hands of Otho or to return to his father:

his atque talibus inter spem metumque iactatum spes vicit.[45]

Ammianus consciously imitates this sentence in a similar context. At the end of Book XX, the eastern emperor Constantius contemplates the prospect of war with Julian as the winter of 360–361 approaches:

his ac talibus imperator inter spem metumque iactabatur. (20.11.31)

Since the two situations are similar, the literary imitation is surely both conscious and deliberate.[46] Another echo of Tacitus may be detected in Ammianus' account of the arrest of Peter Valvomeres. Peter's enormous body and red hair (15.7.4: vasti corporis rutilique capilli) are so characteristic of Germans that they could be considered a commonplace rather than inspired by

---

[43] See, respectively, Fesser, *Beobachtungen* (1932), 23; Fletcher, *Ut pictura poesis* (1955), 85.

[44] Tacitus, *Hist.* 2.1.1.

[45] Tacitus, *Hist.* 2.1.1–2.1.

[46] Rosen, *Ammianus* (1982), 95–96. Similar arguments can be deployed to prove that Ammianus' account of the proclamation of Julian as Augustus (20.4.9–5.7) deliberately copies Tacitus' account of the mutiny of the Rhine armies in 14 (*Ann.* 1.31–49): M. F. Williams, *Phoenix* 51 (1997), 63–68.

the *rutilae comae* of Tacitus' Germans.[47] But Peter is also a *turbarum acerrimus concitor* (15.7.5). Tacitus too has an *acerrimus belli concitor*: he is Antonius Primus at the beginning of the third book of the *Histories*, a convicted forger who is about to seize command of the troops in Pannonia who have declared for Vespasian.[48] Hence it becomes likely that phrases such as *opum contemptor* (25.4.7) and *expediti consilii* (31.5.7) are unconscious echoes of Tacitus,[49] which implies that Ammianus had read him carefully and thoroughly.

Ammianus thus imitates Tacitus both in his presentation of individuals and in his vocabulary.[50] Moreover, the *Res Gestae* began with the accession of the emperor Nerva, exactly where Tacitus ended, and Ammianus' original plan was probably to cover the period from Nerva to Julian in thirty books, which corresponds exactly to the number of books of Tacitus' *Annals* and *Histories* (Chapter III). Hence it is legitimate to believe that, despite the fundamentally Greek nature of his work, Ammianus also thought of himself as a historian who continued, imitated, and emulated Tacitus. Indeed, the two aspects are complementary, not contradictory. For it was precisely his knowledge of Greek historians of the second, third, and fourth centuries that equipped Ammianus to write a history intended to continue and supplement Tacitus for Roman readers who were in the habit of reading the scandalous and salacious imperial biographies of Marius Maximus (28.4.14). The *Historia Augusta* stands as contemporary testimony that "the lonely historian" Ammianus failed to change the literary tastes of Roman aristocrats.[51]

The modern historian whom Ammianus most resembles is not the one with whom he has traditionally been compared.[52] Edward Gibbon blended the historical insights and cynicism of Tacitus with a sentence structure that owes most to the perfectly balanced periods of Isocrates: although he regarded Am-

---

[47] Tacitus, *Germ.* 4.1, cf. *Agr.* 11.2: rutilae Caledoniam habitantium comae, magni artus. According to Jerome, Hilarion healed a Frankish "candidatus Constantii imperatoris, rutilus coma, et candore corporis indicans provinciam" (*Vita Hilarionis* 13.2).

[48] Tacitus, *Hist.* 3.2.1. Editors of Tacitus usually print *concitator*, but the Medicean manuscript has *conciator*, which Orelli emended to *concitor*.

[49] Respectively, Tacitus, *Hist.* 4.5.2: opum contemptor (sc. Helvidius Priscus); *Hist.* 4.42.5: expediti consilii (of Aquillius Regulus); cf. Fletcher, *Rev. phil.*³ 11 (1937), 391; *Ut pictura poesis* (1955), 86.

[50] Löfstedt, *Roman Literary Portraits* (1958), 159–60, drew attention to a shared linguistic preference that may be unconscious, and thus all the more revealing: like Tacitus, Ammianus heavily prefers the archaic preposition *ob*, which he uses 126 times, to its commoner synonym *propter*, which occurs only thrice (15.11.4, 18.2.15, 23.6.87).

[51] Syme, *Ammianus* (1968), 126–210.

[52] E.g., by M. L. W. Laistner, *The Greater Roman Historians* (Berkeley, 1947), 143–44.

mianus highly as a historical source, Gibbon recoiled instinctively from his stylistic excesses.[53] Ammianus' modern congener is not Gibbon, but Thomas Babington Macaulay. Although his essay of 1828 on "history" considers the classic historians Herodotus, Thucydides, Polybius, Sallust, Livy, and Tacitus,[54] the young Macaulay had nothing to say about Ammianus, who did not form part of a normal classical education (then or now):[55] he first read Ammianus in India and pronounced his history "the worst written book in ancient Latin," whose "style would disgrace a monk of the tenth century."[56] Ammianus had no direct influence on Macaulay, who derived his historical approach and his conception of what history ought to be from the novels of Sir Walter Scott and his literary style largely from the Evangelical preaching to which he was exposed when very young.[57] Nevertheless, there are deep affinities between Ammianus and Macaulay, who, despite his revulsion at the ancient writer's style, instinctively recognized in him "many of the substantial qualities of a good historian."[58] Both the *Res Gestae* and the *History of England* strive for formal symmetry, both display strong partiality for or unfairness toward the actors in their narrative, great and small, both allow these personal prejudices to determine their evaluation of evidence, and both employ compositional modes more suited to the novel than to history.

In his journal for 6 February 1854, after a day spent largely on his *History of England*, Macaulay wrote: "I worked hard at altering the arrangement of the first three chapters of the third volume. What labour it is to make a tolerable book, and how little readers know how much trouble the ordering of the parts has cost the writer!"[59] Macaulay strove for strict symmetry between, if not within, volumes.[60] The first two volumes, published together in 1848, have five long chapters each. The first describes England under King James II

---

[53] *Decline and Fall* 2.264, n. 18 (B) = 1.687, n. 16 (W) (quoted in Chapter I).

[54] T. B. Macauley, *Edinburgh Review* 47 (1828), 331–67. On the intellectual context of the essay, see G. P Gooch, *History and Historians in the Nineteenth-Century*[2] (London, 1913), 294–304; J. Clive, *Macaulay. The Shaping of the Historian* (New York, 1973), 98–141.

[55] There seems to be no mention at all of Ammianus in *The Legacy of Rome: A New Appraisal*, ed. R. Jenkyns (Oxford, 1992), despite extensive discussion of Augustine.

[56] G. O. Trevelyan, *Life and Letters of Lord Macaulay*, 1 (Oxford, 1961: first published in 1876), 423: a letter written in Calcutta on 30 November 1836.

[57] See esp. G. Levine, *The Boundaries of Fiction: Carlyle, Macaulay, Newman* (Princeton, 1968), 79–163; W. A. Madden, *The Art of Victorian Prose*, ed. G. Levine and W. Madden (New York, 1968), 127–50; H. R. Trevor-Roper, *The Romantic Movement and the Study of History* (London, 1969), 8, 16–21; Clive, *Macaulay* (1973), 119, 122, 135–36, 248, 498.

[58] Trevelyan, *Life* 1 (1961), 423.

[59] Trevelyan, *Life* 2 (1961), 305.

[60] Modern critics of Macaulay have had virtually nothing to say about the formal structure of his *History*: the omission strengthens the central contention of Chapter III.

and ends with "the first faint indications of a great turn of fortune," and the second begins with James at the height of his power and ends with the interregnum after his flight. The third and fourth volumes, also published as a pair in 1856, each have six long chapters. The third volume begins with the stark sentence "The revolution had been accomplished"; it concludes with William's departure from London in January 1691 after a plot to assassinate him. The fourth begins with William's embarkation for Holland and ends with the treaty of Ryswick in 1697, as a result of which "the cheerful bustle in every seaport and every market town indicated, not obscurely, the commencement of a happier age." The fifth and final volume of his *History*, which was published by Macaulay's sister after his death, concludes with the death of William in 1702 and contains three chapters, probably the number intended by the deceased author.[61]

Like Ammianus, Macaulay has strong likes and dislikes, which he expresses without inhibition in his delineation of the characters whose actions he describes. Like Ammianus too, Macaulay allows his biases to shape and mould his narrative. His hero is William of Orange, who must be exculpated from any blame for the Massacre of Glencoe, his villains King James II and any who made a successful career under him, whatever their subsequent service to William, so that William Penn and John Churchill, Duke of Marlborough, receive very unflattering portaits.[62] Macaulay is as unfair to James as Ammianus is to Constantius, even more inclined to disbelieve ill of William than Ammianus is to suppress Julian's intolerance, fanaticism, and devotion to religious practices of which he disapproved (Chapter XIII).

Ammianus' account of the history of the Roman Empire from 353 to 378 has provided the basis and the framework for almost all modern accounts of the period to almost the same degree as that of Thucydides has for the Peloponnesian War and that of Polybius for Rome's dealings with the Greek world from 220 to 146 B.C. Yet his presentation of events depends on antecedent prejudices that almost always have a personal basis. The biases damage Ammianus' objectivity just as much as Macaulay's prevent his *History of England* from being an impartial account of British history and politics in the late seventeenth century. Macaulay's *History* is now regarded as a work of literature, imagination, and eloquence that reveals more about its author and the nine-

---

[61] That appears to be the clear implication of the letters of October and 14 December 1859 quoted by Trevelyan, *Life* 2 (1961), 395.

[62] C. Firth, *A Commentary on Macaulay's History of England*, ed. G. Davies (London, 1938), esp. 88–90, 201–4, 265–73, 277–303, 334–67.

teenth century than about the "Glorious Revolution" of 1688.[63] The fact that as a historian Ammianus shows such similarities to Macaulay ought to encourage a similar estimation of his *Res Gestae* as a work of imaginative literature.[64] That will in no way diminish the achievement of one who has been saluted as the greatest literary genius that the world produced between Tacitus and Dante.[65] Macaulay declared that "to be a really great historian is perhaps the rarest of intellectual distinctions."[66] Ammianus has secured a permanent place in the select group of really great historians precisely because, like Macaulay's *History of England*, his *Res Gestae* exhibit the creative and imaginative powers of a novelist.

[63] On the manifold ways in which Macaulay resembles the great novelists of Victorian England, see Levine, *Boundaries* (1968), 79–163. It can even be claimed with some plausibility that Macaulay thought of the ideal historian as both novelist and poet: R. Weber, *Papers on Language and Literature* 3 (1967), 216–19. For a general discussion of "History and the Novel," see D. LaCapra, *History and Criticism* (Ithaca, 1985), 115–34.

[64] For a spirited defense of imagination as necessary for the historian, see H. R. Trevor-Roper, *History and Imagination* (Oxford, 1980). Ronald Syme's *Roman Revolution* (Oxford, 1939), will long stand as an example of how to combine detailed and accurate research with the imaginative reconstruction of a past era.

[65] E. Stein, *Geschichte des spätrömischen Reiches* 1 (Vienna, 1928), 331 = *Histoire du Bas-Empire* 1, trans. and rev. J.-R. Palanque (Paris/Bruges, 1959), 215.

[66] *Edinburgh Review* 47 (1828), 365.

APPENDICES

[I]

THE TEXT OF AMMIANUS

The salient facts about the manuscript tradition of Ammianus' *Res Gestae* have been stated with elegance and economy by L. D. Reynolds.[1] The text is transmitted by two Carolingian manuscripts of the ninth century:

M   Fragmenta Marburgensia, the six surviving leaves of a manuscript once at Hersfeld that were rediscovered at Marburg in 1875 and are now in the Landesbibliothek at Kassel (Philol. 2 27).

V   Vatican lat. 1873, from Fulda.

There are also fourteen manuscripts of the fifteenth century that all derive directly or indirectly from V and hence are of value only as repositories of humanist conjectures except where a leaf of V has been lost (31.8.5 *paulatim–* 31.10.18 *incredibile dictu est*).

Although the two Carolingian manuscripts are very close in date, at least on paleographical grounds, it was demonstrated beyond possible doubt in 1936 that V was copied from M.[2] Since M, which broke off at 30.9.6, was employed by Gelenius for his edition of Ammianus (Basel, 1533) before it was dismembered, Gelenius' edition is an important witness to the text. However, considerable care must be exercised when trying to deduce the reading of the lost

---

[1] *Texts and Transmission. A Survey of the Latin Classics*, ed. L. D. Reynolds (Oxford, 1983), 6–8.

[2] R. P. Robinson, *Philological Studies in honor of Walter Miller* (Columbia, Missouri, 1936), 118–40; W. Seyfarth, *Der Codex Fuldensis und der Codex E des Ammianus Marcellinus (Abh. Berlin*, Klasse für Sprache, Literatur und Kunst 1962, Abh. 2). H. Nissen, *Ammiani Marcellini fragmenta Marburgensia* (Berlin, 1876), 18–24, had argued that M was the "archetype" of V, but L. Traube, *Vorlesungen und Abhandlungen* 3 (Munich, 1920), 33–38, dated M slightly later than V on palaeographical grounds and hence held M and V to be independently descended from a lost archetype.

manuscript from Gelenius' text: where Gelenius reproduces the edition of 1518, it cannot simply be assumed that M had the same reading; where he deviates, he has not necessarily corrected from M rather than resorted to conjecture.[3]

The first edition of Ammianus to meet proper critical standards was produced by C. U. Clark, who had previously written a doctoral dissertation on the textual tradition.[4] Although Clark's edition was never properly completed (it lacks both an index and the discussion of the manuscripts promised in the preface), it remains fundamental. What will long be the standard edition, the Teubner of Wolfgang Seyfarth, has brought improvements to Clark's text mainly in matters of punctuation, typography, and the presentation of the paradosis and renaissance conjectures in the *apparatus criticus*.[5] Other texts subsequent to Clark, it must be said with regret, but firmly, have marked a regression to pre-critical standards by too often supplementing lacunae with unsatisfactory fifteenth-century conjectures (the Loeb edition by J. C. Rolfe [1935–1939], the unfinished Budé, whose first volume appeared in 1968, and Roger Blockley's selections.[6]

A complication recently brought to light calls into question the strictness of the evaluation of the paradosis on which Clark and Seyfarth base their constitution of the text. The early humanist Flavio Biondo claimed, in a marginal note found in a manuscript of Ammianus that belonged to Cardinal Bessarion, that he had seen a manuscript that contained the equivalent of a folium in the lacuna at 16.10.4:

hic deest unius folii scriptura ex iis que in exemplari vetusto legisse memini. et est pars multi facienda: a me in Italia apud Ocriculum posita. .B.[7]

---

[3] G. Pasquali, *Storia della tradizione e critica del testo*[2] (Florence, 1962), 81–83, 123.

[4] C. U. Clark, *The Text Tradition of Ammianus Marcellinus* (Diss. Yale, 1904). Clark had studied with Ludwig Traube in Munich and his work was both encouraged and assisted by Mommsen.

[5] On Seyfarth's edition, see R. Cappelletto, *Riv. fil.* 109 (1981), 80–85. Clark printed a double apparatus below his text, with the readings of V and M presented separately from those of the derivative manuscripts and editors; he italicized emendations printed in the text even if the emendation affects only part of a word (e.g., 16.8.1: perpetraban*tur*); and he added a comma after every clausula within a sentence or a clause whether the sense requires it or not, sometimes even where the added comma was likely to confuse a modern reader (e.g., 14.2.18: congesta undique saxa, telaque habentes in promptu). Seyfarth elegantly marks internal clausulae by two typographical devices: an extra space within the line and a hasta when the clausula coincides with the end of a printed line (see Appendix 6).

[6] R. Blockley, *Ammianus Marcellinus: A Selection* (Bristol, 1980). This scholar fails, for example, to mark lacunae in 15.5.14–15, 30, even though an important part of Ammianus' story of how Silvanus' troops were persuaded to desert him appears to be missing and V demonstratively leaves gaps of 15 and 20 or 22 letters in the two passages.

[7] Venice, Biblioteca Nazionale Marciana, lat. Z 388 [= 1850] = W, fol. 48v: best published by R. Cappelletto, *Recuperi ammianei di Flavio Biondo* (Rome, 1983), 19; Tav. I,2, who also re-

Rita Cappelletto, who has republished this marginal note and demonstrated that the attribution to Biondo in another manuscript of Ammianus is correct (N = Paris, Bibliothèque Nationale, lat. 6120, fol. 30v), identified the passage to which Biondo refers: it is indeed found in the entry for Ocriculum in his *Italia illustrata*, which appears to quote from the missing portion of text:

> Siquidem Ammianus Marcellinus, Constantii Caesaris Constantino primo nati adventum a Constantinopoli Romam libro sextodecimo describens, dicit ipsum duxisse in comitatu Ormisdam, Persarum gentis architecturae peritissimum, ius-sisseque illi ut primaria quaeque digniora urbis Romae aedificia diligenter inspecta ordine sibi ostenderet. Et cum Ocriculum de itinere esset ventum, Persam, im-peratore iubente omnium colloquio destitutum, ab Ocriculo Romam prius in-gressum fuisse quam quo in loco urbs inchoasset discernere ac intelligere noverit.[8]

Moreover, Biondo's *Roma triumphans* quotes a statement of Ammianus about Christian clergy riding in carriages not found in the extant manuscripts:

> morem vero hunc, quem Tacitus sacerdotibus concessum fuisse dicit, Ammianus Marcellinus nostros servasse Christianos sacerdotes ut multi quam ornatissimi unico veherentur carpento scribit.[9]

Cappelletto argued that the missing passage that Biondo claims to have read described the flight of Hormisdas from Persia (cf. 16.10.16: cuius e Perside discessum supra monstravimus): she deduced that Biondo had seen a frag-mentary manuscript of Ammianus that probably contained Books XIV and XV, and she identified this fragmentary manuscript as part of the lost manu-script from Hersfeld, separated from the main body of the text in the same way as Book XXXI certainly was.[10]

Alan Cameron has drawn a conclusion of much greater consequence from the evidence discussed by Cappelletto: he argues that, because Gelenius' edi-tion of 1533 repeats from the Froben edition of 1518 the feeble supplement for 16.10.4 that Castelli had added in his edition (Bologna, 1517), the lost M had precisely the same lacuna in this passage as the extant V, not the superior

---

publishes the note in N (28). Clark's apparatus to 16.10.4 quotes the annotation in both W and N; Seyfarth's does not.

[8] Quoted from Cappelletto, *Ricuperi* (1983), 35, who notes Biondo's handwritten alterations to the first edition of *Italia illustrata* in Vatican, Ottobonianus latinus 2369, which she dates c. 1453–1455 (34).

[9] Biondo, *Roma Triumphans* 9.200F, quoted from Cappelletto, *Ricuperi* (1983), 74.

[10] Cappelletto, *Ricuperi* (1983), esp. 40–43 (Hormisdas), 86–91 (arguing that the complete Hersfeldensis had been brought to Italy by Enoch of Ascoli).

supplement known to and used by Biondo.[11] Hence Cameron deduced that a third complete manuscript of Ammianus survived the Middle Ages to become available in Italy in the fifteenth century. That is a bold claim to base on such slender evidence. For, even if the inference could be accepted as plausible a priori, the material assembled by Cappelletto comprises only one apparent quotation in Biondo's *Italia illustrata* that can be tied to a specific passage (16.10.4) and two from his later *Roma triumphans* (of 1457–1459), which cannot: the passage quoted above and an apparent adaptation of an extant passage (17.4.5 on Cornelius Gallus).[12]

The question is an intricate one that hardly admits of a certain answer. Extreme caution is therefore necessary, and the seventeenth-century editor Valesius may have been correct to claim that Biondo was lying about what he had read. In the lacuna at 16.10.4 between *apparatu* and *secunda Orfiti praefectura* Valesius supplied merely *IV Kal. Maias*, which is attested as the day on which Constantius entered Rome in 357 (*Descr. cons.* 357.2).[13] At the place where Biondo claimed a lacuna of a leaf, V marks a lacuna of seventeen letters. Whether or not Biondo should be believed, there is no reason to believe that the differing sizes of the many blank spaces that the scribe of V left to indicate lacunae or illegible passages in his exemplar are in any way accurate indications of how much text has been lost in each case.

Lacunae are extremely frequent in the transmitted text of Ammianus. How frequent can perhaps best be illustrated by the following list of passages in Books XV–XVII, where V marks a lacuna:

1. Passages where little seems to be lost, sometimes only a single word or part of a word:

    XV   3.10, 5.5 (two), 7.3, 11.18

    XVI   2.3, 2.8, 8.6, 8.10, 10.21, 11.6, 12.65, 12.70

    XVII   1.3, 2.2, 13.21, 13.24

2. Passages where more has been lost, perhaps a substantial amount of text:

    XV   4.1–3, 4.6–7, 4.11,[14] 5.2–3, 5.14–15, 5.30

    XVI   4.1–2 (42 letters), 8.13[15]

    XVII   3.6, 12.7

---

[11] Alan Cameron, *HSCP* 92 (1989), 423–36.

[12] Cappelletto, *Ricuperi* (1983), 66–74.

[13] Quoted by Cappelletto, *Ricuperi* (1983), 29, n. 40. Valesius quotes the note in N, reports Biondo's own note, then adds "sed ego Blondio non credo."

[14] Seyfarth marks thirteen separate lacunae in 15.4: most comprise a few letters, but V marks one as more than two lines (2–3) and one as 30 lines (11).

[15] V marks two lacunae, of 19 and 27 letters, respectively, the latter between the words *Aniciique* and *vorum*, where Seyfarth accepts Clark's emendation to *Aniciorumque* without any lacuna at all.

Whatever the cause, Book XXIX seems to be especially lacunose: the account of the campaign of Theodosius against Firmus in Mauretania and Numidia has disappeared (at 5.3–4, 5.30, where V marks a lacuna of two and a half lines), and the loss must be postulated of a substantial passage that registered the *praefecti urbis* who held office between the summer of 372 and the spring of 374 (at 5.1, where V again marks a lacuna of two and a half lines, cf. Appendix 8).

There are also some undeniable lacunae in passages where V does not mark any discontinuity in the text. The most important occurs in 24.7.3, where V reads "hinc opulenta sed ille avidae semper ad ulteriora cupiditatis etc." with no hint that anything is amiss. Grammar alone proves the existence of a lacuna between *opulenta* and *sed ille*, and Valesius saw that a substantial passage has been lost here, which originally contained an account of the activities of Procopius and Arsaces. The forces that they commanded played a vital part Julian's overall strategy in 363 (cf. 23.2.2, 2.5): in Ammianus subsequently states that he explained why they failed to carry out the tasks assigned to them (24.7.8: quod nec adminicula, quae praestolabamur, cum Arsace et nostris ducibus apparebant ob causas impedita praedictas), but this explanation has vanished without trace from the transmitted text.

The paradosis of Ammianus is often corrupt as well as lacunose. Over the centuries editors have brought countless improvements to the text. But many corrupt readings may still stand unquestioned in Seyfarth's text.[16] A pair of examples from the very first page of Book XIV will illustrate. In the very first sentence of the extant text, according to V and most editors, the Caesar Gallus was "ad principale culmen insperato cultu provectus" (14.1.1). What does *cultu* mean here? Seyfarth has defended the transmitted text, taking *insperato cultu* as an ablative of quality attached attributively to *principale culmen*, and renders "mit einem Gepränge, auf das er nie zu hoffen gewagt hätte."[17] But logic and Ammianus' normal use of the word *cultus*,[18] together with two closely parallel passages, commend the conjecture *saltu* proposed by A. Kellerbauer and A. Kiessling.[19] Gallus was unexpectedly proclaimed Caesar as a result of the usurpation of Magnentius: Ammianus elsewhere uses *saltus* of the unjustified promotion of Agilo to replace Ursicinus (20.2.5: immodico saltu

---

[16] See H. Gärtner, *Hermes* 97 (1969), 362–71, whose arguments are not always accepted by Seyfarth.

[17] In his note on 14.1.1, Seyfart also argues that Gallus' appointment as Caesar was "kein Sprung" (1.256, n. 3).

[18] Viansino, *Lexicon* 1.346–47.

[19] A. Kellerbauer, *Blätter für das bayerische Gymnasialschulwesen* 7 (1871), 12; A. Kiessling, *Jahrb. für class. Phil.* 103 (1871), 496. Seyfarth's defense of *cultu* is refuted by K. Bringmann, *Antike und Abendland* 29 (1973), 58–59 n. 62.

promotus) and of Valens' conferring of the title *patricius* on his undistinguished father-in-law Petronius (26.6.7: promotus saltu repentino patricius).

In the second sentence of Book XIV Ammianus states, according to V and all editors, that the Caesar Gallus

> propinquitate enim regiae stirpis gentilitateque etiamtum Constantii nominis efferebatur in fastus, si plus valuisset, ausurus hostilia in auctorem suae felicitatis ut videbatur. (14.1.1)

The word *etiamtum* (= "even then")[20] appears to be misplaced and should perhaps, therefore, be transposed to where it logically belongs, after *fastus*. If this transposition were made, then Ammianus would be saying that Gallus was puffed up by sharing the name of Constantius, and even then (in the summer of 353, before the deaths of Montius and Domitianus) "was disposed, as it seemed, had he possessed any greater power, to venture on a hostile course of action against his benefactor."

An unacknowledged corruption should also be diagnosed in the famous passage describing Constantius' entry into Rome when he sees *lavacra in modum provinciarum exstructa* (16.10.14). Admittedly, translators of Ammianus find no difficulty in rendering the phrase as "the baths built up in the manner of provinces" (Rolfe), "des thermes aux constructions grandes comme des provinces" (Galletier), "die Bäder, so gross wie ganze Provinzen" (Seyfarth) or "the buildings of the baths as big as provinces" (Hamilton and Wallace-Hadrill), and de Jonge claims that "the exaggeration is very attractive and typical of Ammianus." But what can be the point of comparing baths with whole provinces? Hadrianus Valesius conjectured *piscinarum* ("bathrooms like swimming pools"). Seyfarth is right to reject that emendation (with appeal to G. Lumbroso),[21] but the lack of a convincing emendation does not establish *provinciarum* as what Ammianus wrote. Seyfarth was compelled to confess that he could not explain what the text he prints can mean.[22] What is needed is surely a comparison of baths in Rome to some larger structure or structures in the provinces: as a diagnostic conjecture, the emendation *provincialium* <*urbium*> may be offered.

The poor state of the text in general is very relevant to the passage in the second formal excursus on the city of Rome in which Ammianus derides certain

[20] On *etiamtum* in Ammianus, see Viansino, *Lexicon* 1.487–88.

[21] Lumbroso's comments on the passage are reported by G. B. Pighi, *Aegyptus* 13 (1933), 279.

[22] He confessed in the notes to his Latin-German edition that "Der Sinn ist nicht eindeutig" (1 [1968], 296, n. 114).

Roman nobles for sporting pretentious names (28.4.6). Seyfarth, who reproduces the readings of Clark but modifies his punctuation, prints the passage
as follows:

> praenominum claritudine conspicui quidam, ut putant, in immensum semet tol-
> lunt, cum Reburri et Flavonii et Pagonii Gereonesque appellentur ac Dalii cum
> Tarraciis et Ferasiis aliisque ita decens sonantibus originum insignibus multis.

One difficulty in this text is only an apparent one. Ammianus cannot have referred to *praenomina*, since none of the names quoted is a *praenomen*, and the
only *praenomina* in use in the late fourth century were unpretentious ones such
as Quintus.[23] But *praenomina* here could mean "family names,"[24] as it does in
other writers contemporary with Ammianus.[25] However, it might be prema-
ture to exclude the possibility that the transmitted *praenominum* may be a corruption of an original that read either *prae <ceteris> nominum* or *prae <ceteris
cog>nominum.*[26]

The names themselves are problematical: every one of the seven as printed
by Clark and Seyfarth is improbable, even those that are the result of modern
emendation. Hence discussion must begin from the form in which each of
the names is actually attested in V, which presents them as follows:

> cum reburri et flabunii et pagonii gereonisque appellentur ac dalii cum tarracus
> et perrasusque.

Every one of these names is corrupt, including the first. For, although *Reburrus* is a relatively well-attested Spanish *cognomen*,[27] which has been restored by
plausible emendation as the *cognomen* of the *praefectus urbi* in 283 (*Chr. min.*
1.66),[28] it was a low-class name totally devoid of the quality of *claritudo.*[29]

---

[23] E.g., L. Aurelius Avianius Symmachus, *praefectus urbi* in 364–365 (*CIL* 6.1698 = *ILS*
1698), and his son Q. Aurelius Symmachus, consul in 391 (*CIL* 6.1699 = *ILS* 2946; *ICUR* 1.395,
1835; *CIL* 8.24584; *AE* 1966.518), cf. O. Salomies, *Die römischen Vornamen. Studien zur römischen
Namengebung* (*Commentationes Humanarum Litterarum* 82, 1987), 404–13.

[24] B. Salway, *JRS* 84 (1994), 140.

[25] W. Hartke, *Römische Kinderkaiser* (Berlin, 1951), 130–31; P. Veyne, *Rev. phil.*[3] 38 (1964),
253–57, citing *Epigrammata Bobiensia* 8b.9 ("praenomen ductum ex atavis"); *HA, Macr.* 3.4–7;
Diad. 6.2–10. Also *CIL* 3.1228 (Apulum: perhaps third century).

[26] Ammianus uses the phrase *prae ceteris* in three other passages to contrast an individual with
the group to which he belongs (25.6.14; 28.1.19; 29.5.4).

[27] I. Kajanto, *The Latin Cognomina* (*Commentationes Humanarum Litterarum* 36.2, 1965), 238,
registers a total of 69 Reburri, of whom 38 are Spanish. Salomies, *Vornamen* (1987), 131–32, produces a single example of Reburrus as a *praenomen* (*CIL* 2.591).

[28] The name is transmitted as *Titucius Roburrus*: H. Dessau proposed *Reburrus* (*PIR*[1] T 209).

[29] Syme, *Ammianus* (1968), 151.

Adapting and incorporating earlier attempts at correction, Anthony Birley has now restored sense, point, and relevance to the passage by emending the whole series of names (originally eight, of which the last is lost) as follows:

cum Probi et Faltonii et Ragonii Ceioniique appellentur Albini cum Pammachiis et Vitrasiis . . . que.[30]

In each case, at least one contemporary bearer of the name can easily be identified: Sex. Petronius Probus, consul in 371; Faltonius Probus Alypius, *praefectus urbi* in 391; Ragonius Vincentius Celsus, *praefectus annonae* before 391; Ceionius Rufius Albinus, *praefectus urbi* from 389 to 391; Pammachius, whom Jerome saluted as "consulum pronepos et Furiani germinis decus" (*Ep.* 66.6); and Memmius Vitrasius Orfitus, *praefectus urbi* in 353–355 and again in 357–359.[31]

---

[30] A. R. Birley, *Historiae Augustae Colloquia*, N.S. III: *Colloquium Maceratense* (Bari, 1995), 59–60.

[31] Whether or not Birley's precise proposals are all correct, the persons to whom Ammianus alludes are surely to be sought in *PLRE* 1.1133, 1137–38, 1140: Stemmata 7 (Anicii), 11–13 (Caesonii and Ceionii), 16 (Flaviani).

[2]

THE STRUCTURE OF LIVY'S
AB URBE CONDITA

Livy embarked upon his history of Rome from its origins before the Battle of Actium:[1] originally, therefore, he must have intended to conclude the work at some point earlier than 31 B.C., and it seems virtually certain that his original intention was to compose a total of one hundred and twenty books ending either with the death of Cicero in 43 B.C. or approximately at that point.[2] As the work progressed, however, Livy decided to go beyond his original terminus, and he continued his narrative as far as the death of Drusus in 9 B.C., probably crowning the whole work with an epilogue that looked forward to the disaster of Varus in A.D. 9.[3] Since the preface to Book CXXI referred to the death of Augustus, this continuation cannot have been given to the world before September 14.[4] It may be inferred, therefore, that Livy, who was the last of the Republican historians and who was twitted by Augustus for being

---

[1] For proof of this date (which undermines most of what has been written about Livy's attitude to Augustus), see T. J. Luce, *TAPA* 96 (1965), 209–40; A. J. Woodman, *Rhetoric in Classical Historiography* (London/Sydney, 1988), 128–34.

[2] P. G. Walsh, *Livy. Greece and Rome: New Surveys in the Classics* 8 (1974), 9.

[3] The words *clades Quinctilii Vari* at the end of *Periocha* CXLII are known only from the readings of a lost manuscript that P. Pithou copied into the margins of his copy of Sigonius' edition of Livy, but the fact that Julius Obsequens ends with the sentence "multitudo Romanorum per insidias subiecta est" provides apparent confirmation of the report: accordingly, O. Rossbach printed the words in his Teubner edition of the *Periochae* and Julius Obsequens (Leipzig, 1910): for subsequent discussion of their authenticity, see F. Lautenbacher, *BPW* 30 (1910), 1186–93; O. Rossbach, ibid., 1396–98; P. Jal, *Tite-Live: Histoire Romaine 34.1: Abrégés des Livres de l'Histoire Romaine de Tite-Live* (Paris, 1984), 1.ciii–cv, 2.54; J. Briscoe, *Gnomon* 57 (1985), 420–21.

[4] For proof that the heading "Ex libro CXXI qui editus post excessum Augusti dicitur," is authentic, see M. D. Reeve, *CQ*, N. S. 38 (1988), 477–91. On the correct interpretation of the words *editus . . . dicitur*, see A. Klotz, *RE* 13 (1927), 819–20, 823; R. Helm, *Hieronymus' Zusätze in Eusebius' Chronik und ihr Wert für die Literaturgeschichte* (Philologus, Supp. 21.2, 1929), 52–53. There is no substance whatever in the widely accepted theory that Livy died in A.D. 12, two

a "Pompeian" (Tacitus, *Ann.* 4.34.3), observed the cardinal rule of imperial historiography: anyone who wished to write serious history could write only about dead emperors, since the living emperor expected (and deserved) panegyric of the sort that Velleius Paterculus lavished on Tiberius.[5] Livy did not advance beyond his original terminus of 43 B.C. as long as Augustus was still alive, and although he published a continuation after Augustus died, he stopped at the death of Drusus in 9 B.C. so that he could avoid the embarrassing period when the husband of Julia and son-in-law of Augustus withdrew from public life and lived in exile while his political enemies prospered.[6]

The structure of the surviving portion of Livy's history (including the lost Books XI–XX) is in little doubt. Although he may have written and published the first book separately, Livy arranged his vast narrative in groups of five, ten, and fifteen books. The first pentad covered the regal period (I) and the early days of the Republic down to the capture of Rome by the Gauls (II–V). The second and third pentads together described Rome's conquest of peninsular Italy, perhaps with a hardly perceptible break between Books X and XI. The next fifteen books centered on Rome's struggle with Carthage. Book XVI began with an account of the origins and early history of Carthage, and Book XX closed on the eve of the Second Punic War: Livy thus clearly marked off a pentad that covered the years 264–220 B.C. and whose main themes were, first, the First Punic War (XVI–XIX), then Rome's conflicts with the Gauls in North Italy and the so-called First Illyrian War (XX). The ten books devoted to the Second Punic War (XXI–XXX) begin with a formal character sketch of Hannibal and conclude with the triumph of Scipio in 201: they comprise two carefully balanced pentads that present first Carthaginian successes and Rome's refusal to accept defeat, then Rome's gradual and inexorable advance to total victory.[7] The theme of the next fifteen books is Rome's conquest of the Greek world in three pentads that concentrate successively on the wars against Philip V of Macedon (XXXI–XXXV), Antiochus III of Syria (XXXVI–XL), and Perseus (XLI–XLV).[8] Among the extant books, I has a preface to the whole work, II to the history of the Roman

---

years before Augustus, which was developed (though not invented) by R. Syme, *Roman Papers*, I (Oxford, 1979), 414–16: see R. Jeffreys, *CQ*, N.S. 35 (1985), 140–48.

[5] H. Peter, *Die geschichtliche Litteratur über die römische Kaiserzeit bis Theodosius I und ihre Quellen*, I (Leipzig, 1897), 293–94, cf. T. Janson, *Latin Prose Prefaces* (Stockholm, 1964), 100–6.

[6] On this obscure period, see esp. R. Syme, *Roman Papers*, 3 (Oxford, 1984), 912–36; *The Augustan Aristocracy* (Oxford, 1986), 82–103.

[7] On the structure of XXI–XXX, see esp. E. Burck, *Einführung in die dritte Dekade des Livius* (Heidelberg, 1950), 7–56; *Livy*, ed. T. A. Dorey (London, 1971), 21–46; P. G. Walsh, *ANRW* 2.30.2 (1983), 1058–74.

[8] In favor of analyzing Books XXXI–L as two decades, see P. Jal, *Rev. phil.*[3] 49 (1975), 278–85.

Republic, VI to the period after the Gallic capture when Rome was reborn and the historian's materials become *clariora certioraque*, XXI to the Second Punic War, and XXXI to the wider canvas of Rome's dealings with the Hellenistic world ("iam provideo animo . . . in vastiorem me altitudinem ac velut profundum invehi"), while the presumed preface to XLI is lost in a lacuna.

What of the almost one hundred lost books from XLVI onward? Certainty is unattainable. The *Periochae* are unreliable indicators of the emphases that Livy gave his material where they can be checked against the surviving books: therefore, there is no valid reason to suppose them more accurate and trustworthy for the lost books.[9] Until recently, the consensus of scholarship has been that the weight and complexity of his material compelled Livy to abandon his original plan of writing in pentads and decades.[10] However, the analyses of the structure of the whole work by P. A. Stadter and T. J. Luce, even though they disagree in detail, have proved that, if Livy ever abandoned pentadic and decadic structure, he did so only toward the very end of his history.[11] Moreover, G. Wille and R. M. Ogilvie have argued that Livy never abandoned composition in groups of five, ten, and fifteen books: had he lived long enough, they suggest, Livy would have produced a total of 150 books.[12]

Although it is implausible, for reasons that have nothing to do with the structure of his history, to suppose that Livy intended to press on beyond 9 B.C. or that he could have written about Tiberius' exile, close examination of the contents of *Periochae* CXXXI–CXLII renders it highly probable that Livy maintained a structure of pentads and decades through to the very end, so that his account of the reign of Augustus was arranged in two groups of five books. For there is something seriously amiss with the transmitted book numbers of the last few *Periochae*, which ascend to the aesthetically implausible total of one hundred and forty-two. According to the *Periochae*, Livy included the following temporal periods or events in each of the books from CXXXI onward:

CXXXI	Events from late 36 to the end of 35
CXXXII	From Octavian's Dalmatian campaign of 34 to the battle of Actium in August 31
CXXXIII	From Antony's flight from Actium to Octavian's triple triumph of 13–15 August 29

---

[9] P. Jal, *Tite-Live* 34.1: *Abrégés* (1984), 1.lvii–lxxix.

[10] See the conspectus of analyses by scholars from H. Nissen (1872) to R. Syme (1959) tabulated by T. J. Luce, *Livy. The Composition of his History* (Princeton, 1977), 14.

[11] P. A. Stadter, *Historia* 21 (1972), 287–307; Luce, *Livy* (1977), 3–24, cf. P. Jal, *Tite-Live: Histoire Romaine* 11: *Livre XXI* (Paris, 1988), vii–ix.

[12] G. Wille, *Der Aufbau des Livianischen Geschichtswerks* (*Heuremata* 1, 1973), 114–19; R. M. Ogilvie, *PCPS* 210 (1984), 116–25.

CXXXIV	Presumably from 29 and at least as far as Augustus' visit to Gaul in spring 27
CXXXV	The war waged by Crassus in Thrace (presumably campaigns of 28–27); Augustus' conquest of Spain (officially completed in 25); the subjugation of the Salassi (25)
CXXXVI	Lost, but Censorinus reports that it included the Ludi Saeculares of 17[13]
CXXXVII	Lost
CXXXVIII	The conquest of Raetia (15); Drusus' census in Gaul (13); the death of Agrippa (12)
CXXXIX	Events of 13 and 12: Drusus crosses the Rhine, suppresses troubles connected with the Gallic census and dedicates the altar of Rome and Augustus at Lyon.[14]
CXL	The campaigns of Piso in Thrace (12–10) and Drusus in Germany; the death of Octavia, the mother of Marcellus (11)
CXLI	Drusus' campaign of 11; Tiberius' defeat of the Dalmatians and Pannonians; peace with the Parthians, that is, the handing over of the four sons of Phraates in 10[15]
CXLII	Drusus' campaign of 9; his death, funeral, and posthumous honors.

From 29 down to 12 B.C., each book of Livy covered at least three years. According to the transmitted numbers, the last three books covered one year each. That is a priori most improbable. It should be inferred that the transmitted total is erroneous.[16] After the *Periochae* of CXXXVI and CXXXVII had been lost, it seems that someone, in a futile attempt to repair the loss, expanded the summary of Book CXL to cover three books (viz., the *Periochae* of CXL–CXLII). In Livy's original scheme, five books centered on Augustus as a military leader, from his first campaign in Dalmatia to his last active campaign in Spain (CXXXI–CXXXV), with which Augustus had concluded his autobiography,[17] were followed by five books on the campaigns of Drusus and Tiberius, the reigning emperor and his late brother.

[13] Censorinus, *De die natali* 17.9, whence Livy, frag. 65 Weissenborn-Müller = frag. 63 Jal.

[14] On the multifarious problems concerning the altar, R. Turcan, *ANRW* 2.12.1 (1982), 607–44; D. Fishwick, *The Imperial Cult in the Latin West. Studies in the Ruler Cult of the Western Provinces of the Roman Empire* 1.1 (Leiden, 1987), 97–137.

[15] *Res Gestae* 32.2, cf. J. Gagé, *Res Gestae Divi Augusti*[3] (Paris, 1977), 142.

[16] J. Briscoe, *Gnomon* 57 (1985), 420, conjectured that "the author of the *Periochae*" may have had only 140 books in his text of Livy.

[17] Suetonius, *Div. Aug.* 85.1: the fragments are collected by E. Malcovati, *Imperatoris Caesaris Augusti Operum Fragmenta*[5] (Turin, 1969), 84–97.

[3]

AMMIANUS' REFERENCES
TO THE LOST BOOKS

J. F. Gilliam published a useful discussion of the passages in the *Res Gestae* that concern the period from Hadrian (117–138) to Carinus (283–285), including those that make no explicit reference to the lost part of the work.[1] He noted several passages where use of Herodian is clear; in one of them Ammianus follows Herodian against the superior authority of Cassius Dio and the *Historia Augusta* (22.9.6 < Herodian 1.11.1–2; 26.8.15 < Herodian 3.4.1–6; 29.1.17 < Herodian 1.8.5, cf. Dio 72.4.4, *HA, Comm.* 4.2–4; 31.10.18–19 < Herodian 1.15.6). The present appendix confines itself to quoting Ammianus' explicit references to what he had written in the lost books in general support of the thesis about the total number of books advanced in Chapter III.[2] Scholars who accept the transmitted and traditional numeration must perforce argue that most of the lost books contained a relatively brief narrative with few excursus.[3]

14.1.8   ut in Gordianorum actibus factitasse Maximini truculenti illius imperatoris rettulimus coniugem

14.4.2   super quorum [sc. the Saraceni] moribus licet in actibus principis Marci et postea aliquotiens memini rettulisse

---

[1] J. F. Gilliam, *Bonner Historia-Augusta-Colloquium 1970* (Bonn, 1972), 125–47, cf. A. M. Emmett, *History and Historians* (1983), 45, 52 n. 32.

[2] For a catalogue of the phrases that Ammianus uses for cross-references, forward as well as backward, see H. Cichocka, *Eos* 64 (1976), 203–22. Mistaken cross-references and historical allusions misidentified as cross-references are discussed by R. M. Frakes, *Phoenix* 49 (1995), 234–43, whose list of "definite cross-references" misleadingly includes 31.16.9 (243–45).

[3] H. Cichocka, *Eos* 63 (1975), 340.

14.7.7   Serenianus ex duce, cuius ignavia populatam in Phoenice Celsein
          ante rettulimus

Presumably by Jewish rebels in 351 or 352 during the insurrection in Galilee.[4]

14.7.21   Mesopotamia iam digesta, cum bella Parthica narrarentur

Probably in several excursus.[5]

14.10.2   Hermogenis ex magistro equitum filius apud Constantinopolim, ut
          supra rettulimus, popularium quondam turbela discerpti

In early 342 (Jerome, *Chronicle* 236[f]; *Descr. cons.* 342.2).

15.5.16   Lanogaiso vetante, tunc tribuno, quem dum militaret candidatus
          solum affuisse morituro Constanti supra rettulimus

In early 350, shortly after 18 January.[6]

15.6.4   Poemenius raptus ad supplicium interiit, qui, ut supra rettulimus,
          cum Treveri civitatem clausissent Decentio, ad defendendam
          plebem electus est

Apparently in 353, shortly before the final defeat of Magnentius.[7]

16.6.2   Dorus quidam ex medico scutariorum, quem nitentium rerum
          centurionem sub Magnentio provectum rettulimus accusasse Adel-
          phium urbi praefectum

Clodius Celsinus Adelphius was *praefectus urbi* from 7 June to 18 December 351
(*Chr. min.* 1.66).

16.10.12 quod autem per omne tempus imperii nec in consessum vehiculi
          quemquam suscepit nec in trabea socium privatum ascivit, ut fecere
          principes consecrati, et similia multa elatus in arduum supercilium
          tamquam leges aequissimas observavit, praetereo memor ea me ret-
          tulisse cum incidissent

16.10.16 Hormisdas cuius e Perside discessum supra monstravimus

Presumably circa 324: John of Antioch states that it was the emperor Licinius

---

[4] The nature and extent of the rebellion are discussed by M. Avi-Yonah, *The Jews of Palestine. A Political History from the Bar Kokhba War to the Arab Conquest* (Oxford, 1976), 176–81; J. Geiger, *Scripta Classica Israelica* 5 (1979–80), 250–57; P. Schäfer, *Tradition and Re-interpretation in Jewish and Early Christian Literature*, ed. J. W. van Henten (Leiden, 1986), 184–201; J. Arce, *Athenaeum*, N. S. 65 (1987), 109–25; G. Stemberger, *Juden und Christen im Heiligen Land. Palästina unter Konstantin und Theodosius* (Munich, 1987), 132–50; M. Mor, *The Eastern Frontier of the Roman Empire*, ed. D. H. French and C. S. Lightfoot (Oxford, 1989), 335–53. None of them appears to discuss this passage of Ammianus.

Thompson, *Ammianus* (1947), 58, dated the rebellion to 353–354 and deduced that Ammianus deliberately omitted it.

[5] Reference to a single excursus, which occurred in Ammianus' narrative of the period 240–298, is argued by R. M. Frakes, *AHB* 7 (1993), 143–47.

[6] For the evidence, see *Athanasius* (1993), 225–26. Lanaogaisus is otherwise unknown.

[7] *RIC* 9.164–5, Trier 328–37 (coins minted in the name of Constantius as sole Augustus). Poemenius is not in *PLRE* 1.

who received Hormisdas (frag. 178), while Zosimus narrates the story of Hormisdas' flight to Armenia and subsequent reception by Constantine between the defeat of Licinius and his surrender on 29 September 324 (2.27, cf. 3.13.3–4; Zonaras 13.5.13).[8]

18.9.3   Tricensimani Decimanique Fortenses et Superventores atque Praeventores cum Aeliano iam comite, quos tirones tum etiam novellos hortante memorato adhuc protectore erupisse a Singara Persasque fusos in somnum rettulimus trucidasse complures

19.2.3   elephantorum agmina rugosis horrenda corporibus leniter incedebant armatis onusta, ultra omnem diritatem taetri spectaculi formidanda, ut rettulimus saepe

20.1.1   (sc. Julian) verebatur ire subsidio transmarinis, ut rettulimus ante fecisse Constantem

In late January or February 343.[9]

20.6.5   reseratam urbem obsidio superiore docuimus

The "preceding siege" of Singara was presumably raised by the famous night-battle, which (it is now clear) must be dated to 344.[10]

20.11.32   [sc. Constantius] vincere saltem per duces optabat, quod aliquotiens meminimus contigisse

21.8.1   commisit . . . et Iovio quaesturam, cuius in actibus Magnenti meminimus

21.16.7   quod autem nec os tersisse unquam vel nares in publico nec spuisse nec transtulisse in partem alterutram vultum aliquando est visus nec pomorum quoad vixerit gustaverit, ut dicta saepius praetermitto

22.9.6   cuius [sc. the statue of Cybele from Pessinus] super adventu pauca cum aliis huic materiae congruentibus in actibus Commodi principis digessimus per excessum[11]

22.13.3   Asclepiades philosophus, cuius in actibus Magnentii meminimus

22.15.1   res Aegyptiacae tangantur, quarum notitiam in actibus Hadriani et Severi principum digessimus late, visa pleraque narrantes

23.5.7   Gordiani imperatoris . . . cuius actus a pueritia prima exercituumque felicissimos ductus et insidiosum interitum digessimus tempore competenti

---

[8] For what else is known about Hormisdas, *PLRE* 1.443; on the significance of what Ammianus makes him say to Constantius, see R. O. Edbrooke, *Mnemosyne*[4] 28 (1975), 412–17.

[9] *Athanasius* (1993), 225.

[10] *Athanasius* (1993), 220, 312 n. 19; R. W. Burgess, *Continuatio Antiochiensis Eusebii: An Antiochene Continuation of Eusebius' Chronici canones* (forthcoming), no. 37.

[11] For *excessus* = "digression," see 23.6.1, 27.4.1, 28.4.6; for its commoner synonyms, J. Martin, *Antike Rhetorik. Technik und Methode* (Munich, 1974), 89–91.

23.6.2   hoc regnum [sc. Persia] . . . ob causas, quae saepe rettulimus, cum
          apud Babylona Magnum fata rapuissent Alexandrum, in vocabulum
          Parthi concessit Arsacis

23.6.24   qua [sc. Seleucia] per duces Veri Caesaris, ut ante rettulimus,
          expulsata

23.6.50   ubi [sc. in Hyrcania] etiam tigridum milia multa cernuntur feraeque
          bestiae plures, quae cuiusmodi solent capi commentis, dudum nos
          meminimus rettulisse

23.6.83   militari cultu ac disciplina [sc. of the Persians] proludiisque con-
          tinuis rei castrensis et armaturae, quam saepe formavimus

25.4.23   sciant docente veritate perspicue non Iulianum sed Constantinum
          ardores Parthicos succendisse, cum Metrodori mendaciis avidius
          acquiescit, ut dudum rettulimus plene

25.8.5   quod [sc. the town of Hatra] eruendum adorti temporibus variis
          Traianus et Severus principes bellicosi cum exercitibus paene deleti
          sunt, ut in eorum actibus has quoque digessimus partes

27.8.4   quoniam cum Constantis principis actus componerem, motus ado-
          lescentis et senescentis oceani situmque Britanniae pro captu virium
          explanavi, ad ea quae digesta sunt semel revolvi superfluum duxi

Clearly in his account of Constantius' famous winter crossing of the English
Channel in January–February 343.[12]

28.3.8   arcanos genus hominum a veteribus institutum, super quibus aliqua
          in actibus Constantis rettulimus

Ammianus is here describing the exploits of the elder Theodosius in Britain:
he must have explained who the *arcani* were in the context of Constans' British
expedition of 343.

28.4.6   primo nobilitatis [sc. of Rome], ut aliquotiens pro locorum copia
          fecimus,[13] dein plebis digeremus errata

29.5.16   Icosium oppidum, cuius supra docuimus conditores

29.5.18   Caesaream . . . urbem opulentam quondam et nobilem, cuius itidem
          originem in Africae situ digessimus plene

29.6.1   obsessaque ab isdem [sc. the Quadi] Marcomannisque Aquileia
          diu Opitergiumque excisum et cruenta complura per celeres acta
          procinctus vix resistente perruptis Alpibus Iuliis principe Pio quem
          ante docuimus Marco

---

[12] Firmicus Maternus, *De errore profanarum religionum* 28.6; Libanius, *Orat.* 59.139, cf. *Athana-sius* (1993), 225.

[13] Frakes, *Phoenix* 49 (1995), 242, 246, argues that this "could simply refer to 14.6.1–26 and 14.7.1–9."

The Marcomanni and Quadi invaded Italy, besieged Aquileia, and sacked Opitergium when Marcus Aurelius, whom Ammianus oddly calls Marcus Pius, was sole emperor: the precise date appears to be 170.[14]

30.7.1   replicare nunc est opportunum, ut aliquotiens fecimus, et ab ortu primigenio partis huiusce principis ad usque ipsius obitum actus eius discurrere per epilogos breves

31.16.5   Saracenorum cuneus, super quorum origine moribusque diversis in locis rettulimus plura (cf. 14.4.2)

---

[14] A. R. Birley, *Marcus Aurelius: A Biography*[2] (London, 1987), 164, 251.

[4]

CONSULAR DATES IN THE *RES GESTAE*

Ammianus' *Res Gestae* is in no sense an annalistic history, as has often been supposed, since the basic temporal units used in ordering the narrative of Books XIV–XXVI are not consular years (as in Livy and Tacitus), but successive summers or campaigning seasons and winters (Chapter IV).[1] In these books, therefore, Ammianus can use the consular dating formula for any year to emphasize a particular fact or action. The following list describes the context of each pair of consuls noted by the historian and incidentally illustrates the change of narrative structure that occurs between Books XXVI and XXVII (Chapter IV).

354
Noted at the start of Constantius' spring campaign: (14.10.1: caeli reserato tepore Constantius consulatu suo septies et Caesaris ter egressus Arelate).

355
Book XV begins with events of winter 354–55 (15.1–3) and records Constantius' campaign of 355 (4: a very lacunose account), but the text, at least as extant, does not name the consuls until Ammianus states the exact day on which Julian was proclaimed Caesar (15.8.17: haec diem octavum iduum Novembrium gesta sunt, cum Arbitionem consulem annus haberet et Lollianum).

356
Julian's entry on his first consulate is noted in the opening sentence of the

---

[1] The contrary is asserted by Matthews, *Ammianus* (1989), 458: "Ammianus' manner of organising his material was annalistic."

book (16.1.1: Caesar apud Viennam in collegium fastorum a consule octiens Augusto ascitus).

357

Linked with Julian's departure from his winter quarters (16.11.1: at Caesar exacta apud Senonas hieme turbulenta Augusto novies seque iterum consule).

358

The traditional consular dating formula (16.5.1: Datiano et Cereali consulibus) is here used for the first time in the extant books: it stands at the start of a sentence that contrasts success in Gaul with danger on the Persian frontier.

359

Book XVIII opens with a transition from 358 to 359 (18.1.1: Haec per orbis varias partes uno eodemque anno gesta sunt. at in Galliis cum in meliore statu res essent et Eusebium atque Hypatium fratres sublimarent vocabula consulum . . .).

360

Book XX opens with a similar transition (20.1.1: Haec per Illyricum perque orientem rerum series fuit. consulatu vero Constantii deciens terque Iuliani . . .).

361

The entry into office of Florentius and Taurus is linked to the appointment of the former as praetorian prefect of Illyricum (21.6.5: et Anatolio recens mortuo praefecto praetorio per Illyricum ad eius mittitur locum cumque Tauro itidem praefecto praetorio per Italiam amplissimi suscepit insignia magistratus).

362

Ammianus records the consuls of 362 no fewer than three times: (1) in comment on Julian's complaint that Constantine conferred consulates on "barbarians" (21.10.8: brevi postea Mamertino in consulatu iunxit Nevittam);[2] (2) in registering their designation while Julian was in Naissus (21.12.25: Mamertinum promotum praefectum praetorio per Illyricum designavit consulem et Nevittam); and (3) in describing Julian's behavior on 1 January (22.7.1: allapso itaque kalendarum Ianuariarum die cum Mamertini et Nevittae nomina suscepissent paginae consulares).

363

Book XXIII opens with a transition from 362 to 363 (23.1.1: Haec eo anno,

---

[2] Ammianus has misunderstood Julian. Since no consul of non-Roman origin can be discovered under Constantine, by "barbarians" Julian must have meant "non-Hellenes," that is, "Christians": *Constantine* (1981), 403 n. 3; *L'Église et l'empire au IVe siècle* (*Entretiens sur l'Antiquité Classique* 34, 1989), 321.

ut praetereamus negotiorum minutias, agebantur. Iulianus vero iam ter consul
ascito in collegium trabeae Sallustio praefecto per Gallias quater ipse amplissi-
mum inierat magistratum).[3]

364

Ammianus records the consulate of Jovian with his infant son twice within
the space of a page: the infant's crying portended his father's impending death
(25.10.11: et cum introisset Ancyram imperator, paratis ad pompam necessariis
consulatum iniit adhibito in societatem trabeae Varroniano filio suo admodum
parvulo, cuius vagitus pertinaciter reluctantis, ne in curuli sella veheretur ex
more, id quod mox accidit portendebat) and Jovian's father Varronianus knew
from a dream that one of the consuls would be named Varronianus and requested the honor for himself—in vain because Jovian chose his son, not his
father, as his colleague (25.10.17: Varronianus nepos eius, infans etiamtum,
cum Ioviano patre declaratus est ut supra rettulimus consul).

365

Ammianus notes the consuls of 365 twice. First, in his account of the rebellion
of Procopius, he marks the transition from 365 to 366, even though he has not
before stated that the emperors held a joint consulate in 365 (26.9.1: haec adulta
hieme Valentiniano et Valente consulibus agebantur. translato vero in Gra-
tianum adhuc privatum et Dagalaifum amplissimo magistratu). Then, at the
end of Book XXVI he states the date of the tsunami of 21 July 365, drawing
the reader's attention to the temporal regression (26.10.15: hoc novatore
[sc. Procopius] adhuc superstite, cuius actus multiplices docuimus et interitum, diem duodecimum kalendas Augustas consule Valentiniano primum
cum fratre).

366

Book XXVI marks the transition from 365 to 366 during the rebellion of
Procopius (26.9.1, quoted above). Book XXVII opens with a raid by the
Alamanni that lasted into the January (27.1.1) of a year soon identified as 366
in an account of the actions of Dagalaifus (27.2.1: accitoque paulo postea ut
cum Gratiano etiamtum privato susciperet insignia consulatus).

367

Ammianus states emphatically that Valens' Gothic war spanned three years
(27.5.5–7). Other evidence indicates that the three calendar years must be 367,
368, and 369 (Appendix 10), but the transition from 366 to 367 is not noted in
his text.

368

---

[3] On the use made of this consular date, see Chapter V.

369

After the second long digression on Rome (28.4), Ammianus resumes his main narrative with the Saxon raid of 369 (28.5.1: erupit Augustis ter consulibus Saxonum multitudo).

370, 371, 372

373
Possibly lost[4]

374

The transition from 373 to 374 is noted, even though the consuls of 373 are not named in the extant text (30.3.1: secuto post haec anno Gratiano ascito in trabeae societatem Equitio consule).

375, 376

377

Ammianus notes the end of the active season in the Balkans in the year before the fateful campaign of Adrianople (31.8.2: haec Gratiano quater et Merobaude consulibus agebantur anno in autumnum vergente).

378

---

[4] For the large lacuna in Book XXIX, see Appendix 8.

[5]

FORMAL EXCURSUS

What constitutes a formal digression or excursus in Ammianus? A standard history of Latin literature long ago arrived at a total of twenty-six: eleven geographical, eight physical or mathematical, three philosophical or religious, and four social.[1] But that total included as formal excursus evocations of Roman Republican exemplars of conspicuous conduct, such as Sergius and Sicinius Dentatus (25.3.13, 27.10.16), the comparison of Julian at Pirisabora to Scipio Aemilianus at Carthage (24.2.16−17), and even the observation that neither in the case of Jovian's sudden death by suffocation in 364 nor in the similar death of Scipio Aemilianus was any official inquiry conducted (25.10.13).[2] Using a more generous criterion, a survey of excursus in Greek and Latin historians from Herodotus to Ammianus reached a total of thirty-three, including as excursus some (but not all) of Ammianus' obituaries of deceased emperors, his remarks on Adrasteia and the mutability of fortune in his obituary of Gallus (14.11.25−26, 30−34), and his description of the city of Amida (18.9.2), which seems to form part of the main narrative.[3]

In an attempt at a rigorous definition, Helen Cichocka deduced from the four passages where Ammianus refers to his *excessus* (22.9.6, 23.6.1., 27.4.1, 28.4.6) that an excursus must comprise (1) an introduction of the topic ending with an introductory formula, (2) a development of the topic of the ex-

---

[1] M. Schanz, *Geschichte der römischen Litteratur* 4.1[2] (Munich, 1914), 97. Schanz's third category included the important passages on Adrasteia (14.11.25) and guardian spirits (21.14.5), neither of which satisfies the formal criteria laid down here.

[2] H. Finke, *Ammianus Marcellinus und seine Quellen zur Geschichte der römischen Republik* (Diss. Heidelberg, 1904), 6−9.

[3] H. V. Canter, *Philological Quarterly* 8 (1929), 243−44, 247.

cursus, and (3) an ending with a concluding formula. Hence, even though she included in her list of excursus some that do not satisfy her strict criterion, she arrived at a total of only twenty-five.[4] On the other hand, Alanna Emmett included in her total of digressions not only excursus that had either an introduction or a conclusion alone, but also some that lack both and thus counted a total of thirty-four.[5] The first of these definitions seems too strict, the latter too loose. An intermediate criterion is needed. The following list of excursus in the extant books of Ammianus includes only those that he formally designates as such either by using a conventional formula of introduction (e.g., 19.4.1: quae genera morborum unde oriri solent, breviter explicabo)[6] or by formally indicating the transition back to the main narrative (e.g., 20.3.12: verum ad instituta iam revertamur) or by formally marking both the beginning and the end (e.g., 14.4.2: pauca de isdem [sc. the Saraceni] expediam carptim; 14.4.7: hactenus de natione perniciosa; nunc ad textum propositum revertamur).[7] Other passages that have the literary form of a digression, but lack both a formal introduction and an explicit transition back to the main narrative, are not included here (for example, the discussion of how midges kill lions in northern Mesopotamia [18.7.5] and of the mating of palm trees in southern Mesopotamia [24.3.12−13]).[8]

14.4.3−6	Saraceni
14.6.3−25	Rome[9]
14.8.1−15	The provinces of the diocese of Oriens
15.4.2−6	The Bodensee
15.9.2−12.6	Gaul
16.7.4−10	Eutherius and eunuchs
17.4.2−23	Obelisks in Rome
17.7.9−14	Earthquakes

[4] H. Cichocka, *Eos* 63 (1975), 329−40, esp. 334−37. She estimated that on her definition the excursus comprise approximately 17 percent of the preserved text of Ammianus (336, 338).

[5] A. M. Emmett, *Museum Philologum Londiniense* 5 (1981), 15−33; *History and Historians* (1983), 42−53.

[6] Observe that the introductory formula in 15.4.1 (cuius loci figuram breviter, quantum ratio patitur, designabo) may originally have been matched by a concluding formula that has been lost in the lacunae at 4.6−7.

[7] The formulae that Ammianus uses to conclude excursus are conveniently catalogued by T. Wiedemann, *LCM* 4 (1979), 13−14.

[8] On the placing and significance of excursus in Ammianus' text, see Chapters IV, IX.

[9] On various aspects of the two excursus on Rome, which complement each other, see R. Pack, *TAPA* 84 (1953), 181−89; H. P. Kohns, *Chiron* 5 (1975) 485−91; P. van de Wiel, *Hoofdstukken uit de geschiedenis van Rome in Ammianus Marcellinus "Res Gestae"* (Diss. Amsterdam, pub. Utrecht, 1989).

19.4.2−8	Plague
20.3.2−12	Eclipses
20.11.26−30	The rainbow
21.1.7−14	Divination
21.10.3−4	The Pass of Succi
22.8	The coasts of Thrace, the Hellespont, and the Black Sea
22.14.7−8	The Apis bull
22.15.1−16.24	Egypt
23.4.1−15	Military engines
23.6.1−84	The Persian Empire
23.6.85−88	Pearls
25.2.6	Meteors
25.10.2−3	Comets
26.1.2	Atoms
26.1.8−14	Leap year and the bissextile day
27.3.14−15	Christian bishops
27.4.2−14	Thrace
28.1.3−4	Phrynichus
28.1.57	The future punishment of Maximinus, Simplicius, and Doryphorianus
28.4.6−34	The inhabitants of Rome
30.4.3−21	Lawyers
31.2.1−25	The Huns and Alans
31.5.10−17	Previous barbarian invasions of Roman territory: (1) the Cimbri and Teutones, (2) under Marcus Aurelius, (3) during the third century

[6]

AMMIANUS' USE OF
ACCENTUAL CLAUSULAE

In 1891 Wilhelm Meyer laid down the law that has continued since then to bear his name: for twelve centuries from circa 400 onward all writers of Greek literary prose used purely accentual clausulae that totally disregarded the length or prosodic quantity of their constituent syllables. Meyer held that these accentual clausulae required at least two syllables between the last two accented syllables in each and every cadence, and he illustrated his law from Synesius, the earliest author in whom he stated that he had found the law strictly observed.[1] Moreover, in 1905, when Meyer reprinted his original paper of 1891 together with his long review article on Louis Havet's investigation of Latin rhythmical prose, he added to the latter a postscript in which he argued that the clausulae in Ammianus were primarily accentual under the influence of Greek practice, illustrating the point from the obituary of Julian (25.4.22–27).[2]

Later research has modified Meyer's initial findings in several ways that are relevant to Ammianus. The law itself has been shown to need a different and more flexible formulation. Meyer was correct to discern the total predominance of purely accentual clausulae, but mistaken in identifying their primary characteristic as a minimum of two unaccented syllables between the last two accented ones. In 1902 Paul Maas identified the fundamental characteristic of

---

[1] W. Meyer, *Der accentuierte Satzschluss in der griechischen Prosa vom 4. bis zum 16. Jahrhundert* (Göttingen, 1891), 6–15. Meyer himself acknowledged a debt to E. Bouvy, *Poètes et mélodes. Étude sur les origines du rhythme tonique dans l'hymnographie de l'église grecque* (diss. Paris, publ. Nîmes, 1886), esp. 183–220, 353–55. For his reaction to criticism, see his *Gesammelte Abhandlungen zur mittellateinischen Rhythmik*, 1 (Berlin, 1905), 17–22.

[2] Meyer, *Gesammelte Abhandlungen*, 2 (Berlin, 1905), 271–72. Meyer's review of L. Havet, *La Prose métrique de Symmaque et les origines métriques du cursus* (Paris, 1892) had originally appeared in *Gött. Gel. Anz.* 1893, 1–27.

the Byzantine clausula as an even number of unaccented syllables (2, 4, or 6) between the last two accented ones at the end of each clause.[3] The systematic study of prose rhythm in byzantine literature by Wolfram Hörandner, published in 1981, put Meyer's epoch-making study of 1891 into its scholarly context, surveyed, and assessed subsequent investigations, and provided statistical tables that list the percentage of both main and secondary clausulae that have between zero and eight unaccented syllables between the last two accented ones in a wide variety of authors: Hörandner documented a consistent heavy preference ("law" or even "rule" might be too strong a term) for clausulae with either two or four unaccented syllables between the last two accented ones.[4]

Meyer also put the start of the practice too late. In 1899 Wilamowitz showed that Himerius, whose surviving speeches were composed between 340 and the 380s, used accentual clausulae, and he even found accentual clausulae in examples of set pieces in one of the rhetorical handbooks of circa 300 that go under the name of Menander: hence he inferred that the practice went back to teachers of rhetoric in Athens during the third century.[5] Although lack of sufficient material prevents a proper statistical investigation of Menander's clausulae, H. B. Dewing soon documented Himerius' strict "observance of an accentual law": he counted the number of unaccented syllables between the last two accented ones in thirteen Greek authors from Dio of Prusa and Clement of Rome to John Chrysostom and Synesius and concluded that Himerius was indeed the earliest Greek writer who could be shown consciously and consistently to employ accentual clausulae, whereas neither Libanius nor the emperor Julian did so.[6] Hörandner has now provided independent statistical confirmation of Dewing's conclusions about Himerius and Julian.[7] Moreover, G. C. Hansen found that the majority of Themistius' clausulae in his paraphrase of Aristotle's *Physics* have either two or four unaccented syllables between the last two accented ones (about 70 %),[8] and Hörandner has docu-

---

[3] P. Maas, *BZ* 11 (1902), 505.

[4] W. Hörandner, *Der Prosarhythmus in der rhetorischen Literatur der Byzantiner* (*Wiener Byzantinische Studien* 16, 1981), with a full bibliography of the subject (12–15). In what follows I shall, like Hörandner, use the brachylogical expression "Form n" to denote clausulae with n unaccented syllables between the last two accented ones.

[5] U. von Wilamowitz-Möllendorf, *Hermes* 34 (1899), 214–18, quoting Himerius, *Orat.* 61 Colonna, and Menander Rhetor on the *Sminthiakos* (437.27–438.14, 438.30–439.6 Spengel = pp. 208, 210 in the edition by D. A. Russell and N. G. Wilson [Oxford, 1981]). On the dating of Himerius' life and speeches, see *CP* 82 (1987), 206–25.

[6] H. B. Dewing, *AJP* 31 (1910), 321–28.

[7] Hörandner, *Prosarhythmus* (1981), 51–54, 60–61, 160–61.

[8] G. C. Hansen, *BZ* 55 (1962), 235–40. Hansen's figures, reproduced by Hörandner, *Prosarhythmus* (1981), 160, who corrects some minor errors of arithmetic, are as follows: at strong sense-pauses Form 2, 30.5 percent; Form 4, 38.3 percent; Forms 2 + 4, 68.8 percent. At weak

mented the same preference to a much higher degree in the late-fourth-century rhetorical theorist Aphthonius.[9]

The origin of the accentual clausula in Greek has not been fully elucidated. That accentual clausulae were employed by Latin writers at an earlier date is beyond dispute: S. M. Oberhelman has both discovered accentual rhythms in Latin texts of the late second and early third centuries ([Apuleius], *De Platone, De Mundo, Peri Hermeneias, Asclepius*) and shown that the *cursus mixtus*, in which both quantity and accent play a role and which was standard in the fourth and fifth centuries, was used by both Minucius Felix and Cyprian in the middle decades of the third century.[10] Appealing to chronology, Meyer deduced that Greek practice was modeled on or borrowed from Latin practice.[11] But proof positive has yet to be produced. Hence a priori verdicts still hold the field. On the one hand, it seems plausible that, just as purely quantitative verse and prosody were an importation from Greek into Latin, so purely accentual clausulae and prosody were an importation into Greek from Latin, where accent or *ictus* had always played a role, even in verse whose meter was purely quantitative.[12] On the other hand, since it is difficult to imagine a Greek rhetorician circa 300 successfully transplanting a Latin practice into Greek oratory, the change from exclusively quantitative to accentual clausulae may be an independent phenomenon in the two languages.[13] In a later handwritten marginal note to his article of 1902, Maas suggested that Latin practice could have influenced Greek litterati who produced Greek versions of imperial pro-

---

sense-pauses, Form 2, 36.1 percent; Form 4, 35.1 percent; Forms 2 + 4, 71.2 percent. Dewing, *AJP* 31 (1910), 321, arrived at the following figures for Themistius, *Orat.* 9, 19: Form 2, 35.8 percent; Form 3, 12.1 percent; Form 4, 40.9 percent; that is, Forms 2 + 4, 76.7 percent.

[9] Hörandner, *Prosarhythmus* (1981), 61–68, 161. His figures are as follows. (1) At strong sense-pauses: in the main text Form 2, 87.2 percent; Form 4, 10.1 percent; Forms 2 + 4, 97.2 percent. In the illustrative examples, Form 2, 61.4 percent, Form 4, 19.3 percent, Forms 2 + 4, 80.7 percent. (2) At weak sense-pauses: in the main text Form 2, 80.1 percent; Form 4, 11.4 percent, Forms 2 + 4, 91.5 percent; in the illustrative examples, Form 2, 59.7 percent, Form 4, 26.9 percent, Forms 2 + 4, 86.6 percent. He shows that five of the six aberrant clausulae at the ends of sentences (1 Form 0, 3 Form 1, 2 Form 3) can easily be removed either by promoting into the text variant readings from the apparatus criticus of H. Rabe, *Aphthonii Progymnasmata* (*Rhetores Graeci* 10, 1926), or by trivial emendation (62–63).

[10] S. M. Oberhelman, *CP* 83 (1988), 136–49, esp. 145; *CQ*, N.S. 38 (1988), 228–42, cf. R. G. Hall and S. M. Oberhelman, *CQ*, N.S. 35 (1985), 201–14.

[11] Meyer, *Gesammelte Abhandlungen* 2 (1905), 269–70.

[12] See, e.g., D. S. Raven, *Latin Metre: An Introduction* (London, 1965), 22, 31–39, 101–2, 108–9; W. S. Allen, *Accent and Rhythm. Prosodic Features of Latin and Greek: A Study in Theory and Reconstruction* (Cambridge, 1973), 151–99, 335–59. The denial of the importance of accent by W. Beare, *Latin Verse and European Song. A Study in Accent and Rhythm* (London, 1957), 148–92, has not carried conviction.

[13] Hörandner, *Prosarhythmus* (1981), 37–42.

nouncements in the reigns of Diocletian and Constantine.[14] However, the Greek version of Constantine's *Speech to the Assembly of the Saints*, which is an official translation made on the emperor's orders, perhaps even before he delivered it, probably on 16 April 325 in Nicomedia, appears not to strive for accentual clausulae.[15]

In relation to Ammianus, Meyer's observation did not go far enough. In 1910, using Victor Gardthausen's unsatisfactory Teubner text (Leipzig, 1874, 1875), A. M. Harmon analyzed all the clausulae in Book XXII (both final and internal) and the clausulae employed at the ends of sentences in Books XIV–XIX and XXIX–XXXI: out of a total of 3,272 cadences, he counted no fewer than 3,212 as having either two or four unaccented syllables between the last two accented ones. Since these "regular cadences" comprised 98.2 percent of the total, Harmon argued that the sixty examples of irregular cadences printed by Gardthausen in the sample that he analyzed should all be removed by emendation, and he robustly concluded that Ammianus was "entirely indifferent" to quantity in accented syllables and that "in unaccented syllables he observes only quantity due to position."[16] It may be noted in passing that Harmon also showed that Ammianus often retained the original Greek accentuation of Greek names and Latin words of Greek origin, even where this contradicted the normal Latin rules of prosody: for example, the city names *Abdera*, *Antiochia*, *Apamea* and *Arethusa* are accented on the antepenultimate syllable despite their long penultimate syllables.[17]

Harmon's findings were embraced with enthusiasm by his teacher Charles Clark in his critical edition of Ammianus. Although the full introduction that Clark promised was never published, the brief preface to the first volume states his view of Ammianus' clausulae boldly and clearly:

---

[14] P. Maas, *Kleine Schriften* (Munich, 1973), 428: "Quelle die lateinische Prosa?! W. Meyer, kl. Schr. I 19. Doch wohl Ende 3. Jh. und 4. Jh. Übersetzungen lat. Kanzleistücke?"

[15] In *Oratio ad sanctorum coetum* 4, I find the following clausulae at the strong sense-pauses marked as such by I. A. Heikel in his edition (GCS 7, 1902, 157.18–158.9): Form 0, 8.7 percent (2); Form 1, 13 percent (3); Form 2, 34.8 percent (8); Form 3, 26.1 percent (6); Form 4, 8.7 percent (2); Form 5, 8.7 percent (2), that is, Forms 2 + 4, 43.5 percent. For purposes of comparison, I find the following clausulae at strong sense-pauses marked by Heikel in Eusebius' *Panegyric of Constantine* 4 (ibid., 202.19–203.19): Form 0, 11.8 percent (4); Form 1, 17.7 percent (6); Form 2, 41.2 percent (14); Form 3, 5.9 percent (2); Form 4, 11.8 percent (4); Form 5, 11.8 percent (4), that is, Forms 2 + 4, 52.9 percent. On the date of Constantine's speech and the nature of the Greek text preserved by Eusebius, see *The Making of Orthodoxy*, ed. R. W. Williams (Cambridge, 1989), 96, 116–17, n. 5.

[16] A. M. Harmon, *The Clausula in Ammianus Marcellinus* (New Haven, 1910), 170–78, 187, 191, 196–97.

[17] Harmon, *Clausula* (1910), 212–13.

Leges autem clausularum ab Ammiano observatae sunt simplicissimae. Inter duos enim ultimos accentus phrasis vel duae vel quattuor syllabae sine accentu interponendae sunt, numquam una vel tres. Utrum syllabae productae aut correptae sint, parum interest; vocales desinentes numquam eliduntur. Animadvertas *u* et *i* ut vel vocales vel consonantes legi posse. Graeca vocabula fere ubique Graecum retinent accentum.

In other words, Ammianus' clausulae are the three familiar clausulae of medieval Latin:

cursus planus   ó o o ó o

cursus tardus   ó o o ó o o

cursus velox   ó o o o o ó o.[18]

Unfortunately, Clark was carried away by an excess of zeal: he emended away all clausulae that did not conform to one of these three patterns,[19] and he punctuated after each and every clausula, so that, by adding a comma even in the middle of clauses, he introduced an unnecessary obstacle to comprehension for subsequent readers of Ammianus, who find it hard not to interpret his extra commas according to normal conventions of punctuation.[20] Yet Clark's instinct was fundamentally correct. For, if Ammianus indicates by means of clausulae which groups of words belong together as self-contained phrases, then the clausulae materially aid a modern reader's comprehension of his text. The Teubner editor Wolfgang Seyfarth has now ingeniously solved the problem of indicating Ammianus' internal clausulae by using two typographical devices that cannot be confused with conventional punctuation: after each clausula he prints a double space, whether or not there is a mark of punctuation, and if the end of the clausula comes at the end of a printed line, he adds a hasta (/), again whether or not there is a mark of punctuation.[21]

Harmon's demonstration that Ammianus overwhelmingly employed clausulae with either two or four unaccented syllables between the last two accented

[18] Clark, in his edition, 1 (1910), vii, cf. iv.

[19] Blomgren, *Quaestiones* (1937), 9–12, 14, 17, 93–94, defended the readings of V against such emendation: in most of the passages that Blomgren discusses, Seyfarth prints the transmitted nonconforming clausula.

[20] For this standard complaint, see esp. F. Leo, *Gött. Gel. Anz.* 173 (1911), 134; Blomgren, *Quaestiones* (1937), 113–16; W. Seyfarth, *Klio* 48 (1967), 226.

[21] Seyfarth first employed these devices in his edition with German translation (1968–1975), explaining them succinctly in his introduction (1.49).

ones has never been called into serious doubt.[22] It is only recently, however, that S. M. Oberhelman has demonstrated that Ammianus' practice is unique among the Latin writers of Late Antiquity. Oberhelman analyzed the clausulae in more than one hundred Latin texts written between circa 200 and circa 450: although accentual clausulae were completely absent in only nine works, he found that Ammianus' *Res Gestae* "stands apart in its prose rhythms" from all other Latin texts earlier than the sixth century, with the sole exception of three sermons transmitted pseudonymously under the name of Ambrose[23] and that in "a random sample of 557 final clausulae and 405 closings of internal subordinate clauses" 96.4 percent of the final clausulae and 95.6 percent of the internal clausulae "conformed to the three regular forms of the accentual *cursus* system." In other words, "meter plays no role in the formation or structure of the clausula" in Ammianus. Moreover, Oberhelman reaffirms and generalizes Harmon's observation about Ammianus' prosody: he follows "the Greek accentual system that he knew from his rhetorical training." Hence, since Ammianus diverges widely from contemporary Latin, while agreeing so closely with Greek practice, it must be concluded that "Ammianus' prose rhythms are derived from the Greek *cursus*."[24] Ammianus' clausulae, therefore, are yet another powerful indication that he thought in Greek (Chapter VII).

[22] Objections, mostly captious or misguided, were lodged by V. Gardthausen, *Woch. f. klass. Phil.* 28 (1911), 215–17; *Berl. phil. Woch.* 37 (1917), 1508–9; E. Bickel, *Gött. Gel. Anz.* 180 (1918), 292–95. In contrast, a far superior Latinist complimented Harmon on providing full and convincing proof of Clark's working hypothesis (F. Leo, *Gött. Gel. Anz.* 173 [1911], 134). Subsequently, only H. Hagendahl has attempted to claim, with appeal to a private letter from Eduard Norden, that quantity plays a significant role in Ammianus' clausulae (*Eranos* 22 [1924], 188–90).

[23] viz., *Clavis Patrum Latinorum*[2,3] (Steenbrugge, 1961, 1995), no. 181: see S. Oberhelman, *Rhetoric and Homiletics in Fourth-Century Christian Literature* (Atlanta, 1991), 52.

[24] S. M. Oberhelman, *QUCC*, N.S. 27.3 (1987), 79–89, esp. 80–81, 82, 85.

[7]

CORRUPT AND MISTAKEN DATES

The textual transmission of Ammianus Marcellinus is such that the paradosis is often both obviously corrupt and universally agreed to require emendation (Appendix 1). Numbers and dates present a special problem in any ancient author, for both are exposed to easy corruption yet both can often be corrected with certainty from external evidence.[1] The question arises, however, with Ammianus as with other Greek or Latin historians, whether dates and numbers that are wrong in the manuscripts have been corrupted in transmission or were erroneously stated in the original text. It will be well, therefore, to begin with cases where textual corruption is demonstrable before considering passages where modern editors print a text that attributes error to Ammianus himself.

In the statement of the day on which Julian was proclaimed Caesar, M, which is extant at this point, presents the following text: "haec die octalium iduum Novemuriem gesta sunt, cum Arbitionem consulem annus haberet et Lollianum" (15.8.17). The correct spelling of the name of the month (*Novembrium*) was restored by the scribe himself, while a renaissance hand corrected the meaningless *octalium* to *octavo*, and Seyfarth prints Kiessling's conjecture *diem octavum*.[2] In the preceding book, the consular date of 354 is mistakenly stated to be the second consulate of Gallus instead of the third (14.10.2: Constantius consulatu suo septies et Caesaris iterum). Although Seyfarth prints the transmitted text, Valesius was surely correct to emend *iterum* to *ter*. The consuls of 353 were Constantius for the sixth time and Gallus for the second: Ammianus surely registered them to date Constantius' recovery of Gaul to 353 in

---

[1] In mathematical texts, for example, lacunae can often be supplemented with absolute certainty: see, e.g., A. Aaboe, *Episodes from the Early History of Mathematics* (New York, 1964), 36.

[2] A. Kiessling, *Jahrb. für class. Phil.* 103 (1871), 491.

the lost Book XIII, and he can hardly have stated that Gallus was *consul iterum* for both 353 and 354.

Emendation is generally agreed to be necessary to avoid an obvious error in Book XXIII. V states the day on which Julian left Antioch to invade Persia in 363 as *tertium nonas Maias* (23.2.6), but Gelenius, followed by virtually all modern editors, printed *Martias* on the convincing grounds that the correct date must be 5 March 363, not 5 May, as later passages that record dates in March and April make clear (23.3.3, 3.7, 5.1, 5.12).[3]

Two passages where opinions differ on whether the error should be attributed to scribal corruption or to Ammianus himself concern the *dies imperii* and date of death of Constantius. According to the transmitted text, the emperor celebrated the day that marked the end of his thirtieth year as emperor on *diem sextum idus Octobres* in 353 (14.5.1). There is an error over the year that must be attributed to Ammianus himself: in 353 Constantius celebrated the twenty-ninth anniversary of his accession and inaugurated his tricennial year. Since his *dies imperii* was the sixth day before the ides of November, that is, 8 November 324, *Octobres* ought surely to be emended to *Novembres*, as Kiessling proposed.[4] Exactly the same corruption (October instead of November) has occurred in the obituary of Constantius, where Seyfarth prints the following text: "abiit e vita tertium nonarum Novembrium imperii <tricesimo octavo> vitaeque anno quadragesimo quarto et mensibus paucis." (21.15.3). The words *tricesimo octavo*, which are absolutely necessary for the sense, are absent from V: it was Valesius who saw that they needed to be added. As for the month, V has *o[ct]obrium*, which Clark retained, with the result that it is still sometimes believed either that Ammianus misdated the death of Constantius to 5 October,[5] or even, in defiance of all the evidence external to Ammianus, that Constantius died on 5 October 361.[6] However, the day of Constantius' decease is abundantly certified as 3 November.[7] Hence the transmitted *Octobrium* should be emended to *Novembrium*.[8]

---

[3] Kiessling, *Jahrb. für class. Phil.* 103 (1871), 490; A. Kellerbauer, *Blätter für das bayerische Gymnasialschulwesen* 9 (1873), 128. In 23.3.7 Kiessling proposed to add *Apriles* after *diem sextum kalendas*.

[4] Kiessling, *Jahrb. für class. Phil.* 103 (1871), 491, cf. 490.

[5] Sabbah, *Méthode* (1978), 226.

[6] Thus, for example, R. P. C. Blockley, *Studies in Latin Literature and Roman History* 2 (*Collection Latomus* 168, 1980), 487; Matthews, *Ammianus* (1989), 101.

[7] *CP* 88 (1993), 64–65; *Athanasius* (1993), 224. To the evidence there adduced, add the fragment of a Gothic calendar (*PL* 18.878), republished in H. Delehaye, *Anal. Boll.* 31 (1912), 276–77; P. Heather and J. Matthews, *The Goths in the Fourth Century* (Liverpool, 1991), 128.

[8] As persuasively argued by T. Büttner-Wobst, *Philologus* 51 (1892), 561, n. 1 (quoting P. Lehmann).

The opening sentence of Book XXVIII states that Bellona raged in Rome and burned everything, roused from the smallest beginnings to grief-filled massacres *anno sexto decimo et eo diutius post Neptiani exitium* (28.1.1). Since Nepotianus both rebelled and was killed in the month of June in the year 350, the sixteenth year after his suppression was 365–366. But Ammianus states clearly that the trials to which the emotive opening sentence refers began during the urban prefecture of Olybrius (28.1.8), which ran from late September or early October 368 to the late summer or early autumn of 370 and which Ammianus registers separately (28.4.1–2).[9] It has been standard scholarly procedure to accuse Ammianus of either careless error or deliberate distortion of the truth.[10] But is the transmitted numeral correct? The majority of recent translations slide over a difficulty in the received text by taking Ammianus to mean that the trials began shortly after the sixteenth year after the death of Nepotianus, that is, either between July 365 and June 366 or during the calendar year 365 (if the calculation is by consular rather than calendar years). Hence Rolfe renders the chronological marker as "somewhat more than sixteen years after the death of Nepotianus," Seyfarth as "etwas länger als sechzehn Jahre nach dem Tod des Nepotianus," Marié as "quinze ans et davantage après la chute de Népotianus," and Hamilton as "rather more than sixteen years after the death of Nepotian."[11]

A relevant grammatical question has not been asked. Can Ammianus' Latin really mean what it is normally taken to mean? The translations quoted would be correct renderings of an original text that read *paullo plus anno sexto decimo*. But what the text actually has is significantly different. Since the adverb *diutius* normally denotes temporal duration or the passage of time,[12] the transmitted text means "during the sixteenth year after the fall of Nepotianus and lasting beyond it." But if Ammianus' account of the career of Maximinus and of the trials at Rome otherwise reflects a precise and accurate chronology (as argued in Appendix 9), then it should be presumed unlikely that the introduction to his account would commit a gross chronological error. Accordingly, it may be proposed that the transmitted numeral is corrupt and that Ammianus originally wrote either *anno vicesimo* or *anno uno et vicesimo*, and that at

---

[9] Chastagnol, *Fastes* (1962), 178–84.

[10] See Appendix 9, n. 1.

[11] Seyfarth seems to have sensed that something was wrong: his note on the passage refers the reader to Thompson, *Ammianus* (1947), 138–42, for discussion of "die merkwürdige Art und Weise der Datierung."

[12] See *TLL* 5.1565–66. Of the passages there adduced to illustrate the use of *diutius* with an ablative of comparison (which include Ammianus 28.1.1), the most helpful is Cicero, *Pro Quinctio* 37: *annum et eo diutius post mortem circa Quincti fuit in Gallia tecum simul Quinctius* (Quinctius was together with you in Gaul for a year and more after the death of C. Quinctius).

some stage during the transmission of the text either XX or XXI has been deformed into XVI.

Many of the chronological errors and confusions that have been attributed to Ammianus are the corollaries of modern misapprehensions: Julian's appointments at Antioch in January 363 (23.1.3) are only the most conspicuous case where close examination of the other relevant evidence acquits Ammianus of carelessness and redirects the charge against his modern denigrators.[13] There remain, however, two serious errors that are extremely difficult to explain on any rational hypothesis. By a bizarre and presumably fortuitous coincidence, they both involve men called Artemius.

The sarcophagus of Junius Bassus *signo* Theotecnius records that he "went to God as a neophyte" while *praefectus urbi* at the age of forty-two on 25 August 359 (*CIL* 6.32004 = *ILS* 1286 = *ICUR* 1.143.3). Instead of a notice of the usual type for Bassus' prefecture, Ammianus notes that, because Bassus died shortly after his appointment, Artemius, the *vicarius* of the city of Rome, discharged the duties of prefect: during his administration, there were violent riots, but nothing happened worth recording (17.11.5). The placing of this notice, however, indicates unambiguously that Ammianus believed that Bassus died during the summer of 358, not 359 (Chapter IV). No one has yet explained why he has dated Bassus' death a year too early. Artemius was replaced by Tertullus. Appointment in the autumn of 359 is generally deduced from the fact that Ammianus places the notice of Tertullus' prefecture between eastern and western events of the summer of 359 (19.10.1–4).[14] In view of Ammianus' error about Bassus and Artemius, it might be wiser to allow the possibility that Tertullus did not become *praefectus urbi* until 360.

Ammianus presents the lynching of George, the bishop of Alexandria, as a consequence of the execution of Artemius, the former *dux Aegypti*: when they heard the glad news that the latter was dead, they turned their anger on the former (22.11.3, 8). The placing of George's death in Ammianus' narrative firmly and unambiguously dates it to the autumn of 362: Julian was wintering in Antioch (22.10.1: ibi hiemans) and was due to enter on his fourth consulate on 1 January 363 (23.1.1). But the *Historia acephala* reports that the people of Alexandria imprisoned George immediately after the public announcement of the death of Constantius on 30 November 361; then, after a month of incarceration, they took him out, killed him, dragged his body through the streets, and burned it on 24 December 361 (2.8–10 Martin). On

---

[13] *Cognitio Gestorum* (1992), 5–7.
[14] Chastagnol, *Fastes* (1962), 151–53; *PLRE* 1.882–3.

a matter such as this, the testimony of a well-informed local source, which offers an abundance of precise and accurate dates, should not be doubted, even though Dracontius the *praepositus monetae* and Diodorus, whom Ammianus carefully distinguishes (22.11.9), have become conflated or confused in the course of editing or transmission.[15]

Walter Klein attempted to remove the mistake by transposition: he argued that the relevant passage (22.11) originally stood in its chronologically correct position (after 22.3.12), but that a leaf had been misplaced by scribal or mechanical error.[16] If it be objected that such a hypothesis is intrinsically implausible, appeal could be made to the precedent of Tacitus, where a gross error over the activities of Drusus in Illyricum, which are wrongly placed in the annalistic account of the year 19 instead of 18, can (and probably should) be removed by transposition.[17] Klein's hypothesis fails, however, on the directly relevant evidence.

Ammianus explicitly presents the deaths of George, Diodorus, and Dracontius as a consequence of the execution of Artemius (22.11.3: Alexandrini Artemii comperto interitu etc.). In reality, Artemius was tried at Daphne just outside Antioch,[18] hence at a date after Julian arrived in the city in mid-July 362.[19] Furthermore, Julian's letter to the city of Alexandria about the killing of George makes it clear that Artemius was still alive and had not yet been punished for his actions during the reign of Constantius.[20]

---

[15] A. Martin, *Histoire "Acéphale" et Index syriaque des Lettres Festales d'Athanase d'Alexandrie* (*Sources chrétiennes* 317, 1985), 69–106, cf. *JTS*, N.S. 37 (1986), 576–79; *Athanasius* (1993), 4–5. Ammianus' phrase *veluti comes* (22.11.9) does not mean that Diodorus had the official title of *comes*, as is often assumed (e.g., *PLRE* 1.255, Diodorus 2): the Penguin translation correctly renders "who was thought to be in league with him." In an unpublished note, D. Woods plausibly suggests that Constantius had appointed Diodorus *dux Aegypti* in place of Artemius.

[16] W. Klein, *Studien zu Ammianus Marcellinus* (*Klio*, Beiheft 13, 1914), 56–57 ("Über eine Blattversetzung in dem XXII. Buche").

[17] J. Steup, *Rh. Mus.*, N.F. 24 (1869), 72–80, proposed to transpose *Ann.* 2.59–61 to follow 2.67: for a sympathetic, though ultimately negative, assessment of his arguments, see F. R. D. Goodyear, *The Annals of Tacitus* 2 (Cambridge, 1981), 393–96. Somewhat surprisingly, the problem is not discussed at all in the appendix on "Mistakes in the *Annales*" in R. Syme, *Tacitus* (Oxford, 1958), 746–48, nor does Syme's vast bibliography include Steup's paper.

[18] Theodoretus, *HE* 3.18.1; *Passio Artemii* (*BHG*³ 169y, 169z), ed. J. Bidez and F. Winkelmann, *Philostorgius Kirchengeschichte*² (Berlin, 1972), 166–75 (Anhang III); *Passio Artemii* (*BHG*³ 170) 22 (214.1–5 Kotter: this passage was not printed by Bidez in his edition of Philostorgius).

[19] Between the deaths of Artemius and George, Ammianus records the exile of the tribunes of the first and second *scholae Scutariorum* (22.11.2). Although nothing more seems to be known for certain about about either man (*PLRE* 1.768, Romanus 2; 966, Vincentius 2), Ammianus is probably in error here, too: D. Woods, *CQ*, N.S. 47 (1997), 275–76, persuasively assigns their dismissal to early 362, before Julian left Constantinople.

[20] Julian, *Ep.* 60, 379ab = Socrates, *HE* 3.3.10.

Why is the death of George misplaced by almost a year? Ammianus' lapse has been explained and palliated by the hypothesis that he was misled by a written source that wrongly linked the deaths of Artemius and George.[21] But that implies an implausible degree of inattention or carelessness on the part of Ammianus. Moreover, the chronological error is so gross that it is hard to believe that it can be accidental.[22] There remains one explanation—deliberate displacement. Guy Sabbah argued that Ammianus removed the death of George from its correct context for apologetic reasons, so that he might avoid an excessive cluster of negative notices at the very start of Julian's reign as sole emperor.[23] Such a deliberate displacement would probably not be unique in the Res Gestae.

[21] J. Dummer, AfP 21 (1971), 132–35.

[22] M. Caltabiano, Quaderni catanesi 7 (1985), 27–29.

[23] Sabbah, Méthode (1978), 481–82. Sabbah also implausibly suggested that Ammianus may have confused the dates of George's death and the arrival of his library in Antioch (482 n. 91, cf. Julian, Ep. 106, 411cd).

[8]

MISSING *PRAEFECTI URBIS*

The extant books of Ammianus conscientiously note the tenure of every *praefectus urbi* from Orfitus, who entered office on 8 December 353 (14.6, cf. *Chr. min.* 1.69), to Q. Clodius Hermogenianus Olybrius and P. Ampelius (28.4.2–4), who are attested as prefects in the Theodosian Code from January 369 to August 370 and from January 371 to July 372, respectively, and who had both appeared in Ammianus' narrative of the trials at Rome under Maximinus (28.1.8, 22, 32).[1] After Ampelius, Ammianus' coverage appears to change almost completely. Recent fasti of the urban prefecture register no fewer than five prefects as holding office between the late summer of 372 and the death of Valentinian on 17 November 375:

Bappo	22 August 372
Principius	29 April 373
Fl. Eupraxius	14 February 374
Clodius Hermogenianus Caesarius	21 May 374 – 19 July 374
Tanaucius Isfalangius	374 – 375.[2]

The transmitted text of Ammianus registers only one of these five men. Clodius Hermogenianus Caesarius, who is styled Claudius, occurs in a very significant position. His prefecture is the final item of Book XXIX and Ammianus concludes his notice of it with a pregnant reference to the time of

---

[1] On the prefects Olybrius and Ampelius, see Chastagnol, *Fastes* (1962), 178–88; *PLRE* 1.640–1, 57. Chastagnol, *Fastes* (1962), 182, deduces from *Collectio Avellana* 8 that Olybrius was already prefect in October 368: on the date of this letter, see Appendix 9, n. 9.

[2] Chastagnol, *Fastes*, 188–94; *PLRE* 1.1055.

writing. Although the Tiber flooded, Claudius restored many old buildings, including the portico of Bonus Eventus, so named because the temple of this deity was still visible close by (29.6.17–19). When Ammianus penned these words around 390, the continued existence of such temples could not be taken for granted much longer.

What of the other four prefects who are normally believed to have held office before the death of Valentinian? Bappo and Eupraxius are adequately, if not abundantly, documented and their appointments conform to known patterns. Bappo, who is attested by a single piece of extant evidence as *praefectus urbi* on 22 August 372 (*CTh* 6.4.21), has a name that stamps him as Gallic, Germanic, or Frank:[3] Valentinian presumably sent him from court to Rome to impose discipline and order after the embarrassing trials conducted by Maximinus. Eupraxius, too, was a trusted official of Valentinian, but his civilian background (he came from Mauretania) doubtless made him more acceptable to the Senate than Bappo, who was probably his immediate predecessor. Eupraxius is attested on 14 February 374 (*CTh* 11.29.5 + 30.36 + 36.21), and he appears to have been a correspondent of Symmachus.[4]

The remaining pair of prefects are problematical. The only evidence for the prefecture of Principius comprises an imperial constitution with the transmitted date of 29 April 370 addressed "ad Principium p. u." (*CTh* 13.3.10). Seeck emended the year to 373,[5] and his emendation is the only evidence for the postulated prefecture in 373. It is at least equally plausible, as Mommsen proposed, to emend the transmitted year from the joint third consulate of Valentinian and Valens to their joint second consulate, that is, to 368, and to regard the name as an error for Praetextatus, who is well attested as prefect in 367–368 and whose prefecture Ammianus registers at the appropriate point (27.9.8–10).[6] Alternatively, the date could be emended far more radically than either Mommsen or Seeck envisaged, and the addressee identified as the Principius who was praetorian prefect of Italy in 385.[7] As for Isfalangius, there is no compelling reason to assign to these years his undated prefecture, which is also attested epigraphically (*CIL* 6.1672a–b)—for it is circular to argue that

---

[3] A. Piganiol, *L'Empire chrétien* (Paris, 1947), 187, 199; K. F. Stroheker, *Der senatorische Adel im spätantiken Gallien* (Tübingen, 1948), 156, no. 64.

[4] O. Seeck, *Q. Aurelii Symmachi quae supersunt* (*Mon. Germ. Hist.*, Auct. Ant. 6.1, 1883), cxlvi–cxlvii.

[5] O. Seeck, *Hermes* 18 (1883), 291, n. 3; *Regesten* (1919), 31, 35, 244.

[6] For the other evidence relevant to Praetextatus' prefecture, see Chastagnol, *Fastes* (1962), 171–78. Mommsen, ad loc., suggested that *CTh* 13.3.10 may be part of the same constitution as 13.3.8, which is transmitted as having been issued to Praetextatus on 29 January 370: both dates can easily be emended to "iii kal. Feb. (or Mai.) Valentiniano et Valente II AA. conss."

[7] *PLRE* 1.726, Principius 2.

"he was evidently a favorite of Valentinian" and hence held office between 372 and 375 because "there are gaps in the list of prefects in Ammianus."[8]

Ammianus notes that Isfalangius condemned the young Lollianus to death when the case of the latter was referred to him as *consularis* of Baetica (28.1.26, where the epigraphically attested form of the name should be restored by emendation for the transmitted *flalangio*), but he refrains from adding the observation that Isfalangius was later *praefectus urbi*, although the very next sentence records that the accused included "Tarracius Bassus, postea urbi praefectus" (28.1.27). Bassus' prefecture, otherwise known only from an undated inscription (*CIL* 6.1766 = 31894 = *ILS* 6072) has plausibly been assigned to 375–376.[9] Isfalangius could have been prefect much later, perhaps even after Ammianus had completed his *Res Gestae*.

Since Ammianus' narrative of western events continues to November 375, but contains no mention of the prefectures of Bappo and Eupraxius (or of that of Principius), Seeck argued that an account of these three prefects has disappeared in a lacuna in Book XXIX.[10] That theory has been dismissed as unworthy of serious consideration by recent writers, who assume that Ammianus chose not to record the missing prefectures and that there must be a political explanation for such a striking and deliberate omission. Thompson suggested that Ammianus "did not wish to be too specific in his history (especially of Rome itself) of these years."[11] Similarly, Alföldi argued that this "most curious" omission was deliberate and designed to exculpate the omitted trio of prefects "from the odium of those persecutions of the nobility."[12] But Seeck's hypothesis should not be pronounced implausible on a priori grounds. On the contrary, the fact that there are a number of undoubted lacunae elsewhere in Book XXIX (Appendix 1) makes Seeck's postulate of accidental loss preferable to the alternative hypothesis of deliberate omission.

Since Ammianus conscientiously registers all the *praefecti urbis* who held office during the period covered by the extant books with the sole exception of Bappo and Eupraxius, and since it seems unlikely on general grounds that he chose to omit Eupraxius, whom he commends warmly for mitigating Valentinian's outbursts of rage when he was *quaestor sacri palatii* between 367 and 370 (27.6.14, 7.6; 28.1.25), it is reasonable to suppose (1) that he did reg-

---

[8] *PLRE* 1.465, cf. Chastagnol, *Fastes* (1962), 194.

[9] Chastagnol, *Fastes* (1962), 195–96.

[10] O. Seeck, *Hermes*, 18 (1883), 291: "in der grossen Lücke des 29. Buches (5, 1), wo sie ihrer Zeit nach stehen mussten, sind sie uns verloren gegangen." Accepted by W. Klein, *Studien zu Ammianus Marcellinus* (*Klio*, Beiheft 13, 1914), 51–52; R. S. O. Tomlin, *The Emperor Valentinian the First* (Diss. Oxford, 1973), 318.

[11] Thompson, *Ammianus* (1947), 139.

[12] Alföldi, *Conflict* (1952), 70, cf. Matthews, *Ammianus* (1989), 209–15.

ister the prefects Bappo and Eupraxius at the appropriate place, (2) that the notice of their prefectures has been lost in transmission, and (3) that it originally stood where Seeck supposed, in the undoubted lacuna at 29.5.1, which appears to be a substantial one.[13]

[13] The structure of Book XXIX is analyzed in Chapter IV.

[9]

MAXIMINUS AND THE TRIALS
AT ROME UNDER VALENTINIAN

It is commonly believed that not only is Ammianus' account of trials in Rome in the first chapter of Book XXVIII chronologically imprecise or confused, but also that Ammianus was aware of or even admits the fact.[1] In reality, the charge of chronological imprecision should be laid against the modern critics of Ammianus rather than against the historian. For it rests on an uncritical (and so far unchallenged) acceptance of Seeck's date of 371 for Maximinus' departure from Rome to become praetorian prefect of Gaul (28.1.41). Yet the date of Maximinus' promotion is nowhere either stated or directly attested. The evidence adduced for the date of 371 comprises the headings and subscriptions to two documents in the *Codex Justinianus* addressed "ad Maximum." Seeck reasonably emended the name of the recipient of both documents to Maximinus, but no similar justification exists for his claim that Maximinus received them as praetorian prefect in the summer of 371.[2] One of these two imperial constitutions was issued at Contionacum on 7 Au-

---

[1] E.g., Thompson, *Ammianus* (1947), 102–7; Matthews, *Ammianus* (1989), 213. At 28.1.15 Ammianus does not, as Matthews claims, concede that his account "is imprecise in its chronology." What Ammianus emphasizes is the proposition that "non omnia narratu sunt digna quae per squalidas transiere personas": hence the passage should be interpreted as a polemical reiteration of the preface to Book XXVI, where Ammianus argues that history should concentrate on *negotiorum celsitudines* and not investigate the *humilium minutiae causarum* (26.1.1).

[2] Seeck, *Regesten* (1919) 240, 242, followed by W. Ensslin, *RE*, Supp. 5 (1931), 663–64, Maximinus 5; *PLRE* 1.577–78, Maximinus 11; A. Demandt, *Hermes* 100 (1972), 99–100; M. Clauss, *Der magister officiorum in der Spätantike (4.-6. Jahrhundert)* (*Vestigia* 32, 1980), 165–66, 186–87 (the careers of Leo and Remigius); J. Harries, *JRS* 78 (1988), 166–67. Observe that, in his introduction, Seeck had deduced the chronology of Maximinus' career from Ammianus and a careless misdating of *CTh* 14.17.6 to 19 March 369 (*Regesten* [1919], 131, cf. 238, where the constitution is correctly dated 19 March 370).

gust 371: the date and place of issue are confirmed by similar subscriptions to four other constitutions in the Theodosian Code issued by Valentinian at Contoniacum between 12 July and 16 August of that year (*CTh* 11.1.17; 9.3.5; 2.4.3; 4.6.4); but the office of the addressee is not stated, and the fact that its content relates to wills with bequests to the emperor or empress and to wills made by an emperor or Augusta does not exclude the possibility that Maximinus received it while still *vicarius* in Rome (*CJ* 6.22.7). Although the heading of the other constitution, in contrast, does explicitly style its recipient *praefectus praetorio* (*CJ* 11.48.7), it lacks a subscription altogether: hence Seeck's assumption that Valentinian issued it at Contoniacum between 13 and 16 July 371 is a modern conjecture unsupported by any ancient evidence.

The earliest secure and unambiguous attestation of Maximinus as praetorian prefect of the Gauls is on 14 November 374 (*CTh* 9.24.3). His promotion can (and in fact should) be dated from the indications that Ammianus provides. Maximinus was replaced as *vicarius* by Ursicinus (44). Since Ursicinus is attested as *praefectus annonae* on 22 or 23 February 372 (*CTh* 14.3.14), Maximinus' promotion occurred no earlier than the spring of 372, and perhaps somewhat later, conceivably even in 373. There is no call to adopt the extreme (and circular) hypothesis that the Ursicinus attested as *praefectus annonae* on 22 February 372 is a different man from the Ursicinus who succeeded Maximinus as *vicarius urbis Romae*[3] or to offer the ad hoc explanation that, like Maximinus shortly before, Ursicinus temporarily combined the two offices.[4] For there is no conflict in the ancient evidence, only a contradiction between Ammianus and modern conjecture, which should be resolved in favor of the former. The meek acquiescence of subsequent writers in Seeck's authority has obscured the fact that his chronology for the career of Maximinus not only depends on the unsupported supplement of a heading and the unjustified restoration of a subscription in the *Codex Justinianus* but also contradicts the clear indications that Ammianus provides.

Seeck's chronology for Maximinus' career must be rejected and his promotion to the praetorian prefecture of Gaul dated after 22 February 372, when Ursicinus, who replaced him in Rome, was still *praefectus annonae* (*CTh* 14.3.14). For, when Maximinus' career is correctly dated, the charges of imprecision and confusion against Ammianus simply lapse. The following analysis of the first chapter of Book XXVIII discusses the temporal indications in

[3] As *PLRE* 1.987, whose argument that Ursicinus 6 is "probably not identical with Ursicinus 7 since the *praefectus annonae* normally ranked below a *vicarius*," depends on the explicitly stated premise that Ursicinus "succeeded Maximinus 7 as *vicarius urbis Romae* in 371 (when the latter was made PPO)."

[4] Matthews, *Aristocracies* (1975), 38 n. 9.

the text with the intention of demonstrating that Ammianus' narrative has a precise chronology free of inconsistencies.

1–4   Introduction

The transmitted *anno sexto decimo* should be emended to either *anno vicesimo* or *anno uno et vicesimo* to remove the apparent chronological error (Appendix 7).

5–7   Character Sketch and Early Career of Maximinus

Maximinus is introduced as the sometime (or future) *vicarius urbis Romae* (5: regens quondam Romae vicarium praefecturam).[5] Ammianus marks the stages of his official career in precise detail. He began by governing three Italian provinces in succession: Corsica, Sardinia, and Tuscia (6). An inscription provides an approximate date for the second post: it attests Maximinus as governor between the spring of 364 and the late summer of 367 (*Eph. Ep.* 8.781b = *AE* 1889.32 [Sbranagatu]). Subsequently, as *corrector Tusciae*, Maximinus received an imperial constitution dated 17 November 366 (*CTh* 9.1.8: dat. xv kal. Dec. Remis, acc. Florentiae Gratiano nob(ilissimo) p(uero) et Dagalaifo conss.). He was then promoted to be *praefectus annonae* at Rome, temporarily retaining the status of governor of Tuscia since the arrival of his successor had been delayed (7, cf. Jerome, *Chronicle* 246[b] Helm; Rufinus, *HE* 11.10 [1018.2–4]; Socrates, *HE* 4.29.6).[6] The start of the prefecture of the *annona* cannot be dated at all precisely, but Maximinus was still in that office on 19 March 370 (*CTh* 14.17.6).[7]

8–13   The Origin of the Troubles

Trouble began when Chilo, a former *vicarius*, and his wife lodged a complaint before Olybrius, the *praefectus urbi* (8), who held that office from autumn 368 to summer 370.[8] When Olybrius failed to act because of illness (a detail confirmed by *CTh* 11.31.3, addressed to Olybrius on 19 March 370), they requested the investigation to be entrusted to Maximinus, then *praefectus annonae* (9–10). Maximinus took the matter in hand with vigor and continued his inquiries

---

[5] Mistranslated as "formerly vice-prefect of Rome" by Hamilton and Wallace-Hadrill: for *quondam* with a future reference, see *OLD* 1567, s.v. 2.

[6] This detail is confirmed by *Collectio Avellana* 12.3 (singularem urbium atque regionum, quibus temporarie praeest [sc. sinceritas tua]), which is addressed to Maximinus as *vicarius urbis Romae* during the prefecture of Ampelius (see n. 9).

[7] On the career of Maximinus, see now J. Szidat, *Historia* 44 (1995), 481–486, who shows that his rise was due to his education and rhetorical and legal skills, which Ammianus disparages (6: post mediocre studium liberalium doctrinarum defensionemque causarum ignobilem).

[8] Chastagnol, *Fastes* (1962), 178–84. P. Hamblenne, *Byzantion* 50 (1980), 202, dates the beginning of the trials to 368—which seems too early for the other indications given by Ammianus.

after he was promoted to *vicarius urbis Romae* (11–13), in which office he is attested by a pair of imperial letters preserved in the collection of documents relating to the see of Rome conventionally styled the *Collectio Avellana* during the urban prefecture of Ampelius, that is, at some time between 21 August 370 and 22 August 372 (*Collectio Avellana* 11–12 [*CSEL* 35.48–54], cf. *CTh* 2.10.5; 6.4.21).[9]

14–15   The Spread of the Trouble
The first word of 14 (*iamque*) implies temporal progression, but nothing in this section is datable.

16   Cethegus and Others Executed, Alypius Exiled
The precise reference of the introductory *tunc* is unclear.

17–23   The Case of Hymetius
Hymetius had been proconsul of Africa in 366–368.[10] Ammianus marks a clear distinction between two separate episodes. First comes Valentinian's anger over Hymetius' conduct as proconsul of Africa and its immediate consequences (17–21). Then Ammianus turns to Hymetius' subsequent trial by Ampelius and Maximinus, his appeal to the emperor, and the emperor's referral of the case to the Senate (17, 22–23), marking an interval of time between the two episodes with the phrase *post hanc gestorum seriem* (22).

The introductory phrase *eodem tempore* (17) refers to the preceding temporal indications (14, 16). But Ampelius is now *praefectus urbi* in place of Olybrius, who is last attested on 21 August 370 (*CTh* 2.10.5). Moreover, a rescript dated 6 December 371 instructs Ampelius, if he decides that he cannot complete his inquiries when investigating the case of senators accused of magical practices,

---

[9] In chronological order, the eight documents relevant to Maximinus in the *Collectio Avellana* are: (1) three imperial letters to Praetextatus as *praefectus urbi* from the summer of 367 and the following winter, of which the third has a subscription stating that it was written in Trier on 12 January 368 (5–7); (2) a pair of parallel letters written on the same day, probably in the autumn of 368 to the prefect Olybrius and the *vicarius* Aginatius (8–9); (3) a slightly later letter to Olybrius alone as prefect (10); (4) a pair of letters written on the same day to Ampelius as *praefectus urbi* and to Maximinus as *vicarius urbis Romae* (11–12). The date of *Collectio Avellana* 8–10 must lie between 21 September 368, when Vettius Agorius Praetextatus was still *praefectus urbi* (*CTh* 1.6.6), and 1 January 371, when Ampelius had replaced Olybrius in that office (*CTh* 15.10.1): the precise date of 8–9 is hypothetical.

Matthews, *Ammianus* (1989), 212–13, suggests that *CTh* 9.35.1, addressed to Olybrius on 8 July 369, "may embody part" of Valentinian's reply to the *relatio* of Maximinus (28.1.11). That seems to be chronologically impossible, but the ruling that senators may be tortured when charges of *maiestas* are being investigated is clearly relevant to Maximinus' actions.

[10] *Phoenix* 39 (1985), 150, 273.

to send all involved to the emperor with a full documentary record of all the proceedings so far (*CTh* 9.16.10). That seems to have an obvious relevance, but its precise bearing on Ammianus' account is hard to define.

24–29   Other Cases

Ammianus implicitly marks the passing of time: everyone began to be afraid *ob haec et huiusmodi multa* (24), but none of the cases briefly described in this section is precisely datable.

30–56   The Case of Aginatius

The case of Aginatius was long and complicated, and it is most unfortunate that the recent Penguin translation has obscured the coherence of the chapter as a whole by omitting sections 30–35, 37–40, and 48–56.[11] Ammianus begins by explicitly going back in time: Aginatius, who was then *vicarius urbis Romae*, was indignant that the prefect Olybrius had delegated the investigations not to him, but to Maximinus, the *praefectus annonae*, his inferior in rank (31–32). Aginatius' request to Petronius Probus to dismiss Maximinus set in train a series of events that eventually led to his execution (56). The chronological indications that Ammianus provides are clear and consistent. Aginatius had been *vicarius* since autumn 368 (*Collectio Avellana* 8, 9): the reference back to the start of the troubles (32, cf. 9) fixes the date of his letter to Petronius Probus to 369–370. After Maximinus left Rome (41), Ursicinus succeeded him as *vicarius urbis Romae* (44) until he was replaced for being too lenient by Simplicius of Emona (45), who was in turn replaced by Doryphorianus, sent by Maximinus to condemn and execute Aginatius and Anepsia (52–56). All this happened before the death of Valentinian (51, 53).

External evidence supplies some precise dates: Ursicinus is attested as *praefectus annonae* on 22 February 372 (*CTh* 14.3.14) and Simplicius on 23 March 374 (*CTh* 9.29.1), but it should be noted that there is no warrant for the common supposition that the latter was still in office after Valentinian died.[12]

---

[11] Hamilton and Wallace-Hadrill explain that "omitted in this selection is the complex episode of Aginatius and Anepsia" and give the following dates for the three successors of Maximinus: Ursicinus 371–373, Simplicius 374–375, Doryphorianus 376 (469–470, n. 1).

[12] As asserted in *PLRE* 1.270, 844, on the grounds that "he received a letter from Gratian." But Gratian had been a member of the imperial college since 367: hence, when he states, in a letter written between August 378 and January 379, that "our clemency" wrote "ad v. c. Simplicium quondam vicarium" (*Collectio Avellana* 13.3), he means no more than that his name stood in the heading of a letter written by his father as if he were one of its authors, just as that of Valentinian II stands in the heading of his own. The corollary (which contradicts Ammianus) that Aginatius died after Valentinian is duly drawn in *PLRE* 1.29.

Ammianus' statement that Leo preceded Maximinus to court (41) alludes to the appointment of the latter as *magister officiorum* in place of Remigius (30.2.10). The date cannot be determined except by inference from Ammianus.

57   Epilogue

Ammianus promises to relate the subsequent deaths of Maximinus, Simplicius, and Doryphorianus at the appropriate time. In fact, his continuous narrative of western events, which stops with the proclamation of the infant Valentinian II as Augustus on 22 November 375 (30.10), omits the deaths of this trio of malefactors. Simplicius and Doryphorianus were executed shortly after the fall of their patron Maximinus (Symmachus, *Ep.* 10.2.2−3; *Orat.* 4.11−12), who was probably dismissed as praetorian prefect before the end of the winter of 375−376.[13]

[13] Maximinus appears still to have been in office on 15 March 376 (*CTh* 9.6.1 + 2). His tenure of the prefecture is prolonged until 16 April on the strength of *CTh* 9.19.4 by *PLRE* 1.578; Matthews, *Aristocracies* (1975), 65; H. Sivan, *Ausonius of Bordeaux* (London/New York, 1993), 128−29. But 16 April was the day on which the constitution was "p(ro)p(osita) Romae": hence it was issued sometime earlier, perhaps even before 15 March 376.

[10]

THE MOVEMENTS OF VALENS

Ammianus provides a detailed account of Valens' movements from his proclamation on 24 March 364 to the suppression of the revolt of Procopius in May 365. Thereafter, as the nature of his narrative changes, he ceases to chronicle Valens' activities during each campaining season and in the intervening winters, about which, nevertheless, the *Res Gestae* continue to the end to furnish precise and relevant information (Chapter IV). Seeck's standard chronology of the reign concentrates on precisely dated documents, whether or not they emanate from an emperor, and on precisely datable events, whether or not they are related directly to emperors:[1] hence a tabulation of the attested residences and journeys of Valens is apposite.[2]

Principal Residences

364/5	Constantinople
365/6	Ancyra
366/7	Constantinople
367–370	Marcianopolis[3] (possibly with winters in Constantinople)

---

[1] Seeck, *Regesten* (1919), 217–51.

[2] For the format employed, see *New Empire* (1982), 47–87; *Athanasius* (1993), 218–28, covering the years 284–361. A closely similar reconstruction of the movements of Valens is to be found in F. Reiche, *Chronologie der letzten 6 Bücher des Ammianus Marcellinus* (Diss. Jena, pub. Liegnitz, 1889), 15–18, 24–35, 56–60, which I inspected only after composing this appendix.

[3] Zosimus 4.10.3. Zosimus means that Valens resided in Marcianople during the Gothic War, not that he began to campaign in the winter of 366–67 (cf. 10.4–11.1)

370/1   Constantinople
371/2   Caesarea in Cappadocia
372–378   Antioch (winters) and Hierapolis (summers)[4]

Attested Movements

364

March 28	Proclaimed emperor by Valentinian in Constantinople	Ammianus 26.4.3; *Descr. cons.* 364.3
	Proceeds with Valentinian from Constantinople to Naissus	Ammianus 26.5.1
June 11	At Naissus	*CTh* 9.40.6
June 19	At Mediana (an imperial villa three miles from Naissus)	*CTh* 15.1.13, cf. Ammianus 26.5.4[5]
c. Aug.	The imperial brothers divide the empire at Sirmium[6]	Ammianus 26.5.4
Sept. 24	At Heraclea/Perinthus	*CTh* 7.1.8[S]; Sozomenus, *HE* 6.7.8
	Returns to Constantinople	Ammianus 26.5.4

[4] Zosimus 4.13.2 should be construed as a general statement about how Valens conducted himself while residing in the East: he spent the winters in Antioch, the summers on campaign with his main base at Hierapolis, as Constantius had during the 340s (Libanius, *Orat.* 18.207). Theodoretus, *HE* 4.17.1, attests the presence of Valens and his praetorian prefect at Edessa during one of the years between 372 and 377.

[5] For Mediana, see M. Fluss, *RE* 15 (1930), 68; S. Gŭsič, *Roman Imperial Towns and Palaces in Serbia*, ed. D. Srejovic (Belgrade, 1993), 169–77. The place of issue is transmitted as *Med.*, which is normally expanded to *Med*(iolani). But, as Mommsen noted ad loc., "eo die Valentinianus non fuit Mediolani." Accordingly, Seeck, *Regesten* (1919), 224, emended the date to 19 June 365, *PLRE* 1.880 to 20 December 364 ("reading 'XIII Kal. Ian', mss. 'Iun.'"). It is more economical to regard *Med.* as a misleading abbreviation of an unfamiliar name (for the phenomenon, see Seeck, *Regesten* [1919], 106–10). The constitution is addressed to Tautomedes, the *dux* of Dacia Ripensis.

[6] Seeck, *Regesten* (1919), 216, dates the parting of Valentinian and Valens between 4 and 24 August. But Valentinian need not have departed from Sirmium at the same time as Valens returned east: nothing in their content shows whether the constitutions issued in Sirmium in July and early August 364 were issued by both brothers together or by Valentinian alone (*Consultatio* 9.6 [4 July]; CTh 10.7.2[S] [23 July]; 5.15.5 [29 July]; 12.6.7[S] [4 August]).

364–365

Dec. 16–March 19	In Constantinople	CTh 8.11.1 (Dec. 16); 12.12.5 (Dec. 28); Ammianus 26.5.6 (Jan. 1); CTh 8.1.9; 9.34.7 (Feb. 16); 11.16.11 (March 19)[7]

365

Spring	Leaves Constantinople for Syria and travels through Bithynia[8]	Ammianus 26.6.11
Summer	Resides temporarily in Caesarea in Cappadocia	Ammianus 26.7.2; CTh 12.6.5 (4 July)[9]
early Oct.	At Caesarea when he learns of the proclamation of Procopius at Constantinople on 28 Sept.[10]	Ammianus 26.7.2, cf. Descr. cons. 365.2
	Leaves Caesarea and travels through Galatia[11]	Ammianus 27.7.2–3, 13

[7] Seeck, *Regesten* (1919), 223, 225, 33, keeps Valens in Constantinople until the end of July on the strength of CTh 1.16.5 and 12.6.8. The dates of both constitutions are doubtful. First, CTh 1.16.5 is addressed "Secundo p(raefecto) p(raetori)o Orientis." Although its transmitted date of 18 April 329 must obviously be emended, and *PLRE* 1.816 accepts Seeck's emendation to 18 April 365, the correct year could equally well be 362 (cf. Mommsen, ad loc.), when Secundus was praetorian prefect of Julian and with him in Constantinople (*PLRE* 1.815). Second, CTh 12.6.8, also addressed to Secundus as praetorian prefect, is dated 30 July 365 but follows a constitution with the date of 4 August 365 (12.6.7), thus contradicting the principle of strict chronogical order which the compilers of the code were instructed to observe within each title (1.1.5, 6). Mommsen, ad loc., noted crisply: "in die erratum est, neque eo Valens fuit Constantinopoli." The correct date should be some time during the winter of 364–65.

[8] The transmitted text reads: consumpta hieme festinans ad Syriam Valens iamque fines Bithynorum ingressus, etc. Since Bithynia is immediately adjacent to Constantinople, *ingressus* should surely be emended to *egressus*.

[9] Seeck, *Regesten* (1919), 227, emends the date to 2 November.

[10] News of Procopius' proclamation reached Valentinian as he approached Paris *prope kalendas Novembres* (Ammianus 26.5.8). Hence I suspect that the day of issue of CTh 12.1.13, addressed to the proconsul of Africa and received in Carthage on 17 January 366, should be emended from *XV kal(endas) Nov(embres)* to *kal(endas) Nov(embres)*.

[11] Ammianus must be preferred to Zosimus, who implies that the proclamation of Procopius occurred immediately after Valens left Constantinople (4.2) and states that the emperor heard of it in "Phrygian Galatia" (7.3).

	Goes to Nicomedia, then besieges Chalcedon until compelled to retreat to Ancyra for the winter [12]	Ammianus 26.8.2–4, cf. *CTh* 7.4.14
366 Spring	Goes to Pessinus, then advances past Mt. Olympus into Lycia	Ammianus 26.9.1–2
April 4	At Thyatira	*CTh* 4.12.6[S] (mss. Trier), cf. Zosimus 4.8.1 (no precise date)
	Stays in Sardis	Zosimus 4.8.3
May 27	Advances into Phrygia and defeats Procopius near Nacoleia	Ammianus 26.9.7; Zosimus 4.8.3; *Descr. cons.* 366.2; Socrates, *HE* 4.9.8
366–367	In Constantinople	Themistius, *Orat.* 7, 84b, 85d, cf. Zosimus 4.10.1 + 11.4 (residence in the city)
367 May 10–30	At Marcianopolis	*CTh* 12.18.1, 11.17.1
	Crosses the Danube at Daphne	Ammianus 27.5.2
Sept.25	At Durostorum	*CTh* 10.1.1 = 12.6.14
368 March 9–28	At Marcianopolis	*CTh* 10.17.2; Themistius, *Orat.*8 [13]

[12] The fact that *CTh* 7.4.14, which is addressed to the praetorian prefect Secundus, was "acc(epta) kal. Dec. Chalcedone" need not prove that Valens himself was still besieging Chalcedon.

[13] On the dates of Themistius' seventh and eighth orations, see Vanderspoel, *Themistius* (1995), 162, 168.

June–c. Sept.	At Vicus Carporum unable to cross the Danube because of floods	Ammianus 27.5.5
368 c. Oct.–369, May	Winters at Marcianopolis	Ammianus 27.5.5; *CTh* 9.1.10^S, 11^S (mss. 373); 9.34.8 (Nov. 9); 11.24.2^S (Nov. 12: mss. 370); 7.6.2 (Nov. 18); 10.20.4 (Dec. 13); 9.21.7 (March 11); 7.4.15 (May 3)
369 July 3–5	At Noviodunum	*CTh* 10.21.1; 10.16.2
	Crosses the Danube from Noviodunum	Ammianus 27.5.6
369 Aug.–370, spring	Winters at Marcianopolis	Ammianus 27.5.6; *CTh* 11.30.35^S (Aug. 1: mss. 365); 10.10.11 (Dec. 11); 7.13.2^S (Jan. 31: mss. 365)
	Signs treaty with Athanarich on a boat in mid-Danube	Ammianus 27.5.9
370 March	Goes to Constantinople	Ammianus 27.5.10; Socrates, HE 4.14.1, cf. *Descr. cons.* 370 (Church of the Holy Apostles dedicated on April 9)
	At Nicomedia, then travels in haste to Antioch	Socrates, *HE* 4.14.1; Sozomenus, *HE* 6.13.
April 30	At Antioch	*CTh* 10.19.5^S (mss. 369)

[251]

Aug.–Oct.	At Hierapolis	*CTh* 1.29.5 (Aug. 10); 7.13.6 (Sept. 18); 16.2.19[S] (Oct. 17: mss. 365)[14]
Oct. 30	At Antioch	*CTh* 15.2.2[S] (Oct. 30: mss. 369)
370–371 Dec.–May	In Constantinople	*CTh* 11.31.6[S] (Dec. 8: mss. 373); 9.16.8[S] (Dec. 12: mss. 365); 13.10.7 (Jan. 16); 13.5.14 (Feb. 11); 12.1.74 (March 1); 11.21.1 (April 7); 11.1.14[S] (May 1: mss. 366)
371 June 10	At Cyzicus	*CTh* 11.36.17
July 13	At Ancyra	*CTh* 12.1.76
371/2	In Caesarea in Cappaodocia	Gregory Nazianzenus, *Orat.* 43.47–55[15]
372 Jan. 6	In Caesarea in Cappaodocia	Gregory Nazianzenus, *Orat.* 43.52

[14] On Zosimus 4.13.2, see n. 4.

[15] On the chronology of Valens' sojourn in Caesarea, see M.-M. Hauser-Meury, *Prosopographie zu den Schriften Gregors von Nazianz* (*Theophaneia* 13, 1960) 41 n.47; G. May, *Bleibendes im Wandel der Kirchengeschichte*, ed. B. Moeller and G. Ruhbach (Tübingen, 1973), 49–57; P. Rousseau, *Basil of Caesarea* (Berkeley, 1994), 351–53. The traditional (and erroneous) date of 370–371 for Valens' sojourn is repeated by J. Bernardi, *Grégoire de Nazianze: Discours 42–43* (*Sources chrétiennes* 384, 1992), 234. However, the emperor must have passed through Caesarea twice in 370, en route to and from Antioch: hence Basil's first confrontation with Modestus, the praetorian prefect of Valens (Gregory of Nazianzus, *Orat.* 40.30–33; Gregory of Nyssa, *Contra Eunomium* 1.119–46), belongs to the spring or autumn of that year.

	In Antioch	Ammianus 29.1.4, 11; 29.2.17–18
April 4	At Seleucia	CTh 6.4.19
373 Aug. 4	At Hierapolis	CTh 14.13.1^S (mss. 365)
374 Feb. 16–May 21	In Antioch	CTh 10.20.8; 10.22.1 (March 11); 9.21.8
375 June 2	In Antioch	CTh 7.13.7
Dec. 3	In Antioch	CTh 12.1.79
376 May 29–30	In Antioch	CTh 1.28.3; 6.4.24
377 Jan. 25 to Apr. 4	In Antioch	CTh 8.7.14; 7.4.17
July 6–Aug. 9	At Hierapolis	CTh 10.16.3; 7.6.3, cf. 6.2.12 = CJ 12.1.11 (377: month missing)
Winter	In Antioch	Ammianus 31.7.1
378 Spring	Leaves Antioch to campaign against the Goths in Thrace	Jerome, Chronicle 249^b Helm; Ammianus 31.11.1; Philostorgius, HE 9.17; Socrates, HE 4.35.3, 36.1; Sozomenus, HE 6.37.17[16]

[16] Ammianus' narrative clearly puts Valens' final departure from Antioch in the spring of 378: Valens was reluctant to leave Syria, but when he did, he traveled to Constantinople without delay and advanced into Thrace within a few days (31.11.1: excitus Antiochia longitudine viarum emensa venit Constantinopolim, ubi moratus paucissimos dies . . . ad Melantiada villam Caesarianam profectus). Ammianus had already marked a transition from the consular year 377 (31.8.2) to 378 with a reference to *Februario mense* (31.10.4).

	Passes through Caesarea in Cappadocia	Basil, *Ep.* 268 [17]
May 30	Enters Constantinople	*Descr. cons.* 378.1; Socrates, *HE* 4.38.1
June 11	Leaves Constantinople for Melantias	*Descr. cons.* 378.2; Socrates, *HE* 4.38.5; Ammianus 31.11.1
	Advances to Nike, then retires to Melantias [18]	Ammianus 31.11.2, 12.1
Aug. 6	Advances from Melantias to offer battle against the Goths	Ammianus 31.12
Aug. 9	Killed at the Battle of Adrianople	Jerome, *Chronicle* 249 [c] Helm; Ammianus 31.12.10, 13.12–17; *Descr. cons.* 378.3; Socrates, *HE* 4.38.7

[17] On the allusion to the court of Valens, see *Studia Patristica* 29 (1997), 9–12.
[18] On Valens' movements after leaving Constantinople, see Wanke, *Gothenkriege* (1990), 179–87.

BIBLIOGRAPHY

The following bibliography is designed solely as a guide to the modern works cited in the present book. It includes (1) all articles, essays, reviews and papers published in scholarly journals, proceedings of learned academies, or collective volumes, whatever their subject; (2) monographs published in series that are usually catalogued by libraries under their series rather than the author; and (3) all studies whose primary focus is Ammianus Marcellinus, except the works cited by author's name or abbreviated title, which are given in the List of Abbreviations (pp. xi–xiv). (Comprehensive bibliographies of Ammianus are listed in Chapter I n. 35.)

Adler, M. "The Emperor Julian and the Jews." *Jewish Quarterly Review* 5 (1893), 591–651. (A German translation by K. Nicolai is printed as "Kaiser Julian und die Juden," *Julian Apostata* [1978], 48–111.)

Alonso-Núñez, J. M. "The Emperor Julian's *Misopogon* and the Conflict between Christianity and Paganism." *Ancient Society* 10 (1979), 311–24.

———. Review of Elliott, *Ammianus* (1983), and V. Neri, *Ammiano e il cristianesimo: religione e politica nelle Res Gestae di Ammiano Marcellino* (Bologna, 1985). *Journal of Roman Studies* 76 (1986), 328–29.

Andreotti, R. "L'opera legislativa ed amministrativa dell'imperatore Giuliano." *Nuova Rivista Storica* 14 (1930), 342–83. (A German translation by M. Elster is printed as "Kaiser Julians Gesetzgebung und Verwaltung," *Julian Apostata* [1978], 130–190.)

Arce, J. "La rebelión de los Judíos durante el gobierno de Constancio Galo Cesar: 353 d. C." *Athenaeum*, N.S. 65 (1987), 109–25.

Arjava, A. "Divorce in Later Roman Law." *Arctos* 22 (1988), 5–21.

Asmus, R. Review of R. Foerster. *Libanii Opera* 3 (Leipzig, 1906). *Wochenschrift für klassische Philologie* 24 (1907), 151–56.

Athanassiadi-Fowden, P. "A Contribution to Mithraic Theology: The Emperor Julian's Hymn to King Helios." *Journal of Theological Studies*, N.S. 28 (1977), 360–71.

———. "The Oecumenism of Iamblichus: Latent Knowledge and Its Awakening." *Journal of Roman Studies* 85 (1995), 244–50.

Auerbach, E. "Die Verhaftung des Petrus Valvomeres." *Mimesis. Dargestellte Wirklichkeit in der abendländischen Literatur*. Bern, 1946, 56–80. (Translated into English by W. R. Trask as "The Arrest of Peter Valvomeres." *Mimesis. The Representation of Reality in Western Literature*. Princeton, 1953, 50–76.)

———. "Epilegomena zu Mimesis." *Romanische Forschungen* 65 (1954), 1–18.

Aujoulat, N. "Eusébie, Hélène et Julien." *Byzantion* 53 (1983), 78–103, 421–52.

Austin, N. J. E. "Ammianus' Account of the Adrianople Campaign: Some Strategic Observations." *Acta Classica* 15 (1972), 77–83.

———. "Julian at Ctesiphon: A fresh look at Ammianus' account." *Athenaeum*, N.S. 50 (1972), 301–9.

———. "A Usurper's Claim to Legitimacy: Procopius in A.D. 365–66." *Rivista storica dell'antichità* 2 (1972), 187–94.

———. "In Support of Ammianus' Veracity." *Historia* 22 (1973), 331–35.

———. *Ammianus on Warfare: An Investigation into Ammianus' Military Knowledge*. Collection Latomus 165. Brussels, 1979.

Bacher, W. "Statements of a Contemporary of the Emperor Julian on the Rebuilding of the Temple." *The Jewish Quarterly Review* 10 (1898), 168–72.

Baglivi, N. "Da Diocleziano a Costantino: un punto di referimento storiografico in alcune interpretazioni tardoantiche." *Orpheus*, N.S. 12 (1991), 429–91.

———. *Ammianea*. Catania, 1995.

Bagnall, R. S. "Church, State and Divorce in Late Roman Egypt." In *Florilegium Columbanum. Essays in Honor of Paul Oskar Kristeller*, ed. K.-L. Selig and R. Somerville. New York, 1987, 41–61.

Bahti, T. "Auerbach's Mimesis: Figural Structure and Historical Narrative." In *After Strange Texts. The Role of Theory in the Study of Literature*, ed. G. S. Jay and D. L. Miller (University, Ala., 1985), 124–45, 181–82.

Bain, D. "'Treading Birds': An Unnoticed Use of πατέω (*Cyranides* 1.10.27, 1.19.9)." In *"Owls to Athens." Essays on Classical Subjects Presented to Sir Kenneth Dover*, ed. E. M. Craik. Oxford, 1990, 295–304.

Baker, A. "Eunapius' Νέα Ἔκδοσις and Photius," *Greek, Roman and Byzantine Studies* 29 (1988), 389–402.

Banchich, T. M. "Eunapius and Jerome." *Greek, Roman and Byzantine Studies* 27 (1986), 319–24.

———. "On Goulet's Chronology of Eunapius' Life and Work." *Journal of Hellenic Studies* 107 (1987), 164–67.

———. "Julian's School Laws: *Cod. Theod.* 13.3.5 and *Ep.* 42." *Ancient World* 24 (1993), 5–14.

———. "Nestorius ἱεροφαντεῖν τεταγμένος," *Historia* (forthcoming).

Barnes, T. D. "Hadrian and Lucius Verus." *Journal of Roman Studies* 57 (1967), 65–79.

———. "A Law of Julian." *Classical Philology* 69 (1974), 288–91.

———. "Imperial Campaigns, A.D. 285–311." *Phoenix* 30 (1976), 174–93.

———. "The *Epitome de Caesaribus* and Its Sources." *Classical Philology* 71 (1976), 258–68.

BIBLIOGRAPHY

——. "A Correspondent of Iamblichus." *Greek, Roman, and Byzantine Studies* 19 (1978) 99–106.

——. "Proconsuls of Africa, 337–392." *Phoenix* 39 (1985) 144–53, 273–74.

——. "The Career of Abinnaeus." *Phoenix* 39 (1985) 368–74.

——. "The Constantinian Reformation." In *The Crake Lectures 1984* (Sackville, 1986), 39–57. (Reprinted as *From Eusebius to Augustine. Selected Papers 1982–1993* [Aldershot, 1994], no. V.)

——. "Review of A. Martin with M. Albert, *Histoire 'Acéphale' et Index syriaque des Lettres Festales d'Athanase d'Alexandrie. Sources chrétiennes* 317 (Paris, 1985)." *Journal of Theological Studies*, N.S. 37 (1985), 576–89.

——. "The Significance of Tacitus' *Dialogus de Oratoribus.*" *Harvard Studies in Classical Philology* 90 (1986), 225–44.

——. "Regional Prefectures." In *Bonner Historia-Augusta-Colloquium 1984–1985.* Bonn, 1987, 13–23.

——. "Himerius and the Fourth Century." *Classical Philology* 82 (1987) 206–25. (Reprinted as *From Eusebius to Augustine* [1994], no. XVI.)

——. "Christians and Pagans in the Reign of Constantius." In *L'Église et l'empire au IVᵉ siècle.* Entretiens sur l'Antiquité Classique 34. Vandoeuvres-Geneva, 1989, 301–37. (Pages 322–37 are reprinted as *From Eusebius to Augustine* [1994], no. VIII.)

——. "Structure and Chronology in Ammianus, Book 14." *Harvard Studies in Classical Philology* 92 (1989), 413–22.

——. "Panegyric, History and Hagiography in Eusebius' *Life of Constantine.*" In *The Making of Orthodoxy. Essays in Honour of Henry Chadwick,* ed. R. Williams. Cambridge, 1989, 94–123. (Reprinted as *From Eusebius to Augustine* [1994], no. XI.)

——. "Literary Convention, Nostalgia, and Reality in Ammianus Marcellinus." In *Reading the Past* (1990), 59–92.

——. Review of W. Taegert, *Claudius Claudianus: Panegyricus dictus Olybrio et Probino consulibus.* Zetemata 85 (Munich, 1988). *American Journal of Philology* 111 (1990), 414–19.

——. "The Constantinian Settlement." In *Eusebius, Judaism, and Christianity,* ed. Gohei Hata and H. W. Attridge. Detroit, 1992, 635–57. (Reprinted as *From Eusebius to Augustine* [1994], no. IX.)

——. "New Year 363 in Ammianus Marcellinus. Annalistic Technique and Historical Apologetics," *Cognitio Gestorum* (1992), 1–8.

——. "Hilary of Poitiers on His Exile." *Vigiliae Christianae* 46 (1992), 129–40. (Reprinted as *From Eusebius to Augustine* [1994], no. XVII.)

——. "Praetorian Prefects, 337–361." *Zeitschrift für Papyrologie und Epigraphik* 94 (1992), 249–60. (Reprinted as *From Eusebius to Augustine* [1994], no. XIII.)

——. "The Capitulation of Liberius and Hilary of Poitiers." *Phoenix* 46 (1992), 256–65. (Reprinted as *From Eusebius to Augustine* [1994], no. XVIII.)

——. "Ammianus Marcellinus and His World." *Classical Philology* 88 (1993), 55–70.

——. "Derivative Scholarship and Historical Imagination: Edward Gibbon on Athanasius." In *Corolla Torontonensis. Studies in Honour of Ronald Morton Smith,* ed. E. I. Robbins and S. Sandahl. Toronto, 1994, 13–28.

——. "The Religious Affiliation of Consuls and Prefects, 317–361." *From Eusebius to Augustine* (1994), no. VII.

[257]

———. "Scholarship or Propaganda? Porphyry *Against the Christians* and Its Historical Setting." *Bulletin of the Institute of Classical Studies* 38 (1994), 53–65.

———. Review of J. J. O'Donnell, *Augustine: Confessions* (Oxford, 1992). *Classical Philology* 89 (1994), 293–99.

———. "Statistics and the Conversion of the Roman Aristocracy." *Journal of Roman Studies* 85 (1995), 135–47.

———."The Military Career of Martin of Tours." *Analecta Bollandiana* 114 (1996), 25–32.

———. "Emperors, Panegyrics, Prefects, Provinces, and Palaces." *Journal of Roman Archaeology* 9 (1996), 532-52.

———. "Christians and the Theater." In *The Theater in Roman Society*. E. Togo Salmon Papers 1, ed. W. J. Slater. Ann Arbor, 1996, 161–80.

———. "Christentum und Dynastische Politik (300–325)." In *Usurpationen in der Spätantike*, ed. F. Paschoud and J. Szidat. Historia Einzelschriften 111. Stuttgart, 1996, 99–109.

———. "Julian or Constantine? Observations on a Fragmentary Imperial Panegyric." In *Akten des 21. Internationalen Papyrologenkongresses in Berlin 1995*, 1, ed. B. Kramer, W. Luppe, H. Maehler, and G. Poethke. *Archiv für Papyrusforschung*, Beiheft 3. Leipzig, 1997, 67–70.

———. "The Collapse of the Homoeans in the East." *Studia Patristica* 29 (1997), 3–16.

Barnes, T. D., and J. Vanderspoel. "Julian and Themistius." *Greek, Roman and Byzantine Studies* 22 (1981) 187–89.

Barnes, T. D., and R. W. Westall. "The Conversion of the Roman Aristocracy in Prudentius' *Contra Symmachum*." *Phoenix* 45 (1991) 50–61. (Reprinted as *From Eusebins to Augustine* [1994], no. XXIII.)

Bartelink, G. J. M. "L'Empereur Julien et le vocabulaire chrétien." *Vigiliae Christianae* 11 (1957), 37–48.

———. "Eunape et le vocabulaire chrétien." *Vigiliae Christianae* 23 (1969), 293–303.

Barthes, R. "Tacite et le baroque funèbre." *Essais critiques* (Paris, 1964), 108–11. (First published in the literary journal *L'Arc*. Aix en Provence, 1959. Translated into English as "Tacitus and the Funerary Baroque" in Barthes, R., *Critical Essays*, trans. R. Howard. [Evanston, Ill., 1972], 99–102, and reprinted in *A Barthes Reader*, ed. S. Sontag. [New York, 1982], 162–66.)

Bastianini, G. "Lista dei prefetti d'Egitto dal 30° al 299ᵈ." *Zeitschrift für Papyrologie und Epigraphik* 17 (1975), 263–328.

Baynes, N. H. "Rome and Armenia in the Fourth Century." *English Historical Review* 25 (1910), 625–43. (A revised version is printed in his *Byzantine Studies and Other Essays*, ed. R. A. Humphreys and A. D. Momigliano. London, 1955, 186–208.)

———. "Julian the Apostate and Alexander the Great." *Byzantine Studies* (1955), 346–47. (Reprinted from his review of Otto Seeck, *Geschichte des Untergangs der antiken Welt* 4 (Stuttgart, 1911). *English Historical Review* 26 (1912), 755–60.)

Beck, R. "Cautes and Cautopates: Some Astronomical Observations." *Journal of Mithraic Studies* 2 (1977), 1–17.

———. "The Mysteries of Mithras." In *Voluntary Associations in the Roman World*, ed. J. S. Kloppenborg and S. G. Wilson. London/New York, 1996, 176–85.

Bickel, E. Review of Clark's Edition, vol. 2. *Göttingische Gelehrte Anzeigen* 180 (1918), 274–305.

——. "Die Vates der Kelten und die Interpretatio Graeca des südgallischen Matro-nenkultes im Eumenidenkult." *Rheinisches Museum*, N.F. 87 (1938), 193–241.

——. "Zu Ammianus Exkurs über Gallien. Zum Matronenkult." In *Festschrift für August Oxé*. Darmstadt, 1938, 164–69.

Bidez, J. "Le Philosophe Jamblique et son école." *Revue des études grecques* 32 (1919), 29–40.

Billerbeck, M. "Die dramatische Kunst des Tacitus." In *Aufstieg und Niedergang der römischen Welt* 2.33.4. Berlin/New York, 1991, 2752–71.

Birley, A. R. "Indirect Means of Tracing Marius Maximus." In *Historiae Augustae Colloquia. N. S. III: Colloquium Maceratense*, ed. G. Bonamente and G. Paci. Bari, 1995, 57–74.

Bischoff, B., and D. Nörr. *Eine unbekannte Konstitution Kaiser Julians (c. Iuliani de postulando). Abhandlungen der Bayerischen Akademie der Wissenschaften*, Philosophisch-Historische Klasse, N.F. 58. Munich, 1963.

Blanchetière, F. "Julien Philhellène, Philosémite, Antichrétien: l'affaire du Temple de Jérusalem (363)." *Journal of Jewish Studies* 31 (1980), 61–81.

Bleckmann, B. "Constantina, Vetranio, and Gallus Caesar." *Chiron* 24 (1994), 29–68.

——. "Bemerkungen zu den *Annales* des Nicomachus Flavianus." *Historia* 44 (1995), 83–99.

Blockley, R. (P. C.). "Constantius Gallus and Julian as Caesars of Constantius II." *Latomus* 31 (1972), 433–68.

——. "The Panegyric of Claudius Mamertinus on the Emperor Julian." *American Journal of Philology* 93 (1972), 437–50.

——. "Tacitean Influences on Ammianus Marcellinus." *Latomus* 32 (1973), 63–78.

——. "Ammianus Marcellinus on the Battle of Strasburg: Art and Analysis in the *History*." *Phoenix* 31 (1977), 218–31.

——. *Ammianus Marcellinus: A Selection*. Bristol, 1980.

——. "The Date of the 'Barbarian Conspiracy.'" *Britannia* 11 (1980), 223–25.

——. "Constantius II and His Generals." In *Studies in Latin Literature and Roman History*, 2, ed. C. Deroux, Collection Latomus 168, Brussels, 1980, 467–86.

——. "Ammianus Marcellinus on the Persian Invasion of A.D. 359." *Phoenix* 42 (1988), 245–60.

——. "Constantius II and Persia." In *Studies in Latin Literature and Roman History*, 5, ed. C. Deroux, Collection Latomus 206. Brussels, 1989, 465–90.

Boeft, J., den. "Ammianus graecissans?" *Cognitio Gestorum* (1992), 9–18.

Bonfils, G., de. *Ammiano Marcellino e l'imperatore*. Bari, 1986.

Borszák, I. "Von Tacitus zu Ammian." *Acta Antiqua Academiae Scientiarum Hungaricae* 24 (1976), 357–68.

Bowersock, G. W. "The Emperor Julian on his Predecessors." *Yale Classical Studies* 27 (1982), 159–72.

——. Review of Matthews, *Ammianus* (1989). *Journal of Roman Studies* 80 (1990), 244–50.

Bradbury, S. "The Date of Julian's *Letter to Themistius*." *Greek, Roman, and Byzantine Studies* 28 (1987), 235–51.

Brakman, C. *Ammianea et Annaeana*. Leiden, 1909.

——. "Ammianea." *Mnemosyne*² 47 (1919), 100–110.

Bringmann, K. "Ammianus Marcellinus als spätantiker römischer Historiker." *Antike und Abendland* 19 (1973) 44–60.

Briscoe, J. Review of P. Jal, *Tite-Live: Histoire Romaine* 34.1: *Abrégés des livres de l'histoire romaine de Tite-Live* (Paris, 1984). *Gnomon* 57 (1985), 419–24.

Brok, M. F. A. *Die perzische expeditie van Keizer Julians volgens Ammianus Marcellinus.* Diss. Leiden, publ. Groningen, 1959.

———. "Die Quellen von Ammians Exkurs über Persien." *Mnemosyne*[4] 28 (1975), 47–56.

Buck, D. F. "Eunapius on Julian's Acclamation as Augustus." *Ancient History Bulletin* 7 (1993), 73–80.

Büdinger, M. *Ammianus Marcellinus und die Eigenart seines Geschichtswerkes. Denkschriften der kaiserlichen Akademie der Wissenschaften zu Wien.* Philosophisch-historische Classe 44.5. Vienna, 1895.

Büttner-Wobst, T. "Der Tod des Kaisers Julian. Eine Quellenstudie." *Philologus* 51 (1892), 561–80. (Reprinted in *Julian Apostata* [1978], 24–47.)

Burck, E. "The Third Decade." In *Livy*, ed. T. A. Dorey. London, 1971, 21–46.

Burgess, R. W. "Quinquennial vota and the imperial consulship in the fourth and fifth centuries." *Numismatic Chronicle* 148 (1988), 77–96.

Burns, T. S. "The Battle of Adrianople." *Historia* 22 (1973), 336–45.

Calboli, G. " La credibilità di Ammiano Marcellino e la sua arte espositiva." *Bollettino di Studi Latini* 4 (1974), 67–103.

———. "Ammian und die Geschichtsschreibung seiner Zeit." In *Festschrift für Robert Muth*, ed. P. Händel and L. Meid. Innsbrucker Beiträge zur Kulturwissenschaft 2. Innsbruck, 1983, 33–53.

Caltabiano, M. "L'assassinio di Giorgio di Cappadocia (Alessandria, 361 d. C.)" *Quaderni catanesi di studi classici e medievali* 7 (1985), 17–59.

———. "I trionfi di Costanzo II." In *Studi de antichità in memoria di Clementina Gatti. Quaderni di Acme* 9. Milan, 1987, 37–46.

———. "Il carattere delle digressioni nelle *Res Gestae* di Ammiano Marcellino." In *Metodologie della ricerca sulla tarda antichità: Atti del Primo Convegno dell'Associazione di Studi Tardoantichi*, ed. A. Garzya. Naples, 1989.

Cameron, Alan. "The Roman Friends of Ammianus." *Journal of Roman Studies* 54 (1964), 15–28.

———. "Palladas and Christian Polemic." *Journal of Roman Studies* 55 (1965), 17–30.

———. "The Date of Iamblichus' Birth." *Hermes* 96 (1968), 374–76.

———. Review of Syme, *Ammianus* (1968). *Journal of Roman Studies* 61 (1971), 255–67.

———. "The Latin Revival of the Fourth Century." In *Renaissances before the Renaissance. Cultural Revivals of Late Antiquity and the Middle Ages*, ed. W. Treadgold. Stanford, 1984, 42–58, 182–84.

———. "Polyonymy in the Late Roman Arisocracy: The Case of Petronius Probus." *Journal of Roman Studies* 75 (1985), 164–82.

———. "Biondo's Ammianus: Constantius and Hormisdas at Rome." *Harvard Studies in Classical Philology* 92 (1989), 423–36.

———. "Julian and Hellenism." *Ancient World* 24 (1993), 25–29.

———. "Orfitus and Constantius: A note on Roman gold-glasses." *Journal of Roman Archaeology* 9 (1996), 295–301.

Cameron, Alan, and Averil Cameron. "Christianity and Tradition in the Historiography of the Late Empire." *Classical Quarterly*, N.S. 14 (1964), 312–28.

Cameron, Averil. "The 'Scepticism' of Procopius." *Historia* 15 (1966), 466–82.

Camus, P.-M. *Ammien Marcellin, témoin des courants culturels et religieux à la fin du IVe siècle.* Paris, 1967.

Canter, H. V. "Excursus in Greek and Roman Historians." *Philological Quarterly* 8 (1929), 233–47.

Cappelletto, R. Review of Seyfarth's Teubner edition (1978). *Rivista di filologia* 109 (1981), 80–85.

———. *Recuperi ammianei di Flavio Biondo.* Note e discussioni erudite 18. Rome, 1983.

Carroll, K. K. "The Date of Boudicca's Revolt." *Britannia* 10 (1979), 197–202.

Cichocka, H. "Die Konzeption des Exkurses im Geschichtswerk des Ammianus Marcellinus." *Eos* 63 (1975), 329–40.

———. "O Powtórzeniach w 'Res Gestae' Ammiana Marcellina." *Eos* 64 (1976), 203–22.

Clark, C. U. *The Text Tradition of Ammianus Marcellinus.* New Haven, 1904.

Classen, C. J. "Greek and Roman in Ammianus Marcellinus' History." *Museum Africum* 1 (1972), 39–47.

———. "Nec spuens aut os aut nasum tergens vel fricans (Amm. Marc. XVI 10, 10)." *Rheinisches Museum,* N.F. 131 (1988), 177–86.

Clive, J. "Macaulay's Historical Imagination." *Review of English Literature* 1.4 (1960), 20–28. (Reprinted in his *Not by Fact Alone; Essays on the Writing and Reading of History.* New York, 1989, 66–73.)

Colin, J. "Les Vendages dionysiaques et la légende de Messaline (48 ap. J.-C.)." *Les études classiques* 24 (1956), 25–39.

Conduché, D. "Ammien Marcellin et la mort de Julien." *Latomus* 24 (1965), 359–80.

Corbier, M. "Les Familles clarissimes d'Afrique proconsulaire (Ier–IIIe siècle). In *Epigrafia e ordine senatorio (Tituli* 5, 1982, pub. 1984), 685–754.

Craddock, P. B. "Edward Gibbon and the 'Ruins of the Capitol.'" In *Roman Images,* ed. A. Patterson. Selected Papers from the English Institute, N.S. 8. Baltimore/London, 1984, 63–82.

Crump, G. A. *Ammianus Marcellinus as a Military Historian.* Historia Einzelschriften 27. Wiesbaden, 1975.

Cumont, F. "La Marche de l'empereur Julien d'Antioche à l'Euphrate." *Études syriennes* (1917), 1–33.

———. "Les Syriens en Espagne et les Adonies à Séville." *Syria* 8 (1927), 330–41.

Curtius, E. R. "Die Lehre von den drei Stilen in Altertum und Mittelalter (zu Auerbach's *Mimesis).*" *Romanische Forschungen* 64 (1952), 57–70.

Daube, D. "The Marriage of Justinian and Theodora. Legal and theological reflections." *Catholic University of America Law Review* 16 (1966–1967), 380–89.

Dautremer, L. *Ammien Marcellin. Étude d'histoire littéraire.* Diss. Paris, publ. Lille, 1899.

Debru, A. "La Phrase narrative d'Ammien Marcellin." *Revue de philologie*[3] 66 (1992), 267–87.

Delehaye, H. "Saints de Thrace et de Mésie." *Analecta Bollandiana* 31 (1912), 161–300.

D'Elia, S. "Ammiano Marcellino e il cristianesimo." *Studi Romani* 10 (1962), 372–90.

Demandt, A. "Die tripolitanischen Wirren unter Valentinian I." *Byzantion* 38 (1968), 333–63.

——. "Die afrikanischen Unruhen unter Valentinian I." In *Afrika und Rom in der Antike*, ed. H.-J. Diesner, H. Barth, and H.-D. Zimmermann. *Wissenschaftliche Beiträge der Martin-Luther-Universität Halle-Wittenberg*, 1968–6 (C 8). Halle, 1968, 277–92.

——. "Der Tod des älteren Theodosius." *Historia* 17 (1969), 598–626.

——. *Verformungstendenzen in der Überlieferung antiker Sonnen- und Mondfinsternisse. Abhandlungen der Akademie der Wissenschaften und der Literatur, Mainz.* Geistes- und Sozialwissenschaftliche Klasse 1970, Nr. 7, 467–527.

——. "Die Feldzüge des älteren Theodosius." *Hermes* 100 (1972), 81–113.

——. "Das Ende des Altertums in metaphorischer Deutung." *Gymnasium* 87 (1980), 178–204.

——. "Der spätrömische Militäradel." *Chiron* 10 (1980), 609–36.

Desnier, J. L. "Salutius–Salustius." *Revue des études anciennes* 85 (1983), 53–65.

Dewing, H. B. "The Origin of the Accentual Prose Rhythm in Greek." *American Journal of Philology* 31 (1910), 312–28.

Dickison, S. "Claudius: Saturnalicius Princeps." *Latomus* 36 (1977), 634–47.

Dilleman, L. "Ammien Marcellin et le pays de l'Euphrate et du Tigre." *Syria* 38 (1961), 87–158.

Di Maio, M., and W. H. Arnold. "Per Vim, Per Caedem, Per Bellum: A Study of Murder and Ecclesiastical Politics in the Year 337 A.D." *Byzantion* 62 (1992), 158–211.

Dittrich, U.-B. *Die Beziehungen Roms zu den Sarmaten und Quaden im vierten Jahrhundert n. Chr. (nach der Darstellung des Ammianus Marcellinus).* Diss. Bonn, 1984.

Dodds, E. H. "Theurgy and Its Relation to Neoplatonism." *Journal of Roman Studies* 37 (1947), 55–69. (Reprinted in his *The Greeks and the Irrational* [Berkeley, 1951], 283–311.)

——. "New Light on the Chaldean Oracles." *Harvard Theological Review* 54 (1961), 263–73. (Reprinted in H. Lewy, *Chaldean Oracles and Theurgy: Mysticism, Magic, and Platonism in the Later Roman Empire* [2], ed. M. Tardieu [Paris, 1978], 693–701.)

Downey, G. "The Economic Crisis at Antioch under Julian the Apostate." In *Studies in Roman Social and Economic History in Honor of Alan Chester Johnson*, ed. P. R. Coleman-Norton. Princeton, 1951, 312–21.

Drijvers, J. W. "Ammianus Marcellinus 23.1.2–3: The Rebuilding of the Temple in Jerusalem." *Cognitio Gestorum* (1992), 19–26.

Drinkwater, J. F. "The 'Pagan Underground,' Constantius II's 'Secret Service,' the survival, and the Usurpation of Julian the Apostate." In *Studies in Latin Literature and Roman History*, ed. C. Deroux, 3. Collection Latomus 180. Brussels, 1983, 348–87.

——. "Silvanus, Ursicinus, and Ammianus: Fact or Fiction?" In *Studies in Latin Literature and Roman History*, ed. C. Deroux 7. Collection Latomus 227. Brussels, 1994, 568–76.

Dummer, J. "Fl. Artemius Dux Aegypti." *Archiv für Papyrusforschung* 21 (1971), 121–44.

Edbrooke, R. O. "Constantius II and Hormisdas in the Forum of Trajan." *Mnemosyne* [4] 28 (1975), 412–17.

Ehling, K. H. "Der Ausgang des Perserfeldzuges in der Münzpropaganda des Jovian." *Klio* 78 (1996), 186–91.

Ehrhardt, C. T. H. R. "Speeches before Battle?" *Historia* 44 (1995), 120–21.

Ehrismann, H. *De temporum et modorum usu Ammianeo.* Diss. Strassburg, 1886.

Eitrem, S. "La Théurgie chez les néo-platoniciens et dans les papyrus magiques." *Symbolae Osloenses* 22 (1942), 49–79.

Elbern, S. "Das Gotenmassaker in Kleinasien (378 n. Chr.)." *Hermes* 115 (1987), 99–106.

Emmett, A. "Introductions and Conclusions to Digressions in Ammianus Marcellinus." *Museum Philologum Londiniense* 5 (1981), 15–33.

——. "The Digressions in the Lost Books of Ammianus Marcellinus." *History and Historians* (1983), 42–53.

Ensslin, W. "Kaiser Julians Gesetzgebungswerk und Reichsverwaltung." *Klio* 18 (1922–1923), 104–99.

Errington, R. M. "The Accession of Theodosius I." *Klio* 78 (1996), 438–53.

Fesser, H. *Sprachliche Beobachtungen zu Ammianus Marcellinus.* Diss. Breslau, 1932.

Finke, H. *Ammianus Marcellinus und seine Quellen zur Geschichte der römischen Republik.* Diss. Heidelberg, 1904.

Flach, D. "Von Tacitus zu Ammian." *Historia* 21 (1972), 333–50.

Fletcher, G. B. A. "Stylistic Borrowings and Parallels in Ammianus Marcellinus." *Revue de philologie*³ 11 (1937), 377–95.

——. "On Varro, Tibullus, Tacitus, and Ammianus Marcellinus." In *Ut pictura poesis: Studia Latina Petro Iohanni Enk septuagenario oblata.* Leiden, 1995, 75–86.

Fontaine, J. "Ammien Marcellin, historien romantique." *Bulletin de l'Association Guillaume Budé* 28 (1969), 417–35.

——. "Le Julien d'Ammien." In *L'Empereur Julien. De l'histoire à la légende, 331–1715,* ed. R. Braun and J. Riché. Paris, 1978, 31–65.

——. "Valeurs de vie et formes esthétiques dans l'histoire d'Ammien Marcellin." In *Le Transformazioni della Cultura nella tarda Antichità: Atti del Convegno tenuto a Catania, Università degli Studi, 27 sett.- 2 Ott. 1982,* Rome, 1985, 781–808.

——. "Le Style d'Ammien et l'esthétique théodosienne." *Cognitio Gestorum* (1992), 27–37.

Fornara, C. W. "The Order of Events in Ammianus Marcellinus 23.5.4–25." *American Journal of Ancient History* 10 (1985, publ. 1994), 28–40.

——. "The Prefaces of Ammianus Marcellinus." In *Cabinet of the Muses: Essays on Classical and Comparative Literature in Honor of Thomas G. Rosenmeyer,* ed. M. Griffith and D. J. Mastronarde. Atlanta, 1990, 163–72.

——. "Julian's Persian Expedition in Ammianus and Zosimus." *Journal of Hellenic Studies* 111 (1991), 1–15.

——. "Studies in Ammianus Marcellinus I: The Letter of Libanius and Ammianus' Connection with Antioch." *Historia* 41 (1992), 328–44.

——. "Studies in Ammianus Marcellinus II: Ammianus' Knowledge and Use of Greek and Latin Literature." *Historia* 41 (1992), 420–38.

Fowden, G. "Bishops and Temples in the Eastern Roman Empire, A.D. 320–445." *Journal of Theological Studies,* N.S. 29 (1978), 53–78.

Fraenkel, E. "Das Geschlecht von *dies.*" *Glotta* 8 (1917) 26–68. (Reprinted in his *Kleine Beiträge zur klassischen Philologie* 1. Rome, 1964, 27–72.)

——. "Tacitus." *Neue Jahrbücher für Wissenschaft und Jugendbildung* 8 (1932), 309–32. (Reprinted in his *Kleine Beiträge* 2 [1964], 218–33.)

Frakes, R. M. "Ammianus Marcellinus and Osrhoene." *Ancient History Bulletin* 7 (1993), 143–47.

——. "Cross-References to the Lost Books of Ammianus Marcellinus." *Phoenix* 49 (1995), 232–46.

Frank, R. I. "*Commendabiles* in Ammianus." *American Journal of Philology* 88 (1967), 309–18.

Führer, R. "Noch ein Akrostichon in den Kyraniden." *Zeitschrift für Papyrologie und Epigraphik* 58 (1985), 270.

Funke, H. "Majestäts- und Magieprozesse bei Ammianus Marcellinus." *Jahrbuch für Antike und Christentum* 10 (1967), 145–75.

Gärtner, H. *Einige Überlegungen zur kaiserzeitlichen Panegyrik und zu Ammians Charakteristik des Kaisers Julian. Abhandlungen der Akademie der Wissenschaften und der Literatur, Mainz. Geistes- und Sozialwissenschaftliche Klasse* 1968, Nr. 10, 499–529.

———. "Zu Ammianus Marcellinus." *Hermes* 97 (1969), 362–71.

Gardthausen, V. *Die geographischen Quellen Ammians.* Leipzig, 1873. (Also published in *Jahrbücher für classische Philologie,* Supplementband 6 [1873], 509–56.)

———. Review of Clark's edition, vol. 1. *Wochenschrift für klassische Philologie* 28 (1911), 215–17.

———. "Studien zu Ammianus Marcellinus." *Berliner philologische Wochenschrift* 37 (1917), 1471–80, 1505–12.

Garsoïan, N. G. "Politique ou orthodoxie? L'Arménie au quatrième siècle." *Revue des études arméniennes,* N.S. 4 (1967), 297–320. (Reprinted in her *Armenia between Byzantium and the Sasanians.* London, 1985, no. IV.)

Garzya, A. "I Germani nella letteratura greca tardoantica." In *Il mandarino e il quotidiano. Saggi sulla letterature tardoantica e bizantina. Saggi Bibliopolis* 14 (Naples, 1983), 171–98. (Subsequently published in *Byzance: Hommage à André N. Stratos.* Athens, 1986, 425–44).

Geiger, J. "Ammianus Marcellinus and the Jewish Revolt under Gallus: A Note." *Liverpool Classical Monthly* 4 (1979), 77.

———. "The Last Jewish Revolt against Rome: A Reconsideration." *Scripta Classica Israelica* 5 (1979–1980), 250–57.

Ghosh, P. R. "Gibbon's Dark Ages: Some Remarks on the Genesis of the *Decline and Fall.*" *Journal of Roman Studies* 73 (1983), 1–23.

———. "Gibbon Observed," *Journal of Roman Studies* 81 (1991), 132–56.

Gillett, A. "The Date and Circumstances of Olympiodorus of Thebes." *Traditio* 48 (1993), 1–29.

Gilliam, J. F. "Titus in Julian's *Caesares.*" *American Journal of Philology* 88 (1967), 203–03.

———. "Ammianus and the Historia Augusta: The Lost Books and the Period 117–285." In *Bonner Historia-Augusta-Colloquium 1970.* Bonn, 1972, 125–47.

Gilmartin, K. "Corbulo's Campaigns in the East: An analysis of Tacitus' account." *Historia* 22 (1973), 583–626.

Gimazane, J. *Ammien Marcellin. Sa vie et son œuvre.* Diss. Bordeaux, publ. Toulouse, 1889.

Gleason, M. W. "Festive Satire: Julian's Misopogon and the New Year at Antioch." *Journal of Roman Studies* 76 (1986), 106–19.

Goffart, W. "Did Julian Combat Venal *suffragium*? A Note on CTh 2.29.1." *Classical Philology* 65 (1970), 145–51.

———. "Zosimus: The First Historian of Rome's Fall." *American Historical Review* 76 (1971) 412–41. (Reprinted in his *Rome's Fall and After.* London/Ronceverte, 1989), 81–110.)

Gualandri, I. "Fonti geografiche di Ammiano Marcellino XXII 8." *Parola del Passato* 23 (1968), 199–211.

Günther, O. *Quaestiones Ammianeae criticae.* Diss. Göttingen, 1888.

Gutschmid, A., von. Review of V. Gardthausen, "Die geographischen Quellen Ammians." *Litterarisches Cenralblatt für Deutschland* 24 (1873), 737–39. (Reprinted in his *Kleine Schriften*, 5, ed. F. Rühl. Leipzig, 1894, 366–70.)

———. "Cassius Dio Cocceianus." In his *Kleine Shriften*, 5, 1894, 547–62.

———."Ammianus Marcellinus." In his *Kleine Schriften*, 5, 1894, 567–84.

Haehling, R. von. "Ammians Darstellung der Thronbesteigung Jovians im Lichte der heidnisch-christlichen Auseinandersetzung." In *Bonner Festgabe Johannes Straub zum 65. Geburtstag am 18 October 1977 dargebracht*, ed. A. Lippold and N. Himmelmann. Beihefte der Bonner Jahrbücher 39. Bonn, 1977, 347–58.

———. "Ammianus Marcellinus und der Prozess von Scythopolis." *Jahrbuch für Antike und Christentum* 21 (1978), 74–101.

Hagendahl, H. *Studia Ammianea*. Diss. Uppsala, 1921. (Also published as *Uppsala Universitets Årsskrift*, Filosofi, Språkvetenskap och Historiska Vetenskaper 1921.2.)

———. "De abundantia sermonis Ammianei." *Eranos* 22 (1924), 161–216.

Hamblenne, P. "Une 'conjuration' sous Valentinien?" *Byzantion* 50 (1980), 198–225.

Hansen, G. C. "Rhythmisches und Metrisches zu Themistios." *Byzantinische Zeitschrift* 55 (1962), 235–40.

Hansen, M. H. "The Battle Exhortation in Ancient Historiography. Fact or Fiction?" *Historia* 42 (1993), 161–80.

Harmon, A. M. *The Clausula in Ammianus Marcellinus. Transactions of the Connecticut Academy of Arts and Sciences* 16.2 New Haven, 1910, 117–245.

Harries, J. "The Roman Imperial Quaestor from Constantius to Theodosius II." *Journal of Roman Studies* 78 (1988), 148–72.

Hassenstein, G. *De Syntaxi Ammiani Marcellini*. Diss. Leipzig, publ. Königsberg, 1877.

Häussler, R. "Vom Ursprung und Wandel des Lebensaltervergleichs." *Hermes* 92 (1964), 313–41.

Heil, M. "Zwei spätantike Statthalter aus Epirus und Achaia." *Zeitschrift für Papyrologie und Epigraphik* 108 (1995), 159–65.

Helm, R. "Hieronymus und Eutrop." *Rheinisches Museum*, N.F. 76 (1927), 138–70, 254–306.

———. *Hieronymus' Zusätze in Eusebius' Chronik und ihr Wert für die Literaturgeschichte. Philologus*, Supplementband 21.2, Leipzig, 1929.

Helttula, A. "Post Depositum Militiae Munus. Official phraseology in Ammianus Marcellinus." In *Studia in honorem Iiro Kajanto. Arctos*, Supplement 2. Helsinki, 1985, 41–56.

Hengst, D. den. "Ammianus Marcellinus on Astronomy." *Mnemosyne*[4] 39 (1986), 136–41.

———. "The Scientific Digressions in Ammianus' *Res Gestae*." *Cognitio Gestorum* (1992), 39–46.

Henry, M. "Le Témoignage de Libanius et les phénomènes sismiques du IV siècle de notre ère. Essai d'interprétation." *Phoenix* 39 (1985), 36–61.

Hertz, M. "Aulus Gellius und Ammianus Marcellinus." *Hermes* 8 (1874), 257–302.

———. *De Ammiani Marcellini studiis sallustianis dissertatio*. Breslau, 1874. (Prefixed to the *Index Scholarum in Universitate Litterarum Vratislavensi per aestatem anni MDCCCLXXIV habendarum*. Breslau, 1874.)

Hexter, J. H. "Storm over the Gentry." *Encounter* 10 (1958), 22–34. (Reprinted with substantial addenda in his *Reappraisals in History*. Evanston, Ill., 1961, 117–62.)

Heyen, J. "A propos de la conception historique d'Ammien Marcellin (Ut miles quondam et Graecus 31, 16, 9)." *Latomus* 26 (1968), 191–96.

Hohl, E. "Der Prätorianeraufstand unter Otho." *Klio* 32 (1939), 307–24.

Holdheim, W. W. "Auerbach's Mimesis: Aesthetics as Historical Understanding." *CLIO* 10 (1981), 143–56.

Hopkins, K. "The Political Power of Eunuchs." *Proceedings of the Cambridge Philological Society* 189 (1963), 62–80. (Reprinted with revisions in his *Conquerors and Slaves. Sociological Studies in Roman History*, 1 [Cambridge, 1978], 172–96.)

Hunt, E. D. "Christians and Christianity in Ammianus Marcellinus." *Classical Quarterly*, N.S. 35 (1985), 186–200.

———. "Christianity in Ammianus Marcellinus Revisited." *Studia Patristica* 24 (1993), 108–13.

Jacob-Karau, L. *Das Bild der Frau in den "Res Gestae" des Ammianus Marcellinus*. Diss. Berlin, 1971.

Jacques, F. and B. Bousquet. "Le Raz de marée de 21 juillet 365. Du cataclysme local à la catastrophe cosmique." *Mélanges de l'École française de Rome (Antiquité)* 96 (1984), 423–61.

Jal, P. "Sur la Composition de la 'Ve Décade' de Tite-Live." *Revue de Philologie*[3] 49 (1975), 278–85.

Jannacone, S. *Ammiano Marcellino, profilo storico-critico*. Naples, 1960.

Jeep, L. "Die verlorenen Bücher des Ammianus." *Rheinisches Museum*, N.F. 43 (1888), 60–72.

———. "Priscianus. Beiträge zur Überlieferungsgeschichte der Römischen Literatur." *Philologus* 67 (1908), 12–51; 68 (1909), 1–51; 71 (1912), 491–517.

Jeffreys, R. "The Date of Messalla's Death." *Classical Quarterly*, N.S. 35 (1985), 140–48.

Jonge, P., de. "Scarcity of Corn and Corn-Prices in Ammianus Marcellinus." *Mnemosyne*[4] 1 (1948) 238–45.

Kaegi, W. E. "Constantine's and Julian's Strategies of Strategic Surprise against the Persians." *Athenaeum*, N.S. 59 (1981), 209–13.

Kallenberg, H. *Quaestiones grammaticae Ammianeae*. Diss. Halle, 1868.

Karau, L., and I. Ulmann. "Sprachliche Beobachtungen zu einigen Ammian-Stellen." *Klio* 48 (1967), 227–35.

Kellerbauer, A. "Kritische Kleinigkeiten (zu Ammianus Marcellinus)." *Blätter für das bayerische Gymnasialschulwesen* 7 (1871), 11–24; 9 (1873), 81–91, 127–41.

Kiessling, A. Review of F. Eyssenhardt, *Ammiani Marcellini rerum gestarum libri qui supersunt* (Berlin, 1871). *Jahrbücher für classische Philologie* 103 (1871), 481–504.

King, C. "The Veracity of Ammianus Marcellinus' Description of the Huns." *American Journal of Ancient History* 12 (1987, publ. 1995), 77–95.

Klein, W. *Studien zu Ammianus Marcellinus*. *Klio*, Beiheft 13, 1914.

Koch, H. "Comment l'empereur Julien tâcha de fonder une église païenne." *Revue belge de philologie et d'histoire* 6 (1927), 123–46; 7 (1928), 49–82, 511–50, 1363–85.

Kohns, H. P. "Die Zeitkritik in den Romexkursen des Ammianus Marcellinus: zu Amm. Marc.1 4.6.3–26; 28.4.6–35." *Chiron* 5 (1975) 485–91.

Laistner, M. L. W. "Ammianus Marcellinus." In his *The Greater Roman Historians*. Sather Classical Lectures 21. Berkeley/Los Angeles, 1947, 141–61, 180–83.

Lana, I. "Ammiano Marcellino e la sua conoscenza degli autori greci." In *Politica, cultura e religione nell'Impero romano (secoli IV–VI) tra Oriente e Occidente. Atti del Secondo Convegno dell'Associazione di Studi Tardoantichi*, ed. F. Conca, I. Gualandri and G. Lozza. Naples, 1993, 23–40.

Landauer, C. "Mimesis and Erich Auerbach's Self-Mythologising." *German Studies Review* 11 (1988), 83–96.

Lane Fox, R. J. "The Itinerary of Alexander: Constantius to Julian." *Classical Quarterly*, N.S. 47 (1997), 239–52.

Lautenbacher, F. Review of O. Rossbach, *Titi Livi periochae* (Leipzig, 1910). *Berliner Philologische Wochenschrift* 30 (1910), 1186–93.

Lee, A. D. "Campaign Preparations in Late Roman-Persian Warfare." In *The Eastern Frontier of the Roman Empire*, ed. D. H. French and C. S. Lightfoot, British Institute of Archaeology at Ankara, Monograph No. 11. British Archaeological Reports, International Series 553. Oxford, 1989, 257–65.

Lenski, N. "*Initium mali Romano imperio*: Contemporary Reactions to the Battle of Adrianople." *Transactions of the American Philological Association* 127 (1997), 129–68.

Leo, F. *Tacitus. Rede zur Feier des Geburtstags des Kaisers*. Göttingen, 1896. (Reprinted with slight abridgement in his *Ausgwählte Kleine Schriften* 2. Rome, 1960, 263–76. Also reprinted in *Tacitus*, ed. V. Pöschl. Wege der Forschung 97 [Darmstadt, 1969], 1–15.)

——. Review of Clark's edition, vol. 1. *Göttingische Gelehrte Anzeigen* 173 (1911) 132–34.

Lepelley, C. "L'Afrique du Nord et le prétendu séisme universel du 21 juillet 365." *Mélanges de l'École française de Rome (Antiquité)* 96 (1984), 463–90.

——. "Le Présage du nouveau désastre de Cannes: La signification du raz de marée de 21 juillet 365 dans l'imagination d'Ammien Marcellin." *Kokalos* 36–37 (1990–1991), 359–72.

Levenson, D. "Julian's Attempt to Rebuild the Temple: An Inventory of Ancient and Medieval Sources." In *Of Scribes and Scrolls: Studies on the Hebrew Bible, Intertestamental Judaism, and Christian Origins. Presented to John Strugnell on the Occasion of His Sixtieth Birthday*, ed. H. W. Attridge, J. J. Collins, and T. H. Tobin. Lanham, 1990, 261–79.

Lewy, Y. (H.). "Julian the Apostate and the Building of the Temple." In *The Jerusalem Cathedra: Studies in the History, Archaeology, Geography and Ethnography of the Land of Israel*, 3, ed. L. I. Levine. Jerusalem/Detroit, 1983, 70–96.

Liebeschuetz, J. H. G. W. "Ammianus, Julian, and Divination." In *Roma Renascens: Beiträge zur Spätantike und Rezeptionsgeschichte. Ilona Opelt von ihren Freunden und Schülern zum 9.7.1988 in Verehrung gewidmet*, ed. M. Wissemann. Frankfurt, 1988, 198–213. (Reprinted in his *From Diocletian to the Arab Conquest: Change in the Late Roman Empire* [Aldershot, 1990], no. III.)

Liesenberg, F. *Die Sprache des Ammianus Marcellinus: Versuch einer allgemeinen Charakteristik derselben nach Wortschatz, Syntax und Stil. Jahresbericht über das Herzogliche Gymnasium zu Blankenburg am Harz Ostern 1887 bis Ostern 1888*, 1–33; *Ostern 1888 bis Ostern 1889*, 1–21; *Ostern 1889 bis Ostern 1890*, 1–71. Blankenburg, 1888–1890.

Lieu, S. M. C. "From Villain to Saint and Martyr. The Life and After-life of Flavius Artemius Dux Aegypti." *Byzantine and Modern Greek Studies* 20 (1996), 56–76. (An abbreviated version of the article is included in *From Constantine to Julian: Pagan and Byzantine Views*, ed. S. Lieu and D. Montserrat [London, 1996], 213–23.)

BIBLIOGRAPHY

Lightfoot, C. S. "Tilli—A Late Roman *Equites* Fort on the Tigris." In *The Defence of the Roman and Byzantine East*, ed. P. Freeman and D. Kennedy. British Institute of Archaeology at Ankara, Monograph No. 8. British Archaeological Reports, International Series 297. Oxford, 1986, 509–29.

——. "Facts and Fiction—The Third Siege of Nisibis (A.D. 350)." *Historia* 37 (1988), 105–25.

Long, J. "A New Solidus of Julian Caesar." *American Numismatic Society Museum Notes* 33 (1988), 111–18.

——. "Structures of Irony in Julian's Misopogon." *Ancient World* 24 (1993), 15–23.

Luce, T. J. "The Dating of Livy's First Decade." *Transactions of the American Philological Association* 96 (1965), 209–40.

Maas, P. "Rhythmisches zu der Kunstprosa des Konstantinos Manasses." *Byzantinische Zeitschrift* 11 (1902), 505–12. (Reprinted with marginal notes by the author in his *Kleine Schriften*, ed. W. Buchwald [Munich, 1973], 426–34.

Macaulay, T. B. "History." *Edinburgh Review* 47 (1828), 331–67. (Often reprinted: the standard texts are [1] the Albany edition of *The Works of Lord Macaulay* 7 = *Essays and Biographies* 1 [London, 1898], 167–220, [2] the Whitehall edition of *The Miscellaneous Works of Lord Macaulay* 1 = *Critical and Historical Essays* 1 [New York, 1898], 180–238.)

MacMullen, R. "Some Pictures in Ammianus Marcellinus." *The Art Bulletin* 46 (1964), 435–55. (Reprinted in his *Changes in the Roman Empire. Essays in the Ordinary* [Princeton, 1990], 78–106, 301–312.)

McCoy, M. B. "Corruption in the Western Empire: The Career of Sextus Petronius Probus." *Ancient World* 11 (1985), 101–6.

McCulloch, H. Y. "Literary Augury at the End of *Annals* XIII." *Phoenix* 34 (1980), 237–42.

McLynn, N. "The Forth Century *Taurobolium*." *Phoenix* 50 (1995), 312–30.

Madden, W. A. "Macaulay's Style." *The Art of Victorian Prose*, ed. G. Levine and W. Madden. New York, 1968, 127–53.

Malissard, A. "Tacite et le théâtre ou la mort en scène." In *Theater und Gesellschaft im Imperium Romanum*, ed. J. Blänsdorf. *Mainzer Forschungen zu Drama und Theater* 4. Tübingen, 1990, 213–22.

Malotet, A. *De Ammiani Marcellini digressionibus quae ad externas gentes pertineant.* Diss. Paris, 1898.

Manfredini, A. D. "Natalità e legislazione tardoimperiale." *Atti dell'Accademia Romanistica Costantiniana* 8 (Perugia, 1990), 517–33.

Marcone, A. "Un panegirico rovesciato: Pluralità di modelli e contaminazione letteraria nel *Misopogon* giulianeo." *Revue des études augustiniennes* 30 (1984), 226–39.

Marrou, H.-I. "Synesius of Cyrene and Alexandrian Neoplatonism." In *The Conflict between Paganism and Christianity in the Fourth Century*, ed. A. Momigliano. Oxford, 1963, 126–50.

Marshall, A. J. "Ladies in Waiting: The Role of Women in Tacitus' Histories." *Ancient Society* 15–17 (1984–86), 167–84.

Matthews, J. F. "Continuity in a Roman Family: The Rufii Festi of Volsinii." *Historia* 16 (1967), 484–507. (Reprinted as *Political Life and Culture in Late Roman Society* [London, 1985], no. VI.)

———. "Mauretania in Ammianus and the Notitia." In *Aspects of the Notitia Dignitatum*, ed. R. Goodburn and P. Bartholemew. British Archaeological Reports, Supplementary Series 15. Oxford, 1976, 157–86. (Reprinted as *Political Life and Culture* [1985], no. XI.)

———. "The New Traditionalist." *Times Literary Supplement*, 3 November 1978, 1283.

———. "Ammianus Marcellinus." *Ancient Writers: Greece and Rome*, 2, ed. T. J. Luce. New York, 1982, 1117–38. (Reprinted as *Political Life and Culture* [1985], no. I.)

———. "Ammianus' Historical Evolution." *History and Historians* (1983), 30–41. (Reprinted as *Political Life and Culture* [1985], no. II.)

———. "Ammianus and the Eternity of Rome." In *The Inheritance of Historiography, 350–900*, ed. C. Holdsworth and T. P. Wiseman. Exeter Studies in History 12. Exeter, 1986, 17–29.

———. "Peter Valvomeres, Re-arrested." In *Homo Viator. Classical Essays for John Bramble*. Bristol/Oak Park, 1987, 277–84.

———. "Ammianus on Roman Law and Lawyers." *Cognitio Gestorum* (1992), 47–57.

———. "The Origin of Ammianus." *Classical Quarterly*, N.S. 44 (1994), 252–69.

May, G. "Basilius der Grosse und der Römische Staat. Kirchenhistorische Studien." In *Bleibendes im Wandel der Kirchengeschichte*, ed. B. Moeller and G. Ruhbach. Tübingen, 1973, 47–70.

Mendell, C. W. "Dramatic Construction in Tacitus' Annals." *Yale Classical Studies* 5 (1935), 3–53.

Meyer, W. *Der accentuierte Satzschluß in der griechischen Prosa vom 4. bis 16. Jahrhundert*. Göttingen, 1891. (Reprinted with a postscript in his *Gesammelte Abhandlungen zur mittellateinischen Rhythmik*, 2 [Berlin, 1905], 202–35.)

———. Review of L. Havet, *La Prose métrique de Symmaque et les origines métriques du cursus* (Paris, 1892). *Göttingsche Gelehrte Anzeigen* 1893, Nr. 1.1–27. (Reprinted with substantial addenda as "Die rhythmische lateinische Prosa," in his *Gesammelte Abhandlungen*, 2 [1905], 236–86.)

———. "Über Ursprung und Blüte der mittellateinischen Dichtungsformen." In *Fragmenta Burana. Festschrift der königlichen Gesellschaft der Wissenschaften in Göttingen*. Göttingen, 1901, 145–86. (Reprinted in his *Gesammelte Abhandlungen*, 1. [1905], 1–58.)

Michael, H. *De Ammiani Marcellini studiis Ciceronianis*. Diss. Breslau, 1874.

———. *Die verlorenen Bücher des Ammianus Marcellinus. Ein Beitrag zur römischen Literaturgeschichte*. Prog. Breslau, 1880.

Millar, F. "Empire and City, Augustus to Julian: Obligations, Excuses and Status." *Journal of Roman Studies* 73 (1983), 76–96.

Moes, R. *Les Hellénismes de l'époque théodosienne. Recherches sur le vocabulaire d'origine grecque chez Ammien, Claudien et l'Histoire Auguste*. Strasbourg, 1980.

Momigliano, A. "The Lonely Historian Ammianus Marcellinus." *Annali della Scuola Superiore Normale di Pisa*, Classe di Lettere e filosofia, Series III. 4 (1974), 1393–1407. (Reprinted in his *Essays in Ancient and Modern Historiography* [Oxford, 1977], 127–40. Also reprinted in his *Sesto Contributo alla Storia degli Studi Classici e del Mondo Antico*, 1 [Rome, 1980], 143–57.)

Mommsen, T. "Ammians Geographica." *Hermes* 16 (1881), 602–36. (Reprinted in his *Gesammelte Schriften*, 7 [Berlin, 1909], 393–425.)

——. "Die älteste Handschrift der Chronik des Hieronymus." *Hermes* 24 (1889), 393–401. (Reprinted in his *Gesammelte Schriften* 7 [1909], 597–605.)

Mor, M. "The Events of 351–352 in Palestine—The Last Revolt against Rome?" In *The Eastern Frontier of the Roman Empire*, ed. D. H. French and C. S. Lightfoot. British Institute of Archaeology at Ankara, Monograph No. 11. British Archaeological Reports, International Series 553. Oxford, 1989, 335–53.

Moreau, J. "Sur un Passage d'Ammien Marcellin (XXX, 5, 11–12)." In *Mélanges Isidore Lévy. Annuaire de l'Institut de Philologie et d'Histoire orientales de l'Université libre de Bruxelles*, 13. (Brussels, 1953, publ. 1955), 423–31.

Müller-Seidl, I. "Die Usurpation Julians des Abtrünnigen im Lichte seiner Germanenpolitik." *Historische Zeitschrift* 180 (1955), 225–44.

Naudé, C. P. T. *Ammianus Marcellinus in die Lig van die Antieke Geskiedskrywing*. Diss. Leiden, 1956.

——. "Battles and Sieges in Ammianus Marcellinus." *Acta Classica* 1 (1958), 92–105. (This volume was also published separately as *Roman Life and Letters. Studies presented to T. J. Haarhoff* [Cape Town, 1959].)

——. Review of A. Demandt, *Zeitkritik* (1965). *Gnomon* 41 (1969), 481–84.

——. "The Date of the Later Books of Ammianus Marcellinus." *American Journal of Ancient History* 9 (1984, publ. 1990), 70–94.

Neri, V. "Ammiano Marcellino e l'elezione di Valentiniano." *Rivista Storica dell'Antichità* 15 (1985), 153–82.

——. *Ammiano e il Cristianesimo. Religione e Politica nelle "Res Gestae" di Ammiano Marcellino. Studi di Storia Antica*, 11. Bologna, 1985.

——. "Ammianus' Definition of Christianity as *absoluta et simplex religio*." *Cognitio Gestorum* (1992), 59–65.

Nissen, H. *Ammiani Marcellini fragmenta Marburgensia*. Berlin, 1876.

Noonkester, M. C. "Gibbon and the Clergy: Private Virtues, Public Vices." *Harvard Theological Studies* 83 (1990), 399–414.

Nutton, V. "Ammianus and Alexandria." *Clio Medica* 7 (1972) 165–76.

Oberhelman, S. M. "The Provenance of the Style of Ammianus Marcellinus." *Quaderni Urbinati di Cultura Classica* 56 = N.S. 27.3 (1987), 79–89.

——. "The *Cursus* in Late Imperial Latin Prose: A Reconsideration of Methodology." *Classical Philology* 83 (1988), 136–49.

——. "The History and Development of the *Cursus Mixtus* in Latin Literature." *Classical Quarterly*, N.S. 38 (1988), 228–42.

Oberhelman, S. M., and R. G. Hall. "A New Statistical Analysis of Accentual Prose Rhythms in Imperial Latin Prose." *Classical Philology* 79 (1984), 114–30.

——. "Meter in Accentual Clausulae of Late Empire Latin." *Classical Philology* 80 (1985), 214–27.

——. "Rhythmical Clausulae in the *Codex Theodosianus* and the *Leges novellae ad Theodosianum pertinentes*." *Classical Quarterly*, N.S. 35 (1985), 201–14.

——. "Internal Clausulae in Late Latin Prose as Evidence for the Displacement of Metre by Word-Stress." *Classical Quarterly*, N.S. 36 (1986), 208–24.

Ogilvie, R. M. "Titi Livi Lib. XCI." *Proceedings of the Cambridge Philological Society* 210 (1984), 116–25.

Oppolzer, T. von. *Canon der Finsternisse. Denkschriften der kaiserlichen Akademie der Wissenschaften zu Wien*, Mathematisch-naturwissenschaftliche Classe 52. Vienna, 1887. English translation by O. Gingerich, *Canon of Eclipses*, New York, 1962.

Pack, R. A. "Ammianus Marcellinus and the Curia of Antioch." *Classical Philology* 48 (1953), 80−85.

———. "The Roman Digressions of Ammianus Marcellinus." *Transactions of the American Philological Association* 84 (1953), 181−89.

———. "St. Peter in Ammianus." *Harvard Theological Review* 47 (1954), 319−21.

Palanque, J.-R. "Famines à Rome à la fin du IVe siècle." *Revue des études anciennes* 33 (1931), 346−56.

Paschoud, F. "Trois Livres récents sur l'empereur Julien." *Revue des études latines* 58 (1980), 107−23.

———. "Quand parut la première édition de l'Histoire d'Eunape." *Bonner Historia-Augusta-Colloquium 1977−1978* (Bonn, 1980), 149−62.

———. "Eunapiana." *Bonner Historia-Augusta-Colloquium 1982−1983*. Bonn, 1985, 239−303.

———. "Valentinien travesti, ou: De la malignité d'Ammien." *Cognitio Gestorum* (1992), 67−84.

Pearson, B. E. "Theurgic Tendencies in Gnosticism and Iamblichus's Conception of Theurgy." In *Neoplatonism and Gnosticism*, ed. R. T. Wallis and J. Bregman. Studies in Neoplatonism Ancient and Modern 6. Albany, 1992, 253−75.

Peeters, P. "La Date de la fête des SS. Juventin et Maximin." *Analecta Bollandiana* 42 (1924), 77−82.

Penella, R. J. "Julian the Persecutor in Fifth Century Church Historians." *Ancient World* 24 (1993), 31−43.

Perl, G. "Die Zuverlässigkeit der Buchangaben in den Citaten Priscians." *Philologus* 111 (1967), 283−88.

Petschenig, M. "Bericht über die Litteratur zu spätrömischen Geschichtsschreibern bis einschliesslich 1890." *Jahresbericht über die Fortschritte der classischen Altertumswissenschaft* 72 (1892, pub. 1893), 1−74.

Pighi, G. B. "De studiis Jacobi Lumbroso Ammianeis." *Aegyptus* 13 (1933) 275−93.

———. *I discorsi nelle storie d'Ammiano Marcellino*. Milan, 1936.

———. *Nuovi studi ammianei*. Milan, 1936.

———. "Latinità cristiana negli scrittori pagani del IV secolo. I." In *Studi dedicati alla memoria di Paolo Ubaldi. Pubblicazioni della Università Cattolica del Sacro Cuore*, Serie Quinta: Scienze Storiche 16. Milan, 1937, 41−72.

———. *Ammiani Marcellini Rerum Gestarum capita selecta. Bibliotheca Neocomensis* 2. Neuchâtel/Paris, 1948.

———. "Ammianus Marcellinus." *Reallexikon für Antike und Christentum*, 1 (1950), 386−94.

Rea, J. R. "On the Greek Calends." *Proceedings of the XVIII International Congress of Papyrology Athens, 25−31 May 1986*, 2. Athens, 1986, 203−8.

Reeve, M. D. "The Transmission of Florus" *Epitoma de Tito Livio* and the *Periochae*." *Classical Quarterly*, N.S. 38 (1988), 477−91.

Reiche, F. *Chronologie der letzten 6 Bücher des Ammianus Marcellinus*. Diss. Jena, pub. Liegnitz, 1889.

Reinhardt, G. *De praepositionum usu apud Ammianum*. Diss. Halle, publ. Cöthen, 1888.

Reiter, A. *De Ammiani Marcellini usu orationis obliquae.* Prog. Amberg, 1887.

Reynolds, L. D. "Ammianus Marcellinus." In *Texts and Transmission. A Survey of the Latin Classics,* ed. L. D. Reynolds. Oxford, 1983, 6–8.

Richter, W. "Die Darstellung der Hunnen bei Ammianus Marcellinus." *Historia* 23 (1974), 343–77.

Ridley, R. T. "Notes on Julian's Persian Expedition (363)." *Historia* 22 (1973), 317–30.

Rist, J. M. "Basil's 'Neoplatonism': Its Background and Nature." In *Basil of Caesarea: Christian, Humanist, Ascetic. A Sixteen-Hundredth Anniversary Symposium,* ed. P. J. Fedwick. Toronto, 1981, 137–220.

Roberts, M. "The Treatment of Narrative in Late Antique Literature: Ammianus Marcellinus (16.10), Rutilius Namatianus, and Paulinus of Pella." *Philologus* 132 (1988), 181–95.

Robinson, R. P. "The Hersfeldensis and the Fuldensis of Ammianus Marcellinus." In *Philological Studies in Honor of Walter Miller,* ed. R. P. Robinson. University of Missouri Studies 11.3. Columbia, Miss., 1936, 118–40.

Rosen, K. "Beobachtungen zur Erhebung Julians 360–361 n. Chr." *Acta Classica* 12 (1969), 121–49. (Reprinted in *Julian Apostata* [1978], 409–47.)

———. "Wege und Irrwege der römischen Gothenpolitik in Ammians 31. Buch." *Cognitio Gestorum* (1992), 85–90.

———. "Ammianus Marcellinus." *Der neue Pauly. Enzyklopädie der Antike* 1 (1996), 596–97.

Rossbach, O. "Der Schluss des Geschichtswerkes des Livius." *Berliner Philologische Wochenschrift* 30 (1910), 1396–98.

Rota, S. "Ammiano e Libanio: L'Epistola 1063 Förs. di Libanio (A proposito di un articolo di C. W. Fornara)." KOINΩNIA 18 (1994), 165–77.

Rowell, H. T. *Ammianus Marcellinus, Soldier-Historian of the Late Roman Empire.* Cincinnati, 1964. (Republished in *Lectures in Memory of Louise Taft Semple,* First Series: 1961–1965. University of Cincinnati Classical Studies, 1 [Princeton, 1967], 261–313.

———. "The First Mention of Rome in Ammianus' Extant Books and the Nature of the History." In *Mélanges d'archéologie, d'épigraphie et d'histoire offerts à Jérôme Carcopino.* Paris, 1966, 839–48.

Rubin, Z. "The Church of the Holy Sepulchre and the Conflict between the Sees of Caesarea and Jerusalem." In *The Jerusalem Cathedra: Studies in the History, Archaeology, Geography and Ethnography of the Land of Israel,* 2, ed. L. I. Levine. Jerusalem/Detroit, 1982, 79–105.

Russell, D. A. Review of G. Rochefort, *Julien: Oeuvres complètes* 2.1 (Paris, 1963). *Classical Review,* N.S. 15 (1965), 42–43.

Ryberg, I. S. "Tacitus' Art of Innuendo." *Transactions of the American Philological Association* 73 (1942), 383–404.

Sabbah, G. "Présences féminines dans l'*Histoire* d'Ammien Marcellin." *Cognitio Gestorum* (1992), 91–105.

Saffrey, H.-D. "Abamon Pseudonym de Jamblique." In *Philomathes. Studies and Essays in the Humanities in Memory of Philip Merlan.* The Hague, 1971, 227–39.

———. "Les Livres IV à VII du *De Mysteriis* de Jamblique relus avec la *Lettre* de Porphyre à Anébon." In *The Divine Iamblichus. Philosopher and Man of Gods,* ed. H. J. Blumenthal and E. G. Clark. London, 1993, 144–58.

Salway, B. "What's in a Name? A Survey of Roman Onomastic Practice from c. 700 B.C. to A.D. 700." *Journal of Roman Studies* 84 (1994), 124–45.

Samberger, C. "Die 'Kaiserbiographie' in den *Res Gestae* des Ammianus Marcellinus. Eine Untersuchung zur Komposition der ammianeischen Geschichtsschreibung." *Klio* 51 (1969), 349–482.

Scala, R. von. "Doxographische und stoische Reste bei Ammianus Marcellinus. Ein Beitrag zur Geschichte der allgemeinen Bildung des 4. Jahrhunderts n. Chr." In *Festgabe zu Ehren Max Büdinger's von seinen Freunden und Schülern.* Innsbruck, 1898, 117–50.

Schäfer, P. "Der Aufstand gegen Gallus Caesar." In *Tradition and Re-interpretation in Jewish and Early Christian Literature. Essays in Honour of Jürgen C. H. Lebram,* ed. J. W. van Henten. Studia Post-Biblica 36. Leiden, 1986, 184–201.

Scharf, R. "Die Matroniani—Comites Isauriae." *Epigraphica Anataolica* 16 (1990), 147–51.

Scheda, D. "Die Todesstunde Kaiser Julians." *Historia* 15 (1966), 380–83. (Reprinted in *Julian Apostata* [1978], 381–86.)

Schenk von Stauffenberg, A. "Der Reichsgedanke Konstantins." *Das Reich, Idee und Gestalt. Festschrift für Johannes Haller.* Stuttgart, 1940, 70–94. (Reprinted in his *Das Imperium und die Völkerwanderung* [Munich, 1948], 107–27.)

Schickinger, H. "Die Gräcismen bei Ammianus Marcellinus." *Programm des Staats-Gymnasiums in Nikolsburg* 24 (1896–1897), 13–30.

Schlicher, J. J. "The Historical Infinitive." *Classical Philology* 9 (1914), 279–94, 374–94; 10 (1915), 54–74.

Schuffner, M. *Ammianus Marcellinus in rerum gestarum libris quae de sedibus ac moribus complurium gentium scripserit.* Prog. Meiningen, 1877.

Schulze, W. *Zur Geschichte lateinischer Eigennamen. Abhandlungen der königlichen Gesellschaft der Wissenschaften in Göttingen.* Philosophisch-historische Klasse, N.F. 5.5. Göttingen, 1904.

Seager, R. *Ammianus Marcellinus: Seven Studies in His Language and Thought.* Columbia, Missouri, 1986.

——. "*Ut dux cunctator et tutus*: The Caution of Valentinian (Ammianus 27.10)." *Papers of the Leeds International Latin Seminar* 9 (1996), 191–96.

——. "Perceptions of Eastern Frontier Policy in Ammianus, Libanius, and Julian." *Classical Quarterly,* N.S. 47 (1997), 253–68.

Seeck, O. "Die Reihe der Stadtpräfekten bei Ammianus Marcellinus." *Hermes* 18 (1883), 289–303.

——. "Ammianus." *Paulys Real-Encyclopädie der classischen Altertumswissenschaft* 1 (1894), 1845–52.

——. "Zur Chronologie und Quellenkritik des Ammianus Marcellinus." *Hermes* 41 (1906), 481–539.

——. "Die Reichspraefektur des vierten Jahrhunderts." *Rheinisches Museum,* N.F. 69 (1914), 1–39.

Segal, C. "Tacitus and Poetic History: The End of Annals XIII." *Ramus* 2 (1973), 107–26.

Selem, A. "Considerazioni circa Ammiano ed il cristianesimo." *Rivista di Cultura Classica e Medioevale* 6 (1964), 224–61.

Seston, W. "'L'Humiliation' de Galère." *Revue des études anciennes* 42 (1940), 515–19.

Seyfarth, W. *Der Codex Fuldensis und der Codex E des Ammianus Marcellinus. Abhandlungen der*

Deutschen Akademie der Wissenschaften zu Berlin. Klasse für Sprache, Literatur, und Kunst 1962, Abhandlung 2.

——. "Ein Handstreich persischer Bogenschützen auf Antiochia. Sprachliche und historische Rechtfertigung einer Stelle bei Ammianus Marcellinus (23,5,3)." *Klio* 40 (1962), 60–64.

——. "Ammianus und das Fatum." *Klio* 43–45 (1965), 291–306.

——. "Philologische Probleme um Ammianus Marcellinus." *Klio* 48 (1967), 213–35.

——. "Petronius Probus. Legende und Wirklichkeit." *Klio* 52 (1970), 411–25.

——. "Glaube und Aberglaube bei Ammianus Marcellinus." *Klio* 46 (1975), 373–85.

Sicherl, M. "Michael Psellos und Iamblichos De mysteriis." *Byzantinische Zeitschrift* 53 (1960), 8–19.

Solari, A. "Le digressioni erudite di Ammiano." *Rendiconti della Accademia dei Lincei*, Classe di Scienze morali, storiche e filologiche[8] 4 (1949), 17–21.

Sontheimer, W. "Der Exkurs über Gallien bei Ammianus Marcellinus (XV, 9–12) mit besonderer Berücksichtigung des Berichtes über Hannibals Alpenübergang." *Klio* 20 (1926), 19–53.

Speidel, M. P. "Sebastian's Strike Force at Adrianople." *Klio* 78 (1996), 434–37.

Stadter, P. A. "The Structure of Livy's History." *Historia* 21 (1972), 287–307.

Steiner, G. "The Uncommon Reader." In his *No Passion Spent. Essays 1978–1996.* London/Boston, 1996, 1–19. (Apparently composed in 1978.)

Stertz, S. "Ammianus Marcellinus' Attitudes toward Earlier Emperors." In *Studies in Latin Literature and Roman History,* 2, ed. C. Deroux. Collection Latomus 168. Brussels, 1980, 487–514.

Steup, J. "Eine Umstellung im zweiten Buche der Annalen des Tacitus." *Rheinisches Museum,* N.F. 24 (1869), 72–80.

Stoian, A. "À propos de la conception historique d'Ammien Marcellin (Ut miles quondam et Graecus)." *Latomus* 25 (1967), 73–81.

Strauss, B. S. and J. Ober. "No Second Alexander: Why Julian's Persian Expedition failed." In their *The Anatomy of Error: Ancient Military Disasters and Their Lessons for Modern Strategists.* New York, 1990, 216–43.

Süvern, J. W. "Über den Kunstcharacter des Tacitus." *Abhandlungen der historisch-philosophischen Klasse der königlichen Akademie der Wissenschaften zu Berlin aus den Jahren 1822 und 1823* (Berlin, 1825), 73–136.

Sundwall, G. A. "Ammianus Geographicus." *American Journal of Philology* 117 (1996), 619–43.

Swerdlow, N. M. "On the Cosmical Mysteries of Mithras." *Classical Philology* 86 (1991), 48–63.

Syme, R. "Livy and Augustus." *Harvard Studies in Classical Philology* 64 (1959), 27–87. (Reprinted in his *Roman Papers,* 1 [Oxford, 1979], 400–54.)

——. *The Crisis of 2 B.C. Sitzungsberichte der bayerischen Akademie der Wissenschaften zu München,* Philosophisch-historische Klasse 1974, Heft 7. (Reprinted in *Roman Papers,* 3 [Oxford, 1984], 912–36.)

——. "Mendacity in Velleius." *American Journal of Philology* 99 (1978), 45–63. (Reprinted in *Roman Papers,* 3 [1984], 1090–1104.)

——. "The Date of Justin." *Historia* 37 (1988), 358–71. (Reprinted in *Roman Papers*, 6 [Oxford, 1991], 358–71.)

Szidat, J. "Der Feldzug Constantius' II. an der mittleren Donau im Jahre 358 n. Chr." *Historia* 21 (1972), 712–20.

——. "Der Neuplatonismus und die Gebildeten im Westen des Reiches. Gedanken zu seiner Verbreitung und Kenntnis ausserhalb der Schultradition." *Museum Helveticum* 39 (1982), 132–45.

——. "Imperator legitime declaratus (Ammian 30, 10, 5)." In *Historia Testis. Mélanges d'épigraphie, d'histoire ancienne et de philologie offerts à Tadeusz Zawadski*, ed. M. Piérart and O. Curty. Fribourg, 1989, 175–88.

——. "Sabinianus. Ein Heermeister Senatorischer Abkunft im 4. Jh." *Historia* 40 (1991), 494–500.

——. "Ammian und die historische Realität." *Cognitio Gestorum* (1992), 107–16.

——. "Staatlichkeit und Einzelschicksal in der Spätantike." *Historia* 44 (1995), 481–95.

Teitler, H. C. "Ammianus and Constantius. Image and Reality." *Cognitio Gestorum* (1992), 117–22.

Thompson, E. A. "The Historical Method of Ammianus Marcellinus." *Hermathena* 59 (1942), 44–66. (Reprinted with substantial changes and additions in his *Ammianus* [1947], 20–41.)

——. "Ammianus' Account of Gallus." *American Journal of Philology* 64 (1943), 302–51. (Reproduced with minor changes in his *Ammianus* [1947], 56–71.)

Thomsen, P. "Die lateinischen und griechischen Inschriften der Stadt Jerusalem und ihrer nächsten Umgebung." *Zeitschrift des Deutschen Palästina-Vereins* 43 (1920), 138–58, 44 (1921), 1–61, 9–168.

Tihon, A. "Le Calcul de l'éclipse de Soleil du 16 juin 364 p. C. et le 'Petit Commentaire' de Théon." *Bulletin de l'Institut historique belge de Rome* 46–47 (1976–1977), 35–79.

Tomlin, R. S. O. "The Date of the 'Barbarian Conspiracy.'" *Britannia* 5 (1974), 303–9.

——. Review of Bowersock, *Julian* (1978). *Phoenix* 34 (1980), 266–70.

——. "The Army of the Late Empire." In *The Roman World*, ed. J. Wacher, 1, London/New York, 1987, 107–20.

Tränkle, H. "Ammianus Marcellinus als römischer Geschichtsschreiber." *Antike und Abendland* 11 (1962), 21–33.

——. "Der Caesar Gallus bei Ammian." *Museum Helveticum* 33 (1976), 162–79.

Traube, L. "Die Überlieferung des Ammianus Marcellinus." In *Mélanges Boissier*. Paris, 1903, 443–48. (Reprinted in his *Vorlesungen und Abhandlungen*, 3 [Munich, 1920], 33-38.)

Turcan, R. "L'Autel de Rome et d'Auguste 'Ad Confluentem,'" *Aufstieg und Niedergang der Römischen Welt* 2.12.1. Berlin/New York, 1982, 607–44.

Unger, R. *Ad virum clarissimum Theodorum Bergk de Ammiani Marcellini locis controversis epistula critica*. Neustrelitz, 1868.

Veyne, P. "Le 'Prénom' de Naucellius." *Revue de philologie*[3] 38 (1964), 253–57.

Vogt, J. *Kaiser Julian und das Judentum. Studien zum Weltanschauungskampf der Spätantike*. Morgenland 30. Leipzig, 1939.

——. *Ammianus Marcellinus als erzählender Geschichtsschreiber der Spätzeit. Abhandlungen der Akademie der Wissenschaften und der Literatur, Mainz*. Geistes- und Sozialwissenschaftliche Klasse 1963, Nr. 8, 801–25.

Wachsmuth, C. "Pentadenbände der Handschriften klassischer Schriftsteller." *Rheinisches Museum*, N.F. 46 (1891), 329–31.

Walser, G. "Meilen und Leugen." *Epigraphica* 31 (1969), 84–103.

Walsh, P. G. "Livy and the Aims of 'historia': An Analysis of the Third Decade." *Aufstieg und Niedergang der Römischen Welt* 2.30.2. Berlin/New York, 1983, 1058–74.

Warmington, B. H. "The Career of Romanus, Comes Africae." *Byzantinische Zeitschrift* 49 (1956), 55–64.

——. "Objectives and Strategy in the Persian War of Constantius II." In *Limes. Akten des XI. Internationalen Limeskongresses*, (Székesfehérvar, 30. 8.–6. 9. 1976), ed. J. Fitz. Budapest, 1977, 509–20.

——."Ammianus Marcellinus and the Lies of Metrodorus." *Classical Quarterly*, N.S. 31 (1981), 464–68.

Weber, R. "Singer and Seer: Macaulay on the Historian as Poet." *Papers on Laguage and Literature* 3 (1967), 210–19.

Wellek, R. "Auerbach's Special Realism." *Kenyon Review* 16 (1954), 299–307. (Reprinted with slight changes in his *A History of Modern Criticism*, 7 [New Haven/London], 113–21.)

West, M. L. "Magnus and Marcellinus: Unnoticed Acrostics in the Cyranides." *Classical Quarterly*, N.S. 32 (1982), 480–81.

Weyman, C. "Studien zu Apuleius und seinen Nachahmern." *Sitzungsberichte der kaiserlichen bayerischen Akademie der Wissenchaften zu München,* Philosophisch-philologische und historische Classe 1893.2 (1894), 321–94.

Wiedemann, T. E. J. "Nunc ad inceptum redeo: Sallust, *Jugurtha* 4.9 and Cato." *Liverpool Classical Monthly* 4 (1979), 13–16.

——. "Between Men and Beasts: Barbarians in Ammianus Marcellinus." In *Past Perspectives. Studies in Greek and Roman Historical Writing*, ed. I. S. Moxon, J. D. Smart, and A. J. Woodman. Cambridge, 1986, 189–201.

Wiel, P. van de, *Hoofdstukken uit de geschiedenis van Rome in Ammianus Marcellinus Res Gestae.* Diss. Amsterdam, publ. Utrecht, 1989.

Wilamowitz-Möllendorff, U. von. "Lesefrüchte XXIV–XXVIII." *Hermes* 34 (1899), 203–30. (Reprinted in his *Kleine Schriften* 4, ed. K. Latte [Berlin, 1962], 45–71.)

Williams, M. F. "Four Mutinies: Tacitus *Annals* 1.16–30; 1.31–49 and Ammianus Marcellinus *Res Gestae* 20–4.9–20.5.7; 24.3.1–8." *Phoenix* 51 (1997), 44–74.

Wilshire, L. E. "Did Ammianus Marcellinus Write a Continuation of Tacitus?" *Classical Journal* 68 (1972–1973), 221–27.

Winter, E. "On the Regulation of the Eastern Frontier of the Roman Empire in 298." In *The Eastern Frontier of the Roman Empire*, ed. D. H. French and C. S. Lightfoot. British Institute of Archaeology at Ankara, Monograph No. 11. British Archaeological Reports, International Series 553. Oxford, 1989, 555–71.

Wirth, G. "Julians Perserkrieg. Kriterien einer Katastrophe." *Julian Apostata* (1978), 455–507.

——. "Jovian: Kaiser und Karikatur." In *Vivarium. Festschrift Theodor Klauser zum 90. Geburtstag. Jahrbuch für Antike und Christentum,* Ergänzungsband 11. Münster, 1984, 353–84.

Wirz, H. "Ammianus' Beziehungen zu seinen Vorbildern, Cicero, Sallustius, Livius, Tacitus." *Philologus* 36 (1877), 627–36.

Wölfflin, E. "Die hexadische Komposition des Tacitus." *Hermes* 21 (1886), 157–59.

Woloch, G. M. "Ammianus' Route to Cologne." *Arctos* 26 (1992), 137–40.

——. "Ammianus, Alpine Passes and Maps." *Arctos* 27 (1993), 149–53.

Womersley, D. "Gibbon and the 'Watchmen of the Holy City': Revision and Religion in the *Decline and Fall*." In *Edward Gibbon and Empire*, ed. R. McKitterick and R. Quinault. Cambridge, 1997, 190–216.

Woodman, A. J. "Remarks on the Structure and Content of Tacitus, *Annals* 4.57–67." *Classical Quarterly*, N.S. 22 (1972), 150–58.

——. "Amateur Dramatics at the Court of Nero: *Annals* 15.48–74." In *Tacitus and the Tacitean Tradition*, ed. T. J. Luce and A. J. Woodman. Princeton, 1993, 104–28.

Woods, D. "Ammianus Marcellinus and the Deaths of Bonosus and Maximilianus." *Hagiographica* 2 (1995), 25–55.

——. "Julian, Arbogastes, and the *Signa* of the *Ioviani* and *Herculiani*." *Journal of Roman Military Equipment Studies* 6 (1995), 61–68.

——. "A Note Concerning the Early Career of Valentinian I." *Ancient Society* 26 (1995), 273–88.

——. "Ammianus and Some *tribuni scholarum palatinarum* c. A.D. 353–364," *Classical Quarterly*, N.S. 47 (1997), 269–91.

——. "Valens, Valentinian I, and the *Ioviani Cornuti*." In *Studies in Latin Literature and Roman History*, 9, ed. C. Deroux, Collection Latomus. Brussels, 1998.

——. "Ammianus 22.4.6: An Unnoticed Anti-Christian Jibe." *Journal of Theological Studies*, N.S. 49 (1998), 145–48.

Zangemeister, K. "Ungedruckte Emendationen Richard Bentley's zu Nonius und Ammianus Marcellinus." *Rheinisches Museum*, N.F. 33 (1878), 462–77.

Zawadski, T. "Les Procès politiques de l'an 371–372 (Amm. Marc. XXIX 1,29–33; Eunapius, Vitae Soph. VII 6, 3–4; D 480)." In *Labor Omnibus Unus. Gerold Walser zum 70. Geburtstag dargebracht von Freunden, Kollegen und Schülern*, ed. H. E. Herzig and R. Frei-Stolba. Wiesbaden, 1989, 274–87.

Zech, J. *Astronomische Untersuchungen über die wichtigeren Finsternisse, welche von den Schriftstellern des classischen Alterthums erwähnt werden. Preisschriften gekrönt und herausgegeben von der Fürstlich Jablonowoski'schen Gesellschaft zu Leipzig* 4. Leipzig, 1853.

Zuckerman, C. "Cappadocian Fathers and the Goths." *Travaux et Mémoires* 11 (1991), 473–86.

INDEX OF NAMES OF
PERSONS AND PLACES

This deliberately selective index makes no attempt to include all the personal and geographical proper names densely clustered in Chapter IV and Appendices 5 and 10. On the other hand, it does include some institutional titles, collective names, and titles of literary works.

INDEX OF
MODERN SCHOLARS

This index registers modern scholars, critics, and historians who are named or quoted in the main text or in the text of the appendices or whose interpretations of Ammianus are discussed or evaluated. It does not cover bare citations or quotations in footnotes.

PASSAGES OF
AMMIANUS DISCUSSED

The following index includes only passages that are translated and those whose text or interpretation is discussed in the present work. Excluded are passages simply cited or adduced as evidence and the analysis of the structure of the *Res Gestae* in Chapter IV.